DATE DUE

NO 12'02			
NO 9'07			

DEMCO 38-296

GREAT LIVES
FROM
HISTORY

GREAT LIVES FROM HISTORY

American Women
Series

Volume 2
Cho-Gol

Edited by

FRANK N. MAGILL

SALEM PRESS

Pasadena, California   Englewood Cliffs, New Jersey

Library of Congress Cataloging-in-Publication Data
Great lives from history. American women series /
edited by Frank N. Magill.
    p.   cm.
Includes bibliographical references and index.
    1. Women—United States—Biography. 2. Women—
Canada—Biography. 3. Women—United States—His-
tory. 4. Women—Canada—History. I. Magill, Frank
Northen, 1907-   . II. Title: American women series.
HQ1412.G74   1995
305.4′0973—dc20
ISBN 0-89356-892-9 (set)   94-38308
ISBN 0-89356-894-5 (volume 2)   CIP

LIST OF BIOGRAPHIES IN VOLUME TWO

LIST OF BIOGRAPHIES IN VOLUME TWO

GREAT LIVES
FROM
HISTORY

KATE CHOPIN

Born: February 8, 1851; St. Louis, Missouri
Died: August 22, 1904; St. Louis, Missouri
Area of Achievement: Literature
Contribution: Author of the early feminist novel *The Awakening*, Kate Chopin created works that showcased the Louisiana bayou country and often featured women struggling against society's restrictions.

Early Life
Katherine O'Flaherty was born February 8, 1851, in St. Louis. Her father was an Irish merchant and her mother was the daughter of an old French family. Chopin's early fluency with French and English, and her roots in two different cultures, were important throughout her life.

Kate's father, Thomas O'Flaherty, was killed in a train accident in 1855 (the imagined effect on her mother was later depicted in "The Story of an Hour"). Kate lived her preteen years in a female-centered household. Her sophisticated grandmother had a great impact on Kate, encouraging her to reject hypocrisy, to love music and storytelling, and to indulge in unconventional behavior. Kate's formal education began at Sacred Heart Academy, a Catholic school devoted to creating good wives and mothers, while also teaching independent thinking. Kate's readings included fairy tales, *The Pilgrim's Progress*, old-fashioned romances, and contemporary popular novels by women.

The Civil War meant that Kate spent much time at home; she saw the war's violence at first hand. After Kate returned to the academy, her English teacher encouraged her to write. Kate kept a "commonplace book" from 1867-1870, where she recorded observations on her reading and studies. At the age of eighteen, Kate was known as one of St. Louis' prettiest and most popular belles. Her diary, however, reveals that she was torn between social pressures—to attend dances, flirt, and be agreeable—and her passion for voracious reading of authors such as Victor Hugo, Dante, Molière, Jane Austen, and Henry Wadsworth Longfellow. In an age known for producing restless women, Kate also seemed to want something more.

When she was twenty, Kate married Oscar Chopin, a twenty-six-year-old business-man of cosmopolitan background. In their first ten years of marriage, Kate gave birth to five sons and a daughter. Motherhood's joys and demands, as well as societal restraints on women, are important themes in her fiction. During these years, Kate and the children lived three seasons in New Orleans and spent long summers at the Creole resort Grande Isle.

In 1879, Oscar Chopin's money-lending business was in deep trouble. The family moved to Cloutierville, Louisiana, where Oscar ran a general store. Kate Chopin's sophisticated behavior and dress inspired gossip in the small, closely knit town. Her husband, worn down by financial worries, died in 1882, leaving Kate with debts of some $12,000 and six children to rear alone. She decided to manage Oscar's businesses herself. During this time she was romantically linked with Albert Sampite, a handsome and unhappily married man. In 1884, Kate left Cloutierville and Sampite to return to St. Louis, where she lived with her mother.

Her mother's death the following year left Kate devastated; a physician friend suggested that she write for solace—and for much-needed money. Kate's writings at the time indicate that she sometimes longed for the security of marriage, but also recognized that the deaths of the two people closest to her gave her independence unavailable to other women. She later characterized this period as a time of "growth."

Life's Work

These sudden deaths and her own unconventional ideas demanded that Kate Chopin make her own way. She started her first short story in 1888, and became a published author in 1889 when her poem "If It Might Be" appeared in the journal *America*. Her stories and sketches from this early period show that she questioned traditional romance. "Wiser Than a God" depicts a woman who chooses a career as pianist over marriage. Other stories portray a suffragist and a professional woman who try to determine their own lives. Chopin's friends during this period included "New Women"—single working women, suffragists, and intellectuals—who doubtless influenced her previously private questioning of women's role in society.

At Fault (1890), Chopin's first novel, focuses on a woman who renounces her lover after she learns he is divorced. The conflict between morality and sexual attraction is a major theme, and the novel is ahead of its time in depicting an alcoholic woman, the lover's estranged wife. This novel suggests that environment is a greater influence on behavior than heredity—an unpopular idea in the 1890's. *At Fault* was praised for its local color and believable characters, but was attacked by literary moralists, who disliked its subject matter and language. Because one publisher had rejected the novel and Chopin was impatient for publication, she paid to have it printed and distributed.

Chopin also wrote children's stories that appeared in national magazines. Her stature as author began to grow. In her adult stories, she persisted in writing about taboo subjects: "Mrs. Mobry's Reason" (1893), repeatedly rejected, concerned venereal disease; "The Coming and Going of Liza Jane" (1892) focuses on a woman who, longing for a more glamorous life, leaves her husband. Chopin's output from this period is oddly split between formula writing of predictable morality tales and stories of individuals' conflicts with society.

Throughout her career, Chopin gained inspiration from her time in Louisiana. Much of her fiction was set there: she valued its dreamy, less structured and more sensual atmosphere. Chopin was pigeonholed as a regional writer, but badly wanted to reach a national audience. She tried hard to place her collection of Creole stories and finally succeeded. *Bayou Folk* (1894) collected mostly Cane River country stories. Praised for its exotic and bewitching subjects and atmosphere, the collection solidified Chopin's reputation as a local colorist.

The 1890's were a time of achievement for Chopin. *Bayou Folk*'s success led to more short story publications in national magazines and to regional celebrity. "The

Story of an Hour" (1894) recounts the ironic reversal in emotion—from grief to joy—of a woman who mistakenly believes she has been widowed. It is one of Chopin's most powerful—and controversial—stories, and it anticipates *The Awakening* in its depiction of a repressive marriage.

In St. Louis, Chopin held salons where the city's cultural elite could play cards, listen to music, and argue about philosophy and literature. Chopin translated contemporary French writer Guy de Maupassant's tales, and was greatly influenced by his writing. Maupassant was thought to be immoral; his satires, like Chopin's mature fiction, focus on betrayal of ideals, questioning of traditional values, sex, and depression.

Through the mid-1890's, Chopin wrote mainstream fiction, but continued to address more daring subjects such as aging, obsessive love, extrasensory perception, and gambling. *A Night in Acadie* (1897), Chopin's second short story collection, focused on the Cane River country she knew so well. Women characters, some repressed and others rebelling, were prominent. This collection was generally well received, though some reviewers disliked its coarseness—a muted charge that would become a roar with the publication of *The Awakening* in 1899.

The Awakening features a strong female protagonist. After twenty-nine years "asleep" to life's possibilities, Edna Pontellier awakens to the need to find her identity. Like her creator, Edna sometimes feels as if she lives a double life: one that conforms and one that questions. Edna's attraction to both sides is illustrated in her friendships with the conventional "mother-woman" Adele Ratignolle and the eccentric pianist Mademoiselle Reisz.

Edna grows up desiring unattainable men. Believing that she is renouncing the world of illusion, she marries a man for whom she has only fondness and no passion, and settles into motherhood. In a series of small incidents at Grand Isle, however, Edna's rebellion against her rigid role is shown: her unexpected emotional response to Mlle Reisz's concert; her exultation on learning to swim; her desire for Robert Lebrun, a young man with whom she is in sympathy; and her defiance of her husband's wishes.

Edna disproves Victorian ideas about women's moral superiority through her open longing for Robert and her affair with the roguish Alcée Arobin; she moves into her own house and tries to attain fulfillment through painting and an unconventional social life. For a time she behaves solely in accordance with her desires. Eventually Adele summons Edna to her bedside and implores her to think of her children. Edna realizes that she cannot give her children honor and good reputation without sacrificing her independence, her sensuality, and her newfound enjoyment of life. Ironically, freedom means that a "solitary soul" (the novel's original title) will be isolated from society and from sensual experience. Because of her husband's death and her own strength, Chopin was able to escape rigid social convention to an extent. Edna, unable to compromise her desires with her duties, commits suicide.

The Awakening became Chopin's major literary achievement; it was also far in advance of its time. One of the earliest American novels to question marriage as an institution, Edna's discontent and her various attempts to find fulfillment caused a scandal. The novel was attacked as immoral and as unfit for reading. Critics praised the beauty and power of the novel's style and setting, its careful pacing, and its subtly drawn characters, but many questioned Edna's (and Chopin's) morality. Like Norwegian playwright Henrik Ibsen's *A Doll's House*, *The Awakening*'s realistic portrayal of a woman's desire to find her identity outraged many.

Chopin was hurt by the negative reaction to the novel, though she published a tongue-in-cheek "retraction" apologizing for Mrs. Pontellier making such a mess of things and ensuring her own damnation. Chopin's career slowed markedly after 1899. She continued to write poetry and reviews, but published little until her death in 1904. At that time Chopin was eulogized chiefly as a regional writer of note; little was said of *The Awakening* until decades later.

Summary

Kate Chopin's reputation as a writer initially faded soon after her death. After the initial sensation when the novel first appeared in 1899 and in a 1906 reprinting, *The Awakening* was out of print for half a century. By the late 1960's, however, Norwegian writer Per Seyersted rediscovered Chopin and edited *The Complete Works* and a critical biography in 1969. Chopin's reputation blossomed, and her novel is considered a classic, taught in university literature and women's studies courses. Largely through the attention of scholars and critics, Chopin's work has enjoyed a renaissance. Her writing beautifully illustrates a variety of feminist concerns: the clash between individual freedom and social duty; the stifling quality of unequal marriage; the hypocrisy of the sexual double standard; women's desire for creativity and independence. Her characters are utterly believable: complex, thoughtful, and intelligent.

The Awakening is a fine example of the rehabilitation of a "disappeared" writer. Considered out of step with its times, it is a powerfully written novel by a writer whose work had been safely categorized as regional and domestic; these reasons explain its fading from public view. Like several other women's novels enjoying renewed attention as American classics (African American writer Zora Neale Hurston's *Their Eyes Were Watching God* and New Yorker writer Dorothy Parker's cynical comedies, for example), *The Awakening* is being reevaluated by critics and readers. It is a startlingly radical and honest book, which deservedly stands as a classic.

Bibliography

Chopin, Kate. *The Awakening: An Authoritative Text, Contexts, Criticism.* Edited by Margaret Culley. New York: W. W. Norton, 1976. The novel's complete text, including helpful explanatory footnotes that help explain its context. Contains excerpts from writers contemporary with Chopin as well as a sampling of reviews from the novel's first publication to its rediscovery in the 1960's.

_____ . *The Complete Works of Kate Chopin.* Edited by Per Seyersted. Baton Rouge: Louisiana State University Press, 1969. Reprints Chopin's work, including unpublished and uncollected stories, sketches, essays, and poetry. Valuable for the overview these writings give of Chopin's evolution as a writer.

Rankin, Daniel. *Kate Chopin and Her Creole Stories*. Philadelphia: University of Pennsylvania Press, 1932. An early biography that relies on interviews with Chopin's friends and relatives and Chopin's manuscripts and journals. Examines Chopin primarily as writer of unique and rich Creole stories; reprints some stories and sketches.

Seyersted, Per. *Kate Chopin: A Critical Biography*. Baton Rouge: Louisiana State University Press, 1969. A reexamination of Chopin's life and career, using previously unavailable materials. Examines her importance as a writer of realism and her ambitious and assertive life; links Chopin's experience and her work.

Toth, Emily. *Kate Chopin*. New York: William Morrow, 1990. A detailed and fascinating critical biography; gives much valuable information on Chopin's childhood and passionate, secretive life. Shows relationships and influences in Chopin's life and effects on her writing. Includes thorough bibliography of Chopin's writings and criticism of her work, a chronology, and exhaustive footnotes.

Wheeler, Otis. "The Five Awakenings of Edna Pontellier." *Southern Review* XI (January, 1975): 118-128. Focuses on Edna's rejection of "angel in the house" and "scarlet woman" roles; traces Edna's development through her awakenings about personhood, true love, sex, biology, and despair. A useful psychological study of Chopin's most complex character.

Ziff, Larzer. *The American 1890s: Life and Times of a Lost Generation*. New York: Viking Press, 1966. Examines the decade when Chopin flourished as a writer. Ziff puts in context the two impulses of American society—conformity versus individuality—and criticizes the literature of the decade as overly optimistic and unrealistic.

Michelle L. Jones

CONNIE CHUNG

Born: August 20, 1946; Washington, D.C.

Area of Achievement: Journalism

Contribution: A leader in broadcast journalism, Chung advanced through the ranks as a news anchor and hosted several of her own interview news programs before being made the first female coanchor of the *CBS Evening News* in 1993.

Early Life

Constance Yu-Hwa Chung, professionally known as Connie Chung, was born in Washington, D.C., on August 20, 1946. She is the tenth and youngest daughter of William and Margaret Chung and the only one of their children born in America. The other nine children, all female, were born in China. The five eldest children died in China during World War II, a period when it was difficult for civilians to receive proper medical treatment. At the time, William Chung was a diplomat for Chiang Kai-shek's Nationalist government. After enduring several years of the Japanese bombing of Shanghai, he called upon his political connections in America in order to move with his wife and four surviving daughters to the Maryland suburbs of Washington, D.C., in 1944. Following the Japanese defeat in World War II and the subsequent defeat of the Nationalist government by the Chinese Communists in 1949, the Chung family decided to remain in the United States. Connie's father worked first for the Chinese diplomatic service and later for the Washington, D.C., branch of the United Nations.

The Chung family strictly adhered to the traditional Chinese work ethic and the view that education was the surest way to success in the United States. This strong family background provided Connie with much needed strength and encouragement. In elementary school, Connie was a shy and introverted child. In high school, however, she opened up more and became active in school plays, variety shows, and student government. Her awareness of her father's career with the United Nations promoted Connie's interest in current affairs. Connie's experiences in public schools in Washington, D.C., where civics classes regularly visited Capitol Hill, piqued her interest in learning about how the government works.

Like many of her high-school classmates, Connie chose to attend the University of Maryland, where she began her studies as a biology major. During her junior year, she began working as a summer intern for Seymour Halpern, a congressional representative from New York. As an intern, she was actively involved in writing press releases and speeches for Halpern. This exposure to politics and the media had a significant impact on Chung. Believing that television would become more popular than newspapers, Chung decided to pursue a career in broadcast journalism. When she returned to school, she switched her major to journalism and began searching for a job in television. After she applied to several television stations in Washington, D.C., WTTG offered her a part-time job as a copy clerk and she accepted. Her schoolwork in journalism was superior and she received an award for outstanding scholarship. She completed her bachelor of science degree in journalism in 1969.

After graduation, Chung became news department secretary and later a newswriter at WTTG. Within two years, because of her stamina, persistence, and excellent work, she became assignment editor and then an on-the-air reporter for the station. Her reporting included stories on the Vietnam protest demonstrations and congressional activity on Capitol Hill.

At the same time that the Federal Communications Commission began to exert pressure on the major networks to hire more minorities and women, Chung applied to CBS News for a position with the network's Washington bureau. In 1971, she, along with Leslie Stahl, Sylvia Chase, and Michelle Clark (who died in a plane crash in 1972), was hired by CBS News.

Life's Work

Connie Chung began her reporting at CBS News with the assigned task of covering Senator George McGovern's 1971 presidential campaign. During the campaign, she traveled more than 50,000 miles by bus and plane to forty states and to more than two hundred cities. Her thoroughness in preparing for this assignment gave Chung a reputation as a walking encyclopedia on George McGovern. During this early part of her career, Chung established herself as a tenacious reporter and gained enormous respect among her colleagues for her commitment to working extremely long hours, for her willingness to take on any assignment, regardless of the difficulty, and for her interviewing, writing, and reporting skills.

During 1972, Chung covered two of the top news stories of the year, reporting on President Nixon's trips to the Middle East and to the Soviet Union. She was not awarded the assignment to accompany the president on his historic trip to the People's Republic of China. Nevertheless, she prepared stories on Chinese diplomats in the United States and on the Chinese ping-pong team that initiated the historic normalization of relations between the United States and the People's Republic of China. For these reports, she was called upon to use Chinese language skills that she had learned at home.

Chung furthered her reputation as a dogged and persistent reporter during the 1973-1974 Watergate investigations, when she covered such figures as John Dean, a legal adviser to President Nixon; H. R. "Bob" Haldeman, the president's chief of staff; and John Ehrlichman, the chief counsel to the president. She also garnered attention for her coverage of Nelson Rockefeller's vice presidency under Gerald Ford. Despite these high profile reports, Chung decided to move to Los Angeles in 1976 to become the new anchor on KNXT (later KCBS-TV), the local CBS News affiliate where she anchored the 4:30 P.M., 6:00 P.M., and 11:00 P.M. newscasts.

Moving from network to local news was a difficult decision for Chung. Barbara Walters had recently become the first woman to anchor an evening network news program, and Chung wanted an opportunity to become the next. Nevertheless, the experience of anchoring the evening news in the second-largest broadcast market and the substantial salary increase she was offered effectively overcame her reluctance to leave her post as a national correspondent. From 1976 to 1983, Chung also served as a substitute anchor on the *CBS Morning News* and the CBS News weekend and evening broadcasts, and she anchored the network's "Newsbreak" segment for the Pacific time zone. She was credited with improving KNXT's ratings locally from third place to a solid second place, and her annual salary increased to a reported $600,000 by 1983. At the time, this salary made Chung the highest paid local news anchor in the United States.

Eager to become more involved in the coming presidential campaign and to get closer to the national political scene, Chung decided to return to network news in 1983. Unable to land an acceptable position at CBS, she switched to NBC News where she became anchor of the *NBC News at Sunrise* (formerly called *Early Today*). NBC executives expected her to improve the show's ratings as dramatically as she had done for KNXT in Los Angeles. Her other duties included reporting for the *NBC Nightly News*, anchoring the *Saturday NBC Nightly News*, and doing three ninety-second prime-time newscasts a week in New York. She reportedly took a $200,000 cut in salary in this new position. During 1983 she made the first of several appearances as substitute for *Today* show anchor, Jane Pauley. She also continued her grueling work schedule, routinely working eighteen-hour days, six and sometimes seven days a week.

The following year proved to be very important for Chung. She not only served as floor reporter at both the Republican and Democratic national conventions, giving her continued national exposure, but also married her long-time boyfriend Maury Povich, then the anchor of Fox Television's *A Current Affair*. As expected, the ratings for *NBC News at Sunrise* climbed from third to first place in the television ratings.

During the next few years with NBC, Chung served in many high profile positions. In the summer of 1985, she became chief correspondent for *American Almanac*, NBC's prime-time news magazine anchored by Roger Mudd. In 1986, she and Mudd served as coanchors of a new version of *American Almanac*, called *1986*. Chung also became a regular substitute for Tom Brokaw on the *NBC Nightly News*.

From 1987 to 1989, Chung divided her duties between filing stories for *NBC Nightly News* and directing several prime-time documentaries. In "Life in the Fat Lane," a documentary about overweight people in American society, she interviewed several overweight celebrities and talked with Jane Fonda about her bouts with bulimia and anorexia nervosa. Chung's 1987 news special "Scared Sexless," about the effects of the AIDS epidemic on sexual mores, was the highest-rated news program since 1977. Other documentaries included "Stressed to Kill" (1988), "Guns, Guns, Guns" (1988), and "Everybody's Doing It" (1988). She served as political analyst and podium correspondent during the 1988 presidential campaign and political conventions. Chung also returned to China for the first time, in 1987, where she conducted an on-the-air series of interviews with her relatives in Shanghai that she has called one of her most rewarding experiences.

In 1989, Chung rejoined CBS News as anchor of a revamped *West 57th Street*, a prime-time news magazine that soon became *Saturday Night with Connie Chung*. She also became anchor of the *CBS Sunday Night News* and the primary substitute for Dan Rather for the *CBS Evening News*. *Saturday Night with Connie Chung*, despite its high ratings, was criticized for dramatizations and recreations of news events. On this program she reported on such stories as the American Hostages in Lebanon and the bombing of Pan Am Flight 103. She also interviewed Joseph Hazelwood, captain of the Exxon *Valdez*, in his only appearance on national television.

Chung became anchor of her own Emmy Award-winning CBS News prime-time series, *Face to Face with Connie Chung*, in 1990. The following year, she served as rotating anchor and contributing correspondent for CBS News' coverage of the Persian Gulf War and served as coanchor with Dan Rather on *America on Line,* an interactive CBS News special examining the nation's reaction to President Bush's 1992 State of the Union Address. In 1992, she contributed to CBS News' coverage of "Campaign 92."

On June 17, 1993 she was named coanchor of the *CBS Evening News* and anchor of *Eye to Eye with Connie Chung*, a prime-time news program. These two positions have made her one of the top newscasters in television history.

Summary

Through hard work and determination, Connie Chung became one of the most prominent and most respected news reporters and interviewers working in broadcast news. During her career in broadcast journalism, she has received many awards. She is the recipient of three national Emmy Awards, including two for Best Interview/ Interviewer. While in Los Angeles she was honored by an award for best news reporting from the Los Angeles Press Club, won the Portraits of Excellence award and the First Amendment award from the B'nai Br'ith, and won Emmys for consistently outstanding television performances. Among her other broadcast honors, she received the prestigious George Foster Peabody Award. Connie Chung has excelled in broadcast journalism, a field previously dominated by men. In so doing, she has become a role model for not only Asian American and other minority women, but for all who seek, through persistence and dedication, to reach their full potential.

Bibliography

Malone, Mary. *Connie Chung: Broadcast Journalist*. Hillside, N.J.: Enslow Publishers, 1992. A good overall account of Connie Chung's early life to her rise in broadcast journalism. Written for the middle and high school audience, this work is a part of the series entitled *Contemporary American Women*.

Morey, Janet, and Wendy Dunn. *Famous Asian Americans*. New York: E. P. Dutton, 1992. A well-written work that chronicles the lives and accomplishments of Chung and thirteen other Asian Americans, including Maxine Hong Kingston, June Kuramoto, Michael Chang, An Wang, and Wendy Lee Gramm.

Paisner, Daniel. *The Imperfect Mirror: Inside Stories of the Television Newswomen*. New York: William Morrow, 1988. An informative set of interviews with contemporary newswomen, including Connie Chung. Places Chung within the context of her female peers.

Trotta, Liz. *Fighting for Air: In the Trenches with Television News*. New York: Simon & Schuster, 1991. An excellent introduction to television news including stories of the journalists' careers.

Ricchiardi, Sherry, and Virginia Young. *Women on Deadline: A Collection of America's Best*. Ames: Iowa State University Press, 1991. Provides a collection of interviews with some of America's top female journalists. The interview with Chung is quite informative.

Gregory A. Levitt

LIZ CLAIBORNE

Born: March 31, 1929; Brussels, Belgium

Area of Achievement: Fashion
Contribution: A designer of affordable, casual, mix-and-match sportswear separates for working women, Liz Claiborne has expanded her enterprises to become one of the few women to head a *Fortune 500* company.

Early Life

Elisabeth Claiborne was born on March 31, 1929, in Brussels, Belgium. Her parents, Omer Villere and Louise Carol Claiborne, were American citizens from New Orleans, Louisiana. On her father's side, Liz Claiborne was a direct descendant of William C. C. Claiborne, who was the governor of Louisiana during the War of 1812. Liz spent her childhood in Brussels and returned with her family to New Orleans in 1939, right before the Nazi invasion of Belgium.

From her father, who was a banker with the Morgan Guaranty Trust Company, Liz acquired a love of painting and an aesthetic appreciation of art. From her mother, a homemaker, she learned to sew at an early age. Liz never graduated from high school because her old-fashioned father did not think it was essential for her to acquire a formal education. In 1947, she returned to Europe to study fine arts in Brussels and in Nice, France, in 1948, because her father wanted her to become an artist.

Although she did not desire to become a painter, Liz went along with her father's wishes. Later in life, she admitted she was glad to have received such art training. This training taught her color, proportion, and many other things that she might not have learned in design school. By day she went to art classes, and at night she took pattern-making courses. Because Liz loved to draw and to sew, she became a designer.

Her Roman Catholic family opposed her decision to pursue a career in fashion, but on her own initiative, at the age of nineteen, Liz entered a national design contest. It was sponsored by *Harper's Bazaar*, and she won the contest with a sketch of a woman's high-collared coat with a military flair. In 1951, Claiborne defied her father, cut off her hair, and left for New York. Living with an aunt, she landed a job in the Seventh Avenue garment district as a sketcher for Tina Lesser, one of the few sportswear designers at the time.

In the same year, Liz married Ben Schultz, a designer for Time-Life Books (they were later divorced). Unlike most women in the 1950's, Liz decided to continue working as a designer after she gave birth to her only child, Alexander G. Schultz.

Life's Work

Seeking a diversified career experience, Liz Claiborne moved from one designer to another. After working for Tina Lesser, Claiborne went on to work for Ben Rieg, who designed tailored clothes, and then she became Omar Kiam's assistant at the Seventh Avenue house. In the midst of a five-year association (from 1955 to 1960) with the

New York City firm of Dan Keller, Claiborne, on July 5, 1957, married her second husband, design executive Arthur Ortenberg, whom she had met earlier while working for the Rhea Manufacturing Company of Milwaukee. During these early years, Claiborne became known as a top designer of dresses, despite her own avowed preference for wearing pants.

In 1960, Claiborne began her fifteen years of employment as chief designer for Youth Guild, the junior dress division of Jonathan Logan. Her boss, Arthur Lefkowitz, gave her the decision-making freedom designers cherish. Along with this responsibility, she had greater financial responsibility for her family. Her husband, Arthur Ortenberg, began to experiment with different designs at his own company, but eventually went out of business. For a while, Ortenberg went from job to job. Although these were difficult years, Liz was primarily frustrated because she recognized from her own experience that there was a gap in the market for moderately priced career clothes. She was unable to persuade the Youth Guild management that the time had come for mix-and-match coordinated sportswear for a neglected segment of the market—working women. She marked time and waited until her son and two stepchildren finished college before she left Youth Guild in December, 1975.

Then, on January 19, 1976, Claiborne launched her company, Liz Claiborne, Inc., which was financed by personal savings and money from her family, friends, and business associates. Claiborne became the head designer and president of the sportswear company, and her husband, an expert in textiles and business administration, served as secretary and treasurer. When Claiborne founded her company, she was determined to expand the wardrobe choices available to working women. She recognized that they actually purchased two distinct wardrobes: work clothes and casual weekend clothes. Claiborne herself disapproved of the limitations imposed by the standard corporate attire for women: the business suit, consisting of a coordinated jacket and skirt paired with a tailored shirt and floppy bow tie. Claiborne decided to develop clothes, not only for women executives and office workers but also for women who worked as teachers and doctors, those who worked in Southern California and Florida, and those who worked in the fashion industry itself. Because her fashions liberated the working woman from the stiff navy, gray, or black suit uniform, Claiborne came to be called "the working woman's best friend."

In the first year, she showed some thirty-five pieces in her first group of clothes for the fall of 1976. Among those pieces included knickers, pleated skirts, tattersall shirts, shirt jackets, and hunting jackets. These pieces could be worn in a variety of combinations. As a result, sales in the first year passed the $2 million mark, and the company was in the black. In addition to designing clothes for working women, Claiborne had a realistic pricing policy. She strove to consider the value of her merchandise from the customer's point of view in determining prices.

Her best-sellers in 1977 were a velour peasant blouse followed by a crepe de chine version a season later. She made women confident about accepting culottes as a refreshing variation in dressing for daytime. For spring 1978, Liz designed full skirts, loose tunics, and vests, mainly in rust and plum. That year, sales reached $23 million.

In 1980, Liz Claiborne became the first woman in the fashion industry to be named Entrepreneurial Woman of the Year, and in June, 1981, her firm went public. It raised $6.1 million by selling stock for nineteen dollars per share. This was an unusually successful debut in the midst of the recession of the early 1980's. The price of the Liz Claiborne, Inc., stock jumped thirty-one dollars in the first six months and split, two for one, in 1983. This performance led Merrill Lynch to identify Claiborne's company as a success story. During the recession, Liz Claiborne, Inc., prospered while other clothing companies experienced declining sales. ˙

There are several other reasons for Claiborne's success in the fashion industry. First, she listened to requests and complaints from both customers and retailers. Second, she kept abreast of trends by analyzing statistical figures produced by a computerized system, unique to her company, known as System Updated Retail Feedback. The marketing department was provided with weekly reports which revealed the styles, colors, and sizes that were sold in a cross-section of stores. Third, Liz's company added two lines of merchandise to the traditional four, generating a continuous flow of fresh merchandise that increased inventory turnover.

As the company grew rapidly, Claiborne's company diversified into new areas, increasing its phenomenal growth. Added to the basic lines of active sportswear and a slightly dressier collection was a petite sportswear, in 1981, proportioned for women under five feet four. A dress division was launched in 1982, followed by a unit for shoes in 1983.

After a disappointment with a girl's line from 1984 to 1987, a new "Lizwear" line was introduced in 1985, featuring jeans and other casual wear. At the same time, Liz Claiborne, Inc., purchased the Kaiser-Roth Corporation, which produced accessories, including handbags, scarves, gloves, belts, and hats. It was during this period that Liz Claiborne, Inc., reached the half-billion dollar summit. When retail sales hit $1.2 billion in 1986, the company broke into the *Fortune 500* list of the largest industrial companies in the United States, ranked at 437. It was one of the youngest enterprises to scale that height and the first one started by a woman.

In June, 1989, Claiborne and her husband, who own 5.6 million shares of company stock worth almost $100 million, retired from active management to pursue environmental, social, and personal interests.

Summary

As a fashion designer, Liz Claiborne spotted an untapped market not being fully served by the clothing industry. She recognized women's desire for reasonably priced and attractive clothes to wear to work, and opened the purse strings of America's working women.

Claiborne has been unwilling to rest on her laurels, even though she has retired from active management. Claiborne and her husband have committed themselves to perpetuating the creative spirit of the company by turning it over to young management. Her design philosophy has been continuously nurtured in an extensive staff of talented designers and design assistants. She continues to devote time teaching and guiding the new division heads. For this reason, Liz Claiborne's aesthetics or wish list are clearly present in cleanly sculptured silhouettes and in a tangy dash of color in apparel.

As the 1980's came to a close, Americans were facing a deepening recession and high unemployment figures. The freewheeling spending of previous years came to an abrupt halt as people tightened their purse strings. American designers, including Claiborne, increasingly took to creating secondary and less expensive collections. In the late 1980's, Liz Claiborne, Inc., had moved into retailing and her stores, named First Issue, sold sportswear and accessories in the $40 to $100 range. The First Issue stores were designed to compete with youth-oriented retail outlets such as The Limited, The Gap, and Banana Republic. With her realistic pricing policy and far-sighted corporate decisions, Liz Claiborne has cemented her reputation as one of the most admired corporate executives in America.

Bibliography
Better, Nancy Marx. "The Secret of Liz Claiborne's Success." *Working Woman* 17 (April, 1992): 68-73. Includes the secrets behind Claiborne's success and how she started the company.
Davis, Fred. *Fashion, Culture, and Identity*. Chicago: University of Chicago Press, 1992. A thorough discussion is given on the role clothing plays in communicating the individual's social identity. Antifashion in contemporary society is delineated.
Feldman, Elane. *Fashions of a Decade: The 1990's*. New York: Facts on File, 1992. Provides an overview of the decade, examining fashion developments in the light of trends in the arts, technology, politics, and living patterns. It includes eight chapters highlighting key individual fashion themes.
Grigsby, David W., and Michael J. Stahl. *Strategic Management Cases*. Boston: PWS-KENT, 1992. Provides comprehensive, timely cases featuring a wide range of organizations. The authors focus on Liz Claiborne, Inc., to examine its strategic decision making in the fashion apparel industry.
Morgenson, Gretchen. "The Feminization of Seventh Avenue." *Forbes* 149 (May 11, 1992): 116-120. Reports how men still dominate the fashion news, but it is women designers and executives who move the merchandise on Seventh Ave. It profiles women designers, including Liz Claiborne.
Morris, Michele. "The Wizard of the Working Woman's Wardrobe." *Working Woman* 13 (June, 1988): 74-77. Profiles Elisabeth Claiborne Ortenberg, president and chief executive officer of Liz Claiborne, Inc., the first company started by a woman to make the *Fortune 500* list. It describes Claiborne's background and her career in the fashion industry.

Bill Manikas

PATSY CLINE

Born: September 8, 1932; Gore, Virginia
Died: March 5, 1963; near Camden, Tennessee
Area of Achievement: Music
Contribution: A pioneering force in bringing women to the forefront of country music, Patsy Cline proved not only that a female could become a significant star but also that her singing could appeal across many musical boundaries.

Early Life

Virginia Patterson Hensley was born the daughter of Sam Hensley, a World War I veteran, and his second wife, Hilda Patterson Hensley, in the town of Gore near Winchester, Virginia, on a September day amid the darkest days of the Great Depression. Young Virginia grew up in the Shenandoah Valley of Virginia. Her family was poor, and during the 1930's, they moved every year, sometimes more, as father Sam searched for work. A frequent stop was Sam's hometown of Elkton, Virginia, a small town nestled up against the newly established Shenandoah National Park. Their financial situation improved during the years between 1941 and 1945 when the family moved to Portsmouth and her father worked as a master blacksmith and engineer at the naval shipyards near Norfolk, Virginia. Growing up, Virginia Hensley attended Baptist church services and loved to sing the familiar hymns and traditional spirituals she heard at church.

It was radio, however, that provided a constant link to the outside world, enabling Virginia to learn to mimic her country music favorites, from Patsy Montana to Roy Acuff. Virginia's impressive memory enabled the precocious youngster to sing almost any country song after she had heard it only two times. She could never read a note of music and never took a singing lesson in her life. During early adolescence, Virginia developed a serious throat infection during a bout with rheumatic fever. After her recovery, Virginia lost her childlike voice and began to sound more like an Ethel Merman or Kate Smith. After World War II ended, the Hensley family settled in the rail and trading hub of Winchester, but in 1947, Sam Hensley deserted his wife and their three children (Virginia, younger brother Sam, Jr., and younger sister, Sylvia.) Hilda found work as a seamstress and Virginia quit high school at the beginning of her sophomore year to help support the family. During the day, she worked behind the soda fountain in the local drugstore. At night, she sang in local Moose and American Legion Halls to earn a bit more income.

In 1952, she professionally became "Patsy" Hensley as a Saturday night regular at the Moose Hall in Brunswick, Maryland, located some forty miles up the Potomac River from Washington, D.C. Soon, she found steady work in music and was able to quit her day job. Literally across the street from a rail yard, she belted out her renditions of current hits for fifty dollars a performance. One year later Patsy moved to nearby Frederick, Maryland, married Gerald Cline, and became known professionally as Patsy Cline.

Life's Work

Patsy Cline's break came with radio and then television work in Washington, D.C. Country music impresario Connie B. Gay found work for Cline singing for the city's ABC-TV affiliate and performing live on radio station WARL in Arlington, Virginia, across the river from the nation's capital. Patsy Cline, Jimmy Dean, and Roy Clark, all of whom became legends in the country music business, were then newcomers, happy to appear seven days a week on television and radio as well as making public appearances in a circuit which stretched from Hagerstown to Baltimore, Maryland, and Washington, D.C., down to Richmond, Virginia.

From 1955 through 1956, Cline appeared with Jimmy Dean on *Town and Country Time*, which aired on a forty-station regional television network stretching from Salisbury, Maryland, to Harrisonburg, Virginia. Gay's Hillbilly Midnight Cruises sailed the Chesapeake Bay, with 2,000 fans jammed aboard an open-decked boat, and his Hillbilly Air Shows featured biplanes and country music. At the height of her success as a regional performer, Patsy Cline appeared on the CBS television show *Arthur Godfrey's Talent Scouts* and seemed to be on the verge of becoming a national star. Wearing a conservative party dress, not the usual cowgirl outfit sewn by her mother, Patsy Cline earned thousands of new fans with her rendition of "Walkin' After Midnight."

The song proved to be her first hit record. Although Patsy Cline seemed to be on her way, it was not to be. Her follow-up records did not sell well. Connie B. Gay's empire developed in directions that did not include Patsy Cline. She was divorced from Gerald Cline, moved back to her mother's house on Kent Street, and married a Winchester neighbor, Charlie Dick. After their wedding on September 15, 1957, Charlie and Patsy found a house down the street from Patsy's mother in an area considered to be on the wrong side of the tracks. Charlie had been drafted into the U.S. Army and was soon sent to Fort Bragg, North Carolina. The couple's daughter Julie was born in Winchester on August 26, 1958. Leaving her infant daughter in her mother's care, Patsy Cline resumed her musical career on the regional club circuit, traveling wherever she could find work in Maryland, West Virginia, and Virginia. She sang at drive-in movie theaters before the features began. Those performances featured Cline in her homemade cowgirl outfit, jumping on the back of a flatbed truck and belting out new country tunes. July 4, 1958, Patsy Cline served as the Grand Marshal of the Jubilee Parade held in her father's birthplace of Elkton, Virginia, and even sang before minor league baseball games in Front Royal, Virginia.

In February, 1959, Charlie Dick was discharged by the Army and returned to Winchester. Despite her husband's discharge, Cline continued to receive child support payments from the Army. In October of 1959, Patsy and Charlie cashed these checks and moved to Nashville, Tennessee. Iron-willed Patsy Cline wanted to risk one more attempt at fame and fortune.

After struggling to find work and make recordings throughout 1960 into the spring of 1961, Patsy Cline finally achieved a hit with the new Nashville Sound. Her lush and emotional recording of "I Fall to Pieces" rose to number one on the country music charts in August, 1961, soon followed by another chart climber, "Crazy," written by Willie Nelson. Thereafter, for eighteen heady months, through the latter half of 1961 and all of 1962, Patsy Cline became a star and was one of the popular regulars on the legendary broadcasts from the stage of Nashville's Grand Ole Opry. *The New York Times* hailed Cline's appearance at Carnegie Hall. Although she was nearly killed in a horrible car accident after recording "I Fall to Pieces," Cline continued to perform during her recuperation. By the end of 1962, Patsy Cline had deposed Kitty Wells as the reigning queen of country music.

Patsy Cline developed her popular Nashville Sound recording style under the direction of producer Owen Bradley, a former pop music pianist. Bradley surrounded Patsy Cline with the best musicians Nashville offered, and located songs that appealed to both country and pop music audiences. Fans loved Patsy Cline's smoothly evoked heartache and pain so tenderly expressed in "Sweet Dreams," "Faded Love," "Crazy Arms," "So Wrong," and "Three Cigarettes in an Ashtray." Even when surrounded by cool, elegant orchestral arrangements, she evoked a tension, a dynamic, a subtlety that quickly made her one of country music's top attractions.

Cline's body of work was characterized by her magnificent vocal stylings, subtly accenting each word and note. She had the ability to stretch musical phrases without breaking her voice; her control was both precise and pleasing, her presentation smooth and sure. Her unique and complex singing style—perfected through years of work in and around Washington, D.C.—ensured that her reputation and popularity continued to grow.

Sadly, her success proved short-lived. Patsy Cline died in a light plane crash on her way back from a concert in Kansas City. She was buried on March 10, 1963, in a simple cemetery near Winchester, Virginia. Her record label Decca (later MCA Records) kept releasing songs that Patsy Cline had recorded before her death and these posthumous releases continued to sell for several years thereafter.

Summary

Patsy Cline represents one of the most famous and most influential singers of country music. Indeed her very style defined a particular country music genre—the Nashville Sound. Cline's crossover appeal brought her fame well beyond the country music market as the first female country singer to achieve such national and later international fame within the field of mainstream popular music.

Portrayed by Beverly D'Angelo in the Loretta Lynn film *Coal Miner's Daughter* (1980) and by Jessica Lange in the celebrated film autobiography *Sweet Dreams* (1985), and commemorated on a postage stamp issued in September of 1993, Patsy Cline had an enduring appeal that continued to influence a new generation of fans. Her election into the Country Music Hall of Fame in 1973, a decade after her tragic death, kept her in the country music record buying public's consciousness. Thereafter, admirers issued tributes such as Loretta Lynn's album entitled *I Remember Patsy* (1976), and covers of Cline's most famous songs were recorded by such contemporary stars as Emmylou Harris and Reba McEntire. Avant garde country singer K. D. Lang recorded covers of several Patsy Cline songs in the 1980's and named her backup band the Reclines in Cline's honor.

Patsy Cline's recordings are constantly reissued. In 1992, her *Greatest Hits* album passed 4 million in sales, and was still selling well. Through her recordings, Patsy Cline lives—a great talent constantly rediscovered and seemingly alive to new generations of fans. By the close of the twentieth century, Patsy Cline had become such a national icon that during the 1992 presidential election, third party candidate Ross Perot used Patsy Cline's version of *Crazy* as his campaign theme song. Few singers have ingrained themselves further into the national consciousness than Patsy Cline.

Bibliography

Brown, Charles T. *Music U.S.A.: America's Country & Western Tradition.* Englewood Cliffs, N.J.: Prentice-Hall, 1986. This valuable textbook survey of the history of country music in the United States contains a valuable section on Patsy Cline. Well illustrated, the best part of the survey is its bibliography and textual musical analysis.

Bufwack, Mary A., and Robert K. Oermann. *Finding Her Voice: The Saga of Women in Country Music.* New York: Crown, 1993. Here is a well-documented history of the impact of women in country music in the United States. Chapter 10 is one of the best surveys of Patsy Cline's career. Contains illustrations and an extensive thirty-page bibliography.

Jones, Margaret. *Patsy: The Life and Times of Patsy Cline.* New York: HarperCollins, 1994. Based on extensive interviews with those who were Cline's contemporaries on the country music scene, this biography presents a sympathetic account of Cline's turbulent life and the intense drive to succeed that fueled her pursuit of country music stardom. Includes illustrations, bibliographic references, and a discography.

Kingsbury, Paul, and Alan Axelrod, eds. *Country: The Music and the Musicians.* New York: Abbeville Press, 1988. A lavish, beautifully illustrated, oversized coffee table book that contains sixteen essays covering all the basics of the history of country music. The selected discography and bibliography are fundamental. An entire chapter assesses, at some length, the considerable accomplishments of Patsy Cline.

Lewis, George H., ed. *All That Glitters: Country Music in America.* Bowling Green, Ohio: Bowling Green State University Popular Press, 1993. The work of Joli Jensen is crucial to understanding the music of Patsy Cline. A doctoral candidate at the University of Illinois, Jensen completed a Ph.D. dissertation on the Nashville music scene in 1984, but that fine work has, sadly, not been turned into a book. Most accessible is this essay in this valuable collection which covers many facets of country music history and the pioneering place of Patsy Cline.

Malone, Bill C. *Country Music U.S.A.* Rev. ed. Austin: University of Texas Press, 1985. This work stands as the standard one-volume scholarly history of country music. The career of Patsy Cline is treated in considerable detail, again emphasizing her key role in opening doors for women in what had long been a business dominated by males. The extensive bibliography of more than one hundred pages ought to be required reading for anyone seriously interested in this genre of popular music.

Nassour, Ellis. *Honky Tonk Angel: The Intimate Story of Patsy Cline.* New York: St. Martin's Press, 1993. Based on a popular biography issued in 1981, this revised life history offers the most complete account of the career of Patsy Cline. The detail gathered from interviews is considerable; the photographs are rare and the best of any available book. Nassour's work suffers badly when compared to scholarly biography of comparable music figures; his insights are all too rare and his views consist primarily of undigested pop psychology.

Douglas Gomery

HILLARY RODHAM CLINTON

Born: October 26, 1947; Chicago, Illinois

Areas of Achievement: Law and government and politics
Contribution: A highly regarded lawyer and activist for children's rights and comprehensive health care, Clinton also became her husband's most important adviser when he served as governor of Arkansas and president of the United States.

Early Life

Hillary Diane Rodham was born on October 26, 1947, in Chicago, Illinois. Her father Hugh was a textile merchant who married Dorothy Howell in 1942. Hugh's success in making draperies for hotels and corporate offices enabled the family to move to the upper-middle-class suburb of Park Ridge in 1950.

Growing up in a tightly knit family with her two brothers provided Hillary with what she later called her "core values." Along with her parents' unconditional love and support came their high expectations for achievement and a demand for responsible behavior and hard work. Hillary responded by becoming an honor student in high school who excelled at numerous extracurricular activities, including debate and student government. Her interest in politics led her to work as a volunteer in the 1964 presidential campaign for Barry Goldwater, a Republican candidate who reflected the conservative beliefs of her family and neighborhood.

The Methodist church was another early influence in Hillary's life. The emphasis upon the social mission of the church as well its teachings on personal faith and growth appealed to her. Youth minister Don Jones was particularly influential. He took youth groups to meet inner-city teens, and he encouraged Hillary to help organize day care services for migrant farm workers. In 1962, Jones took a youth group to hear an address from the Reverend Martin Luther King, Jr., who spoke on the need to eradicate social injustice. Jones also introduced Hillary to the writings of liberal theologians Paul Tillich and Reinhold Niebuhr, works concerned with alienation and the search for meaning. Hillary later acknowledged that Jones not only whetted her intellectual curiosity but also demonstrated to her the necessity of helping those less fortunate than herself.

The evolution of her values was accelerated when Hillary entered Wellesley College near Boston, Massachusetts, in 1965. Amidst the turbulence of the late 1960's, Hillary became a social activist. She worked at a Head Start center in the Roxbury neighborhood of Boston, joined in an effort to recruit more minority students to Wellesley, organized teach-ins on the Vietnam War, and won election as president of Wellesley's student government.

The culmination of her undergraduate experience came when her classmates selected Hillary to deliver the first student commencement address at Wellesley. She offered a message common to that era, arguing that her generation was seeking an alternative to the "competitive corporate life" and wanted to find "more immediate, ecstatic, and penetrating modes of living." Her commencement message attracted national attention when *Life* magazine published a photo of her and quotations from her address. The next logical step for Hillary, a political science major whose senior thesis was on poverty and community development, was Yale Law School, an institution known for its "social" approach to law.

Life's Work

Besides compiling an excellent academic record, Hillary Rodham met two important people during her time at Yale. In 1970, Marian Wright Edelman, who headed an advocacy group for poor children, made a speech on the campus. Hillary was so impressed by Edelman's appeal that she decided to work as an intern with her in Washington, D.C., during the summer of 1970. Eager to learn more about the problems of children, Hillary worked at the Yale Child Study Center upon her return to law school and began a study of child development and children's rights. From this research, Hillary wrote an article entitled "Children Under the Law" that appeared in the *Harvard Educational Review* in 1974.

The other significant person Hillary met at Yale was a Rhodes scholar from Arkansas named Bill Clinton. Although he was initially intimidated by Hillary, Bill quickly found that they were intellectually as well as romantically compatible. The two traveled to Texas in 1972 to work on George McGovern's presidential campaign. Following graduation the next year, however, Hillary became a staff attorney for Marian Wright Edelman's Children's Defense Fund in Cambridge, Massachusetts, and Bill accepted a position on the faculty of the University of Arkansas Law School at Fayetteville.

In January of 1974, Hillary joined the legal team headed by John Doar, special counsel to the House Judiciary Committee, selected to conduct the impeachment investigation of President Richard Nixon. One of only three women among the forty-three lawyers picked, Hillary helped establish the procedural guidelines for the investigation. After President Nixon resigned in August of 1974, Hillary decided to join Bill Clinton on the faculty of the University of Arkansas Law School and helped organized his congressional campaign against long-time incumbent Republican John Paul Hammerschmidt. Although he lost in a close contest, Bill made a name for himself in Arkansas politics and ran successfully two years later for the post of attorney general.

Bill and Hillary, who had married on October 11, 1975, moved to the state capital in Little Rock, Arkansas, in 1976. Both had worked in the Jimmy Carter presidential campaign that year, Bill in Arkansas and Hillary in Indiana. Impressed by her efforts in the campaign and her legal expertise, President Carter appointed Hillary in 1977 to serve on the board of the Legal Services Corporation, an agency that administered funds for legal services to the indigent. She also became the first female associate in the Rose Law Firm in Little Rock, where she specialized in family law and commercial litigation.

Beginning in 1978, Hillary was a crucial figure in her husband's six campaigns for governor, all of which he won except the 1980 race. An effective and tireless speaker, she also became a valued adviser on campaign tactics and issues. Despite her expertise, Hillary was perceived by some as hindrance to the success of her husband's gubernatorial races. After her marriage, Hillary kept her maiden name until 1982 because she had developed her professional reputation as Hillary Rodham. Traditionalists in Arkansas, however, disapproved. They also did not want the state's first lady to continue her career. More serious were charges that her continued affiliation with the Rose Law Firm brought the governor into a conflict of interest whenever the firm did legal work for the state.

Such concerns did not prevent Governor Clinton from appointing his wife to chair some significant statewide committees. The most important appointment came in 1983 when she headed the Arkansas Education Standards Committee. She tackled the challenge in a way that presaged her effort a decade later to reform health care. She spoke to civic groups around the state and held hearings in every Arkansas county. In all, she heard from thousands of citizens; from those exchanges, she crafted a package of reforms for the legislature's consideration. An improved curriculum, reduced class size, mandatory student testing, improved teacher salaries, and a sales tax increase to pay for the improvements were approved by the legislature and began to be implemented in 1987.

While Hillary impressed most with her organizational skills, excellent speeches, and an impressive two-hour presentation to the Arkansas House, she angered many teachers. Believing that demonstrating teacher competency was the only way to convince voters to support a tax increase, Hillary included mandatory tests for all public schoolteachers in Arkansas in the reform package approved by the legislators. Demanding accountability from those benefiting from reform became a hallmark of Hillary's efforts.

Hillary's life was not consumed entirely by campaigning and serving on committees. She devoted time to caring for her daughter Chelsea, who was born on February 27, 1980, and in carrying out some of the traditional ceremonial functions of the state's first lady. Hillary also found time to advance her career. After the Rose law firm made her partner in 1979, she branched out into patent infringement and other intellectual property cases. Acknowledging her growing influence, several enterprises, including the nation's leading retailer Wal-Mart, selected her to serve on their boards. Hillary's considerable accomplishments brought her numerous honors. Most notable, in both 1988 and 1991, the *National Law Journal* named her one of the hundred most influential lawyers in the nation.

When Bill Clinton joined the race for the 1992 Democratic presidential nomination, Hillary became a campaign issue. During the 1992 Republican Convention, for example, some speakers portrayed Hillary as a radical feminist who represented a threat to the traditional family. Most damaging to the Clintons, however, were charges of Bill's infidelity. Rumors of marital problems had plagued the couple in the 1980's in Arkansas, but these rumors became headline stories when Gennifer Flowers, a former Arkansas television reporter and lounge singer, claimed she had had a twelve-year affair with Bill Clinton. While all the questions were not answered, Hillary played a major role in defusing the story in an appearance she made with Bill on the CBS news program *60 Minutes* in January of 1992. She not only vigorously defended her husband's character but also told a national audience that everyone, including political candidates, should "have some zone of privacy."

Following his inauguration, President Clinton demonstrated his faith in Hillary's abilities by naming her to head the most important commission of his new administration, the Task Force on National Health Care Reform. As she had done in the Arkansas legislature a decade earlier, Hillary impressed the national media and congressmen alike with her knowledge and poise in two days of hearings in the House of Representatives. Throughout 1993, she enjoyed high ratings in public opinion polls. The only significant concern with the First Lady's performance were questions about the legalities involved in the Clintons' investments in the Arkansas Whitewater Development Corporation. In April of 1994, she held a special press conference to answer questions and counter criticism that she had been less than forthcoming about her role in the corporation's activities.

Summary

In the eyes of many, Hillary Rodham Clinton became a role model in demonstrating the gains resulting from the changing status of women. While she refused to discard the roles of wife and mother, Hillary was not reluctant to embrace a career in both the private and public sectors. That she was highly regarded in both areas was a testament to her intelligence, ambition, and skills as a politician. These achievements were not without costs. As they observed her rise to prominence, some portrayed Hillary as overbearing and arrogant, charges that ambitious, successful women often faced in the late twentieth century.

Most of her public struggles—for children's rights, better schools, and quality health care accessible to all—are best understood as an effort to help families fulfill their societal obligations. In pursuing these reforms, Hillary was doing more than following the social mission she learned as a teen in the Methodist Church. She was also demonstrating that the old labels of liberal and conservative were no longer useful for many reformers in the late twentieth century. She advocated the use of government power to extend rights to citizens, but she also demanded that those citizens be accountable, that they demonstrate a sense of responsibility. In helping to redefine the relationship between government and the people, Hillary Rodham Clinton found the political meaning she had been seeking.

Bibliography

Kelly, Michael. "Saint Hillary." *The New York Times Magazine*, May 23, 1993, 22-25, 63-66. Kelly offers a critical discussion of Clinton's efforts at reform. He sees her as one of a long line of do-gooders seeking to impose her view of morality on the populace.

Martin, Nina. "Who Is She?" *Mother Jones* 18 (November/December, 1993): 34-38,

43. In a largely complimentary article, Martin describes Hillary Rodham Clinton as a moderate reformer. More important, as she discusses Hillary's career, the author explores how marriage to Bill Clinton restricted Hillary's options.

Nelson, Rex, and Philip Martin. *The Hillary Factor.* New York: Gallen Publishing Group, 1993. This work by the political editor and a political columnist for the *Arkansas Democrat-Gazette* offers the perspective of reporters who covered Hillary Rodham Clinton during her almost two decades in Arkansas politics.

Radcliffe, Donnie. *Hillary Rodham Clinton: A First Lady for Our Time.* New York: Warner Books, 1993. The author, a *Washington Post* reporter, offers a full-length biography of Clinton. One of the virtues of the book is that the author was able to draw upon two extensive interviews with Clinton.

Wills, Garry. "H.R. Clinton's Case." *New York Review of Books* 39 (March 5, 1992): 3-5. Through an examination of her articles and speeches, Wills offers an analysis of Clinton as an activist for children's rights. He concludes that she was one of the most important scholar-activists of the 1970's and 1980's.

Larry Gragg

GLENN CLOSE

Born: March 19, 1947; Greenwich, Connecticut

Areas of Achievement: Film and theater and drama
Contribution: A talented actress who has received awards for her performances in film, theater, and television, Glenn Close has played characters whose careers, problems, and situations reflect women's social and political issues.

Early Life

Glenn Close was born on March 19, 1947, in Greenwich, Connecticut, and reared on her grandfather's five-hundred-acre estate. As a child, she read extensively; she later commented that her earliest memories were of pretending to be someone else. By the time she was seven, she had decided to become an actress and fantasized about being discovered by Walt Disney. Her life was both privileged (her parents, William and Bettine Close, had the money and durable New England ancestry to belong to Greenwich society) and isolated. When her father, a surgeon working with Moral Re-Armament, went to the Belgian Congo (now Zaire) to establish a medical clinic, her isolation increased, for she divided her time between Africa, Connecticut, and Switzerland, where she went to boarding school. She has stated that her parents' move made her feel a bit rejected. Finally, like her mother and grandmother, she entered Rosemary Hall, an exclusive boarding school for girls, where her interest in dramatics was stimulated. With five friends, she formed the acting group *The Fingernails, the Group with Polish*, which performed skits. She also appeared in school productions, culminating with her role as Romeo in the senior play.

Like her father, Close was affiliated with Moral Re-Armament, and after her high school graduation in 1965 postponed college, instead touring the country with singing groups, including the upbeat Up with People ensemble, for whom she wrote songs and sang. About this "dropout" phase of her life, which she has termed her "lost life," she has mixed feelings; while she had the opportunity to perform, she also felt manipulated and out of place. In 1969, she married rock musician Cabot Wade; a year later, they entered the College of William and Mary, a state university in Virginia where she had performed on tour. Although the marriage ended before she was graduated, her life at the university was beneficial to her career. She majored in theater, appeared in several productions, and was graduated Phi Beta Kappa in 1974. Howard Scammon, her mentor, encouraged her to audition for the Theater Communication Group, and in the finals, conducted in Chicago, she did so well that she was asked to audition for small roles and to understudy several female leads.

Life's Work

Glenn Close's first break as an actress came with the New Phoenix Repertory Company. As an understudy to lead Mary Ure, Close replaced her in William Congreve's *Love for Love* after Ure was fired. Close's performance led to two more roles with the New Phoenix Repertory Company in the 1974-1975 season, after which she appeared in regional theater productions of dramatic "classics," Off-Broadway plays by lesser-known dramatists, and the Broadway musical *Rex*. In 1978, her supporting role in Paul Giovanni's *The Crucifer of Blood* won critical acclaim. She appeared in two made-for-television films in 1979, but it was her 1980 role as Charity Barnum in the musical *Barnum* that was the pivotal point in her career. Director George Roy Hill had seen Close in *Barnum* and, impressed with the "charged stillness" she projected in a scene that called for her to be motionless, hired her to play Jenny Fields, Garp's mother in *The World According to Garp* (1982). Her portrayal of the sexless, nurturing, independent Jenny won her an Oscar nomination for best supporting actress and many job offers.

In the next two years Close played, as she had in the past, a variety of theatrical roles, including the androgynous title character in a 1982 Off-Broadway production of *The Singular Life of Albert Nobbs* (for which she won an Obie award) and the highly sexed, exuberant Annie in a 1984 Broadway production of Tom Stoppard's *The Real Thing* (for which she won a Tony Award). In the made-for-television film *Something About Amelia* (1984), Close garnered attention for her portrayal of a woman who finally realizes that there is an incestuous relationship between her husband and her adolescent daughter.

Despite her versatility, Close appeared to have been typecast for feature-film roles during this period—roles she termed "daughters of Jenny." In *The Big Chill* (1983), she played Sarah, a strong, nurturing woman whose emotional shower scene earned for Close a second Oscar nomination for best supporting actress. In *The Stone Boy* (1984), she portrayed a caring wife and mother stricken with grief over the unexpected death of her son. Released from a commitment to act in the film adaptation of Henry James's *The Bostonians*, Close was awarded the role of Iris Raines opposite Robert Redford in *The Natural* (1984). Made pregnant by her high-school sweetheart, baseball prospect Roy Hobbes, Iris waits fifteen years before reappearing in his life, informing him of his paternity, and being reunited with him. Criticized for her "Earth Mother" roles, Close insisted she wanted to avoid long-suffering, nurturing roles and break out of such typecasting.

With *Maxie* (1985), Close broke out of this mold. As a good woman possessed by the spirit of a Roaring Twenties "vamp," Close demonstrated her comedic talent, but the film did poorly at the box office. In the thriller *Jagged Edge* (1985), she was cast as Teddy Barnes, a divorced San Francisco attorney who eventually sleeps with her client, a man accused of murdering his wife. It was not until she appeared in the thriller *Fatal Attraction* (1987), however, that her break with past stereotyping was complete. In the film, Close plays a psychotic career woman named Alex Forrest whose weekend fling with Dan Gallagher (Michael Douglas) turns sour when he returns to his wife and child. While incorporating elements of the horror genre, the film's riveting drama afforded Close an opportunity for demonstrating her sexuality and emotional range, and her success resulted in another Oscar nomination, this time as best actress.

Fatal Attraction garnered public attention because of the way Close's character was depicted. In the original version, the film ended with Alex carefully staging her own suicide in such a way that Dan Gallagher was framed for her murder. After preview audiences registered their indignation over the film's callous destruction of the Gallagher family, the ending was altered to depict Close's character as psychotic, not suicidal, and to reunite the Gallaghers. Feminists were further outraged by this skewed portrait of the career woman, and the film became a catalyst for much serious discussion.

Close's success in *Fatal Attraction* was followed by her role as the calculating Marquise de Merteuil in *Dangerous Liaisons* (1988). Close's role as a woman who represses her feelings in order to achieve control in the male-dominated eighteenth century French society won critical recognition. As in *The Big Chill*, her character maintains her composure so well that the final emotional outburst shocks and electrifies the audience. As Sunny Von Bulow in *Reversal of Fortune* (1990), Close played a brutally boozy character from the newspaper headlines; in *Immediate Family* (1989) she played a married woman who discovers she is infertile and decides to adopt a child; and as Gertrude in *Hamlet* (1990), she portrayed a sexually provocative but weak mother opposite Mel Gibson in the lead role. In *Meeting Venus* (1991), she again demonstrated the extraordinary range of characters she was able to portray. Her appearance as an opera diva in love with her conductor gave Close an opportunity to exhibit her singing skills.

Despite her success with films, Close did not abandon the stage. In 1991, she appeared in *Brooklyn Laundry*; in 1992, she appeared in *Death and the Maiden*; and in 1993, she starred in the Los Angeles production of Andrew Lloyd Webber's *Sunset Boulevard* in the Gloria Swanson role. As she stated in an interview at the American Film Institute, "I like what they do in England—they do everything." She herself was the coexecutive producer and star of *Sarah, Plain and Tall*, a Hallmark Hall of Fame production for CBS television. The film was a property that interested her and was so popular it spawned a sequel, *Skylark* (1993).

In 1994, Close returned to the motion picture screen in two Hollywood studio releases: She appeared in *The Paper*, directed by Ron Howard, and in *House of Spirits*, a film adaptation of a novel by Isabel Allende. In the latter film, Close appears in a supporting role opposite Meryl Streep as her friend and rival; as a sexually repressed woman in love with her brother's wife, Close has a rich role as a composed woman whose emotions finally erupt.

Summary

Glenn Close has enjoyed critical and popular success in a variety of roles in film, theater, and television. Moving freely between the media, she has been unwilling to restrict her performing to one field; and she has recently begun producing shows in addition to acting in them. She is not a conventional "star" whose personality dominates her roles; she is an actress who submerges her personality and becomes the characters she plays, even when those characters are not young, attractive, or wholesome. Despite playing characters of all ages, backgrounds, and classes in a variety of historical and cultural settings, she has tended to be attracted to complex roles featuring strong, independent women intent on control, but unable ultimately to check their emotions and passions. Sexual politics, whether treated overtly as in *The World According to Garp* or conveyed covertly as in *House of Spirits* or *Fatal Attraction*, is the theme of many of her films, and conflicts between characters often represent ideological tensions. The subject matter of her films and plays (infertility, incest, disturbed children) has also dealt with women's issues. Although early in her career she claimed that feminism seemed "rather hollow," her subsequent performances have established her as a feminist actress.

Bibliography
Allen, Bonnie. "Glenn Close: Sitting Pretty." *Ms.* 18 (November, 1989): 46-50. Excellent overview of Close's film career, which Allen sees as a transition from stereotypical "Earth Mother" roles to more varied parts beginning with the pivotal *Fatal Attraction*. Allen also traces Close's life story from her childhood to her stint with Up with People to the Broadway triumphs that led to her first screen role. Asked about her earlier statement that feminism "seems rather hollow," Close requested a retraction of the comment.
Buckley, Peter. "Close Encounter." *Horizon* 27 (April, 1984): 50-54. Focuses on Close's possible award-winning performances on Broadway in Tom Stoppard's *The Real Thing* (Tony), on television in *Something About Amelia* (Emmy), Off-Broadway in *The Singular Life of Albert Nobbs* (Obie), and in Kasdan's film *The Big Chill* (Oscar). Buckley provides some biographical details and some discussion of Close's "theatrical" work at Rosemary Hall, her exclusive Connecticut boarding school.
Michener, Charles. "She's Not Meryl Streep, But She's Close." *Esquire* 112 (November, 1989): 136-140. Besides discussing Close's varied roles, Michener comments on her acting methods, using a distinction between actors who perform a role (Meryl Streep) and those who become the role (Close). He further develops the contrast between the actresses in a discussion of Wendy Wasserstein's *Uncommon Women and Others*—both Streep and Close played the role of Leilah. Close declares her admiration for Bette Davis, who, like Close, often played unattractive characters "with only the hope that people understand them in the end."
Segrave, Kerry, and Linda Martin. *The Post-Feminist Hollywood Actress*. Jefferson, N.C.: McFarland, 1990. Mingles biographical information and critical evaluations of Close's work in television, theater, and film. The authors regard *Fatal Attraction* as providing a "departure from type" for her. The essay also contains a filmography and a comprehensive list of sources, including some film reviews.
Spotnitz, Frank. "Glenn Close." *American Film* 16 (November-December, 1991): 22-27. Interesting interview conducted at the American Film Institute. Close answers, at length, questions about her acting method, her judgments of scripts, the qualities of a good director, and her future plans to produce films. Her com-

ments about her character in *Fatal Attraction* (suicidal rather than psychopathic) and in *Dangerous Liaisons* (attempted puppeteer rather than puppet) are especially interesting.

Wetzsteon, Ross. "Too Close for Comfort." *American Film* 9 (May, 1984): 16-21. In conversation on the set of *The Natural*, Close discusses film versus stage acting and comments on her readiness to escape the roles she played after *The World According to Garp*, the "daughters of Jenny," "motherly, strong, serene." Wetzsteon provides a great deal of information about Close's stage career.

Thomas L. Erskine

JACQUELINE COCHRAN

Born: c. 1910; Pensacola, Florida
Died: August 9, 1980; Indio, California
Area of Achievement: Aviation
Contribution: A pioneer in women's aviation and a savvy businesswoman, Jacqueline Cochran paved the way for female American pilots of the future.

Early Life

Although she may have been born sometime in 1910, Jacqueline Cochran chose to commemorate May 11, 1912, as her date of birth. Orphaned at an early age, she was adopted by a poor family of factory workers who worked in the sawmill camp towns of northern Florida and southern Georgia. At the age of eight, she worked in the mills for six cents an hour on twelve-hour shifts.

Unwilling to suffer the fate of her foster parents, Cochran moved to Montgomery, Alabama, as a teenager. There, she secured a position in a beauty shop. Encouraged by a customer who was impressed with her potential, Cochran entered and finished nursing school. Convinced she could make a difference, she returned to the mill towns where she grew up to practice nursing. It was not long before she abandoned that endeavor. After assisting in the difficult delivery of a sick, scrawny baby, Cochran decided her limited efforts could do nothing to ease the plight of the poor.

Determined to make something of herself, Cochran returned to work in a beauty shop, this time in Pensacola, Florida. In 1929, she went to New York, where she talked herself into a hairdresser's job at Antoine's Salon, Saks Fifth Avenue. During the winter social season, she worked at Antoine's shop in Miami Beach. It was there, in 1932, that Cochran met the wealthy Floyd Bostwick Odlum. Noting the popularity of barnstorming exhibitions and air races, Odlum encouraged her to train as a pilot in order to help promote the cosmetics industry. The following summer, she obtained her pilot's license on Long Island during her three-week vacation from the beauty salon. She eventually followed up with more training to increase her competency.

Meanwhile, with the help of Odlum she started her own company, Jacqueline Cochran Cosmetics, Incorporated, in 1935. Her interest in aviation flourished, too, as she began to compete in air races. In 1934, she entered the McRobertson London-Melbourne Race. She was the only woman to enter the Bendix Transcontinental Race in 1935 and to win it in 1938. Taking a break from competition, Cochran and Odlum were married in 1936; it was a match that lasted for forty years. When Cochran began racing again, she received the coveted Clifford Burke Harmon trophy as the outstanding woman flier in the world.

Life's Work

Jacqueline Cochran's numerous flight records endeared her to the American public as she continued to pioneer a path for female aviators. In 1939, she achieved a new altitude record for women; later, she became the first woman to make a blind landing.

Two of her speed records in 1940 broke the existing speed records that had been established by men. As a result of her accomplishments and her husband's connections with President Franklin D. Roosevelt, Cochran suggested to Eleanor Roosevelt that a female air corps could be established in order to perform noncombatant duties, such as flying troop transport and supply planes and ferrying fighter planes overseas.

To demonstrate that women had a role to play during World War II, Cochran planned to deliver a bomber to England. To prove herself worthy of the task, she endured a three-day flight test of sixty takeoffs and landings before she was cleared for the transatlantic flight. As soon as her intentions were announced, male ferry pilots threatened to strike, arguing that to allow women to perform these duties would be to put their own abilities into question. To solve the conflict, Cochran had to relinquish the controls to her male copilot, Captain Grafton Carlisle, on takeoff and landing. She completed the flight successfully, but stayed in England only long enough to visit Pauline Gower, the director of the British women pilots in Britain's Air Transport Auxiliary.

Returning to the United States, Cochran tried to organize a similar group. Supported by General Hap Arnold, Cochran tried unsuccessfully to convince the U.S. government that it should employ female pilots. Upon General Arnold's reassurance that America would rely on the women in an emergency, Cochran followed his suggestion to recruit American women to fly for the British Air Transport Auxiliary. She kept the detachment small, selecting forty women from her files and narrowing the list down to twenty-five before sending them to England. These American pilots completed a three-month Air Transport Auxiliary Program. They were acknowledged as first-class fliers and most of them finished their eighteen-month contracts.

When Cochran returned home in the fall of 1942, she was surprised to find that the United States had already begun to mobilize women fliers. Under the Army Air Force Air Transport Command, a Women's Auxiliary Ferrying Squadron was activated. Nancy Harkness Love commanded this squadron. Although Cochran commended Love as an excellent pilot, she surmised that Love did not wish to head a completely female squadron under military rules. Cochran's assumption proved correct. Nancy Love only wished to supplement the male forces with women's pilots. The government activated the Women's Auxiliary Ferrying Squadron at the end of 1941 when the United States entered World War II. Instead of being inducted directly into the Army Air Force, these women were hired as civil service employees, ostensibly because the government made no provision for flight pay for women pilots. Cochran protested vigorously that the government had overlooked her proposition because of an unwillingness to accord women professional respect as military pilots. Washington conceded and decreed that there would be two programs: Love's elite Women's Auxiliary Ferrying Squadron and a Women's Flying Training Detachment organized by Cochran. Cochran had more than twenty-five thousand applicants for the program, some from other countries. The first class consisted of twenty-eight women who met in Houston for training in November, 1942. Cochran met them with an enthusiastic speech of welcome. The trainees remained in good spirits despite a lack of uniforms and the difficulties of a makeshift training program.

By May of 1943, the Training Detachment had shifted to Avenger Field in Sweet-water, Texas. In Sweetwater, Cochran could easily enforce militaristic standards. First, she outfitted her trainees with blue uniforms and berets. She determined that the recruits could not be efficient and reliable unless they were subject to military discipline. An Army major commanded Avenger Field and an Army staff administered it. Flight instructors were civilians and mostly male. Cochran expected her trainees to conform to military regulations as well as a rigid code of conduct. They participated in parades and infantry drills, stood roll call, and withstood barracks inspections. Training included ground school, flight training, and calisthenics. Eventually the women pilots would carry side arms and fly aircraft loaded with secret equipment restricted to all but military personnel.

Once Cochran moved the trainees to Sweetwater, she convinced the Army Air Force to combine the Women's Auxiliary Ferrying Squadron and her trainees under one command—her own. On August 5, 1943, the two branches merged into one organization known as the Women Airforce Service Pilots. Cochran became Director of Women Pilots and Nancy Love became the executive on the staff of the Air Transport Command's ferrying division.

Cochran assumed that the government would militarize the women pilots and thus make them eligible for hospitalization, insurance, and the same veterans' and death benefits to which other military personnel were entitled. Congress, however, defeated the bill to militarize women pilots on June 21, 1944. This defeat occurred in part because civilian male pilots under contract to the Army feared that militarized female pilots would automatically have priority ferrying assignments.

Under the leadership of Jacqueline Cochran and Nancy Love, the Women Airforce Service Pilots were a highly efficient and enthusiastic group of women. They excelled in virtually every kind of flying, but did not perform combat and overseas ferrying duties. In spite of its effectiveness, the Women Airforce Service Pilots Program was halted on December 20, 1944. Military losses were smaller than expected and male pilots began returning home to take over their jobs. Although General Arnold and Cochran pushed to continue the program, they could not justify doing so unless the women pilots were militarized.

Although she no longer had any duties as director of the Women Airforce Service Pilots Program, Cochran continued to fly and break records. In 1953, she broke the world speed records for both men and women in a Sabre jet; in that year she also became the first woman to fly faster than the speed of sound (Mach 1); in 1961, she was the first woman to fly at twice the speed of sound (Mach 2).

Jacqueline Cochran retired in 1970 from the Air Force reserve as a colonel. She then continued as a special consultant for the National Aeronautics and Space Administration (NASA). Her autobiography, *The Stars at Noon*, was published in 1954. In 1977, Cochran was pleased to learn that women pilots would finally receive military orders and full training, although not for combat missions. She died in Indio, California, on August 9, 1980.

Summary

Rising above her humble beginnings, Jacqueline Cochran was an adventurer who flew for the pure experience of it. She set out to make and break new records, to advance herself and her gender in a male dominated occupation. As a businesswoman, Cochran first considered her aerial exploits as a means to promote the cosmetics industry. Her stunts drew attention and thus promoted sales. It was, however, as an aviator that Cochran made her greatest impact on American society.

Unlike most female pilots before her, Cochran put women to work as pilots. She made it possible for these women to serve their country in an efficient and highly successful manner. Flight for women became a career path, not merely a promotional stunt. In essence, Cochran paved the way for female test pilots, astronauts, and women in military service. The excellent service provided by the Women Airforce Service Pilots pushed the United States military to accept women as a viable and useful part of its organization. Cochran lived to see the government honor these women retroactively as military veterans.

A flamboyant and adventurous woman, Jacqueline Cochran set out to make her mark. In 1937, before two hundred listeners, she delivered a eulogy to honor the memory of her friend and fellow pilot, Amelia Earhart. She noted that one could mourn the loss of such a pilot but one should admire her efforts as well. Cochran claimed that Earhart had merely passed on the torch to others. Seeing herself as a successor, Jacqueline Cochran carried that torch admirably.

Bibliography

Cochran, Jacqueline, with Floyd Odlum. *The Stars at Noon.* New York: Arno Press, 1980. A reprint of the original 1954 edition. In addition to providing a lively glimpse of Cochran's personality, this autobiography provides a firsthand glimpse of the challenges that faced women pilots during the early years of aviation and the strong opposition they faced from their male counterparts in military during World War II and beyond.

Douglas, Deborah G. *United States Women in Aviation, 1940-1985.* Washington, D.C.: Smithsonian Institution Press, 1990. This encyclopedic study by the Smithsonian Institution is the third in a series of studies about the women who contributed to American aviation. It presents several career related biographies of female aviators who played vital roles in World War II and the postwar era.

Moolman, Valerie. *Women Aloft.* Alexandria, Va.: Time-Life Books, 1981. This informative work provides a chronological history of women and flight. It includes brief biographies and pictures of female pilots from all over the world beginning with the balloonists and ending with the women aviators of World War II.

Noggle, Anne. *For God, Country, and the Thrill of It.* College Station: Texas A&M University Press, 1990. Photographer and former Women Airforce Service Pilot Anne Noggle presents an enlightening and easy-to-read book combining an extensive pictorial history with descriptive written accounts of Women Airforce Service Pilot training at Sweetwater, Texas.

Oakes, Claudia M. *United States Women in Aviation, 1930-1939.* Washington, D.C.: Smithsonian Institution Press, 1985. This factual publication is the second in a series presented by the Smithsonian Institution on American women in aviation. It gives a concise interpretation of the struggles and victories endured by female aviators and their efforts to prove their flight capabilities during the 1930's.

Scharr, Adela Riek. *Sisters in the Sky.* 2 vols. Gerald, Mo.: Patrice Press, 1986-1987. A thorough and personal account of the Women Airforce Service Pilots and their contributions to the war effort. The author details aircraft, pilots, and participants of the WASP program with factual accuracy and depth.

Verges, Marianne. *On Silver Wings: The Women Airforce Service Pilots of World War II, 1942-1944.* New York: Ballantine Books, 1991. A well-researched book based on interviews and personal experience. Provides an interesting and conversational account of the Women Airforce Service Pilots program and of the people who made it possible.

Dover C. Watkins
Elisabeth A. Cawthon

MARVA COLLINS

Born: August 31, 1936; Monroeville, Alabama

Area of Achievement: Education
Contribution: Founder of the Daniel Hale Williams Westside Preparatory School, Marva Collins has spent her time educating inner-city children who are labeled at risk and ineducable.

Early Life
Born to Bessie May Nettles Knight and Henry Knight, Jr., on August 31, 1936, in Monroeville, Alabama, Marva Knight enjoyed the life of a privileged middle-class child. She later referred to herself in interviews and in her autobiography, *Marva Collins' Way* (1982), as a "daddy's girl." She grew up in a large home with several bedrooms and was accustomed to dressing in store-bought dresses and pinafores.

Her father was a very successful African American businessman. Henry Knight, Jr.'s business holdings included an inherited grocery store and other properties. After inheriting his father's businesses, he utilized his entrepreneurial acumen to expand into other areas. He purchased a mortuary and a ranch. Knight's successful acquisitions during the 1930's and 1940's were especially unusual given the prevalence of Jim Crow racism in the South.

Marva's father became a major influence throughout her childhood and in adult life. He introduced her to the many phases and intricacies of the business world. Marva was schooled in the world of enterprise, accompanying him on business trips and working in his stores. Her admiration of her father grew as she not only witnessed his social standing in the community but also his seeming lack of fear when confronting threats, discrimination, and prejudice from whites in their community.

Marva's mother was a somewhat less influential factor in her early years because of the time Marva spent with her father. The lavish physical signs of love in the form of hugs, kisses, and gifts that were shared between father and daughter seemed to have been lacking between Marva and her mother. Although she later described her mother as distant and aloof, Marva appreciated her mother's gifts as an excellent homemaker.

Marva's idyllic existence was shattered in 1948, when her parents filed for divorce. After the divorce became final, Marva and her mother moved to Atmore, Alabama. Her daily access to her father ceased and her influences were limited primarily to her mother and her maternal grandmother. Her mother remarried and gave birth to Marva's half sister Cynthia.

Saddened by her parents' divorce, Marva found some solace in school. She was enrolled in Bethlehem Academy before attending Escambia County Training School, an all-black high school. It was at Escambia that she exhibited the independence and ambition she had learned so well from her father. All female students were to enroll in home economics as a requirement for graduation. Marva vehemently objected and opted instead to enroll in a typing class. She believed that acquiring office skills would be more useful and would halt the notion that African American women should be prepared only for domestic positions. She became the only female in the history of Escambia County Training School to graduate without fulfilling the home economics requirement.

After graduating from high school, Marva attended Clark College, a liberal arts college for black women in Atlanta, Georgia. While at Clark, she continued to pursue secretarial training and took additional courses in education. She was graduated with a bachelor's degree in secretarial science in 1957 before returning to Alabama. During her collegiate years, Marva experienced the normal activities of the college student. She dated, socialized, and prepared herself academically for the working world.

Since secretarial positions for blacks in Jim Crow Alabama were scarce, Marva chose the one profession that attracted many women—teaching. She taught at Monroe County Training School for two years before moving north to Chicago, Illinois. Armed with some instructional experience, she reveled in her newfound independence by finding an apartment and new employment as a medical secretary at Mount Sinai Hospital. Less than two years later, she met Clarence Collins, a drafter employed by the Sunbeam Corporation. After a brief courtship, the couple was married in September of 1960.

Life's Work

Almost immediately after her marriage, Marva Collins quickly left her position as a medical secretary and sought a teaching position in one of Chicago's public schools. Without having taken any education classes to prepare her for public instruction, Collins was assigned to teach second grade at the Calhoun South Elementary School. She demonstrated an apparent love for children and teaching. Possessed with the enthusiasm of youth, she quickly developed a style which would be later termed renegade and in complete contradiction to the curriculum of the school.

Collins taught according to the individual student's needs and pace. She criticized the treatment of African American students, believing that many African American children were stigmatized and stereotyped as being poor students and ineducable because of their low socioeconomic backgrounds. Despite her efforts to bring about change, Collins left Calhoun South Elementary within the year.

Collins eventually returned to the education field after the birth of her first child, Eric. After spending some time with her young son, she was assigned to Delano Elementary School. Her educational philosophy would soon pit her against colleagues and administrators. As she became more discontented with the politically charged atmosphere around her and with the curriculum changes that interrupted her own teaching methods, Collins resigned her job and decided to found her own private academy.

The year 1975 began a new chapter in Marva Collins' life. It was in this year that the Daniel Hale Williams Westside Preparatory School was established. Housed in the basement of the Daniel Hale Williams University, the Westside Preparatory School gained support from the college, residents, and the Alternative Schools Network.

Space and equipment were given gratis by the college, while Collins' salary was financed by the Alternative Schools Network. During the school's first months, Collins was its director, curriculum developer, and sole instructor. She spent much of her free time requisitioning educational supplies and materials of all kinds. Although the enrollment was small—only twenty students by the school's fourth month—it was rapidly outgrowing the limited space provided by the university. The decision was made to move the school to her home. With the help of her husband, Collins was able to renovate the top floor of her home in time to open the doors of Westside Preparatory in September of 1976.

It is vital to comprehend what makes Collins' school unique, innovative, and successful. In founding her school, Collins provided another choice for students who were considered rejects from all other types of educational facilities. According to Collins, the public and private schools of Chicago were failing to nurture these students academically and emotionally. She believed in teaching the entire child. Drawing on her childhood experiences with her father, Collins believed in instilling pride, self-confidence and self-esteem in each child. She realized early in her teaching career that many children deemed unteachable were, in reality, mislabeled. She made it her life mission to alter the public's notion that these "rejects" were doomed to fail.

The focus of her educational technique was reading. She believed that the key to all learning was reading. She also promoted self-respect, courage, and self-reliance. In addition to the vital character components of values and ethics, she believed that all instruction must be life applicable. Collins dressed neatly and appropriately for her occupation as a teacher, believing that her appearance reflected her own self-confidence, and would encourage students to respect her as an authority figure. She encouraged students to respect themselves and others by dressing and talking properly. Most of all, Collins motivated them to aim high and never run from a challenge.

Collins believed that students' cognitive skills were enhanced through the use of a variety of learning materials. She taught Shakespearean plays and Greek mythology in order to encourage better learning skills, creativity, and a love for the "challenge." Challenging one's brains, she was convinced, made education more pleasurable and fun. In 1979, the television news magazine *60 Minutes* featured a segment on Marva Collins that attempted to document her teaching methods. The sight of young elementary school pupils reciting Shakespeare and reading Greek tragedies mesmerized a nation. With reading and math scores of her students escalating annually, Collins became a media phenomenon of the 1980's. Magazines and newspapers clamored for interviews. She was interviewed by *Time, Ebony, Essence, Jet, Black Enterprise, People, Good Housekeeping*, and the *Chicago Sun-Times*. In 1981, *The Marva Collins Story* was featured as a Hallmark Hall of Fame television special starring Morgan Freeman as Clarence Collins and Cicely Tyson as Marva Collins.

To many, such media attention might have seemed the pinnacle of success and achievement. Yet to Collins, it was not personal accolades that she desired, but recognition of the American public school system's weaknesses—particularly its inability to provide adequately for a particular sector of the population. With this broad public exposure, Collins was able to obtain funding more easily and quickly. Soon, the school moved to a two-office building in Chicago's Garfield Park area. Grants and fees from her public speaking engagements were sufficient to purchase the space necessary for her rapidly expanding school. The school's staff expanded as did the student population, and the waiting list numbered into the hundreds.

Despite her achievements and struggles, Collins was not without her critics. Many have been skeptical about her success. Old colleagues and disgruntled former employees have made rumblings about what they perceive as Collins' personal frailties and shortcomings. For every one critic, however, there are numerous individuals who support Collins and her educational crusade.

Collins' success with children cannot be ignored or denied. Many of her students have gone on to excel in their secondary and collegiate pursuits. Celebrities such as Prince and Mr. T have been contributors and staunch supporters of the Marva Method. Parents, students, and underwriters of grants have given testimony of her success. Her awards and honors have included several educator of the year awards from various agencies as well as the Sojourner Truth Award, Fred Hampton Image Award, and the Legendary Woman of the World Award. She is affiliated with the National Institute of Health, the National Advisory Board on Private Education, the National Department of Children, the Youth and Family Services, as well as the President's Commission on White House Fellowships. Collins has served as the director of Right to Read and is an honorary degree holder from Howard University, Chicago State University, Amherst College, Dartmouth College, and Washington University. She has authored many articles for journals and other publications. Collins has taken particular pride in serving as the founder of the Westside Preparatory National Teacher Training Institute to help other teachers employ her educational methods.

Summary

Marva Collins continues to be an outspoken advocate for pupils who have been neglected by mainstream educational organizations. Refusing high ranking positions she has been offered in federal and local government, she has continued to reside and work in the Garfield Park area of Chicago. With the continued support of family, friends, students, parents, and neighborhood residents, Collins has continued to instill in her students the pride, self-esteem, strength, and self-confidence that she herself learned from her father. Through perseverance and dedication, Marva Collins has demonstrated that race and socioeconomic status are not necessarily the sole determinants of academic success. She has shown that proper academic training, confidence building, and ethics are major components of success and can help students overcome obstacles posed by racial discrimination. With her innovative and "renegade" style, she has managed to instill the notion that success comes from within and is enhanced through proper education and ethical training. Happier to serve as a model of achievement by her commitment to education rather than her fleeting celebrity, Collins has continued to persevere, believing in the adage that "Good teachers see the future in a child's eyes."

Bibliography

Collins, Marva, and Civia Tamarkin. *Marva Collins' Way*. Los Angeles: Jeremy P. Tarcher, 1982. An autobiography of Marva Collins from her childhood to adulthood. Emphasis is placed on her parental relationship, educational background, and creation of the "Marva Method."

Keerdoja, Eileen, et al. "Report Card on Marva Collins." *Newsweek* 101 (June 27, 1983): 13. A critical analysis of the teaching techniques used by Collins. The authors include a discussion of Collins' success in improving students' scholastic achievements at Westside Preparatory school.

Lanker, Brian. *I Dream a World*. New York: Stewart, Tabori, & Chang, 1989. A coffee-table book full of impressive photography, Lanker's work includes profiles of famous African American individuals who have made a difference.

Reed, S. "Marva Collins: 'I Take the Kids No One Else Wants!'" *Instructor* 91 (January, 1982): 18-19. Appearing in a leading professional publication for educators, this brief profile of Collins chronicles her development of her educational method and her commitment to rescuing students who have been neglected and ignored.

Smith, Jessie Carney, ed. *Notable Black American Women*. Detroit: Gale Research, 1992. A collection of biographical portraits of prominent African American women from all areas of achievement. The entry on Collins provides an excellent introduction to her life and career and includes bibliographic sources for further study.

Annette Marks-Ellis

BETTY COMDEN

Born: May 3, 1917; Brooklyn, New York

Areas of Achievement: Film, music, and theater and drama

Contribution: In her lifelong writing partnership with Adolph Green, Betty Comden collaborated as a lyricist, dramatist, and screenwriter for some of the most notable musicals produced on Broadway and in Hollywood, ranging from *On the Town* (1944; film version, 1949) and *Singin' in the Rain* (1952) through *The Will Rogers Follies: A Life in Revue* (1991).

Early Life

Betty Comden was born Elizabeth Cohen, the daughter of Leo Cohen, a lawyer, and his wife Rebecca Sadvoransky Cohen, a schoolteacher. As a young girl growing up with her brother in the New York City borough of Brooklyn, Betty developed a great appreciation for music and for dramatics. She received piano lessons at a young age, enjoyed dressing up and performing original skits at home, and often visited the opera with her parents. As a seventh grade student at the Brooklyn Ethical Culture School, Betty made her acting debut when she was cast in the role of Rebecca in a school production of Sir Walter Scott's *Ivanhoe*.

During her years at Erasmus Hall High School, Betty became interested in the Manhattan entertainment scene and began to frequent the Clay Club in Greenwich Village. After graduating from high school, she went on to attend New York University (NYU), where she took a variety of education courses before settling on a major in dramatics. She earned a bachelor of science degree from New York University in 1938 and began to work in summer stock with the Studio Players. While making the rounds of theater auditions on Broadway, Betty became active with a little theater group known as Six and Company. The group included Adolph Green, another aspiring actor whom she had first met through a mutual friend at NYU.

Green learned of an opportunity to perform at a Greenwich Village coffeehouse known as the Village Vanguard, and he gathered together Alvin Hammer, Betty Comden, her friend John Frank, and a somewhat reluctant Judy Tuvim (later known as Judy Holliday) to form an acting group. Known as the Revuers, the five group members learned to improvise their skits in the club's cramped quarters. Earning only five dollars each per night, they were unable to pay royalties to use other people's material, so they met together to write their own satirical skits and songs. Soon, their audiences began to grow as word spread about their amusing cabaret act. They became a featured act several nights a week and began to compile the best of their numbers into a permanent act. During some of their performances in 1939, the Revuers were accompanied by Green's friend Leonard Bernstein, and they appeared at another venue on a bill with actor/dancer Gene Kelly. In November of 1939, the Revuers took their show to the Rainbow Room, a sophisticated Manhattan nightclub, but their satire evidently fell flat and did not appeal to the club's clientele. Nevertheless, their appearances at the Rainbow Room publicized the Revuers' work, and they were invited to perform on the NBC Radio network in a weekly half-hour variety show. In 1940, they were invited to perform at the Radio City Music Hall between film showings, and they began making the rounds of the New York nightclub circuit and performed in regional supper clubs on the East Coast and in the Midwest.

With the entry of the United States into World War II, life began to change for Betty Comden. On January 4, 1942, she was married to Siegfried Schutzman, a young artist who soon was inducted into the Army Engineers and later changed his name to Steven Kyle. Shortly thereafter, Betty's husband was called overseas, and her brother went off to serve in the war as a doctor. New performing opportunities were scarce, and the Revuers went out on the road again. Not long afterward, they lost founding member John Frank, who dropped out of the group in order to seek treatment for his drinking problem.

Comden and the three other remaining Revuers decided to accept an offer from a Hollywood agent and traveled to Los Angeles in the summer of 1943 to perform in a film version of a radio show known as *Duffy's Tavern*. After their arrival, the Revuers learned that the film had been canceled (it was later made by Paramount Pictures in 1945). They quickly found work performing at the famed Trocadero nightclub, where Judy Tuvim came to the attention of casting agents. She eventually signed a contract with Twentieth Century-Fox after being assured that the Revuers would appear together in her first film. They joined the cast of *Greenwich Village* (1944) and were allowed to perform two of their own sketches. Unfortunately, their scenes were cut from the final film, and only Tuvim was kept under contract after changing her name to Judy Holliday. Although Alvin Hammer decided to remain in Hollywood to try his luck, Betty Comden returned to New York to rejoin her husband, who was on furlough, and Adolph Green soon followed.

Life's Work

Although they had returned home with little to show for their Hollywood sojourn, Betty Comden and Adolph Green's work with the Revuers laid the foundation for their songwriting and scriptwriting partnership, and they soon received the big boost that launched their successful career. The two had found work as an act appearing at New York's Blue Angel nightclub. They were visited there one evening by Leonard Bernstein, who wanted to discuss ideas for a new musical. Bernstein had written music for the ballet *Fancy Free*, choreographed by Jerome Robbins, and the two men had been contacted about adapting the ballet as a musical. Bernstein invited Comden and Green to write the book and lyrics for the new musical. Drawing on their long experience as collaborators on material for the Revuers, the duo expanded the contemporary story of three sailors on leave in New York City and wrote clever lyrics to accompany Bernstein's jazz-flavored score. When the resulting musical, *On the Town*, went into production, Comden and Green auditioned for and won the roles of Claire the anthropologist and Ozzie the sailor, respectively. The musical opened in December of 1933 at New York's Adelphi Theatre under the guidance of veteran

Broadway director George Abbott and went on to win rave reviews for its freshness and originality.

Spurred on by the success of their first writing venture, Comden and Green immediately began writing another musical. Set in the era of the Roaring Twenties, *Billion Dollar Baby* focused on the social-climbing antics of a beauty pageant contestant who abandons a faithful young boyfriend for the company of speakeasy gangsters before marrying a millionaire whose enormous fortune disappears on their wedding day in the 1929 Stock Market Crash. Choreographer Jerome Robbins and director George Abbott again contributed their talents, but since Bernstein was unavailable as a composer, Morton Gould provided the musical score. *Billion Dollar Baby* opened on Broadway in December of 1945, and featured Joan McCracken in the lead role of Maribelle Jones. Some critics found the show to be uneven, appreciating the clever lyrics and satirical jabs at the social pretensions of an era, but criticizing the show's failure to strike a balance between its comedic spoofs and the melodramatic elements of the plot. Nevertheless, the show continued for more than 200 performances before it closed and was considered a modest success.

Comden and Green's next project resulted in their return to Hollywood. After being contacted by Metro-Goldwyn-Mayer (MGM), the pair expected to work on an original project of their own, but were invited instead to work with film producer Arthur Freed on a new adaptation of the stage musical *Good News*. Although they were firmly discouraged from altering the basic story line about college life in the 1920's, Comden and Green did manage to write a new screenplay that incorporated most of the show's original songs while also including an original song of their own called "The French Lesson." The film, which starred June Allyson and Peter Lawford, was released in 1947 and was a box-office success.

After their next musical, *Bonanza Bound!* (1947), failed during its pre-Broadway run, Comden and Green returned to work with the Freed production unit at MGM studios in Hollywood. They were asked to prepare an original musical screenplay to showcase the talents of Judy Garland and Fred Astaire, who were being cast together again in the wake of their successful pairing in *Easter Parade* (1948). Comden and Green wrote a script which went into rehearsal, but Garland had to leave the production because of health problems. She was replaced at the last minute by Astaire's old screen partner, Ginger Rogers, and thus several songs written for Garland were dropped and other changes were incorporated into the script. Although the part had not been written for her, Rogers managed to carry off her role as Dinah Barkley with flair, and the reunited team of Astaire and Rogers made *The Barkleys of Broadway* one of the top box-office films of 1949.

After working on the film version of *On the Town* and providing the lyrics for Gene Kelly's film *Take Me out to the Ball Game* in 1949, Comden and Green began working on what became their most acclaimed film musical, *Singin' in the Rain* (1952). Reunited with the Arthur Freed unit at MGM and working closely with their good friend Gene Kelly, the pair worked diligently to come up with the right opening scene for their new project. Unable to choose between the three possibilities they had sketched out, they were stuck until Comden's husband Kyle suggested that they use all three together. The film, which featured their clever lyrics on "Moses Supposes," earned for Comden and Green their second Screenwriters Guild Award. Beloved by audiences, the film went on to be named one of the ten best American films of all time by the American Film Institute and was ranked number three among the ten best films of all time by a prestigious circle of international film critics in the 1980's.

Comden and Green continued to work on both coasts as new projects developed for film and stage. The year 1953 saw the release of their film musical *The Band Wagon*, featuring Fred Astaire, and the Broadway opening of their musical *Wonderful Town*, based on the 1940 play *My Sister Eileen*. In 1956, they were reunited with their old colleague from the Revuers, film star Judy Holliday, when they designed a musical specifically to showcase her talents. *Bells Are Ringing* was a success on Broadway, earning a Tony Award for Holliday. Although they were reluctant to interrupt their busy theatrical schedule, Comden and Green adapted the play for its film release in 1960, thus creating the final film role for Holliday before she died of cancer in 1965.

The 1960's marked the beginning of a string of collaborations between Betty Comden and Adolph Green as lyricists with composer Jule Styne. The three of them worked together on the Broadway adaptation of Garson Kanin's story *Do Re Mi* (1960), on a Broadway musical featuring Green's wife Phyllis Newman called *Subways Are for Sleeping* (1961), on an original musical for television called *I'm Getting Married* (1967), and on the Tony Award-winning *Hallelujah, Baby!* (1967).

Although these projects enjoyed modest success, Comden and Green went on to create two of the most successful Broadway musicals of the 1970's: *Applause* (1970), featuring Lauren Bacall and based on the popular film *All About Eve*, and *On the Twentieth Century* (1978), featuring Imogene Coca, Kevin Kline, and John Cullum. *Applause* won six Tony Awards, including honors as best musical and to Comden and Green for best book. *On the Twentieth Century* won five Tony Awards, including ones to Comden and Green for best score and best book. Although Comden and Green remained active on Broadway, none of their work achieved such acclaim during the 1980's. They were not allowed to make changes to the story for the 1985 Broadway adaptation of *Singin' in the Rain* and were said to have been banned from the set by director Twyla Tharp; the resulting musical was severely panned by critics. Instead, they received more attention for a variety of cameo roles they themselves performed, particularly Comden's appearance as Greta Garbo in the 1984 film *Garbo Talks* (Green also had a small role) and Green's cameo as a television producer in the 1982 film *My Favorite Year*.

The year 1991 brought new laurels for Comden and Green. They collaborated on the Tony Award-winning lyrics for *The Will Rogers Follies*, which went on to earn five other Tony Awards; the show's cast album went on to earn a Grammy Award for the pair in 1992. Shortly after the musical opened on Broadway in May of 1991, Comden and Green were presented with the Johnny Mercer Award for Lifetime Achievement by the Songwriters Hall of Fame. In December of that year, the two were presented with Kennedy Center Honors for Lifetime Achievement in the Performing Arts. Many longtime friends and colleagues, including Gene Kelly and Lauren Bacall, paid tribute to Comden and Green.

Summary

Although she has been a talented performer in her own right, it is as part of a writing team—creating librettos and lyrics for musical comedies—that Betty Comden has received her greatest acclaim as an artist. Her work with Adolph Green has demonstrated the pair's complete familiarity with a sophisticated urban milieu and their uncanny ability to skewer the social pretensions and foibles of the many individuals who inhabit such an environment. At the same time, Comden and Green became adept at creating a wide variety of likable and sympathetic characters and a host of memorable, lighthearted songs. Comden and Green's collaborative work, spanning more than fifty years on stage and screen, is a testament to their dazzling and acerbic wit, their love of show business, and their deep respect for each other. Although many women lyricists and songwriters have found it difficult to achieve recognition and respect on par with their male colleagues, Comden enjoyed equal billing in her writing partnership from the very beginning and always found that peers and critics appreciated the hard work and dedication that both she and Green have exhibited throughout their productive career as a writing team. Despite the fact that credit for their work behind the scenes has brought Comden and Green less name recognition in their later years, one critic has aptly summarized their contribution to musical comedy: "If the names of Comden and Green were removed from the record, great blank stretches would be left in the history of the Broadway musical. [The public] would lose some of the happiest interludes on Hollywood celluloid as well."

Bibliography
Laffel, Jeff. "Betty Comden and Adolph Green." *Films in Review* 43 (March-April, 1992): 74-85, 154-156. A chatty interview with Comden and Green that highlights episodes in their early career. They reminisce about their work with Broadway producer George Abbott, with film producer Arthur Freed, and with directors Vincente Minelli, Gene Kelly, and Stanley Donen. The article discusses the extraordinary fact that *Singin' in the Rain* was overlooked for Academy Award consideration for best screenplay.
McDaniell, Tina, and Pat McGilligan. "Betty Comden and Adolph Green: Almost Improvisation." In *Backstory 2: Interviews with Screenwriters of the 1940s and 1950s*, edited by Pat McGilligan. Berkeley: University of California Press, 1991. This dual interview focuses on the pair's writing strategies, yet is also useful for its discussion of their working relationships with various directors, producers, and actors. Other interviews in the collection discuss the works of Comden and Green's screenwriting contemporaries, including Garson Kanin.
Robinson, Alice M. "Betty Comden." In *Notable Women in the American Theatre: A Biographical Dictionary*, edited by Alice M. Robinson, Vera Mowry Roberts, and Milly S. Barranger. Westport, Conn.: Greenwood Press, 1989. This overview of

Comden's career as performer, dramatist, screenwriter, and lyricist gives a complete account of her early life and career with the Revuers. Many of the details found here are explored in further detail in Robinson's bio-bibliography, cited below.

——————. *Betty Comden and Adolph Green: A Bio-Bibliography.* Westport, Conn.: Greenwood Press, 1994. The most comprehensive biographical source on Comden to date. Provides a thorough biography of Comden as well as of Green and discusses the full range of their work together. Includes a useful chronology, a complete discography, and individual summaries of the stage musicals and films for which they wrote as well as their own performances on stage and in film. The bibliography, while exhaustive, is unannotated.

Roddick, Nick. "Betty Comden and Adolph Green." In *Dictionary of Literary Biography: American Screenwriters, Second Series*, vol. 44, edited by Randall Clark. Detroit: Gale Research, 1986. A biographical sketch on Comden and her writing partner, this article briefly acknowledges their Broadway successes while focusing primarily on their achievements as Hollywood screenwriters. Provides useful chronology of their pictures, theatrical productions, and books based on their work.

Wendy Sacket

MAUREEN CONNOLLY

Born: September 17, 1934; San Diego, California
Died: June 21, 1969; Dallas, Texas
Area of Achievement: Sports
Contribution: Before a serious injury cut short her dazzling career at the age of nineteen, Maureen "Little Mo" Connolly established herself as one of the most powerful and effective women's tennis players in modern history. She was the first women's tennis player to achieve the Grand Slam in 1953.

Early Life

Maureen Catherine Connolly was born in San Diego, California, on September 17, 1934, to Martin Connolly, a naval officer, and Jassamine Wood Connolly. When Maureen was only four, her father abandoned the family, and her parents were later divorced. Maureen's mother had wanted to be a concert pianist and hoped her daughter might follow her in that career. Instead, Maureen's first love was horseback riding. Her mother could not afford that sport for young Maureen and tennis was the next alternative. Maureen took to the game at once. Tennis became the most important thing in her life from the moment that she first picked up a racquet at the age of ten.

Maureen's first coach was Wilbur Folsom. Impressed with her budding ability, he offered to give her lessons and changed her natural left-handed stroke to a right-handed game. She practiced diligently from nine in the morning until it was time for dinner in the evening. She knew already that she wanted to reach the top of women's tennis. As Maureen's tennis instruction progressed, she became a student of Eleanor "Teach" Tennant, a famous and demanding coach who had been associated with the development of such other women's stars as Helen Wills and Alice Marble. To strengthen Maureen's competitive instincts, Tennant refused to allow her student to converse or associate with other women's tennis players. Maureen approached tennis with an intense hatred for her opponents, a trait that Tennant encouraged. Maureen believed that she could not win if she did not despise her opponent. Winning became a single-minded pursuit for the talented youngster.

By her early teens, Maureen was winning tournaments in Southern California against most of the top women players. She won the national championship for girls eighteen and under in 1949 when she was fifteen years old—the youngest woman to do so up to that time. She repeated her victory in that division the next year in 1950. A sportswriter gave her the nickname "Little Mo," in contrast to the famous battleship U.S.S. *Missouri,* known as "Big Mo." Maureen graduated from Cathedral High School in 1951 and set out to make tennis her life. That summer she was selected to the United States Wrightman Cup team and helped her country defend its title to that international women's tennis trophy.

Life's Work

Maureen Connolly's run of important tennis victories began at the United States

National Championships at Forest Hills, New York, during the late summer of 1951. Convinced by her coach that Doris Hart, her friend and fellow women's tennis star, had disparaged her, Connolly went out and beat Hart in the semifinals. She followed that triumph up with a hard-fought three-set victory over Shirley Fry in the finals, 6-3, 1-6, 6-4. With this victory, Maureen Connolly became the youngest women's champion in the history of the U.S. Open up to that time (with her win in 1979, Tracy Austin superseded Connolly as the youngest woman to win). She came off the court and told Tennant that she wanted to go home and work on the offensive phase of her game.

The strength of Connolly's tennis rested on her ability to hit winning shots from the baseline with precision and consistency. Her serve was not strong and she did not like to volley. She was so accurate and deadly from the baseline that these drawbacks did not hamper her. Sportswriters raved about her engaging blend of teenage charm and killer instinct on the court. Fueled by her intense passion to win, her drive and energy on the court swept her past all of the best women players of her day. Later in life she remarked about the fear that drove her and the talent that she displayed.

After her victory in the U.S. Open, Connolly learned that her coach had deceived her about Doris Hart's attitude toward her. Connolly apologized to Hart and their friendship resumed. The revelation of what Tennant had done produced strained relations between coach and player that came to a climax at the Wimbledon Championships in 1952. Connolly experienced a slight shoulder strain just before the tournament opened. Convinced that the injury was serious, Tennant wanted Connolly to default. Her own determination, however, led Connolly to enter the tournament. Following her first-round victory, she called a sudden press conference, an unheard-of act for even a top player in those days. She announced that she was breaking her ties with Tennant and stated that anything that Tennant said was without Connolly's authority; her goal was to play Wimbledon and win. The episode underlined Maureen Connolly's willpower and determination to excel. Her relations with Tennant were severed from that time forward.

Connolly had a difficult third-round match against Susan Partridge at Wimbledon in 1952. Only two points from defeat in the third set, Connolly drew even at 30-all in the decisive game. Needing a word of encouragement, she heard an American serviceman in the stands shout for her to win. This unexpected boost from a total stranger restored her confidence, and she won the game and the match. She went on to defeat Louise Brough in the finals for her first Wimbledon title, 7-5, 6-3. The press predicted that Connolly would have a long reign at the top of women's tennis.

Following up on her Wimbledon success, Connolly defended her U.S. Open title later that summer. She had a difficult match in the semifinals against Shirley Fry and then swept past Doris Hart in the finals, 6-3, 7-5. By this time, Connolly had a new coach: Australian Davis Cup captain Harry Hopman. His wife, Nell, acted as Connolly's chaperon. The Hopmans brought stability and serenity to Connolly's career, and she intended to make 1953 a banner year. She had gained confidence in her volleying and overhead, and practice had strengthened her service.

Up to that time, no woman had won the Australian, French, Wimbledon, and U.S.

Open crowns during the same year for the fabled Grand Slam. Don Budge had accomplished this feat in men's tennis fifteen years earlier, and no one else had matched his accomplishment since. Connolly began her quest for the Grand Slam by winning the Australian in January without losing a set. She dropped one set during the French championships on the famous red clay of Roland Garros Stadium in Paris during May of 1953, but gained that prestigious trophy as well. At Wimbledon, she played an epic final with Doris Hart that brought her another triumph, 8-6, 7-5. The two women were both at the top of their form, and the result was one of the hardest-fought final matches that spectators at the All-England Club had ever witnessed. Connolly completed the Grand Slam at the U.S. Open with a 6-2, 6-4 defeat of Doris Hart. The press called it one of Connolly's finest performances. She stood atop the world of women's tennis.

In 1954, Connolly added the French and Wimbledon championships to her glittering record. Down 5-2 in the second set in the Wimbledon final against Louise Brough, Connolly feared she might lose. At that point, however, she began to hit with her old authority. She went for the lines and hit winner after winner. She won 6-2, 7-5. It seemed that a brilliant career was ahead of her. Students of the game were calling her one of the best tennis players of all time.

Then came sudden and unexpected personal tragedy. Resting at home after Wimbledon, she went riding on her horse, Colonel Merryboy, on July 20, 1954. As she was proceeding down a narrow side road, a passing cement truck hit Connolly's horse and caught her leg. She was thrown to the ground with serious injuries, including a broken bone and severed calf muscles in her right leg. Connolly endured a four-hour operation to repair her leg and was under sedation for four days. With her customary drive and determination, she began a lengthy program of rehabilitation and planned for a comeback, intending to announce her decision to become a professional. Despite her efforts, her recuperation suddenly stalled, and she realized that she would not regain her full abilities. Connolly never played competitive tennis again. She told the public that she had lost her enjoyment for the game.

After she announced her retirement from tennis, Connolly married Norman Brinker of Dallas, Texas, in June of 1955. Brinker, a former member of the United States Equestrian team, shared his wife's love for horses. The couple had two daughters, Cindy and Brenda. Maureen Connolly Brinker became a coach for the British Wightman Cup team during its American visits, and she covered tennis matches for several newspapers in England and the United States. Friends remarked on the warmth of her personality and generous kindness. She had long since put aside the hatreds and passions on the court that had driven her to reach the heights of women's tennis. With her husband and her coaching friend Nancy Jeffett, she set up the Maureen Connolly Brinker Foundation to encourage the development of young tennis players in Texas. She was elected to the National Lawn Tennis Hall of Fame in 1968.

In 1967, Maureen began to complain of pain. She was diagnosed with cancer, and fought the disease with the same intensity that she had brought to her years in big-time tennis. After a long struggle, she died in Dallas, Texas, on June 21, 1969.

Summary

Maureen Connolly was one of the major sports celebrities of the post-World War II era. During her brief reign at the top of women's tennis, she dominated the sport for three and a half years and was ranked number one in the world among women players from 1952 to 1954. She lost only five matches during that period. Although her career-ending injury prevented her from setting records that would equal the achievements of future women's champions such as Chris Evert, Billie Jean King, and Martina Navratilova, Maureen Connolly is regarded by many tennis experts as one of the best women's players of all time. Her achievement of the Grand Slam in 1953 has only been equalled twice, by Margaret Smith Court and Steffi Graf. Her coaching work and the foundation she created have perpetuated her name and reputation for generations of tennis fans who never got to see "Little Mo" in her prime. The passage of time has not dimmed her accomplishments or the luster of her game.

Bibliography

Brown, Gene, ed. *The Complete Book of Tennis.* New York: Arno Press, 1980. A compilation of columns that first appeared in *The New York Times*, this history of tennis contains accounts of most of Connolly's most famous matches.

Connolly, Maureen. *Forehand Drive.* London: Macgibbon & Kee, 1957. This autobiography recounts Connolly's emotional struggles on and off the tennis court.

Danzig, Allison, and Peter Schwed, eds. *The Fireside Book of Tennis.* New York: Simon & Schuster, 1972. A collection of sportswriting about tennis, the volume contains many of the newspaper articles about Connolly's rise to prominence during her brief career.

Hart, Doris. *Tennis with Hart.* Philadelphia: J. B. Lippincott, 1955. A tennis memoir by Hart, who was one of Maureen Connolly's toughest competitors, this work provides anecdotes on the women's rivalry and friendship on and off the court.

King, Billie Jean, with Cynthia Starr. *We Have Come a Long Way: The Story of Women's Tennis.* New York: McGraw-Hill, 1988. A general history of women's tennis with a very useful section about Connolly and her impact on the sport.

Lumpkin, Angela. *Women's Tennis: A Historical Documentary of the Players and Their Game.* Troy, N.Y.: Whitston, 1981. A combination of history and bibliography about women's tennis, this book has references to many of the magazine articles that were written about Connolly.

Tinling, Ted. *Love and Faults: Personalities Who Have Changed the History of Tennis in My Lifetime.* New York: Crown, 1979. A memoir by a renowned designer of women's tennis dresses with several informative chapters on Connolly's career.

Wade, Virginia, with Jean Rafferty. *Ladies of the Court: A Century of Women at Wimbledon.* New York: Atheneum, 1984. There is a perceptive and insightful chapter on Connolly's Wimbledon record in this survey of the role of women at this prestigious championship.

Karen Gould

MARTHA COOLIDGE

Born: August 17, 1946; New Haven, Connecticut

Area of Achievement: Film
Contribution: After an early career in documentary filmmaking, Coolidge became a
successful feature film director of teen comedies, coming-of-age dramas, and social
satires.

Early Life
Born on August 17, 1946, into an upper-middle-class family in New Haven,
Connecticut, Martha Coolidge explored her family and personal history through her
early documentary films. After studying acting with Lee Strasberg and Stella Adler,
Coolidge attended the Rhode Island School of Design to learn animation; these
experiences along with further graduate work in film in New York provided Coolidge
with the necessary skills to begin her documentation of the triumphs and tragedies of
her young life. Her first short documentary *David: Off and On* (1972) interviews her
brother about his life as an alienated youth in Haight-Ashbury and his alcohol and
drug dependency. In *Old-Fashioned Woman* (1973), Coolidge, like many feminists of
the era, finds inspiration in the life of an ancestor, in this case, her eighty-seven-year-
old grandmother, Mabel Tilton Coolidge. This loving portrait also investigates the
changing roles of women as Martha, narrator and participant in the family action,
attempts to understand Mabel's life as matriarch of her large family and keeper of the
magnificent ancestral home.

Coolidge's most painful yet significant exploration of her personal history, however, occurs in *Not a Pretty Picture* (1975), a feature-length documentary about and
dramatic re-creation of her own date rape at age sixteen. Coolidge skillfully blends
past and present, fact and fiction, interview and dramatization to show what happened
to her and how it affected her life in the twelve years that followed. Boundaries
between actor and role disappear as the girl playing young Coolidge, Michele
Manenti, confesses details of her own real-life rape to director Coolidge as they
discuss the scene she is to play.

The critical acclaim for these three award-winning documentaries helped Coolidge
make the transition in the late 1970's from the East Coast to Hollywood and from
documentary filmmaker to feature film director. Her theatrical background taught her
how to work with actors, and independent documentary exposed her to the many
technical facets of filmmaking while forcing her to work on a limited budget and
instilling in her a respect for reality. In an *American Film* interview, Coolidge credits
these early "portrait" films, with their fresh and personal point of view, for getting her
noticed by Hollywood.

Life's Work
Once in Los Angeles, Martha Coolidge first worked as an American Film Institute

Academy intern with director Robert Wise on the production of *Audrey Rose* in 1977. Next, she was hired by Francis Ford Coppola in 1978 to develop a rock 'n' roll musical to be called *Photoplay*. After putting more than two years of work into the project, Coolidge learned a hard lesson about the film business when Zoetrope Studio went bankrupt and the film was canceled. Difficulties also plagued her next project, a Canadian tax-shelter production that she took over in December of 1980 after the first director was fired. Originally conceived as an exploitative film about a female photographer's quest for sexual fulfillment, Coolidge reworked the script to reflect contemporary feminist concerns about career and independence. When financial problems threatened to cancel that film, Coolidge convinced noted director Peter Bogdanovich to finance its completion as *City Girl* (1983).

Although it did not receive wide commercial release, the film attracted the attention of writer-producers Andy Lane and Wayne Crawford, who were looking for a woman to direct their teen comedy script. Coolidge was hired only weeks before shooting was to begin and given a low budget of about $350,000. To accomplish the difficult task of bringing the film in under budget, Coolidge carefully storyboarded each scene, thoroughly rehearsed the actors to prevent unnecessary takes, and filmed no more than three takes of each shot. *Valley Girl* (1983) was an immediate success, earning more than $17 million in domestic release.

Transcending the short-lived "Valley girl" craze, the film creates an updated version of the Romeo and Juliet love story that is rich with details about contemporary teen culture and sensitive to a woman's coming of age. In this comedic version of the star-crossed lovers, the consumer-conscious WASPish teens of the San Fernando Valley are pitted against the trendy hipster outcasts of Hollywood. Through an amazing array of quirky characters, Coolidge provides insight into the eternal problems of growing up without villainizing, exploiting, or blaming any one group. The parents of the heroine are endearing leftover hippie types who embarrass their daughter with their 1960's values. Although the heroine's Valley friends are not totally sympathetic, Coolidge shows some genuine moments of friendship and fun between the girls. An effective visual and musical montage of dates between Julie (Deborah Foreman) and Randy (Nicolas Cage) captures the pure magic and delight of first love without condescension. Despite a rather silly brawl at the Senior Prom and an unsatisfyingly abrupt reunion of the lovers as the credits roll to Modern English's "I Melt with You," Coolidge creates a charming romantic fable.

Her success with *Valley Girl*, however, threatened to stereotype Coolidge as a director of teen sex comedies. She was brought in to save the doomed production of *The Joy of Sex* (1984), a film that several other directors and screenwriters had worked on and then abandoned. Miraculously, Coolidge finished shooting the film in twenty-six days; she later admitted that the only good thing about this project was that she met her husband, producer Michael Backes. The story involves the adventures of a teenager who, mistakenly thinking that she is dying, sets out to lose her virginity, a task that ends up being more complicated than she thought it would be, even in the seemingly sex-crazed milieu of the American high school.

Coolidge's next filmmaking experience was much more positive, but because of distribution problems, *Real Genius* (1985) did not receive the popular attention that it deserved. Coolidge expanded her directorial skills, however, in this techno-comedy, a film with complicated action sequences, special effects, an Academy Award-winning crew, widescreen cinematography, and a budget of $17 million. *Real Genius* is a teen comedy about gifted college students at Pacific Tech (a school loosely modeled on the California Institute of Technology) who play at making scientific discoveries and learn about accepting the consequences of their inventions, all while they try to make friends, fall in love, and balance serious intelligence with childhood silliness. Rich in character detail and atmosphere, briskly paced, and filled with excellent performances (by a young Val Kilmer in his first major role and a Coolidge regular, Michelle Meyrink), the film suffered by being released at the same time as several similarly themed films—*Weird Science* and *My Science Project.*

Because the producers of the film *Plain Clothes* (1988) wanted a more human form of comedy in their comedy-detective picture, Coolidge was selected two years into the project's development. She was attracted to the mystery element of the plot, the dark satire, and the fast-paced action. In the film, an undercover cop (Arliss Howard) disguises himself as a student to infiltrate the local high school to solve the murder of a teacher and clear his brother's name. In addition to her usual collection of teen types, Coolidge also introduces some interesting adult characters. Ultimately disappointed with the film's poor reception in limited release, Coolidge also was upset that studio pressures forced her to eliminate much of the pertinent social satire: "Everything in it that had something to do with being about something was cut out . . . in the fear on the part of the studio that it would detract from the comedy."

During this time Coolidge became increasingly involved in directing for television, beginning with several episodes of *The Twilight Zone* for CBS in 1985. In 1987, she directed the ABC pilot for the short-lived offbeat detective spoof series *Sledge Hammer!*, starring Jackie Cooper. Coolidge took on the challenge of the made-for-television film when she directed *Trenchcoat in Paradise* (1989), a comic murder mystery made for CBS that featured a number of soap opera stars. In *Bare Essentials* (1990), also for CBS, Coolidge satirizes the Yuppie lifestyle by returning to one of her favorite themes—the clash of two different cultures—when a high-powered lawyer couple, stranded on a deserted island, are introduced to the world of a beachcomber and a native beauty. Coolidge's concern for the lives of women emerges in *Crazy in Love* (1991), a film made for cable network Turner Network Television (TNT) starring Holly Hunter, Gena Rowlands, and Julian Sands. Hunter plays a documentary film-maker who, fearing that her husband is unfaithful, gets involved with a visiting photographer. This character study is unique in its use of three generations of women—grandmother, mother, and daughters—in their ancestral home to explore the heredity of emotions and the effect of past on present.

The influence of Coolidge's documentary *Old-Fashioned Woman* can be seen not only in *Crazy in Love* but also in Coolidge's *Rambling Rose* (1991). She even screened her early documentary to show her cinematographer and art director some of the historical ambience that she wanted to create in the script by Calder Willingham from his personal reminiscence novel of the same name. Although the script's setting and characters are southern, Coolidge was reminded of her own grandmother and knew that she had to make the film. A complex preproduction process began in the mid-1980's, and Coolidge ultimately convinced Laura Dern to play the role of Rose, cast Robert Duvall as the family patriarch, and persuaded action film director Renny Harlin to produce the film.

Although the story centers on the coming of age of its male protagonist, the catalyst for that change is Rose, a sexually active young woman desperately seeking love and affection. When she comes to work for the Hillyer family, Rose finds an ally in the slightly eccentric matriarch (played by Dern's real life mother, Diane Ladd) and makes a conquest of the love and imagination of the young son (Lukas Haas). The family and town are threatened and confused by Rose's naïve yet insatiable sexuality. When a doctor who is infatuated with Rose attempts to perform a radical hysterectomy to curb Rose's behavior, the film reaches a poetic epiphany in Mrs. Hillyer's defense of Rose and of the female principle in the universe. The warm nostalgic tone, the rich visual textures, and the transcendent performances by the actors contribute to the film's success and demonstrate Coolidge's remarkable directorial advances.

Coolidge's next theatrical release after the success of *Rambling Rose* was the 1994 film *Angie*, which was released by Walt Disney's Hollywood Pictures division and starred Geena Davis. A contemporary story set in the Italian American neighborhood of Bensonhurst in Brooklyn, New York, *Angie* follows the transformations that occur in the life of a young working-class woman who discovers she is pregnant and finds herself unwilling to relinquish her independence in order to settle down into an expected marriage with her boyfriend. Although *Angie* drew mixed reviews, particularly for its casting of Davis as a Brooklyn native, the film explored issues of identity and self-discovery that were hallmarks of Coolidge's earlier efforts.

Summary

As a director, Martha Coolidge has managed to survive and prosper within the confines of the notoriously male-dominated Hollywood system. Part of her success is the result of her ability to work within the system, taking on projects that others have rejected and completing them under difficult circumstances. Instead of being inhibited by formulaic genres, she has injected new life into her projects through realism and complex character development. Since she is not making overtly political or "serious" films, Coolidge is allowed some leeway in the creation of her nonexploitative, human comedy. Though cautious of being labeled a "feminist" director, she continues to make films with interesting female characters and has taken a rather feminist approach to her creative collaboration with other artists. In an interview published in *American Film* magazine in June of 1984, Coolidge acknowledged Hollywood's misconception of women directors: "[T]here is this idea that a woman cannot handle authority and cannot be a so-called boss. The real truth is that if you know what you want as a director, and can get that across, everyone will be happy." Her main difficulty in adjusting to the Hollywood system has been accepting her role as "the sandwich person," the person between the creative people in the cast and crew and the producers who hired her. Coolidge seems to have worked out an ideal balance of genre and originality, commercial success and artistic integrity, feminism and humanism, collaboration and control. A gifted director of comedy, Coolidge is limited only by the quality of the scripts she chooses to film.

Bibliography
Cook, Pam. "Martha Coolidge." In *Women in Film: An International Guide*, edited by Annette Kuhn and Susannah Radstone. New York: Fawcett Columbine, 1991. Biographical introduction to Coolidge with consideration of her feminist contributions to filmmaking.
"Dialogue on Film: Martha Coolidge." *American Film* 9 (June, 1984): 15-18. Interview with Coolidge about production of *Valley Girl*, her documentary background, and her views of women in Hollywood.
"Dialogue on Film: Martha Coolidge." *American Film* 13 (December, 1988): 14-19. Coolidge discusses a variety of issues concerning the production of *Plain Clothes* and *Real Genius*.
Horton, Robert. "Connecticut Yankee." *Film Comment* 27 (November/December, 1991): 16-20. A critical evaluation of Coolidge's career. Focuses primarily on her work on *Rambling Rose*.
Schickel, Richard. "Hollywood's New Directions." *Time* 138 (October 14, 1991): 75-76. An assessment of the factors behind the increasing presence of women directors in Hollywood. Coolidge's work on *Rambling Rose* in placed within the context of other 1991 films directed by women, including Katheryn Bigelow's *Point Break*, Randa Haines's *The Doctor*, Jodie Foster's *Little Man Tate*, and Lili Fini Zanuck's *Rush*.

Carol M. Ward

GERTY CORI

Born: August 15, 1896; Prague, Austro-Hungarian Empire (later Czech Republic)
Died: October 26, 1957; St. Louis, Missouri
Area of Achievement: Biochemistry
Contribution: The research carried out by Gerty Cori, and her husband Carl, led to an understanding of the metabolic processes involved in the enzymatic synthesis of glycogen and its subsequent cleavage into glucose. She was awarded a Nobel Prize in 1947, only the third woman to receive that award in science.

Early Life

Gerty Theresa Radnitz was born on August 15, 1896, the eldest of three daughters belonging to Otto Radnitz and Martha Neustadt Radnitz. Her father was a successful businessman and manager of several sugar refineries. Relatively wealthy, Gerty and her sisters had private tutors until the age of ten, at which time they entered a private school for girls. The emphasis at the school was development of social graces, rather than training in mathematics or science. Nevertheless, Gerty developed an interest in chemistry, and following graduation in 1912, she decided on a career in medicine. In this endeavor, she was strongly encouraged by an uncle who was a professor of pediatrics at Carl Ferdinand University.

Aided by a teacher from the Tetschen Realgymnasium, she mastered, in a year, the Latin, mathematics, and science necessary for admission to medical school. In 1914, Gerty passed the examinations at the Tetschen Realgymnasium and entered the medical school of the German branch of Carl Ferdinand University (later, the University of Prague).

While at medical school, Gerty met another student, Carl Cori. They began to collaborate as a research team on biochemistry experiments, even publishing a scientific paper together. Soon, their professional collaboration developed into a romantic relationship. In 1914, Austria entered World War I; during his third year in medical school, Carl Cori was drafted into the Sanitary Corps. Gerty spent the war as an assistant in the school, reuniting with Carl in 1918. The couple received their medical degrees in 1920 and were married on August 5 of that year.

After graduation, Carl Cori joined the staff at the University of Vienna, while Gerty was hired at the nearby Carolinen Children's Hospital. Interested in research rather than clinical practice, Gerty published a number of papers on studies of the thyroid and spleen. The war had devastated many of the older cities of the former empire, however, and left little opportunity or sources of funds for the Coris to carry out their research.

In 1922, Carl was offered a position as biochemist at the State Institute for the Study of Malignant Diseases (later named Roswell Park Memorial Institute), in Buffalo, New York. Soon after, Gerty was offered a position there as assistant pathologist, and the Coris came to the United States. They were to spend nine fruitful years at the institute, laying the groundwork for subsequent discoveries in the area of glycogen metabolism. In 1928, during the course of their tenure at Buffalo, the Coris also became American citizens.

Life's Work

The work carried out by Gerty and Carl Cori at Buffalo initially centered on metabolic processes carried out within cancerous tumors. Carbohydrate chemistry as exhibited even by normal cells or tissues was not well understood at the time, however, and they quickly found themselves working in this area. It was an exciting time for those interested in the metabolism of sugars. Sir Frederick Banting and his student, Charles Best, working at the University of Toronto, had recently isolated a chemical from the pancreas, insulin, which was shown to be critical in the utilization of glucose by the body. The Coris took this discovery a step forward, addressing the question of what specific effects the presence of insulin and a second hormone, epinephrine, had on the metabolism of sugar.

Glycogen, a highly branched polymerized form of glucose, had been discovered by the French physiologist Claude Bernard in 1857. Bernard had observed that animals fed a sugar-free diet nevertheless secreted glucose from the liver, and that glycogen was the likely source. It would later be shown that glycogen represents the major carbohydrate stored in the body—primarily in the liver, but to a lesser extent in muscle cells.

In 1925, the Coris began their studies on regulation of this glycogenic function of the liver. They found that when laboratory rats were maintained on a diet of glucose and fructose, that most of these sugars were either stored as glycogen, or oxidized to lactic acid. Further, the rate of glycogen storage was determined by insulin levels, while the conversion of glycogen to glucose was regulated in part by epinephrine. In 1929, they proposed that this process, known as the Cori cycle, regulated the relative levels of both liver and muscle glycogen, and blood glucose and lactic acid. Specifically, they proposed that liver glycogen is depolymerized to form blood glucose, itself converted to muscle glycogen. The muscle glycogen is eventually metabolized to form lactic acid, some of which is released into the blood. The blood lactic acid is further metabolized back to liver glycogen. A "by-product" of lactic acid by the muscle was hexosemonophosphate. Though modified during ensuing years (in part by the Coris themselves), the cycle has been shown to be essentially correct.

In 1931, Carl Cori received an offer for a position as chair of the department of pharmacology at Washington University School of Medicine in St. Louis, Missouri. The university also offered Gerty an appointment as research associate with her own laboratory. The nature of these appointments was in part a reflection of the role played by women in collaboration with their male counterparts at the time. Rarely were women given the primary appointment, or even one at an equal level. Gerty Cori had proven ability, yet she willingly accepted a post as research associate—usually considered a position of lesser responsibility and recognition—because it allowed her to concentrate on the laboratory research she loved.

In St. Louis, the Coris continued their work on glycogen metabolism, investigating intermediates in the pathways. They centered their investigations on the hexose monophosphates, esters which result from reactions between six-carbon sugars and phosphate. Glucose-6-phosphate, a compound in which phosphate is attached to the number six position on the sugar, had been previously known. The Coris were able to isolate a precursor to this compound, glucose-1-phosphate (Cori ester), and eventually purified the enzymes which carry out each step in the process. By the early 1940's, the Coris had elucidated each step in the process by which glycogen is converted to glucose: Glycogen is depolymerized to glucose-1-phosphate, a reaction catalyzed by the enzyme phosphorylase. Glucose-1-phosphate was converted to glucose-6-phosphate by the enzyme phosphoglucomutase. Glucose-6-phosphate can in turn either be converted back to glycogen, or metabolized to lactic acid. An additional enzyme which led to the branched structure of glycogen was also isolated. The Coris confirmed this work in 1943, carrying out the first test-tube synthesis of a naturally occurring compound (glycogen) by incubating glucose with the correct sequence of enzymes. These studies formed the basis of the Nobel award for the Coris in 1947.

As the Coris completed this aspect of their work on glycogen metabolism, they turned to the investigation of glycogen storage disease. These inherited defects in glycogen metabolism result in abnormally large accumulation of glycogen in various parts of the body. Based on their earlier studies of glycogen metabolism, the Coris logically believed that the heritable nature of these disorders was likely the result of defects of specific enzymes within the glycogen pathway. This proved to be the case. Type I storage disease (von Gierke's disease), characterized by buildup of glycogen in the liver and kidneys, was found to be due to a glucose-6-phosphate dehydrogenase deficiency, while Type III disease (Cori's disease), characterized by a similar buildup of abnormally branched glycogen in the liver or heart, was found to be caused by a defect in the branching enzyme. These studies, completed in the early 1950's by Gerty working independently from her husband, represented the first demonstrations that human genetic disease could be due to loss of a specific enzyme.

In 1947, the Coris were jointly awarded the Nobel Prize in Physiology or Medicine (along with Bernardo Houssay of Argentina). Though this year was one of international recognition, it was also the period in which Gerty Cori was diagnosed with myelofibrosis, a bone marrow disorder characterized by abnormal development of marrow tissue. Nevertheless, it would be ten years before Gerty would succumb to the disease. In the meantime, she was appointed professor of Biochemistry in 1947. Despite the increasing severity of her illness, Gerty continued her research. Using the enzymes she had previously isolated, she finally determined the chemical structure of glycogen. Gerty Cori died in 1957 from kidney failure brought on by her illness.

Summary

Gerty Cori's life was a sterling example, not only for women, but to all humanity. Without question, her death was a loss to the scientific world. The isolation and purification of specific enzymes led to an understanding of critical metabolic processes. These same enzymes also enabled the Coris to define the structure of a macromolecule: glycogen. Her awards in addition to the Nobel Prize included, among many others, the American Chemical Society Midwest Award in Science (1946), the Squibb Award in Endocrinology (1947), the Garvin Gold Medal (1948), and the Borden Award of the Association of American Medical Colleges (1950). In 1947, she became only the fourth woman elected to the National Academy of Sciences.

Perhaps even more important than her honors, Gerty Cori was recognized for her kindness and love of humankind. She had a rich, engaging personality that reached out to those in need. Her work on the genetic basis of glycogen storage disease was no accident, but represented a sincere desire to eliminate suffering among children, a trait stemming from her observations during World War I. In addition, her collaboration on research with her husband and decision not to pursue full teaching responsibilities allowed her to juggle her responsibilities as a working mother responsible for rearing her son Carl Thomas.

Cori never lost her childhood belief in the moral goodness of humankind. Yet she was not naïve; she had seen too much of war and suffering. Rather, Cori's actions served as examples of attributes of which humans were capable: kindness, generosity, and interest in others. Ironically, at the time of her death she had an unfinished letter written to a friend whose husband was ill. She was inquiring as to his health and expressing the hope he would soon recover. Cori expected much of others, but no more than the demands she made on herself.

Bibliography
Cori, Carl F. "The Call of Science." *Annual Review of Biochemistry* 38 (1969): 1-20. An excellent discussion of the life and career of Gerty Cori, written by her husband. The article also provides a fine discussion of the progression of their work.
Fruton, Joseph S. "Cori, Gerty Theresa Radnitz." In *Dictionary of Scientific Biography*, edited by Charles Gillispie. New York: Charles Scribner's Sons, 1971. A brief biography of Cori, with a synopsis of her work. Though not detailed, the article provides a good overview of her career.
Kass-Simon, Gabriele, and Patricia Farnes, eds. *Women of Science: Righting the Record*. Bloomington: Indiana University Press, 1990. Divided into chapters based on the field, this book provides both a concise biography of the subject, and a general description of their work. A brief discussion of the Coris' contributions is provided, along with a list of some of their important works.
Miller, Jane. "Carl F. Cori and Gerty T. Cori." In *The Nobel Prize Winners: Physiology or Medicine*, edited by Frank N. Magill. Vol. 2. Pasadena, Calif: Salem Press, 1991. An excellent description of the lives and careers of the Coris. Also included is their Nobel lecture, and a list of their major works.
Rossiter, Margaret. *Women Scientists in America: Struggles and Strategies to 1940*. Baltimore: The Johns Hopkins University Press, 1982. A good general discussion of struggles faced by women scientists during a particular era. Little is found specifically on Cori, but the book does provide a fine synopsis of contributions by women to scientific fields.

Yost, Edna. *Women of Modern Science.* New York: Dodd, Mead, 1960. Reprint. Westport, Conn.: Greenwood Press, 1984. Includes a fine, concise biography of Gerty Cori. The chapter is based in part on correspondence with the subject prior to her death, and then later discussions with her husband. Emphasis is placed on Cori's concern for humanity, along with some discussion of her work.

Richard Adler

KATIE COURIC

Born: January 7, 1957; Arlington, Virginia

Area of Achievement: Journalism
Contribution: An award-winning television journalist, Couric has made notable contributions to reporting and producing the news of issues, events, and figures at both national and international levels.

Early Life

Katherine Anne Couric was born in Arlington, Virginia, on January 7, 1957. She grew up in this suburb, located just across the Potomac from the nation's capital and famous for its national cemetery on the grounds of what was originally the private home of Civil War Confederate General Robert E. Lee. In a red brick, white-trimmed house, young Katie lived with her mother, Elinor; her father, John; her elder sisters, Emily and Clara, nine and six years her senior; and her brother John, Jr., older by a little more than a year than Katie. John Couric, Sr., earned his living as a journalist and public relations specialist, while Elinor Couric maintained the home and household, volunteered her services to the community, and worked as a saleswoman and a sometime floral designer. Here in their traditional-style home, amid warm and supportive family ties and surrounded by neighborhood friends, the Couric family flourished. The young Courics were each expected to share a newly learned word at the nightly gatherings for dinner. Katie, who had a naturally friendly and ebullient nature, always followed her mother's dictum to make sure her presence was noted. By the time she graduated from Yorktown High School in 1975, Katie had succeeded in making her presence known as a member of the cheerleading squad, as a gymnast, as a competitive runner, as a member of the National Honor Society, and as a writer for the school paper. At the University of Virginia in Charlottesville, she embarked upon a major in American studies and was graduated in 1979 with honors. During her undergraduate years, she joined Delta Delta Delta sorority and worked as associate editor of the University of Virginia student paper.

Life's Work

In 1979, following her graduation from the University of Virginia, Katie Couric applied for work at the Washington, D.C., news bureaus of both the American Broadcasting Company (ABC) and the Columbia Broadcasting System (CBS) networks. Enthusiastic about the prospect of a career in broadcast journalism, Couric hoped to get her start as a writer for the television news-reporting business at the national level. She was offered a position as a desk assistant at ABC, where she worked with Sam Donaldson and Frank Reynolds, sometimes sitting in on White House briefings. When George Watson, ABC's Washington news bureau chief, moved to the newly forming Cable News Network (CNN) in 1980, Couric moved with him as an assignment editor at the new network's Washington bureau. Not long afterward, she won a spot on camera, although this post was short-lived. Still at CNN, she was transferred to production, working behind the scenes in Washington, as well as in Miami and Atlanta, until she polished her on-air image sufficiently to earn a much desired position on camera. As producer of the news program *Take Two* in Atlanta, she had the opportunity to appear on air occasionally under the aegis of her mentors, *Take Two* coanchors Don Farmer and his wife, Chris Curle.

Always eager to accomplish more than was required or expected of her, Couric produced an exclusive three-hour live show for CNN from Cuba in 1982. Working with limited resources in a hotel room in downtown Havana, and doing her own research surrounded by books and a Spanish-speaking crew, Couric managed to impress her boss, CNN President Reese Schoenfeld, with her own on-air production of a program on Ernest Hemingway. Soon after this, Couric became a political correspondent for CNN, assigned to cover the 1984 presidential campaign. From 1984 to 1986 she worked as general assignment reporter for WTVJ in Miami. Her documentary on child pornography, written and produced in Miami, won a prize, and her police-crime productions won the notice of Fred Francis, chief Pentagon correspondent for NBC.

In 1986, Couric again obtained an on-air position as general news assignment reporter with WRC-TV, the National Broadcasting Company affiliate in Washington, D.C., where her work won her an Emmy and an Associated Press Award. Then, in July 1989, she joined National Broadcasting Company News as deputy Pentagon correspondent. She became well liked and respected among both her colleagues from competing networks and the senior military officer community who trusted the accuracy and discretion she displayed in her reports. In July of 1990, she moved to NBC's *Today* show as a national correspondent based in Washington. In August and September of that year, after the United States had deployed American troops and ships to the Middle East in what was later to become known as the Persian Gulf Crisis, Couric conducted a memorable series of interviews with fighting men and women, not to mention their flag-ranked commanders, broadcasting from Saudi Arabia. Throughout the Persian Gulf War, Couric served as special correspondent to the Pentagon, as well as substitute coanchor for the *Today* show. Couric was officially named as the morning show's cohost on April 4, 1991.

On camera every weekday morning during *Today* show's two-hour format, Couric is a highly visible role model for young women around the world. She is well aware of this aspect of her career and consciously tries to project her self-image as a knowledgeable, assertive woman, able to defend herself without being strident. As a feminist, she maintains her own personal life goals and agenda, while at the same time she adheres closely to the highest principles of a serious, credible journalism that have contributed to her notable success. Her strong personality is equal to that of her strong coanchor, Bryant Gumbel. The cohost position requires Couric to keep abreast of international political events as well as current national news. At the same time, she is expected to present information on relatively trivial popular minutiae. Couric is an admitted star watcher, welcoming the chance for informal chats with visiting celebrities. Her empathy for others is a major part of her appeal. Careful attention to detail prepares her for the times when, unrehearsed and unplanned, a golden moment for interviewing arises. The interview questions she poses to her guests are fair, yet thought-provoking. She attempts to avoid either a liberal or conservative bias in her reporting, thus widening her potential for broader audiences and her access to credible sources. As a result, her interviews have given her a reputation for being fair, direct, and quick-witted. These attributes, along with Couric's dynamic, improvisational style and her ability to maintain an unaffected charm, are credited with returning the *Today* show to first position among its competitors in network television's morning news programs.

Some of Couric's more noteworthy interviews have included an impromptu meeting with President George Bush just after finishing an exclusive White House interview with his wife, First Lady Barbara Bush, in October of 1992. This encounter produced an unscheduled, unrehearsed, and unprecedented informal twenty-minute visit with the president that won Couric new fans everywhere. Earlier, in June of 1992, she had engineered a viewer phone-in show featuring then-undeclared presidential candidate, H. Ross Perot. The accompanying interview made television history. Following the Persian Gulf War, Couric conducted prestigious interviews with General Norman Schwarzkopf and King Hussein of Jordan. At other times, she has interviewed such diverse personalities and/or celebrities as former Ku Klux Klan leader and political hopeful David Duke, law professor Anita Hill, comedian George Burns, actor Warren Beatty, and comedian Whoopi Goldberg.

Couric has hosted many prime-time programs and specials. In May of 1993, she anchored the first one-hour prime-time interview granted by First Lady Hillary Rodham Clinton. In 1992, Couric also coanchored NBC's prime-time election coverage and cohosted NBC's morning coverage of the Summer Olympics in Barcelona. Among her other duties, Couric cohosted the Metropolitan Opera's Silver Anniversary Gala in 1991, taking viewers behind the scenes with some of the opera's most illustrious stars, including Luciano Pavarotti and Placido Domingo. In August of 1993, NBC inaugurated a prime-time news magazine *Now* that teamed Tom Brokaw and Katie Couric. This new assignment signaled the network's respect for Couric's journalistic talents and also gave her more opportunities to focus on the hard news stories she had had the chance to cover in her early career.

Summary

Watched by millions of viewers each morning, Katie Couric maintains one of the highest profiles of any contemporary woman. After working her way through the ranks and learning the fundamentals of broadcast journalism, Couric became one of the first morning show coanchors to have a solid background in covering serious news stories. Her work in interviewing government and military officials during her stint as a Pentagon correspondent provided her with a good foundation for later assignments on the *Today* show. Couric's determination to work as a team player and to learn from her colleagues allowed her to gain the trust and respect of network executives. Her decision to balance the demands of her career with her responsibilities to her growing family helped to encourage her women viewers to emulate her example.

Bibliography

Diamond, Edwin. "The Couric Effect." *New York* 24 (December 9, 1991): 20-22. In an analysis of the ratings races of the networks' morning television shows, Diamond emphasizes the way in which success hinges on the personalities of the performer-journalists. He compares the many changes dictated by behind-the-scenes producers to the complicated plot lines of television soap operas. In Diamond's assessment, the hiring of Couric to replace Deborah Norville is seen as a major coup for NBC, primarily because of Couric's solid journalistic credentials.

Flander, Judy. "The Two Faces of Katie Couric." *Washington Journalism Review* 14 (May, 1992): 26-30. The author analyzes Couric's contributions to NBC's resurgence in the morning show ratings race and how her appeal has translated into high advertising revenues for the network. She ascribes Couric's success to her ability to conduct herself as both a cheerful and charming cohost and as a tough interviewer.

Kessler, Judy. *Inside Today: The Battle for the Morning.* New York: Villard Books, 1992. Kessler, who worked as a booking agent for the *Today* show, draws upon her own experiences to provide an account of the stormy behind-the-scenes maneuvering that led to Jane Pauley's departure from the show. Critical of the limited power given to the women who worked in front of and behind the camera at the *Today* show, Kessler attributes blame to the producers, who tried to avoid any redistribution of power that might upset or upstage host Bryant Gumbel. Although the book contains little information on Couric, it does provide a background for understanding the working environment Couric confronted when she landed her assignment as cohost.

Scott, Sophfronia. "Here We Go Again: Today's Norville Moves Out. But Is Musical Chairs Over?" *Time* 137 (April 15, 1991): 57. Critical response to news of Couric's promotion to coanchor of the *Today* show as announced by Michael Gartner, president of NBC News. One *Today* show staff member summarized the opinions of many people by noting that the decision to appoint Couric as a permanent replacement for Deborah Norville as cohost was popular because of Couric's ability to project herself as friendly and outgoing in addition to being a credible journalist.

Zoglin, Richard. "Today Show." *Time* 140 (July 13, 1992): 77-78. In this overview of midsummer television interviews granted by the 1992 presidential candidates, Zoglin gives high marks to Katie Couric for encouraging callers to grill Ross Perot with follow-ups on tough questions during a call-in session televised on the *Today* show.

Betsey Pender

PRUDENCE CRANDALL

Born: September 3, 1803; Hopkinton, Rhode Island
Died: January 28, 1890; Elk Falls, Kansas
Areas of Achievement: Education, social reform, and women's rights
Contribution: A Quaker who became devoted to a range of social reforms, Crandall
  dedicated her life to education, especially for black females, and also to women's
  suffrage.

Early Life

Prudence Crandall was born in Hopkinton, Rhode Island, on September 3, 1803, one of Pardon and Esther Carpenter Crandall's four children. In 1813, the Quaker family moved from the uncomfortable shadow of Esther Crandall's parents to a farm near Canterbury, Connecticut. Curious and inquisitive as a child, Prudence received a "guarded" Quaker education at the finest coeducational boarding school, New England Yearly Meeting School, or Brown Seminary, which was located on land in Providence belonging to Moses Brown, an abolitionist. There she studied the practical subjects as well as Latin and the sciences. In the Quaker tradition, the cultural environment of the school was plain. Although the focused religious orientation may have accentuated her sense of separation from mainstream American society, Prudence thrived there. After she finished her schooling, she returned to Connecticut, where she taught for a short while. By this time, her brother Reuben considered her very obstinate, a reputation she evidently shared with her father.

In 1831, Prudence was appointed director of the new Canterbury Female Seminary in Canterbury, Connecticut, at a time when there was an undercurrent of change in the town, occasioned by new mills and new towns populated by bumptious workers; attacks on the long-standing fraternal organization of freemasonry; the advent of revival sects with their frenetic enthusiasm; and the popularization of organizations such as the American Colonization Society that advocated sending free blacks to settle the colony of Liberia in West Africa.

Life's Work

Soon after she moved into the seminary's quarters in the elegant Paine mansion, Prudence Crandall opened the school to twenty white female students. Mariah Davis, a black "family assistant" at the school, was engaged to the son of William Harris, an agent for *The Liberator.* When Harris' seventeen-year-old daughter Sarah asked to attend the school but live at home, Crandall agreed. Although the community disregarded Sarah's attendance for a short while, soon the Episcopal minister's wife expressed her disapproval, threatening that, when all the white parents withdrew their daughters, the school would sink. With little hesitation, Crandall replied, "Let it sink."

After consulting with William Lloyd Garrison, the fiery and fearless editor of *The Liberator,* and other prominent abolitionist leaders including Samuel J. May, the local Unitarian minister, Crandall advertised for a new student body. On February 24, 1833, the High School for Young Colored Ladies and Misses opened with approximately twenty "well-bred colored girls" from Providence, Boston, and Philadelphia. A major controversy erupted. Some Canterbury lawyers uncovered an obsolete pauper and vagrant law stating that, if strangers remained in the village without the approval of town authorities, they would be fined $1.67 per week. The tension mounted while prominent citizens, such as attorney Andrew T. Judson, kept the issue agitated. Crandall was asked to move her school to a "more retired situation," away from the town center. Many citizens expressed their fear that, instead of leaving town to teach at schools in black communities, these educated young black women would remain in Canterbury and marry white men or provoke trouble—situations that seemed likely to ruin the reputation of the community and its inhabitants.

When Crandall refused to move or to close her school, the Canterbury merchants and physicians boycotted her school, refusing to provide any services. Next, the legislature passed the Black Law on May 24, 1833, targeting anyone who set up an educational institution for colored persons who were not inhabitants of Connecticut or anyone who taught or boarded such persons. By restricting their freedom of movement and residence, the law implied that blacks were not citizens. Moreover, the new statute imposed heavy fines: $100 for the first offense, $200 for the second, and double for each offense thereafter.

Soon after, the twenty-nine-year-old Crandall was arrested on a series of charges, including the crime of keeping a boarding school for colored girls in the state of Connecticut and for instructing these girls, who were not inhabitants of the state, without having first obtained written permission to do so.

The abolitionist movement was strengthened as free-thinking citizens realized that the Colonization Society, which prided itself on liberating blacks by sending them to Liberia, actually protected the institution of slavery. William Lloyd Garrison, leader of the abolitionist movement, covered the situation extensively in *The Liberator*; and Charles C. Burleigh, backed by wealthy merchant and philanthropist Arthur Tappan, created a weekly called *The Unionist* expressly to distribute news of Crandall's trials, the Black Law, and the national implications of the controversy all over New England. During the three trials, Connecticut citizens were confronted with difficult questions: What was the intention of the framers of the Constitution? Were persons of color equal? Were they citizens?

At Crandall's first trial on August 22, 1833, the defense strategy tried to prove the wrongful nature of the Black Law by arguing that the Constitution gave citizens in each state the rights and privileges of citizens of other states when they were temporarily residing there. Thus, the abolitionist lawyers argued, the black students were citizens. Because the jury was split, no decision resulted. Crandall was arrested again on the same charges on September 26, 1833. In her retrial, Chief Justice David Daggett ruled categorically that black people were not citizens. As a result of his ruling, Crandall was found guilty, but the decision was immediately appealed on technical points.

A pacifist by nature who was aided by abolitionists and members of her own family,

Crandall tried to concentrate on teaching the young girls, but the continuing harassment interrupted the lessons. Instigators dumped manure in the school's well, blew horns and beat drums whenever the girls went out, threw rocks in the windows, mutilated and impaled a black and white cat on the fence post, and finally set the mansion on fire.

Crandall's appeal was heard on July 26, 1834 in the Supreme Court of Errors. Although her lawyers focused again on the unconstitutional nature of the Black Law, the case was ultimately dismissed on the technicality of insufficient information. The court ruled that the Black Law was applicable only to unlicensed schools and that the original complaint had not stated that Crandall's school was unlicensed. Although pleased that Crandall was free, the abolitionist lawyers were disappointed that they would be unable to test their argument in the Supreme Court. The constitutional question of citizenship for black people had been evaded.

Soon after the trial, on August 12, 1834, Crandall married Calvin Philleo, acknowledged by her biographers as an overbearing Baptist minister from Ithaca, New York. When harassing men entered the mansion a month later, ravaged it and traumatized the students, Philleo ordered her to abandon the school. Crandall sold the house and moved with her husband to upstate New York and then later, without her wandering spouse, to Troy Grove, Illinois, where she opened the Philleo Academy on the prairie and resumed teaching. Her unstable husband and her own relatives depended so heavily on her that she had little freedom in her midlife to participate actively in the politics of reform efforts, but she remained an outspoken abolitionist and a fervent advocate of women's rights, especially suffrage. During this time, she abandoned the Quaker religion and became a Unitarian spiritualist, as she called it, and later became interested in Christian Science. After the death of her husband in 1874, Crandall resumed a lively schedule of lecturing on peace, temperance, and women's rights.

Crandall expressed great satisfaction in 1885, when more than one hundred citizens of Canterbury signed a petition to the Connecticut legislature asking that reparation be given to her for the "cruel outrages" committed against her while she taught in Canterbury. In 1886, a bill established a pension of $400 annually for the duration of her life. With the first payment, Crandall bought a two-story wooden house in Elk Falls, Kansas. Always a woman of principle, Crandall was pleased that her criminal conviction was expunged from her record and that her dignity was restored. Crandall died on January 28, 1890, at the age of eighty-six.

Summary

Prudence Crandall was among the first women to be actively involved in the abolitionist movement at a time when most women were relegated to the traditional role of raising funds for the cause. Because defiance was uniquely hers and she was so prominently identified, Crandall suffered the opprobrium and persecution that went with the notoriety. Yet the "little known episode of Canterbury," as biographer Edmund Fuller termed it, had linkages and ramifications that reached far beyond Crandall and the little town.

As a result of Crandall's unswerving stand in Connecticut, the United States and England were alerted to the need to educate black children. Unfortunately, the need was accomplished by the establishment of separate and unequal schools for blacks—a legacy which was increasingly denounced until the decision in *Brown v. Board of Education* in 1954 legally required integration of public schools in the United States.

To the end, Crandall remained a woman of principle. Her ideas were consistent throughout her life, and she never wavered in adhering to them in her search for truth, even when she was considered an outspoken and dangerous rebel. In an interview with journalist George B. Thayer late in her life, Crandall acknowledged that her life had been one of opposition. She revealed that even her husband had opposed her, not letting her read the books that he himself read. Despite his disapproval, she reveled in the fact that she read them after all, and plenty of others. Earlier in her life, Garrison had described her in *The Liberator* as "the Ornament of Her Sex"; but Ellen Larned, nineteenth century historian of Windham County, Connecticut, best epitomized Crandall's contribution to history when she wrote, "Miss Crandall did not succeed in teaching many colored girls but she educated the people of Windham County."

Bibliography

Fuller, Edmund. *Prudential Crandall: An Incident of Racism in Nineteenth-Century Connecticut*. Middletown, Conn.: Wesleyan University Press, 1971. The original, somewhat biased, biography of Prudence Crandall with careful attention to the "little known episode" in Canterbury and its ramifications. A word of caution: the dates used for major events in Crandall's life are often one year later than those cited by Strane in her biography. A final chapter concentrates on Crandall's last years and includes George B. Thayer's journalistic report of his two-day visit with Crandall in Elk Falls, Kansas.

Litwack, Leon F. *North of Slavery: The Negro in the Free States, 1790-1860*. Chicago: University of Chicago Press, 1961. "Education: Separate and Unequal," chapter 4, is a succinct but detailed summary of the controversy over the Canterbury boarding school in Connecticut. Sets the controversy in the larger context of abolitionism and educational reform.

May, Samuel J. *Some Recollections of Our Antislavery Conflict*. Reprint. New York: Arno Press, 1968. Recollections printed as a series of articles for the editor of *The Christian Register* and organized under the two headings of "The Rise of Abolitionism" and "Antislavery Conflict." May recounts how he was drawn into the violent conflict and the "shameful, cruel persecution of Miss Prudence Crandall."

Strane, Susan. *A Whole-Souled Woman: Prudence Crandall and the Education of Black Women*. New York: W. W. Norton, 1990. An engaging and definitive biography that sets Crandall's life within the context of the social changes that transformed American culture during nineteenth century. This biography is especially notable for its coverage of the years after Crandall's move to Illinois and Kansas. Corrects some minor factual errors in the Fuller biography. The notes and bibliography are unusually thorough.

Yates, Elizabeth. *Prudence Crandall: A Woman of Courage*. New York: Aladdin Books, 1955. A lightly fictionalized biography for younger readers that concentrates on the boarding school controversy and the resulting trials. The epilogue uses excerpts from Crandall's letters to cover the latter years of her life. There are no bibliographical sources.

Deborah Elwell Arfken

CHERYL CRAWFORD

Born: September 24, 1902; Akron, Ohio
Died: October 7, 1986; New York, New York
Area of Achievement: Theater and drama
Contribution: A prizewinning producer and director with unequaled influence in American theater for more than fifty years, Crawford served as casting director for the Theatre Guild early in her career before going on to help found the Group Theatre, the Actors Studio, and the American Repertory Theatre.

Early Life

Cheryl Crawford was born just after the turn of the century in the small midwestern city of Akron, Ohio. Located on the Cuyahoga River in the northeastern part of the state, Akron had a bustling economy dominated by the activities of the Quaker Oats cereal company. Cheryl's father, Robert Kingsley Crawford, was a real estate broker known by his nickname of "King"; her mother, Luella Elizabeth Parker Crawford, reared Cheryl and her three younger brothers. The Crawford home was a solid Victorian structure built to house a large family, and included such amenities as a large library and space in which to hold amateur theatrical productions. As an elder sister to three brothers, Cheryl was something of a tomboy and an enthusiastic participant in climbing trees, racing bicycles, and even boxing in gloved matches. When her youngest brother Robert was born in 1915, Cheryl served as his surrogate mother and enjoyed regaling him with the ad-libbed stories that were her great specialty.

King Crawford served as superintendent of the Congregational Sunday School, where he taught a young men's Bible class. A staunchly religious individual, he insisted on saying grace before every family meal. Cheryl later complained of the overly puritanical atmosphere of her childhood home, but learned to appreciate her father's insistence on discipline when she later took charge of unruly actors and theatrical personnel.

Cheryl's maternal grandmother, Lavinia Lynn Parker, was an important influence during Cheryl's early years. Lavinia Parker lived with the Crawfords and served as an unofficial babysitter, rocking Cheryl to sleep night after night to the tune of old Civil War songs and other musical favorites. Cheryl's grandmother also told thrilling stories about the night that Abraham Lincoln had been assassinated, drawing on the memories of her father, who had been a member of the posse that hunted John Wilkes Booth. Lavinia Parker particularly enjoyed watching silent pictures and often took her grandchildren with her to watch installments of *The Perils of Pauline.*

The Crawford family was sufficiently well off to afford a variety of lessons for Cheryl. In the area of music, she studied violin, piano, guitar under various tutors and teachers; she also took lessons in swimming, horseback riding, and ballroom dancing. Trained at the Emerson School of Elocution in Boston, her mother taught Cheryl the basics of elocution and coached her in the use of dramatic gestures. King Crawford also coached Cheryl in acting and speech. Her dramatic training was evident in her graduation day monologue as Lady Macbeth. In Cheryl's performance of the famous sleepwalking scene, her waist-length hair caught fire from the candle she was holding. Never once stepping out of character, she put out the fire with her hands and finished the monologue without a pause despite horrified outbursts from the audience.

Life's Work

In 1921, Cheryl Crawford left home to attend Smith College, a women's college located in the Berkshire Mountains of western Massachusetts. During her freshman year, she pursued her passion for drama by performing in a number of one-act plays. Crawford also discovered two other treasured subjects: philosophy and English literature. She made a name for herself in the role of the Count in a performance of *A Marriage of Convenience* at the famous Academy nearby. Having found her calling, Crawford improved her study habits and attained excellent grades worthy of Phi Beta Kappa membership by her sophomore year.

In her junior year, she served as president of the Dramatic Association at Smith. With the guidance of a professor who instructed her in playwriting and dramatic history, Crawford produced and directed a spectacular outdoor performance of a classic Indian play. In her staging, she constructed a long trench through the lawns and gardens surrounding the residence of the college president and commandeered the hoses of the Northampton Fire Department in order to create a continuous line of fountains that provided a curtain for the play. The magnificent effect of the fifteen-foot-high curtain of water, lit up by a combination of multicolored stage lights as well as smoke candles donated by the local railroad station, enhanced the Oriental ambience created by burning incense cones. The play drew packed audiences and set a nearly impossible precedent for future dramatic productions.

During the summer before her senior year, Crawford traveled to Cape Cod in hopes of performing with the famous Provincetown Players acting troupe. Driving an old car purchased by means of a bequest from her grandmother Parker, Crawford made the journey to Provincetown only to discover that the playhouse itself was no longer in existence. Undaunted, she joined the Players, built scenery for the troupe's productions, and reveled in the bohemian life enjoyed by these summer exiles from New York's Greenwich Village. At the end of the summer, Crawford returned to Smith College for her final year of studies and was graduated with honors in 1925.

After her graduation, Crawford announced her intention to find theater work in New York City. Back in Akron, her parents were concerned about her future and tried to dissuade her from pursuing acting. Nevertheless, with the help of the bequest from her grandmother, Crawford went ahead with her plans. She sought an interview at the Theatre Guild Company, considered to be the top acting school in Manhattan, with producer Theresa Helburn. Dressed in an outfit devised to convey a chic and sophisticated persona, Crawford persuaded Helburn to take her on as an acting student even though her actual purpose was to learn as much about the techniques of theater production as possible.

After locating an apartment on Bedford Street across from a former residence of

Edna St. Vincent Millay, Crawford began her acting studies under the tutelage of Alfred Lunt and other notable Guild actors. By graduation day, the enrollment in her class had been reduced considerably, and all were hired as part of a stock company. Crawford was awarded the position of assistant director. Many of her ideas were disregarded, and she began to encounter the type of strong prejudice directed at women who held positions in theater other than that of actor. Despite this discouragement, she continued to make the rounds of various theatrical offices in search of employment. Finally, Philip Loeb, her former dramatic coach and director at the Guild, offered her the chance to take his place as casting secretary. She agreed to take the position with the proviso that she also be hired as third assistant stage manager for the Guild's next play.

During her career as the Guild's casting director from 1926 to 1930, Crawford met and worked with a number of notable actors, including Edward G. Robinson, Claude Rains, and Henry Fonda. Among other young actors cast by Crawford during her early years were Katharine Hepburn, whom she advised to return to Bryn Mawr College to complete her undergraduate degree, and Bette Davis. Crawford also collaborated with playwrights such as Eugene O'Neill and Noel Coward, among others. Through her friendship with Harold Clurman, she was introduced to Lee Strasberg, who had studied in the Stanislavsky method of acting under Madame Ouspenskaya and the Polish-born stage director Richard Boleslavsky. Strasberg told Crawford that there was a definite technique that could be taught in order to eliminate the staged gestures, mannered posturing, and clichés that made theatrical productions stale. Intrigued by the idea of this new technique, Crawford joined Clurman and Herbert Biberman in order to form the new Theatre Guild Studio. Their first stage production was *Red Rust*, a Russian work. The threesome tried to hire a young Clark Gable to play the lead in their second play, Philip Barber's *Dead or Alive*, but the company folded shortly before the production was staged.

During the early part of the Depression, Crawford and her colleagues Strasberg and Clurman broke with the Theatre Guild Company in 1931. They formed their own company, known as the Group Theatre, with twenty-eight actors, among them Franchot Tone and Clifford Odets. The new company's first play, Paul Green's *The House of Connelly* (1931), incorporated as much of method acting as Strasberg could instill in the members during one short summer in Brookfield Center, Connecticut. When the production opened in New York that autumn, the audience was so enthusiastic that they gave the cast twenty-three curtain calls. The actors were also excited about this new method of coping with individual talents and faults while also compelling performers to call upon their inner resources in order to create fresh interpretations. Like many others, Crawford embraced "the Method" with messianic fervor.

As part of the Group Theatre from 1931 to 1937, Crawford directed and produced four plays by Clifford Odets as well as the works of Maxwell Anderson, Theodore Dreiser, and Kurt Weill, among others. After a memorable transatlantic crossing aboard the *Ile de France* and a train trip across Europe, Crawford visited the Moscow Art Theatre in 1935 and was inspired to pursue an independent career. She eventually left the Group Theatre. Her independent theatrical productions met with a notable lack of success, however, and she was forced to take a new approach. She formed a New Jersey-based stock company known as the Maplewood Theatre that was dedicated to producing a play per week. Crawford also formed numerous road companies featuring stars such as Ethel Barrymore, Helen Hayes, Ingrid Bergman, and Paul Robeson. New performers, including Oona O'Neill, found Crawford's companies provided them with a welcome proving ground for their budding talents.

In 1942, Crawford achieved Broadway success with a revival of George and Ira Gershwin's *Porgy and Bess*. Intrigued with musical theater, Crawford cast Mary Martin in an independent production of *One Touch of Venus* (1943) and went on to stage Alan Jay Lerner and Frederick Loewe's *Brigadoon* (1947) and *Paint Your Wagon* (1951). Despite her forays into musical theater, Crawford never entirely abandoned her interest in dramatic theater. After helping found the American Repertory Theatre with Eva Le Gallienne and Margaret Webster, Crawford staged classical productions by William Shakespeare, Henrik Ibsen, and George Bernard Shaw under the aegis of the newly formed company in 1946. She was involved in the production of four plays by Tennessee Williams—*The Rose Tattoo* (1951), *Sweet Bird of Youth* (1959), *Camino Real* (1953), and *Period of Adjustment* (1960). During this same period, she worked on an early Leonard Bernstein production as well as works by Berthold Brecht (*Mother Courage and Her Children* in 1963), Sean O'Casey, James Thurber, Eugene O'Neill, and Roald Dahl. At the Actors Studio Theatre, Crawford produced James Baldwin's *Blues for Mister Charlie* in 1964. During the 1970's, she staged a theatrical adaptation of Isaac Bashevis Singer's *Yentl* in 1975. Her final theatrical production was *So Long on Lonely Street*, which appeared shortly before her death in 1986 in New York City at the age of eighty-four.

Summary

Throughout her long and distinguished career as a theatrical director and producer, Cheryl Crawford never limited herself to a single dramatic genre, choosing instead to produce a wide range of musicals, operas, comedies, and serious dramas. She also refused to let her gender limit her advancement in her chosen profession. Starting from the lowest ranks, Crawford mastered the details of casting, stage management, script analysis, and directing through observation and firsthand experience before progressing as a director and producer in her own right. During Crawford's fruitful association with the Group Theatre, she worked with many of the leading playwrights and actors of the 1930's and established a reputation as a shrewd and practical executive. Whether working as an independent producer or as an associate of the American Repertory Theatre, the American National Theatre and Academy (ANTA), or the Actors' Studio, Crawford continued to collaborate with leading figures in Broadway and regional theater. Convinced that artistic risk-taking was essential to the survival of meaningful theater, Crawford took the opportunity to work on many avant-garde and challenging productions instead of limiting her attention solely to theatrical works by notable and commercially successful playwrights.

Bibliography
Adams, Cindy. *Lee Strasberg: The Imperfect Genius of the Actors Studio.* Garden City, N.Y.: Doubleday, 1980. This comprehensive biography of Strasberg contains extensive references to his work with Crawford at the Actors Studio. Its coverage of the Moscow Art Theatre and Stanislavsky provide an excellent frame of reference for understanding the origins of the "Method" as used by Strasberg and Crawford.

Crawford, Cheryl. *One Naked Individual.* Indianapolis: Bobbs-Merrill, 1977. Crawford's frank and unpretentious autobiography provides an informal, humorous, and self-deprecatory account of American theatrical life as she lived it. Reviewers who expected this memoir to be filled with gossip and scandal about the lives of Crawford's famous friends were disappointed, but Crawford stayed true to her principles and refused to demean her work with such details.

Garfield, David. *A Player's Place: The Story of the Actors Studio.* New York: Macmillan, 1980. Beginning with the origins of the Actors Studio in the Group Theatre, this history traces the studio's development through its influence on contemporary acting in film and television. The appendix contains a complete list of all performers who studied there, a selected bibliography of additional sources, and detailed notes.

Hirsch, Foster. *A Method to Their Madness: The History of the Actors Studio.* New York: W. W. Norton, 1984. Hirsch gives an alternate history of the Actors Studio, crediting its founding to Crawford, Elia Kazan, and Robert Lewis. Written from the perspective of an audience member and observer rather than a participant, this work provides a slightly different view of events at the studio.

Betsey Pender

RUTH CRAWFORD-SEEGER

Born: July 3, 1901; East Liverpool, Ohio
Died: November 18, 1953; Chevy Chase, Maryland
Area of Achievement: Music
Contribution: A pioneer among innovative twentieth century classical composers, Ruth Crawford-Seeger was active in avant-garde musical circles in the 1920's and 1930's. Later, her scholarly research in the area of American folk music resulted in transcriptions of more than 300 works from the Library of Congress Archives.

Early Life

Ruth Porter Crawford was born on July 3, 1901, in East Liverpool, Ohio, where her father was a Methodist minister. After living in several midwestern towns, the family settled in Jacksonville, Florida. Clark Crawford died when his daughter was just thirteen years old; thereafter, Clara Crawford supported Ruth and her brother Carl by operating a boarding house.

An intellectually and musically inquisitive child, Ruth began piano lessons at the age of six. She also kept a diary from about age twelve that illustrates her powerful imagination and literary gifts. The writing also reveals the strong sense of self-discipline and high standards which were present as well in her professional life and shows the influence of her parents' puritanical, yet altruistic, ideals.

After graduation from high school in 1918, Ruth taught piano and took classes at the School of Musical Arts in Jacksonville, Florida. In 1920, she left to continue her education at the American Conservatory of Music in Chicago. There she studied piano with Heniot Levy and Louise Robyn and theory and composition with Adolf Weidig and John Palmer. In time, the young pianist developed a chronically painful condition as a result of tension in the arms. This problem provoked a change in focus in Ruth's musical studies from piano to composition. After graduating from the conservatory with a diploma (1923) and a bachelor's degree (1924), Ruth took advanced composition studies with Weidig toward the master's degree (1927). In addition to composing, Ruth taught piano at the American Conservatory (1924-1929) and at Elmhurst College of Music (1926-1929).

In 1924, she began to study piano in Chicago with Mme Djane Lavoie-Herz. A woman whose influence extended beyond the lessons, she introduced Crawford to musical and artistic circles that included important members of the avant-garde. It was also through Herz that Ruth first became associated with composer Henry Cowell and poet Carl Sandburg. These figures represent the two areas that would receive the major musical and intellectual energy for the rest of her life, namely, progressive musical composition and the perpetuation of American folk music.

Alfred Frankenstein, clarinetist and music and art critic for the *San Francisco Chronicle*, befriended Crawford after meeting her at musical soirées held at the home of Mme Lavoie-Herz. He introduced Crawford to a vast amount of contemporary music as well as to Carl Sandburg, who kindled her lasting interest in folk music and children's literature. Her love of Sandburg's writing and her respect for his philosophy of life led Crawford to use several of his poems as texts for her songs. She later assisted Sandburg in the preparation of the *American Songbag* (1927), a collection of his poems set to music.

Life's Work

Ruth Crawford's years in Chicago served to establish her as a professional musician whose work was slowly but steadily gaining recognition. Compositions that resulted from this period include *Adventures of Tom Thumb* (for piano and narrator) in 1927, for which she received a Sigma Alpha Iota award; two sets of piano preludes (1927-1928); and *Suite for Five Wind Instruments* (1927, revised 1929). The piano preludes and the instrumental works exhibit qualities characteristic of her Chicago years in which harmonic elements reflect the music of Claude Debussy and Aleksandr Scriabin. The compositions were dominated by nonlyrical melody, avoidance of conventional scale and chordal patterns, and a preference for dissonance.

The year 1929 proved to be a landmark in Crawford's musical career. Several aspects of her life took new directions. She spent her summer composing at MacDowell Colony in Petersboro, New Hampshire. Composer and teacher Marion Bauer, a fellow resident, became an important female friend and mentor to Crawford and encouraged her to continue her composition. Another major turning point was Crawford's decision, upon the urging of Henry Cowell, to leave Chicago for New York. Cowell arranged for her to spend the winter with Blanche Walton, a wealthy widow, and then embarked upon his scheme to have Crawford accepted into the studio of his former composition teacher, Charles Seeger. Seeger became convinced of her talent, and she began lessons with him. Under Seeger's tutelage, Crawford produced a number of compositions that led to her being named a recipient of a Guggenheim Foundation fellowship to study composition in Europe.

Rather than work with one particular teacher following her intensive work with Charles Seeger, Crawford chose to spend time interviewing active composers such as Alban Berg, Béla Bartok, and Maurice Ravel. Her subsequent work in the 1930's showed the influence of especially Bartok and Berg. Up to this time, Crawford had encountered few impediments because of her sex; however, at Universal Editions in Vienna, she was informed that general policy would make it difficult for any woman to have her compositions published. Greatly assisted by letters of introduction provided by the Guggenheim Foundation, Crawford quickly became aware of the importance of knowing the right people and making the right connections in the professional world. This method of operation offended her personal ideals, however, and she avoided it whenever possible.

Crawford's most impressive compositions were products of her stay in Europe: *Three Chants for Women's Voices*; "In Tall Grass," one of the set called *Three Songs* based upon poems of Carl Sandburg; and her most famous work, the *String Quartet* of 1931. The unique quartet combined contemporary compositional techniques that included use of contrapuntal dynamics (where each instrumental line has separate dynamic indications) and complete nontraditional reorganization of pitch, rhythm, dynamics, and instrumentation into prescribed patterns. She also employed the process of retrograde in the last movement wherein the second half is a backward progression of the first. The *String Quartet* has become recognized as one of the most notable and expressive works in twentieth century string literature.

Another major event occurred during this period of Crawford's life: Her relationship with Charles Seeger changed dramatically. The two were married on October 3, 1932, and Ruth Crawford-Seeger's energies became directed more toward rearing a much-wanted family, which eventually consisted of one son and three daughters.

Ruth's involvement with her family and the Seegers' activity with a group in New York called the Composer's Collective brought about a realization that the avant-garde style in which they had been producing works was not one in which they were able to communicate with the general public. As an alternative, they turned to folk music—"the music of the people." The Seegers' scholarly research in the field was the best of its kind and brought about the transcription of much American music that had long been kept alive strictly through oral tradition. The Archives of American Folk Music in the Library of Congress was the source of many recordings of folk music which were edited, arranged, transcribed, and sometimes provided with piano accompaniments by Ruth. They also shared their interest with other well known musicians in the field, the most important being John and Alan Lomax. At their invitation, Ruth wrote a book of transcriptions which they published called *Our Singing Country*. Her introduction to the songs is a valuable source of information for folk music performers. The Seegers moved to Silver Spring, Maryland, near Washington, D.C., in 1935 and found substantial support for their work in folk music from the Resettlement Administration and the Federal Music Project through which Charles worked.

Crawford-Seeger's musical output during the 1940's and 1950's was mostly limited to efforts that combined easily with the demands of child rearing. It is not surprising then that this period produced collections such as *American Folk Songs for Children* (1948), *Animal Folk Songs for Children* (1950), and *Christmas Folk Songs for Children* (1953), which have been highly acclaimed by music educators.

Although her time to write was greatly diminished, her ambitions as a composer were not abandoned; however, her compositions were few in number. *Rissolty, Rossolty*, her second and final orchestral essay using original folk materials was a product of 1939, and in 1952, she wrote the *Suite for Wind Quintet*, which resembled the more abstract style of her works from the 1920's and 1930's. The *Suite* won a first place award from the District of Columbia chapter of the National Association of American Composers and Conductors.

Ruth Crawford-Seeger's work was cut short in 1953 when, after several months of severe illness, she died of cancer. Various projects, including new collections of folk music and of her own compositions, were left unfinished at the time of her death.

Summary

Ruth Crawford-Seeger was a versatile and gifted musician who was loved and respected among her colleagues for the integrity she displayed in her personal life as well as in her work. She worked steadily at her profession throughout her lifetime and every period was rich in accomplishments. Persevering in her chosen profession at a time when female composers were still more the exception than the rule, she was in her own way a pioneer. She had mentors among men and women in the field and collaborated professionally with important musicians of both sexes. When responsibilities of home and family limited her time for working on serious classical compositions, she turned to other creative outlets, such as folk music and educational materials, which could be completed more quickly. Each facet of her work was approached with the utmost musical and intellectual energy, and the products which resulted were exemplary. Although she was not known specifically for activity as a feminist, Crawford-Seeger strove to prove through her work that her gender should not be an issue for herself or others. Both before and after her marriage, she exhibited an independence in her work that allowed her not only to use her creative genius but also to serve as a strong role model for other women in society.

Bibliography
Ammer, Christine. *Unsung: A History of Women in American Music*. Westport, Conn.: Greenwood Press, 1980. Crawford is discussed in the chapter "American Composers in European Idioms" along with other musicians whose training was grounded in nineteenth century European musical language. A brief biography along with details about her work and interaction with contemporaries is provided.
Bowers, Jane, and Judith Tick, eds. *Women Making Music: The Western Art Tradition, 1150-1950*. Urbana: University of Illinois Press, 1986. Women from different periods of music history are examined in separate essays. Matilda Gaume, author of a 1971 Ph.D. dissertation on Crawford's life and works, provides a comprehensive chapter devoted to Crawford that includes a complete list of compositions and a discography.
Chase, Gilbert. *America's Music*. 2d ed. New York: McGraw-Hill, 1966. This historical overview of American music provides good background for the study of American composers and singles out Crawford in its discussion of innovative and experimental composers.
Cowell, Henry, ed. *American Composers of American Music: A Symposium*. Rev. ed. New York: Frederick Ungar, 1962. Originally published in 1933, this collection includes an insightful essay by Charles Seeger that discusses the style and form of his wife's works in a thorough, analytical fashion. Also addressed are the personal characteristics which he perceived as influential in her composition.
LePage, Jane W., ed. *Women Composers, Conductors, and Musicians of the Twentieth Century: Selected Biographies*. 3 vols. Metuchen, N.J.: Scarecrow Press, 1980-1988. LePage's collection of biographies includes an informative section on Crawford complete with lists of works and available recordings.
Reis, Claire R. *Composers in America: Biographical Sketches of Contemporary Composers with a Record of Their Works*. Rev. ed. New York: Macmillan, 1947.

Crawford is included among three hundred composers dating from 1915-1945 whose biographies are complete with information concerning awards, commissions, and broadcasts. Lists of compositions are grouped according to type indicating duration, publisher, and date. Although the material is dated, it gives the reader a glimpse of the composer's position among her contemporaries.

Thomson, Virgil. *American Music Since 1910*. London: Weidenfeld and Nicolson, 1971. An American composer and premier music critic and author in his own right, Thomson includes Crawford among his biographical sketches of more than one hundred American composers of the twentieth century. Thomson's assessments help place Crawford's work within the context of that of her peers.

Sandra C. McClain

RACHEL CROTHERS

Born: December 12, 1870; Bloomington, Illinois
Died: July 5, 1958; Danbury, Connecticut
Area of Achievement: Theater and drama
Contribution: A prolific and successful playwright and director for more than thirty years, Crothers often focused on the lives of women who faced dilemmas posed by changing sex role expectations.

Early Life

Rachel Crothers was born December 12, 1870, in the central Illinois community of Bloomington. Her father, Eli Kirk Crothers, was a physician who moved to Bloomington to begin his practice in 1850. Her mother, Marie Louise De Pew Crothers, embarked on her own medical studies when Rachel was a child and eventually established a practice in Bloomington in 1883, becoming the town's first woman doctor. Rachel's older sister Louise (known as Lulu) carried on the family's medical tradition by becoming a registered pharmacist, but Rachel's early interests led her in a different direction. The youngest of four surviving children, Crothers later recalled spending hours as a child acting out stories with her paper dolls. At the age of thirteen she and a friend May Fitzwilliam wrote and performed all the roles in a melodrama entitled *Every Cloud Has a Silver Lining.*

While a student in the high school of the Illinois State Normal University in the neighboring town of Normal, Crothers formed a dramatic club with friends and produced several plays. After graduating from University High School in 1891 (her schooling had been delayed by a serious attack of typhoid), Crothers studied for one term at the New England School of Dramatic Instruction in Boston. Back in Bloomington by February of 1892, she presented dramatic readings or "elocution recitals" in Bloomington, Normal, and other communities.

In 1896 or 1897, Crothers joined the throng of talented young people who yearly descended upon New York City seeking careers in the arts. Unable to find a job, she enrolled in the Stanhope-Wheatcroft School of Acting. After completing at least one term, she was invited to stay on as a teacher and director of the one-act plays that the school produced to showcase the acting talents of the students. Crothers considered her four years at the school as an invaluable apprenticeship in directing, a field in theater generally closed to women. While still associated with the school, she made her acting debut with the E. H. Sothern Company. Her ambition, however, was to write, not act, and Stanhope-Wheatcroft gave her the opportunity to write and produce her own one-act plays for the student showcase. In the process, she prepared herself for her first professionally produced full-length play *The Three of Us* (1906). She was poised for a remarkable thirty-year career in the theater.

Life's Work

The Three of Us was a success for the young Rachel Crothers. It also established a pattern that would become a hallmark of a number of Crothers' plays. The central character of this and other Crothers' works is an appealing, autonomous woman who ultimately bows to the conventions of traditional womanhood.

It would be ten years before Crothers would have another play as successful as the first, although six of her works were produced in between. The plays of this period were social problem plays that tackled issues such as prostitution, the double standard, the moral responsibility of women, conflict between marriage and career. Two of the social problem plays are among Crothers' most interesting and thought-provoking works.

A Man's World (1909), while not a commercial success, did generate much critical and journalistic comment at the time. The heroine, Frank Ware, a successful novelist, has adopted the child of a deceased friend and is rearing him on her own. In love with newspaperman Malcolm Gaskell, Ware is devastated to learn that it is he who fathered her adopted son, Kiddie, and abandoned Kiddie's unwed mother. When Ware confronts Gaskell with this knowledge, he expresses no remorse nor assumes any responsibility for his actions. She cannot accept the double standard of the man's world and severs her relationship with Gaskell. The play prompted playwright Augustus Thomas to write a rebuttal in defense of the double standard in his play *As a Man Thinks*, produced the following year in 1910.

Crothers' play *He and She* (pr. 1911) features a New Woman heroine who must choose between her career and her domestic responsibilities. Ann and Tom Herford, both sculptors, enter designs for a frieze to be judged in a national competition. Ann wins the $100,000 prize, much to her husband's chagrin. Reconciliation comes only when she turns over the commission she has won to her husband in order to meet the needs of their teenage daughter. The essential tragedy of Ann's situation is acknowledged by a contrite Tom when he tells her there will be times when the artist in her will yell to be released. In a 1920 revival of *He and She*, Crothers played the role of Ann herself, having been dissatisfied with previous interpretations of the part. Despite critical acclaim, neither the play nor the actress succeeded in winning over audiences.

With the advent of World War I, Crothers turned from social problem plays to sentimental blends of comedy and romance and with this formula found the commercial success that had eluded her since her first play. Of the six plays she wrote from 1914 to 1919, three were great successes: *Old Lady 31* (1916), which was adapted from a novel by Louise Forsslund and later made into a film entitled *The Captain Is a Lady* in 1940; *A Little Journey* (1918), which was nominated for a Pulitzer Prize; and *39 East* (1919), which drew on her own early boarding house experiences in New York. It was also during this period that Crothers began directing and overseeing all aspects of production for her plays.

After the United States entered World War I in April of 1917, Crothers helped found and then served as president of the Stage Women's War Relief Fund. This organization of women from all areas of theater work provided assistance to families of theater men in military service and raised funds to bring entertainment to servicemen in military camps and in New York City.

Crothers' plays of the 1920's and 1930's constitute a third phase of her career. Written between 1921 and 1937, these plays are comedies of manners, marked by witty dialogue, irony, and satire. The characters are most often rich and worldly, facing dilemmas caused by changing manners and morals. Although Crothers had featured men as the central characters in a majority of her sentimental formula plays, she returned to a more consistent focus on women in her postwar pieces. Like her earliest heroines, the women in the later plays are caught in conflicts arising from new freedoms for women. In these, as in the earlier plays, heroines espouse liberated lifestyles but come to accept traditional ones.

One theme that Crothers revisited was the double standard of sexual behavior. In the successful comedy *When Ladies Meet* (1932), the wife and the "other woman" in a romantic triangle meet without knowing one another's identity. They immediately like each other. When they discover that their relationships are with the same man, they realize he is not worth the love of either of them.

Seven of the ten or so plays from 1921 to 1937 had successful runs and two were award-winning. *When Ladies Meet* won the Dramatist Guild's Megrue Prize for best comedy of the 1932 season and *Susan and God* (1937), Crothers' last new play produced during her lifetime, won the Theater Club's gold cup. A film version of the latter play, starring Joan Crawford, appeared in 1940.

Through the last phase of her career and into her retirement, Crothers' humanitarian impulses were called forth first by the Great Depression and then by World War II. In the early 1930's as the Depression closed theaters, Crothers helped organize the United Theatre Relief Committee to assist unemployed theater people by making loans available to them and giving them access to basic necessities through a food commissariat and a used clothing shop. The committee raised funds from individual contributors and from benefit performances of plays on Broadway.

At the end of the decade, Rachel Crothers was honored for her work as a playwright and director and for her leadership in relief work during World War I and the Depression. On April 25, 1939, at a dinner ceremony in the White House, Crothers received the Chi Omega National Achievement Award from First Lady Eleanor Roosevelt. Chi Omega, a national collegiate sorority, had presented the award annually since 1930 to individuals who had made outstanding contributions in the arts, sciences, politics, or public service.

As war once again grew imminent, Crothers was a leading figure in founding the American Theatre Wing in 1940. Established to assist British war relief efforts, the group operated war services for Americans after 1941. Its most famous service was the Stage Door Canteen in New York City, where servicemen were provided with hospitality, food, and entertainment. Crothers served as the executive director of the American Theatre Wing until 1950.

Although Rachel Crothers completed a final comedy entitled *We Happy Few* in 1955, it was not produced. The playwright spent most of her retirement years at her home in Connecticut, where she died in her sleep at the age of eighty-seven on July 5, 1958.

Summary

Rachel Crothers was a success in the "man's world" of early twentieth century American theater. She wrote more than thirty plays, most of which were produced, and she was accounted one of America's best directors by her contemporaries. Although she was not known as an innovator, her early serious social problem plays contributed to the advent of realistic modern American drama and her comedies of manners to a more worldly sophistication in American theater. She used her position of influence in the world of theater to found and guide three theater-based relief organizations during times of national crisis.

Critics and commentators have been divided over the issue of whether Crothers' plays present a truly feminist point of view. Because many of her female characters ultimately opt for traditional solutions to their problems, a number of critics have viewed the plays as falling short of endorsing feminist ideals. Nevertheless, Crothers raised a series of important questions relating to women's lives, aired a variety of opinions through the voices of her casts of characters, and often treated the traditional solution as tragic or heavily ladened with irony. Throughout her career, her emphasis on women's lives provides a kind of commentary on early twentieth century women, providing insights into the conflicts and ambiguities facing women in times of heady social change.

Bibliography

Clark, Larry D. "Female Characters on the New York Stage in the Year of Suffrage: Enter Advocacy, Quietly, Stage Left." *Theatre History Studies* 7 (1987): 51-60. Clark analyzes Crothers' *He and She* and John Ervine's *Jane Clegg* as the only two New York plays of 1920, the year of woman suffrage, that rose above stereotypical portrayals of women.

Flexner, Eleanor. "Comedy." In *American Playwrights 1918-1938: The Theatre Retreats from Reality*. New York: Simon & Schuster, 1938. Chapter six in this dated but still useful survey of early twentieth century American theater gives a compact assessment of Crothers' work. It is the author's premise that the playwright's later work did not measure up to the promise of her social problem plays.

Gottlieb, Lois. "Looking to Women: Rachel Crothers and the Feminist Heroine." In *Women in American Theatre*, edited by Helen Krich Chinoy and Linda Walsh Jenkins. Rev. ed. New York: Theatre Communications Group, 1987. This essay interprets Crothers' early social problem plays and later comedies as essentially feminist in outlook. Introductory material by the editors and other essays in the collection help place Crothers in a larger context.

_____ . *Rachel Crothers*. Boston: Twayne, 1979. This book, the only published full-length study of Crothers' life and work, presents biographical information about Crothers, but is primarily a critical assessment of her plays. Special attention is given to the nature of the feminism implicit in Crothers' work. The bibliography includes a listing of all of her published plays.

Shafer, Yvonne B. "The Liberated Woman in American Plays of the Past." *Players*

Magazine 49 (Spring, 1974): 95-100. The author considers Crothers the first woman playwright to deal with the subject of women's liberation. She discusses five of her plays and those of other playwrights, male and female, with feminist perspectives.

Sutherland, Cynthia. "American Women Playwrights as Mediators of the 'Woman Problem.'" *Modern Drama* 21 (September, 1978): 319-336. While the title refers to playwrights, the focus in this article is on Crothers. Sutherland studies the female characters in Crothers' plays as mediators of conflicting views of woman's place in society.

Sandra D. Harmon

IMOGEN CUNNINGHAM

Born: April 12, 1883; Portland, Oregon
Died: June 23, 1976; San Francisco, California
Area of Achievement: Photography
Contribution: Cunningham demonstrated that an unqualified humanistic approach to using the camera could celebrate the individual subject as well as the art form.

Early Life

Imogen Cunningham was the fifth child of ten in the family of Isaac Burns Cunningham and Susan E. Johnson Cunningham. The family was poor, and Isaac took on various jobs over the years in order to support his large family. He was an extremely independent and strong-minded man—qualities that his daughter absorbed in order to sustain her art throughout her life. At the time Imogen was born, he operated a small wood and coal business in Seattle, Washington. Imogen was close to her father, who recognized her intelligence and appreciated her desire for an education. She did not begin school, however, until she was eight because the family home was somewhat remote from town. From that time on and with her father's encouragement, she took art lessons on the weekends and during school vacations.

Imogen Cunningham eventually attended the University of Washington in Seattle, where she could live at home and work as a secretary to pay for her education. She had already decided by her second year of college that she wanted to become a photographer, and a faculty member suggested that she major in chemistry in order to achieve that goal. The following year, she bought her first camera from the American School of Art and Photography in Scranton, Pennsylvania, and began to process her photographs in a woodshed darkroom her father made for her. During her senior year, she worked in the studio of Edward S. Curtis, famous for his photographs of Native Americans. From Adolf F. Muir, the studio technician, she learned the skills of retouching and platinum printing.

Completing her course work at the University of Washington in three and a half years, Cunningham won a fellowship from her college sorority that provided her with $500 to study in Germany. With this money and an additional loan, she spent a year studying photochemistry at the Technische Hochschule in Dresden with Robert Luther, an internationally known photochemist. Luther developed her earliest awareness of the need to incorporate the personality of her sitters into their portraits. While in Dresden, she saw an international photography exhibition and developed a heightened awareness of photography as an art form.

On her way home to Seattle in 1910, Cunningham visited Paris, London, and New York. In London, she arranged to meet photographer Alvin Langdon Coburn. She met photographer Alfred Steiglitz, at his avant-garde New York gallery "291." During her visit to New York, she also met Gertrude Käsebier, who particularly impressed Cunningham by demonstrating that strong photographic images could be made by women.

With a studio of her own, Cunningham immediately began to create commercial portraits to support herself and adopted the pictorialist style for her art photographs. The ascendent style of that period, pictorialism employed a romantic soft focus technique for the human figure often posed in landscape. A narrative association was often suggested through the title and the theatricality of the pose. After her marriage to Roi Partridge, an etching artist, in 1915, Cunningham used him as a nude model in a series of wilderness portraits. The publication of these photographs caused a scandal in Seattle, no doubt increasing her disregard for other people's response to her art.

Cunningham gave birth to her first child, a boy, in 1916. In 1917, she and her husband moved first to San Francisco, where their twin boys were born, and then to nearby Oakland, California, where Partridge taught art at Mills College, a women's school. Unfortunately, little work exists from Cunningham's early period; during the first move, Cunningham smashed most of her glass negatives because they were too heavy to transport.

Life's Work

During the years 1916 to the early 1920's while her children were very young, Imogen Cunningham was necessarily tied to home. She continued to photograph people, including her children, using the pictorialist style; at the same time, she began to use the plants in her backyard as subjects. This change proved to be serendipitous. She not only developed an intense interest in botanical subjects but also changed from a pictorialist approach to a hard focus one. The hard focus style brings a sharpness to the presentation of the subject, a sharpness she emphasized by photographing in strong light. Strong dark-light contrasts produced abstract effects that Cunningham incorporated into her mature style. Cunningham photographed the material up close and often cropped the image to concentrate on the portion she wanted to present. For example, in *Magnolia Blossom (Tower of Jewels)* (1925), only the pistils and stamens of the blossom are shown, with the petals severely cropped to allow the viewer's knowledge to fill in the rest of the blossom. Cunningham's flower and plant forms are among her best-known work. She was always willing to try new subject matter and different ways to manipulate prints and negatives. During these years when she was confined at home, she was forced to investigate what was close to her and she found a way to make this a strength.

People who knew Cunningham have remarked that throughout her life she was an experimental artist, always willing to try something new. At the same time, they have acknowledged that she was a sloppy technician. She probably learned very early that, with active children around, she had to get work in her basement darkroom done quickly or it would not get done at all.

In the late 1920's, Cunningham came into contact with work of the Precisionist artists, who applied sharp focus to machines and industrial buildings to show these subjects as beautiful abstract forms. Cunningham tried this, too, and turned out satisfying prints. The humanist in her was not satisfied with this new approach for long, but it was a useful expansion of her success with plant forms. By the end of the

1920's, she was regarded by some as the most sophisticated and experimental photographer working on the West Coast. Her friends during these years included many photographers who, along with Cunningham, were exhibiting in the San Francisco area and, in 1929, in an international photography exhibition held in Stuttgart, Germany.

Cunningham began to apply her art photography techniques to her commercial photos in 1931, when she began working as a freelance photographer for *Vanity Fair* magazine, published in New York City. Her new subjects were famous artists and film stars. In these photographs, she combined many of the techniques that she had explored for several years: close ups, sharp focus, and multiple exposures. She sharpened her skill in working with the subjects by conversing with them and waiting for the right moment that would allow their personality to reveal itself.

In 1932, Cunningham was one of three major founding members of a new group, Group f.64 (Ansel Adams and Edward Weston were the other major members). The group was short-lived, existing primarily to put on an exhibition, but their influence was immediate and long lasting. The name derived from the smallest aperture available on a large format camera resulting in the greatest depth of focus and sharp detail. They theorized, in keeping with a realist emphasis in twentieth century art philosophy, that negatives should be printed on glossy paper without manipulation, for example, no retouching or double exposures. Group f.64 not only followed an idea to its logical conclusion but also remained an inspiration for generations to come in advancing these ideas. True to her experimental nature, Cunningham did not follow this approach for long. From this time on, she exhibited with increasing frequency as her reputation steadily grew.

In 1934, *Vanity Fair* invited Cunningham to work for the magazine in New York City. Her husband could not accept that she had an independent life as a professional; when she would not defer the trip, he initiated divorce proceedings against her. In order to support herself in these Depression years, she had to increase greatly her commercial work, largely working for magazines as well as making private portraits. She continued to work for *Vanity Fair* from the West Coast. Cunningham said that of all the informal movie star portraits she made during this time, she liked doing the homely men best, such as Wallace Beery and Spencer Tracy, because they had no illusions about themselves.

Cunningham replaced her clumsy large format camera in 1936 with her first small camera. The new camera did not change her style, but it must have made her work much easier. Cunningham was only five feet four inches tall, had a slight build, and was in her fifties when she made the substitution.

In 1946, Cunningham moved to San Francisco, where she lived for the rest of her life. Although she became a standard fixture of the art scene, enjoying some measure of celebrity, she never allowed her public character to detract from the seriousness of her work. In 1954, a new San Francisco gallery, the Limelight Gallery, became the first to exhibit and sell photographs exclusively. Cunningham was asked to be part of the gallery's inaugural exhibition; a solo show followed the next year. The prestigious

International Museum of Photography in Rochester, New York, acquired a large collection of her work in 1959. *Aperture*, a highly respected art photography magazine, published the first monograph on her when it devoted an entire issue to Cunningham in 1964. Exhibitions of her work were mounted in important museums around the country: at the George Eastman House in Rochester, New York, in 1959; at the Chicago Art Institute in 1964; and at the Metropolitan Museum of Art in New York City in 1973. By this time, she had already exhibited at most of the museums in the Bay Area.

In her eighties, Cunningham became concerned about the disposition of her life's work, began sorting it and discovered negatives she didn't know she had. Several decisions resulted. She applied for and received a Guggenheim Fellowship in 1970, when she was eighty-seven, to print negatives from throughout her career that she had never had the time or money to pursue. Rather than give her work to a museum, she created the Imogen Cunningham Trust in 1975 to preserve her photographs and negatives and make decisions after her death about their promotion, exhibition, and sale. To make this decision public, she accepted an offer to appear with Johnny Carson on *The Tonight Show* and, typically for her, stole the show. During her lifetime she received many honors, including election as a Fellow of the National Academy of Arts and Sciences in 1967.

After turning ninety in 1973, Cunningham undertook a significant new photography project, a book called *After Ninety*. She sought out and photographed a large collection of people over the age of ninety because she wanted others to see and appreciate the vitality and diversity of older people. She died at the age of ninety-three, working up until the end in spite of suffering from periods of vertigo.

Summary

Imogen Cunningham's photography career did not really get under way until she was in her forties. She had worked hard at her chosen field until then experimenting with new ideas of all kinds and incorporating what worked. This willingness to try everything within her means remained a lifelong strength which others saw and imitated. She proved at the same time that it was not necessary to own the latest equipment to produce interesting work which was on the cutting edge. She was always willing to teach what she had learned to others. Her ability to photograph people sympathetically and interestingly has created a standard against which any photographer must be measured.

Bibliography

Dater, Judy. *Imogen Cunningham: A Portrait*. Boston: New York Graphic Society, 1979. A host of people who knew Cunningham personally are interviewed: family, friends, art world associates, and people she photographed.

Cunningham, Imogen. *Imogen Cunningham: Selected Tests and Bibliography*. Edited by Amy Rule. Boston: G. K. Hall, 1992. The book contains a biography, chronology, writings by Cunningham, texts referring to her, and a bibliography.

Lorenz, Richard. *Imogen Cunningham, Frontiers: Photographs 1906-1976.* Berkeley, Calif.: The Imogen Cunningham Trust, 1978. Ten of Cunningham's photographs are accompanied by a short biography.
White, Minor. "Imogen Cunningham." *Aperture* 11 (1964): 134-175. The entire issue is a monograph of Cunningham.

Ann Stewart Balakier

/

ALEXANDRA DANILOVA

Born: November 20, 1904; Peterhof, Russia

Area of Achievement: Dance
Contribution: An internationally acclaimed ballerina from the 1930's to the 1950's, Danilova carried on the traditions of classical ballet and helped bring them to the United States, where she worked as a master teacher from the 1960's through the 1980's.

Early Life

Alexandra Danilova was born in 1904 in Peterhof, a royal suburb of St. Petersburg. Details of her early childhood are somewhat sketchy: After their parents died, she and her younger sister Elena were shunted between their relatives and godparents before being placed in adoptive families. Alexandra was taken in by a wealthy society woman, Lidia Mstislavna Gototsova. Shortly after adopting Alexandra, Gototsova obtained a divorce from her philandering husband and later married Mikhail Ivanovich Batianov, a high-ranking Tsarist general who had received numerous military honors.

The elderly Batianov's extended family included children from his first two marriages as well as his grandchildren. The entire family was apparently gracious to the new wife and her adopted daughter. Nevertheless, Alexandra found herself to be somewhat of an outsider, even though one of the general's unmarried daughters, Machuta, took a special interest in her. Alexandra later remarked that her unsettled and occasionally lonely childhood had schooled her in self-reliance.

Like many children reared in genteel families of the period, Alexandra received lessons in ballroom dancing. Chosen to dance a solo in her grammar-school Christmas pageant, Alexandra evidently impressed her family so much that they submitted an application for her to attend the ballet school of the Maryinsky Theater, the home of the Russian imperial opera and ballet. Despite the school's policy of only accepting children between the ages of nine and twelve, Alexandra passed the required physical and artistic examinations and entered the Maryinsky school as a boarding student at the age of eight. She continued to see her sister Elena from time to time, and General Batianov continued to regard Alexandra as his own adopted child; nevertheless, Alexandra began to consider her fellow students to be her real family. One of those students was Georgy Balanchivadze—later to gain fame as George Balanchine, a renowned choreographer and founder of the New York City Ballet.

The children of the Maryinsky School not only took academic courses but also performed in ballets and operas at several of the imperial theaters. Alexandra was singled out for many of the featured children's roles and received a scholarship, a rare reward given only to those who showed great promise. The school gave her more than a technical education in dance; it gave her a solid grounding in music and the other fine arts and it established within her a habit of discipline. She later remarked that all of these elements were essential to the making of an intelligent dancer.

The Maryinsky School survived the Russian Revolution of 1917, although not without tremendous hardships. Families and teachers were scattered, the facilities had no heat or water, and the school did not function for nearly a year. Eventually, it did reopen, and Alexandra graduated in 1920. She was immediately invited to join the school's performing company, renamed the State Academic Theater of Opera and Ballet.

Life's Work

In the midst of a society racked by hunger and civil war, the former Maryinsky company offered Alexandra Danilova a level of stability she desperately craved. With two hundred dancers and a repertoire retained from pre-Soviet times, the State Academic Theater provided Danilova with her professional debut in its corps de ballet. She soon graduated to larger roles in classics such as *La Bayadère* and *Swan Lake* as well as solo roles in *Une Nuit d'Egypte* and *Coppélia*. Her first principal role came as the title character in *The Firebird*. Danilova had performed so well in her first two years with the company that its directors offered her a much-welcomed bonus—a full winter's supply of firewood.

In spite of Danilova's own successes, material hardship and the state's increasing interference in the private lives of its citizens augured a bleak future in the Soviet Union. The ballet theater itself seemed to become more rigid and blinkered. When Vladimir Dmitriev, a former light-opera singer, proposed leaving Soviet Russia for a summer tour of western Europe in 1924, Danilova eagerly agreed to accompany Balanchine and five other dancers on the tour. All of them assumed that they would be returning home for a new season of theatrical engagements in the fall.

The group toured Germany and Austria and, despite threats of dismissal from their Soviet ballet company, stayed on tour through the fall to accept an engagement in Great Britain. In London, they were contacted by impresario Sergei Diaghilev, founder of the famous Ballets Russes. His company's Russian Seasons in Paris in 1909-1910 had created an immediate sensation and had changed the course of ballet history. Interested in adding new performers to the Ballets Russes, Diaghilev offered contracts to Danilova, Balanchine, Tamara Geva (Balanchine's wife), and Nikolai Efimov.

The Ballets Russes not only had introduced Russian performers to the West but also had ushered ballet into the modern age. Programs read like a roster of twentieth century genius, with musical scores written by Igor Stravinsky, Eric Satie, Maurice Ravel, Sergei Prokofiev, and Francis Poulenc and sets and costumes designed by Pablo Picasso, Henri Matisse, Georges Braque, Aleksandr Benois, and Léon Bakst. Despite these innovations, the company also performed many of the classics, including *Swan Lake*, *Les Sylphides*, and excerpts from *Sleeping Beauty*. In her appearances with the company, Danilova performed a wide range of principal roles in these traditional pieces. She also danced the lead in new ballets created by Balanchine in the Romantic vein, *The Triumph of Neptune* and *The Gods Go A-Begging*, as well as his innovative *Apollo Musagète* and *The Prodigal Son*, both of which became signature pieces.

Although she was not yet an established ballerina like older counterparts from the Maryinsky such as Tamara Karsavina and Olga Spessivtseva, Danilova was on the brink of stardom when the company was suddenly dissolved after Diaghilev's death in 1929. Most of the dancers scattered to find work wherever they could. At the same time that her professional career was in limbo, Danilova's personal life was also in flux. Since 1926, she had been living with Balanchine, but his work as a choreographer was taking him further afield. She began having doubts about the direction of their future as a couple. When she was offered the chance to dance in a London musical entitled *Waltzes from Vienna* in 1931, Danilova took the role and wrote Balanchine to announce her decision to break off their relationship. Believing that someone not involved in the arts might make a more reliable partner, Danilova was married to Italian businessman Giuseppe Massera later that same year.

The marriage faltered when Massera announced that he expected Danilova to abandon her ballet career after their wedding. Instead, Danilova joined Colonel de Basil's Ballets Russes de Monte Carlo, a troupe that sought to carry on Diaghilev's legacy. Although de Basil had neither the aesthetic taste nor the entrepreneurial skills of Diaghilev, he did create a strong company that showcased the talents of Léonide Massine, a former Diaghilev dancer and choreographer. As part of the new company, Danilova had to contend with the so-called baby ballerinas that were heavily promoted by de Basil, but once she performed a principal role, she usually kept it. Partnered by Massine, Danilova danced the lead in the troupe's production of his ballet *La Boutique fantasque*. Her performance as the Street Dancer in *Le Beau Danube* added a new signature role to her repertoire. The Ballets Russes de Monte Carlo toured constantly in Europe and America; by the end of the 1930's, Danilova had become an internationally known ballerina.

Despite the strength of its dancers, the Ballets Russes de Monte Carlo was chaotic and ill-run. When economic chaos began encroaching on the artistic direction of the company, Danilova decided that it was time for her to leave. Léonide Massine had left the company earlier to become balletmaster of the new Ballets Russes de Monte Carlo; in 1937, he invited her to join the new company. He was able to mount a production of his long-promised new version of *Coppélia* featuring Danilova, and engaged artist Raoul Dufy to design the costumes and sets. The production was a tremendous success, and Swanilda became one of Danilova's most famous roles. Balanchine, who occasionally worked as a guest choreographer with the company, reentered Danilova's life—this time on a friendly but purely professional basis. She danced in Balanchine's *Danses Concertantes*, to a jazz-influenced score written by Stravinsky. Balanchine rechoreographed his ballet *Mozartiana* especially for her, and a year later created *Night Shadow* (later known as *La Somnabula*), an entirely new one-act ballet featuring Danilova. Together, they revived *Raymonda*, a full-length ballet from the Maryinsky repertoire that had always been popular in Russia but was little known in the West. By the late 1940's, Danilova herself had completed a select body of choreographed work; her most notable piece was *Paquita*, a reworking of another Maryinsky standard.

Giuseppe Massera, who had never granted Danilova a divorce, died in 1936. While Danilova was touring in the United States with the new Ballets Russes in 1941, she was married to Casimir Kokic, another dancer with the troupe. Their marriage lasted until 1949. The Ballets Russes had spent the war years touring in the United States, and the company decided to stay there permanently after the war. Having established her residency, Danilova became an American citizen in 1946.

During the postwar years, dance in the United States was on the rise. The Ballets Russes began losing many of its stars—including Alicia Markova, Igor Yuskevich, and others—to new companies such as Ballet Theatre (later the American Ballet Theatre). Although Danilova at first turned down offers to leave, she was disheartened by both the quality and the artistic management of the Ballets Russes and ultimately left in 1951. After her departure from the Ballets Russes, Danilova danced with smaller companies such as the Slavenska-Franklin Ballet and the Markova-Dolin Ballet. In 1956, Danilova founded her own small concert troupe known as "Great Moments in Ballet"; in addition to touring the United States and Canada, the troupe toured South America, Japan, and the Pacific. Although she later appeared for a season on Broadway, Danilova gave her farewell performance as a ballerina in Japan in 1957. She then worked for two successful seasons as a choreographer for the Metropolitan Opera in New York City.

Danilova launched a new career in 1963, when Balanchine invited her to teach a variations class at the School of American Ballet, a school affiliated with the New York City Ballet. In 1964, she became a full member of the faculty and taught and coached there until her retirement in 1989. Although she had left the stage, Danilova gave one more major public performance—this time as herself, coaching young dancers in the 1976 film *The Turning Point*. In 1989, Danilova received both a Kennedy Center Award and New York City's Handel Medallion for her contributions to the arts.

Summary

As a performer, Alexandra Danilova was known for a stage presence that combined quick grace, sophistication, and allure. Although she was often cast in the standard soubrette role, she had a wide range as a prima ballerina and proved her dramatic power in the leads of such ballets as *Swan Lake*, *The Firebird*, and *La Somnabula*. She was one of the stars of international ballet for nearly three decades. Early in her career she helped introduce modern art and movement to conservative ballet audiences; later, she helped introduce the classics to new viewers unfamiliar with the world of ballet. Struggling against sexism and social conventions that would limit her career as a dancer, Danilova chose to sacrifice many of her personal relationships in order to find lasting fulfillment in her art. The dedication and discipline she learned during her childhood at the Maryinsky School translated into a thoroughgoing professionalism and devotion to the fundamentals of her art as an adult. These traits established

Danilova as a model for younger dancers onstage and off. As both a dancer and a teacher, Danilova was herself a link between the classical traditions of the imperial Russian ballet, particularly the choreography of Marius Petipas, and the innovation of twentieth century choreographers such as Léonide Massine and George Balanchine. Providing the foundation for the growth of ballet in the United States, Danilova and her fellow émigrés served as an inspiration to a later generation of dancers who defected from the Soviet Union in search of artistic freedom in the West.

Bibliography

Anderson, Jack. *Ballet and Modern Dance: A Concise History.* 2d ed. Princeton, N.J.: Princeton Book Company, 1992. Although Danilova herself is mentioned only in passing ("the scintillating Danilova"), this work provides essential background information on her art. It includes chapters on Diaghilev's Ballets Russes and on the development of American ballet.

Danilova, Alexandra. *Choura: The Memoirs of Alexandra Danilova.* New York: Alfred A. Knopf, 1986. Danilova's memoirs are the only source available for information on her childhood. Long on verve and charm while short on dates, these memoirs assume that the reader is familiar with ballet terminology and repertoire.

Dunning, Jennifer. *"But First a School": The First Fifty Years of the School of American Ballet.* New York: Viking, 1985. A history of the school founded by George Balanchine and Lincoln Kirstein to train dancers for work with the New York City Ballet. Danilova's classes and teaching style are discussed; she herself is often quoted. Includes a glossary of ballet terms.

Garafola, Lynn. *Diaghilev's Ballets Russes.* New York: Oxford University Press, 1989. A thorough and detailed history of Diaghilev's company. Particularly useful for providing an overview of the company's struggle for survival, its cultural milieu, and its far-ranging influence on ballet and dance theater in the twentieth century.

Walker, Kathrine Sorley. *De Basil's Ballets Russes.* New York: Atheneum, 1983. An account of the company from 1931 to 1952, with a critical look at the much-maligned impresario himself. Discusses Danilova's many roles and reviews as well as the entire company's impact on the dance world. The book includes a list of all productions by de Basil, including dates and names of choreographers, composers, and librettists; it also includes a list of dancers and their tenure with the company.

Jane Ann Miller

BETTE DAVIS

Born: April 5, 1908; Lowell, Massachusetts
Died: October 8, 1989; Neuilly-sur-Seine, on the outskirts of Paris, France
Areas of Achievement: Film and theater and drama
Contribution: With a screen persona comprised of equal parts talent, passion, and
   intelligence, Bette Davis was, at the height of her career, the leading film actress of
   her generation.

Early Life

Ruth Elizabeth Davis was born on April 5, 1908, in the industrial city of Lowell,
Massachusetts. Her only sister, Barbara, followed eighteen months later. Her parents,
patent attorney Harlow Davis and his wife, Ruth, were divorced several years later.
After the divorce, Mrs. Davis—always called "Ruthie" by her children—moved to the
town of Newton with the girls. The years that followed were sometimes difficult as
Ruthie supported her family first as a governess and later as a photographer, and she
and her daughters forged strong emotional bonds that would remain the mainstay of
her elder daughter's life even at the height of her Hollywood career.

After adopting the name "Bette" from Balzac's novel *La Cousine Bette*, Bette Davis
decided in her early teens to pursue a career as an actress. Her first taste of the power
of acting came during a potentially tragic accident: While she was appearing in a
school Christmas pageant, her costume caught fire and she decided on impulse to
pretend that she had been blinded. After recovering from her injuries, she began
appearing in school plays and attending drama classes.

Following her graduation, Davis went to New York City, where she enrolled as a
student at the Robert Milton-John Murray Anderson School of the Theatre. In addition
to her acting classes, her studies there included dance classes with the legendary
Martha Graham. She soon began appearing in small parts and ingenue roles in
regional and summer stock theaters, making her Broadway debut in 1929 in Henrik
Ibsen's *The Lady From the Sea*. This was followed by a critically acclaimed run in the
comedy *Broken Dishes* (1929) and an unsuccessful screen test for Samuel Goldwyn.
She spent another year in stock theater and on Broadway before making a second
screen test, this time for Universal. In 1930, she was hired by the studio as a contract
player.

Life's Work

Bette Davis arrived in Los Angeles accompanied by her mother in December of
1930. Hollywood legend has it that the studio representative sent to meet her train
returned without her, stating that he had not seen anyone disembarking who looked
like an actress. In many ways, the incident set the stage for Davis' Hollywood career;
the unconventional looks and manner that seemed to many to be a handicap in the
beginning would become famous throughout the world by the decade's end, captivat-
ing film audiences and setting Davis apart from her peers.

At its inception, however, Davis' film career seemed headed for failure. Finding Davis lacking in glamour and sex appeal, studio executives insisted that her hair be dyed Jean Harlow blond and then cast her in a series of forgettable films. Davis' debut in *Bad Sister* (1931), one of several films she would make with Humphrey Bogart, offered little hint of the power and electricity that would mark her later work, and Universal did not renew her contract when it expired. Davis was contemplating a return to New York and the stage when she was hired by Warner Bros. to appear opposite George Arliss in *The Man Who Played God* (1932). The film established Davis' reputation as one of Hollywood's most gifted young actresses and was the beginning of her almost twenty year association with the studio.

As a studio contract player, Davis had no say over the films in which she appeared and soon became disenchanted with the roles that Warner Bros. offered her. Her finest work from this period occurred when she was loaned to RKO studios to appear opposite Leslie Howard in *Of Human Bondage* (1934). The following year she received her first Academy Award for her performance in *Dangerous* (1935), and she appeared with both Howard and Bogart in *The Petrified Forest* in 1936. These roles were the exception, however, to the parts she was usually assigned. In 1936, Davis defied the studio and attempted to break her contract by sailing for England to work with Italian producer Ludovico Toeplitz. The dispute was settled in the studio's favor by the English courts, however, and Davis returned to Hollywood.

Although she had lost her legal case, the event marked an important turning point in Davis' career. Upon her return to Warner Bros., she began to be offered the sorts of roles she had long sought; in 1938, she received her second Oscar for her performance in *Jezebel*. Over the next decade, Davis reigned as one of Hollywood's leading actresses, earning acclaim for the wide variety of roles she undertook and becoming the yardstick against which other actresses of her generation were measured. She was one of the leading contenders for the coveted role of Scarlett O'Hara in *Gone with the Wind* (1939) and she lost her third bid for an Oscar to the actress who eventually won the role, Vivien Leigh.

Davis' nomination that year came for one of her best-loved films, *Dark Victory* (1939), in which she plays a spoiled rich girl who finds love only after learning that she is dying of a brain tumor. The film's plot typified what would come to be known as the "woman's picture," and Davis, along with many actresses of the period, found a rich variety of dramatic roles within the genre. The films were characterized by strong female characters who suffered loss, hardship, and heartbreak, often growing in wisdom and spirit through their experiences. In *The Old Maid* (1939), Davis portrays an unwed mother of the 1860's struggling to rear her unsuspecting child, while *The Great Lie* (1941) finds her rearing another woman's illegitimate child. In *All This and Heaven Too* (1940), she plays a governess wrongly accused of murdering her employer; in *The Letter* (1940), she is indeed guilty of the crime, cast as a married woman who shoots her lover. In perhaps the definitive woman's picture, *Now, Voyager* (1942), Davis portrays an emotionally crippled spinster who blossoms as a result of her affair with a married man and then informally adopts his troubled daughter.

Throughout this period of her career, which also saw her play the central role in the screen adaptation of Lillian Hellman's *The Little Foxes* (1941), Davis enjoyed tremendous critical and popular success. She was the first woman to serve as president of the Academy of Motion Picture Arts and Sciences (AMPAS) and would become one of the most-nominated actresses in Oscar history, surpassed only by Katharine Hepburn. Toward the end of the 1940's, however, Davis once again became dissatisfied with the roles offered to her by the studio, and in 1949 she severed her relationship with Warner Bros.

Davis' first film prior to leaving the studio proved to be one of her best: the Academy Award-winning *All About Eve* (1950). Her career throughout the rest of the 1950's, however, was largely unrewarding, and she returned to the stage in 1961 in Tennessee Williams' *The Night of the Iguana*. The 1960's brought an unexpected turn in Davis' career, sparked by her appearance opposite Joan Crawford in the offbeat 1962 horror film, *What Ever Happened to Baby Jane?* Davis received her tenth and final Oscar nomination for her role as a deranged former child star who torments her wheelchair-bound sister, and the film was the first in a series of gothic thrillers for the actress. The final years of Davis' career were marked by occasional work in films and on television, increasingly limited by ill health. In 1977, she was awarded a Lifetime Achievement Award from the American Film Institute. Her last completed film, *The Whales of August* (1987), in which she costarred with silent film star Lillian Gish, captured on film the ravages of her battles with cancer and a stroke. It also conveys the fierce, indomitable spirit that characterized her work as a whole and helped make her a legendary figure in Hollywood history. Davis died at her home outside Paris in 1989.

Summary

Bette Davis' remarkable film career was aided both by her own extraordinary talent and screen presence and by the Hollywood studio system, which depended for its success on the studios' ability to provide their stars with strong material. Davis' magnetic screen persona, characterized by intelligence, dramatic power, and an almost ferocious energy, captured the filmgoing public's imagination in a series of roles that showcased her talents even as they helped define the genre of the woman's picture. Despite the sometimes double-edged message that these films held for women, with their stories of heroines ennobled by suffering, they offered images of women who were strong, often resourceful, and always emotionally complex. Davis carved out a place for herself in an industry that initially doubted her ability to hold an audience's attention, and she did it with uncompromising determination and integrity. Her personal style, her speech, even the way in which she smoked her trademark cigarettes, became an integral part of Hollywood imagery and legend. Talent alone, however, is not enough to secure a place in film history; the greatest stars also share a quality that can only be described as larger than life. To watch Bette Davis on the screen is to watch a performer who seems to define the term.

Bibliography
Davis, Bette. *The Lonely Life*. New York: G. P. Putnam's Sons, 1962. Davis' intelligent, highly readable autobiography covers her life and career from her childhood until shortly before her appearance in *What Ever Happened to Baby Jane?*
_____, with Michael Herskowitz. *This 'N That*. New York: G. P. Putnam's Sons, 1987. Written near the end of her life, Davis' second book covers primarily her later years in an entertaining, anecdotal fashion.
Higham, Charles. *Bette*. New York: Macmillan, 1981. A comprehensive look at Davis' life and career, this biography includes behind-the-scenes stories of both a personal and professional nature.
Hyman, B. D. *My Mother's Keeper*. New York: William Morrow, 1985. Davis' daughter, Barbara Davis Hyman, presents a no-holds-barred account of her relationship with her mother and the stormy contest of wills that eventually led to their bitter estrangement. Although far from balanced in its treatment of Davis, this biography presents important insights into her private life.
Quirk, Lawrence J. *Fasten Your Seat Belts: The Passionate Life of Bette Davis*. New York: William Morrow, 1990. Completed near the time of Davis' death, Quirk's biography often focuses on scandalous details from the actress' private life.
Ringgold, Gene. *The Films of Bette Davis*. New York: Bonanza Books, 1966. This chronological look at each of Davis' films up to *The Nanny* includes cast, credits, a synopsis, and excerpted reviews.
Stine, Whitney. *"I'd Love to Kiss You . . ." Conversations with Bette Davis*. New York: Pocket Books, 1990. As its title suggests, this book contains a series of conversations the author had with Davis during the final decades of her life.
Stine, Whitney, with commentary by Bette Davis. *Mother Goddam*. New York: Hawthorn Books, 1974. Stine's detailed examination of Davis' career contains highlighted passages by Davis, who offers a running commentary throughout the book.

Janet Lorenz

GEENA DAVIS

Born: January 21, 1957; Wareham, Massachusetts

Areas of Achievement: Film and television

Contribution: Known for her strong feminist roles as an actor, Davis won an Academy Award as Best Supporting Actress in 1989 for her role in *The Accidental Tourist* (1988) and was nominated in the same category in 1991 for her role as Thelma in *Thelma and Louise* (1990).

Early Life

Virginia Phyllis Davis was born on January 21, 1957, in the small town of Wareham, Massachusetts. Both of her parents were natives of Vermont. Her father, William Davis, worked as a civil engineer, while her mother Lucille worked as a teacher's aide. Virginia was nicknamed "Geena" while she was still a baby and grew up under the watchful eye of her older brother, Dan. In high school, Geena was a natural as a hurdler and high-jumper at Wareham High School. During her senior year, she studied abroad in Sweden as a foreign exchange student and learned to speak Swedish fluently.

After returning to the United States, Geena Davis studied drama at New England College in New Hampshire before transferring to Boston University's School of Fine Arts to complete a degree in theater arts in 1979. During the course of earning her degree, she also studied dance and took voice lessons. Davis' acting career began when she performed summer stock with the Mount Washington Repertory Theater Company in New Hampshire. Soon after graduation, Davis moved to New York City in order to find work. Finding few opportunities as an actor or as a model, she waited tables and worked as a salesperson in a retail clothing store to pay her living expenses. Eventually, she landed a job with the Zoli modeling agency and was given assignments modeling for various catalogs. After the agency branched out into theatrical work, Davis began appearing in television commercials and was sent out to audition for film roles in preparation for her professional acting debut.

Life's Work

After two years of modeling, Geena Davis made her big-screen debut in *Tootsie* (1982). In the gender-bending film featuring Dustin Hoffman as an out-of-work actor who disguises himself as a woman to land a role in a long-running soap opera, Davis had a minor part as a young soap opera actress who shared a dressing room with Hoffman's character. She received good notices for her performance. Although her acting career began to flourish at this point, Davis' personal life was in some turmoil. In 1981, Davis had married New York City restaurateur Richard Emmolo; after she became interested in pursuing an acting career in Hollywood, they were divorced in 1983 after less than two years of marriage.

Having appeared with Dabney Coleman in *Tootsie*, Geena Davis found work in

May of 1983 on the NBC television series *Buffalo Bill*, which starred Coleman as Bill Bittinger, the arrogant and abrasive host of a popular television talk show in Buffalo, New York. Hired to play Wendy Killian, a naïve young research assistant working for Bittinger, Davis conveyed the character's offbeat combination of dim-witted charm and genius while managing deftly to deflect the amorous attentions of her boss. During the course of the short-lived series, Davis also wrote some scripts for the show.

After *Buffalo Bill* was canceled, Davis was given a starring role in a midseason comedy replacement on NBC called *Sara*. The show, which ran from January through May of 1985, was set in a law office in San Francisco. Davis played Sara McKenna, a young career woman who shared law offices with three other struggling attorneys, including a gay man (played by Bronson Pinchot) and an African American woman (played by Alfre Woodard). Billed as an updated version of *The Mary Tyler Moore Show*, *Sara* attempted to strike a balance between the personal and professional aspects of its protagonist's life, but Davis lacked the experience and name recognition to repeat Moore's success in headlining a long-running situation comedy. During the same year, Davis made guest appearances on two episodes of the hit television series *Family Ties*.

Turning her attention to film roles, Davis was cast in a cameo role as an assistant to Chevy Chase in the comedy detective film *Fletch* (1985). In the same year, she appeared as a seductive vampire in the horror spoof *Transylvania 6-5000*. Although the latter film was a failure at the box office, it did give Davis the opportunity to meet costar Jeff Goldblum, whom she married in 1987. Davis and Goldblum starred together in David Cronenberg's 1986 remake of the science fiction horror classic *The Fly* and were praised for their ability to convey the tragic dimensions of the ill-fated romance between their characters. They also appeared in the comedy spoof *Earth Girls Are Easy* (1989), featuring Davis as a goofy Valley girl manicurist who becomes romantically involved with a space alien (played by Goldblum).

Davis' next comic role was equally offbeat. She played a young wife who dies in a car accident shortly after attaining her dream house and remains as a ghost to scare off the obnoxious New York interlopers who become the home's new owners in Tim Burton's *Beetlejuice* (1988). Cast opposite Alec Baldwin and Michael Keaton, Davis gained new exposure in this box-office hit. By her fifth film, she won an Academy Award as Best Supporting Actress for her role as Muriel Pritchett in Lawrence Kasdan's *The Accidental Tourist* (1988) and held her own in the company of her notable costars, William Hurt and Kathleen Turner. In 1990, Davis costarred with Bill Murray and Randy Quaid in the likable but unremarkable comedy *Quick Change*.

Geena Davis appeared with Susan Sarandon in Ridley Scott's *Thelma and Louise* in 1991. (Shortly after the film wrapped, Davis filed for divorce from Goldblum.) For her role as Thelma, Davis was nominated for both the Oscar and the Golden Globe Award for best actress. Davis won best actress honors from the Boston Society of Film Critics, and tied with Sarandon for the same honor from the National Board of Review. After *Thelma and Louise* hit the screen, some reviewers criticized the film for its man-bashing attitude, which they saw as evident in its one-dimensional male characters and its justification of the violence committed against these men. Other critics praised the politically provocative issues raised by the film and the transformation of Davis' Thelma from an insecure, repressed homemaker into a take-charge woman who believes in herself. Incorporating the images of outlaw camaraderie from films such as *Butch Cassidy and the Sundance Kid* (1969) and *Easy Rider* (1969), *Thelma and Louise* reverses these same images by establishing a relationship between two women on the run. While many critics focused on the guns and violent retribution portrayed in the film, Davis and others contended that the film used these elements as metaphors to represent how women can find and assert power in a society where they have been socialized to be powerless. Unprepared for the furor unleashed by the film, Davis commented on the irony that few people have reacted as strongly to the vast majority of Hollywood films that have portrayed women as one-dimensional carica-tures and have exploited women as sexual objects, but that the whole world seemed to react negatively when one film portrayed women with the guns and the power.

Thelma and Louise also transformed Davis' own life to a certain degree, since the controversial responses to the film caused her to be more aware of her responsibility to other women. She saw more clearly how women are trained not to assert them-selves. Davis admitted that she was taught to be silent so as not to risk being categorized as aggressive and unattractive for voicing her thoughts and feelings. After appearing in *Thelma and Louise*, Davis found that she was more willing to risk her reputation as an actor in order to stand up for her beliefs. She also commented that Susan Sarandon served as an example to Davis because of her strength as an actor, as a working single mother, and as a social activist.

Subsequently, the next two films that Davis appeared in also featured her in strong female roles. In 1992, she had a starring role as an outstanding catcher and the backbone of a softball team called the Rockford Peaches in *A League of Their Own*, directed by Penny Marshall. Set during World War II, when few women were encouraged to have careers as athletes, the film focuses on the All American Girls Professional Baseball League, which became an outlet for many women athletes to pursue their dreams to play baseball on a legitimate team. In this film, Davis appeared with an ensemble cast that included Tom Hanks, Madonna, Rosie O'Donnell, and Lori Petty. A few days after completing *A League of Their Own*, Davis began filming on *Hero* as a successful Chicago television journalist named Gale Gayley who is rescued from a plane crash and becomes embroiled in a convoluted search to find her rescuer. Although the film was not a popular success, it did offer Davis a chance to display her comic talents.

In September of 1993, Davis married Finnish director and producer Renny Harlin, best known for his work on the action film *Cliffhanger* (1993). Together, they worked to promote a production company called Genial Pictures to develop film projects for Davis. In 1994, Davis headlined the cast of *Angie*, a film about the voyage of self-discovery that takes place when a young Italian American woman from Brooklyn finds herself pregnant and goes in search of her own mother.

Summary
Despite the strong female roles that Geena Davis has played, and the awards she has won for acting, it is hard to find significant material written on her in popular literature. The focus of many of her interviews still tends to be more on her beauty rather than on her character and accomplishments. This oversight, however, is more a reflection of the pervasive stereotype of the film goddess in the minds of Hollywood promoters than it is of Davis' stature as a serious actress.

Although women have tended to figure more prominently in film than in any other art that is dominated by men, more women have remained in front of the camera as actors than have found power and success behind the camera as producers, screenwriters, directors, or other critical roles. Geena Davis stands at the forefront of a new breed of Hollywood women who are using their clout as box-office stars to develop film vehicles that will showcase their talents in strong, ambitious, intelligent roles. Because of her commitment to other women as well as herself, Geena Davis has become an example of what a woman can accomplish if she believes in herself and pursues her dreams.

Bibliography
Brown, Mary Ellen. *Television and Women's Culture*. Newbury Park, Calif.: Sage Publications, 1990. A realistic insight into women's culture as it relates to television. The focus is on women as audiences and critics, discussing their positions concerning the overall television genre.
Diamond, Jamie, and Max Vadukul. "Geena: The Goddess Next Door." *Vogue* 182 (September, 1992): 538-543. An overview of Davis' college years and early acting career. An emphasis on Davis' self-expression.
Handy, Bruce. "What's So Strange About Geena Davis?" *Rolling Stone* 548 (March 23, 1989): 43-44. A look into Davis' life, interests, and accomplishments.
Haskell, Molly. *From Reverence to Rape: The Treatment of Women in the Movies*. New York: Holt, Rinehart and Winston, 1974. An in-depth study of women and film. A realistic look at the stereotypes, humiliations and ultimate transcendence women have confronted historically through acting and film. The chapters begin with "The big lie" and move chronologically from the 1920's through the 1970's with a focus on women actors, films, and the overall culture specifically surrounding each decade. Provides a brutal reality check.
Jerome, Jim. "Riding Shotgun." *People Weekly* (June 24, 1991): 90-96. This interview, published in the wake of Davis' appearance in *Thelma and Louise*, emphasizes her expertise as accomplished actor, producer, and feminist. She particularly discusses the dearth of strong roles available for women in Hollywood films.

Carla Stoner

LUCY S. DAWIDOWICZ

Born: June 16, 1915; New York, New York
Died: December 5, 1990; New York, New York
Areas of Achievement: Historiography and education
Contribution: Dawidowicz was the author of several important studies about the life of Eastern European Jews in the period before World War II and their experiences during the Holocaust perpetrated by the Nazis.

Early Life

Lucy Schildkret was born on June 16, 1915, in New York City in a neighborhood settled by Jewish immigrants. Her parents, Max Schildkret and Dora Ofnaem Schildkret, had emigrated to New York from Poland, then a province within czarist Russia, sometime around 1908, when they were still in their teens. At first, they worked in the New York sweatshops. After their marriage, her parents tried their hand at several small business, but all of these endeavors failed. In 1927, they purchased a new four-family house in a developing section of the Bronx; by 1937, they were unable to make mortgage payments, and the bank foreclosed.

Although both of Lucy's parents were reared in a religious environment of Orthodox Judaism, they ultimately rejected orthodoxy. Theirs was a secular faith expressed through the celebration of the Jewish holidays; pride in Jewish history; preservation of Yiddish, the vernacular language of Eastern European Jews; and advocacy of a Jewish socialist ideology. They were avid readers of the New York Yiddish press and wanted their daughter to have an understanding of Eastern European Jewish culture as well as American culture.

Education was the central focus of Lucy's life. As a young child, she attended the Sholem Aleichem Folk Institute to learn to read and write Yiddish. From 1928 to 1932, she went to classes at the elite Hunter College High School and, on the weekends, also attended the Sholem Aleichem *Mitlshul*, a Yiddish high school.

Despite the family's economic hardship, Lucy entered Hunter College in September of 1932. At that time, the United States was in the depths of the Great Depression, and Hitler's Fascist domination of Germany was an imminent reality. During her undergraduate years, Bolshevik communism in the Soviet Union deeply affected her intellectual and emotional development. Nevertheless, she rejected the communist ideology by the time she was graduated from college.

After her graduation from Hunter College in 1936, Lucy was unable to find a job. Her mother encouraged her to return to school to study for a master's degree. In September of 1936, Lucy enrolled at Columbia University, choosing courses in art, poetry, and philosophy. Despite her initial enthusiasm, she dropped out of the program after only a few weeks. Instead, her interest turned in the direction of Jewish studies, particularly the history and culture of Polish Jews. The disappearance of Yiddish culture in Poland seemed imminent, since contemporary Jews in Poland were experiencing severe poverty, and outbreaks of anti-Semitic violence were becoming commonplace. In 1937, Lucy was accepted for readmission to Columbia, and she made plans to begin a research project on the Yiddish press in England.

Eventually, Lucy applied for a 1938-1939 postgraduate fellowship at the Yiddish Scientific Institute (YIVO) in Vilna, Poland. In the late 1930's, YIVO had become the center for research and study in Yiddish linguistics, history, social studies, and pedagogy. Lucy's decision to study at YIVO was an expression of her ardent belief that this institution might eventually become an international center of a self-sustaining Yiddish culture. Ignoring her family's objections to her decision to go to Poland when it stood at the brink of war, Lucy accepted a fellowship to YIVO and embarked on the Polish ocean liner *Batons* on August 1, 1938.

Life's Work

Although her fellowship year at YIVO, surrounded by some of the most creative scholars of Yiddish life in Poland, was rich in cultural experiences, Lucy Schildkret decided to leave Vilna after one year because of the heightened threat of war. As she later recalled in her 1989 memoir *From That Place and Time*, "[E]very night we lay down to sleep and to dream the dark dreams of our fears." Although she felt guilty about leaving her friends and colleagues behind, Lucy was able to return to the United States shortly before the Nazis invaded Poland on September 2, 1939.

During World War II, Lucy lived in New York City and worked as a researcher and archivist at the newly established American branch of the YIVO. The Vilna branch of the institute was taken over first by the Lithuanian Soviet Socialist Republic; later, in 1941, the German army occupied Vilna. During the German occupation of the city, many of YIVO's precious books and manuscripts were confiscated. Although a major portion of the collection was transported to Germany, numerous books and documents were destroyed. Some materials were saved from destruction by Polish Jews such as the poet Abraham Sutzkever, who hid portions of the archives in the Jewish ghettos in Vilna.

Desperate to learn the fate of her friends, Lucy was horrified to hear of the methodical extermination of Polish Jews once this news became public. During the war, she had immersed herself in the study of Yiddish literature and Jewish history in the hope that she could help preserve Jewish culture as a legacy to the postwar world. An opportunity to put her knowledge to use arose in 1946, when the New York branch of YIVO learned that all the collections of Judaica found in Germany had been deposited in Offenbach, near Frankfurt. The Office of Military Government of the United States (OMGUS) had been given responsibility for these collections, which were cataloged and administered by a section of OMGUS known as Monuments, Fine Arts, and Archives. It was the task of this office to advise the military on how best to ensure the security of such valuable properties, to protect them from further deterioration, and to identify their rightful owners.

Lucy returned to Europe in 1946 ostensibly to work with Jewish survivors in Munich, Germany, then under the administration of American occupation forces. She was appointed to the position of education officer with the Jewish American Joint

Distribution Committee (JDC). Her work eventually led her to the Judaica collections held in Offenbach. In 1947, the YIVO in New York was informed that the Vilna YIVO collection was to be placed under its ownership and care. Lucy was then appointed by the New York YIVO to coordinate with OMGUS to identify and prepare the "orphaned" volumes, documents, and photographs for shipment to the United States. By the end of May, 1947, cases of materials originally belonging to the Vilna YIVO were sent to New York.

On her return to the United States in 1948, Lucy married Szymon M. Dawidowicz, a refugee who had been an activist with the socialist Jewish Labor Bund in Poland. For the next twenty-one years, Lucy Dawidowicz worked as a research analyst and was named research director of the American Jewish Committee (AJC), the oldest Jewish defense organization in the United States. At the AJC, she was instrumental in sponsoring scientific studies on prejudice and anti-Semitism. During these years, she had time to complete her master's degree at Columbia University. She also cowrote *Politics in a Pluralist Democracy* (1963) with L. J. Goldstein and coedited the essay collection *For Max Weinreich on His Seventieth Birthday: Studies in Jewish Languages, Literature and Society* (1964). After leaving the AJC in 1969, Dawidowicz joined the faculty of Yeshiva University in New York City, where she served as a professor of social history and was named to two special chairs as professor of Holocaust studies from 1970 to 1978.

A turning point in Dawidowicz's scholarly life occurred in 1967, with the publication of *The Golden Tradition: Jewish Life and Thought in Eastern Europe*, an anthology of individual memoirs and personal documents which she edited. Her introductory historical essay to this collection poignantly conjured up the lost world of Eastern European Jewry before the Holocaust. It was a powerful work, amplifying and reconstructing the past.

Dawidowicz was not satisfied, however, with merely reconstructing the nostalgic past. She felt compelled to assess the historical impact of the Holocaust. In 1975, she published *The War Against the Jews, 1933-1945*, which won the Anisfield-Wolf prize in 1976 and was translated into Hebrew, French, German, and Japanese. In this influential work, Dawidowicz argued that the destruction of the Jews by the Nazis was not merely incidental to World War II; the Nazis' racial ideology, with its stated intention to eliminate every Jew, was an end in itself. The following year saw the publication of Dawidowicz's *A Holocaust Reader* (1976).

Many other historians were also involved in interpreting the Holocaust, assessing its importance in human history. Certain historians focused on the particular role of the Jewish community during the Holocaust. There were historians who blamed the Jews for the catastrophe, claiming either that the Jews were collectively passive or that Jewish communal organizations had collaborated with the Nazis to bring about their fate. Others blamed American Jews for their lack of prompt reaction to news of the Holocaust and their failure to act decisively to pressure the United States and its allies to intervene on behalf of European Jews. To place her own interpretation of anti-Semitism and the Holocaust in perspective, Dawidowicz wrote *The Jewish*

Presence: Essays on Identity and History (1977) and *The Holocaust and the Historians* (1981). In this latter work, she categorically repudiated any indictments of Jewish historical blindness, cowardice, or complicity in their own destruction. Although there were scholars who contested her interpretation, Dawidowicz held firmly to her convictions and continued to do battle with her critics in the pages of *Commentary* magazine, *The New York Times Book Review*, and various academic publications.

As one of the founders of Holocaust studies in the United States, Dawidowicz was invited to teach and give special lectures at several universities during the 1970's and 1980's. During this same period, she was awarded several honorary doctorates and won a number of prestigious awards, including a Guggenheim fellowship in 1976. She was appointed by President Jimmy Carter to serve on the President's Commission on the Holocaust from 1978 to 1979, and she served on the board of directors of the Leo Baeck Institute in New York City. Her husband, Szymon, died in 1979. Lucy Dawidowicz died in New York City in 1990 at the age of seventy-five.

Summary
Lucy S. Dawidowicz distinguished herself as an author and professor of Holocaust studies. A first-generation Jewish American woman scholar, she had a special affinity for her Polish heritage and feared that the wartime extermination of numerous Eastern European Jews might extinguish their unique thousand-year-old culture as well. In her writings, she sought to keep alive the spark of the lost world of Eastern European Jewry.

Her scholarly focus on the fate of Jews and Jewish communities in Eastern Europe during World War II remains a vital part of the ongoing debate about the origins and expression of bigotry, violence, and destruction in the twentieth century. Although her work came under critical attack during her later years, Dawidowicz was recognized as a serious scholar, a meticulous researcher, and a passionate seeker after moral truth.

Although she was among the first Jewish women of her generation to excel in the academic world and to achieve acclaim in a long career, Dawidowicz did not identify herself as a feminist. Unlike other prominent Jewish women, she did not lend her voice to the American feminist movement of the 1960's and 1970's. Turning from these secular concerns, she instead became increasingly more orthodox in religion and even wrote in defense of the Orthodox Jewish practice of separate seating for men and women in the synagogue. Nevertheless, her dedication and her contributions to scholarship set a vibrant example for the generation of women who followed.

Bibliography
Bernstein, Richard. "Lucy S. Dawidowicz, Seventy-five, Scholar of Jewish Life and History, Dies." *The New York Times*, December 6, 1990, p. B12. Describes Dawidowicz's role in Holocaust studies and lauds her for her excellent scholarship and profound moral impact.
Dawidowicz, Lucy S. *From That Place and Time: A Memoir, 1938-1947.* New York: W. W. Norton, 1989. This memoir traces Dawidowicz's experiences at YIVO in

Vilna before the war through her escape from Poland and her postwar return to Eastern Europe to retrieve books and archival materials. Her emotions and her intellectual judgments are portrayed with passion and clarity.

Dubkowski, Michael. "Anti-Semitism." In *Jewish-American History and Culture: An Encyclopedia*, edited by Jack Fischel and Sanford Pinsker. New York: Garland, 1992. This article gives historical background about anti-Semitism and sets Dawidowicz's concepts alongside those of other twentieth century scholars.

Kozodoy, Neal. "In Memoriam: Lucy S. Dawidowicz." *Commentary* 93 (May, 1992): 35-40. In addition to describing her personal life and career, this obituary traces Dawidowicz's intellectual development and discusses the political implications of her views regarding Nazi responsibility for the Holocaust.

Marrus, Michael R. *The Holocaust in History*. Hanover, N.H.: University Press of New England, 1987. In his comprehensive assessment of modern Holocaust historiography, Marrus places Dawidowicz's ideas about the final solution in the context of other historians' interpretations.

Norma Fain Pratt

DOROTHY DAY

Born: November 8, 1897; Brooklyn, New York
Died: November 29, 1980; New York, New York
Areas of Achievement: Journalism and social reform
Contribution: Cofounder of a radical Catholic social movement, the Catholic Worker (CW), and editor and publisher of its paper, Day linked traditional piety to immediate relief for the needy and to nonviolent direct action in order to end injustice and war.

Early Life

The third of the five children of John I. Day and Grace Satterlee, Dorothy Day was born on November 8, 1897, in Brooklyn, New York, into a comfortable home. At the time of Dorothy's birth, John Day, the ambitious son of an impoverished Confederate surgeon, was a clerk, but advanced to sports editor, columnist, and partner in the Hialeah Racetrack venture later in life. During prosperous periods, the family employed a domestic servant. Reared in Protestant churches, the Days were not regular churchgoers when their children were growing up. On her own initiative, Dorothy was baptized into the Episcopal church as a teenager.

Shortly after Dorothy started school, the family moved across the continent to the San Francisco Bay Area, where John Day accepted a position as sports editor at one of the city's major papers. The 1906 earthquake devastated the family's home and ruined John Day's employer. Resettled in Chicago, the Days experienced unaccustomed poverty. The family rented a grim tenement apartment above a saloon, and Grace Day assumed the duties once performed by the maid.

Parental protectiveness failed to shield the children from social reality and radicalism. Their seedy neighborhood provided an observant child such as Dorothy with an education about injustice. A precocious reader, she devoured the writings of muckrakers and socialists, whose lurid realism inspired progressive reform during the early twentieth century. She enjoyed writing and performed well enough in high school to win a coveted Hearst scholarship to the University of Illinois. As an undergraduate, Dorothy nurtured her talent in the Scribblers' Club and reinforced her radical leanings by joining a Socialist group, experiencing student poverty, and reading whatever interested her. In 1916, after two years of mediocre academic performance, she quit the university and joined her family in New York, where John Day had assumed a promising position after the failure of still another of his employers.

Life's Work

At age eighteen, armed with a thin portfolio of writings from small-town newspapers, Dorothy Day became a reporter, despite her father's edict that women belonged at home. Hired as a lowly features writer by a New York-based socialist daily, the *Call*, Day wrote vividly about women workers, a series much admired by the reform-minded Russell Sage Foundation. Soon the *Call* sent Day to cover strikes, riots, birth control activists, and the peace movement. Perhaps the rookie reporter's greatest coup was an interview of Russian revolutionist Leon Trotsky weeks before the czar was overthrown.

Day's career was boosted when Floyd Dell hired her to assist him with the editing of *The Masses*, Greenwich Village's chic radical monthly. Within a few months, wartime censorship shut down the magazine, leaving Day without regular work. At the urging of a friend, she traveled to Washington and picketed for woman suffrage in front of the White House. The pair was arrested a few times and jailed, along with members of the militant National Woman's Party. At the notorious Occoquan Workhouse Day, the women engaged in a hunger strike, and Day scuffled with guards over inmate conditions. Ironically, Dorothy Day never voted in a national election on principle. Throughout her life, she preferred direct action, especially picketing, to the debates and deals of politicians. She joined in this demonstration out of boredom and a desire to address the treatment of political prisoners in American penal institutions.

Between 1918 and 1924, a period of drift, Day fell in and out of love, was married and divorced, and traveled throughout Europe and the United States. She published a novel of disillusionment, *The Eleventh Virgin* (1924), patterned on her life, and entered into a common-law marriage with Forster Batterham, a biologist with whom she had a daughter, Tamar. Her search for self-purpose led her into the Catholic church in 1927, which precipitated a break with Batterham, whose commitments to anarchism and atheism made him hostile to organized religion. Day tried to maintain her friendships with radicals and for a few years sought work within the radical movement. Before 1931, she wrote a few articles for the *New Masses*, a Communist literary magazine, and was a propagandist for a Communist front group.

Accepting a contract to write dialogue in Hollywood, Day moved with Tamar to California. Uncomfortable in this bourgeois setting, she left for Mexico. Upon their return to the United States, Day wrote for Catholic magazines but felt unfulfilled. A radical at heart and a Catholic convert with a social conscience, Day wanted to help change the social order that created injustice. Writing about it was not enough, especially when she saw the human suffering caused by the Depression.

In 1932, she met the person who helped her to resolve her vocational crisis. Peter Maurin, twenty years Day's senior and a French immigrant, was a devout Catholic, well read in Catholic and social issues, and committed to nonviolent revolution. Encouraged by her platonic friend, Day founded *The Catholic Worker*, a tabloid edited, published, and at first largely written by her. Within five years, the paper reached nearly 200,000 readers each month. Lively writing about work and social injustice and a sense of urgency attracted readers, many of whom wanted to put radical Catholic social ideals into practice. The bold works of art that graced its pages, as well as its trademark penny cover price, added to the paper's appeal.

The Catholic Worker movement started with the paper, the feeding of the hungry, and later the establishment of houses of hospitality, where homeless people could find shelter without the annoying difficulties of welfare bureaucracies and the condescension of do-gooders. A clothing room outfitted the tattered. All were to be treated with dignity, each person an ambassador of Christ. Peaceful protests aroused social consciences. Catholic Workers picketed with striking workers, taught black children in Harlem how to draw, and spoke at the Capitol against the military draft. The movement spread to other American cities, including Boston, St. Louis, Washington, and Seattle. By 1941, twenty-seven cities had Catholic Worker houses.

Like her contemporaries in the radical movement, Dorothy Day predicted that the Depression of the 1930's was evidence that American capitalism was dying from its own structural weaknesses. To replace it, she envisioned Christian community: voluntary, cooperative, nonviolent, egalitarian, and distributist, based on production for need and not for profit. A just society would help to prevent evil. In the meantime, Day and the Catholic Worker movement supported stopgap measures, the right of workers to unionize, earn fair wages, and improve industrial safety. Maurin's "green revolution," an alternative to industrialism and urbanization, was translated into Catholic Worker farming communes, the first of which was founded within a few years. On the communes, Catholic Worker families, volunteers, and guests theoretically would live in rural simplicity and produce food for their own use. The contrasts between theory and reality posed some of the more problematic aspects of the Catholic Worker movement. Intellectuals, unemployed industrial workers, and the frail were rarely equipped to run a farm.

A socialist opponent of World War I, Dorothy Day was predisposed to Christian pacifism. Clinging to the belief that the possession of arms leads to war, the Catholic convert believed that human life was sacred and must be protected. Since she understood violence to be an ever-escalating condition, each conflict breeding greater violence to counter it, Day found no moral justification for war. To critics who scoffed at nonviolence, she replied that spiritual weapons, prayer, penance, and fasting, were the best defense against evil. During World War II, however, the novelty of Catholic pacifism divided the Catholic Worker movement. Dissenting volunteers claimed that war was a lesser evil than fascism.

Day put pacifism into practice in several ways. She opposed the military draft and supported the right of conscientious objection. Urging noncooperation with the war effort, Day suggested that workers should not take jobs in defense plants, and she refused to pay war taxes. When Japanese Americans were sent to armed detention camps for the duration of the war, she was one of a handful who criticized the federal government order. The use of the atomic bomb on civilian targets likewise sparked her outrage. In the Cold War era, Day promoted peace through nonviolence and was arrested for challenging compulsory Civil Defense air raid drills. The nuclear arms race and its potential for global holocaust emboldened Dorothy Day to educate the bishops of the Catholic church about pacifism when they gathered in Rome for the Second Vatican Council. During the Vietnam War, she supported new Catholic peace groups and was widely credited for building the foundation of modern Catholic pacifism.

Weakened by heart trouble for more than a decade and barely able to write her monthly column, Dorothy Day died in 1980 at the age of eighty-three.

Summary
   Dorothy Day revitalized American Catholicism. She found ways for volunteers to work for a nonviolent revolution within the church and to care for the immediate needs of the poor and oppressed. Her inclusive understanding of Christian community led to the establishment of the first true Catholic pacifist movement in the United States. Her steady leadership for nearly fifty years made the Catholic Worker one of the most durable of American alternative movements. Her deep faith and good judgment preserved CW religious orthodoxy and prevented church officials from silencing her or dismantling the controversial movement.
   Dorothy Day's powerful writing attracted volunteers and introduced pacifism and nonviolent direct action to Catholics. During the Second Vatican Council (1962-1965), Day was among those who moved the Catholic church toward pacifism. She was justly celebrated for her contributions to nonviolent change by the American bishops in a 1983 pastoral statement on peace.
   Since 1933, the Catholic Worker has challenged many injustices: poverty, war, and racism. In death, Dorothy Day lives through her writings, the work of her followers, and in the memories of all who have been touched by her deep faith in Christian radicalism. *The Catholic Worker*, still sold for a penny, and Catholic Workers throughout the United States, England, Canada, Australia, and Mexico bring Day's message of nonviolent revolution to a new generation.

Bibliography
Coles, Robert. *Dorothy Day: A Radical Devotion*. Reading, Mass.: Addison-Wesley, 1987. Psychiatrist Coles's brief study features excerpts from taped interviews with Day, but offers surprisingly little psychological analysis.
_____. *A Spectacle unto the World: The Catholic Worker Movement*. New York: Viking Press, 1973. A generous selection of photographs accompanies a short text about Day and the Catholic Worker movement. Largely ignores the revolutionary aspects of the movement by focusing on activities at the House of Hospitality.
Day, Dorothy. *Dorothy Day, Selected Writings: By Little and by Little*. Edited by Robert Ellsberg. Maryknoll, N.Y.: Orbis Books, 1992. A wide-ranging anthology of Day's writings on social and spiritual issues drawn from published works. Ellsberg's well-crafted biographical introduction is based on a personal relationship with Day and careful scholarship.
_____. *The Long Loneliness*. New York: Harper & Row, 1952. An autobiography written primarily to explain her conversion and the work of the Catholic Worker movement especially relating to the poor, the labor movement, gospel pacifism, and nonviolent social revolution. Weak on the period from 1918 through 1924.
Klejment, Anne, and Alice Klejment. *Dorothy Day and "The Catholic Worker": A Bibliography and Index*. New York: Garland, 1986. Helpful for researchers. Lists all known publications by Day, indexes *The Catholic Worker* from 1933 through 1983, and comments on selected titles.

McNeal, Patricia. *Harder than War: Catholic Peacemaking in Twentieth-Century America*. New Brunswick, N.J.: Rutgers University Press, 1992. Examines leading American Catholic peace organizations and peace advocates with emphasis on the formative role played by Day and her movement in the emergence of Catholic pacifism.

Miller, William D. *A Harsh and Dreadful Love: Dorothy Day and the Catholic Worker Movement*. New York: Liveright, 1973. Dated, but an interesting history of the Catholic Worker movement with portraits of many key figures and quotes from volunteers.

O'Connor, June. *The Moral Vision of Dorothy Day: A Feminist Perspective*. New York: Crossroad, 1991. Views Day as a writer, woman, convert, radical, and moralist and presents her as an occasionally antifeminist feminist.

Piehl, Mel. *Breaking Bread: The Catholic Worker and the Origin of Catholic Radicalism in America*. Philadelphia: Temple University Press, 1982. A demanding but rewarding work that explains the religious context of the movement. Roughly covers events to 1965.

Roberts, Nancy L. *Dorothy Day and the Catholic Worker*. Albany, N.Y.: State University of New York Press, 1984. One of the most readable accounts of Day's life at the Catholic Worker with a focus on Day the advocacy journalist.

Anne Klejment

DOMINIQUE DE MENIL

Born: March 23, 1908; Paris, France

Areas of Achievement: Patronage of the arts and philanthropy

Contribution: In addition to her influential humanitarian work, Dominique de Menil has commissioned works from and inspired numerous artists of the late twentieth century while also bringing art and art education to the general public.

Early Life

Dominique Schlumberger was born in Paris on March 23, 1908, the second of three daughters of Conrad Schlumberger, a geophysicist, and Louise Delpech Schlumberger. From an early age, Dominique showed a great interest in collecting, gathering objects such as fossils, stamps, butterflies, and matchboxes. Descended from a cultured family that had built a textile fortune during the late twentieth century, Dominique's father and her uncle, Marcel Schlumberger, created an even larger fortune. They developed technology in the area of geologic exploration that came to be known as well logging, based on a device invented by Conrad that measured the electrical resistance of underground formations in order to locate petroleum deposits. After establishing their own corporation, Schlumberger, Ltd., in 1934, the brothers expanded their operations worldwide and amassed a substantial fortune from the burgeoning global petroleum market.

Dominique was reared in comfortable circumstances and decided to pursue her education at the University of Paris. After completing her course work, she received her bachelor of arts degree in mathematics in 1927 and went on to pursue postgraduate work in mathematics and physics at the Sorbonne. She met her future husband, John de Menil ("Jean" by birth), at a ball held in Versailles in 1930; she later claimed that it was a party that neither had planned to enjoy attending. John de Menil had been born into a titled military family, but had grown up in impoverished circumstances. He had dropped out of school to work as a bank clerk and ultimately received his first degree from the University of Paris by attending night classes. Despite the differences in their backgrounds, the two fell in love and were married on May 9, 1931. When she married John de Menil, Dominique converted to his Catholic faith, despite the fact that her own parents were agnostics who came from Protestant family backgrounds.

After seven years of marriage, John de Menil was invited to join the Schlumberger family business. At a time when Europe was on the brink of war, Dominique found herself alone while her husband traveled abroad to oversee the company's interests. After the Nazi invasion of France, she fled Paris in 1941 with her three young children, finding refuge in Spain before boarding a ship bound for Cuba. She was met in Havana by John, who had arrived in Cuba after leaving the Schlumberger oil operations in Romania. Together, the family traveled to the company's American headquarters in Houston, Texas. After settling in Houston, Dominique had two more children, and she became a United States citizen in 1962.

Life's Work

Dominique de Menil's career as one of the world's leading art collectors began in earnest after her arrival in the United States. During the 1940's and 1950's, she and her husband made frequent trips to New York City, where they came under the artistic tutelage of Father Marie-Alain Couturier, a French Dominican priest and amateur painter who cultivated the couple's appreciation for modern art. A wealthy woman as a result of her family inheritance, Dominique de Menil indulged herself in an impressive collecting spree, acquiring works by Paul Cézanne, Georges Braque, and Pablo Picasso before concentrating on works by the Surrealists. Eventually, she and her husband amassed a collection that came to be considered one of the best collections of twentieth century art in the United States. Consisting of more than ten thousand pieces of art, almost half of which are rare books, prints, and photographs, the collection includes a large number of works by twentieth century masters such as Braque, Cézanne, Picasso, René Magritte, Max Ernst, and Fernand Leger as well as a wide range of Mediterranean antiquities, Byzantine and Medieval European artworks, and the art of various African tribal cultures.

In the 1960's, she and her husband established themselves as important patrons of Houston's Museum of Fine Arts, but eventually discontinued their association with the museum because of conflicts with other museum trustees. Inspired by her own exposure to modern art, she began to organize art exhibitions in 1964 to share her collections with the general public. Eager to display their art at home, the de Menils bucked the Houston trend of living in a formal Southern mansion by commissioning architect Philip Johnson in 1948 to design a starkly modern, sprawling single-story house. After construction was completed, Dominique commissioned clothing designer Charles James to decorate the house. James designed felt coverings for the doors and a paint scheme that incorporated highly unusual color combinations designed to enhance the artworks exhibited throughout the house.

Dominique's art patronage extended to the area of art education. Beginning in the late 1940's, she and her husband gave generous donations to St. Thomas University, a private Catholic college located in Houston. Their patronage included the establishment of fully staffed and funded departments in art and art history, the purchase of additional real estate holdings to facilitate expansion of the school, and the donation of important works of art. Although appreciative of the de Menils' support, the Basilian Fathers who operated the college believed that the emphasis on secular art and art history threatened to overwhelm the school's identity as a Catholic institution. Sensitive to the school's concerns, Dominique and John de Menil turned their attention to encouraging artistic scholarship at nearby Rice University.

During the 1960's, the de Menils became involved in a range of civil rights activities. Conservative Texas society accused them of dabbling in "radical chic" because of their support for Martin Luther King, Jr. In addition, the de Menils fostered the political career of Congressman George "Mickey" Leland of Houston, who served as a member of the Texas legislature from 1973 to 1978 before serving in Congress from 1978 until his death in an airplane crash in Ethiopia in 1989. The couple entertained many African American leaders and cultural figures at their dinner table and were known for their iconoclasm. Dominique and John de Menil were proud of their European heritage, were willing to endorse radically liberal political views, and provided enthusiastic support to artists outside the established mainstream. Dominique's husband John died of cancer in December of 1973, but she continued to carry on his political and cultural legacy.

The Menil Collection museum was commissioned by Dominique and her husband with detailed stipulations that ensured that only works from their collection as it existed before John's death would be included as permanent exhibits. The museum, which was built at a cost of $25 million, was designed by Italian architect Renzo Piano and built on a three-acre property located in the Montrose area of Houston, a community well known for its diverse cultural life. In order to maintain an intimate atmosphere, the museum exhibits only a small number of artworks at a time on a rotating schedule. Nearly ninety percent of the collection is maintained in open storage within eight rooms on the museum's second floor. These rooms are accessible by appointment to scholars and other visitors with a special interest in a particular work.

Among her other activities, Dominique de Menil began sponsoring a lengthy research project in 1961 to address the image of black people in Western art. By the 1990's, the project had produced volumes on images in antiquity, in the Middle Ages, and in the nineteenth century; three additional volumes covering the sixteenth, seventeenth, and eighteenth centuries were scheduled for publication in 1997.

In the years after her husband's death, Dominique continued to support many of the social causes that had been important to him, including efforts on behalf of international human rights and religious freedom. In addition to helping to address civil rights issues affecting minority groups in the United States, she has supported reform efforts in India, Africa, and the Arab world. Her funding of various humanitarian awards brought her to the attention of former president Jimmy Carter; together, they founded the Carter-Menil Human Rights Prize, an award of $100,000 that has been given annually since its inception in 1986.

Summary

Dominique de Menil has established a reputation as a dynamo on the international art scene and is considered one of the leading art patrons of the late twentieth century. Despite the fact that the economic recession of the 1980's and the volatile market of the early 1990's diminished the buying power of her investments in Schlumberger oil concerns, Dominique de Menil has continued to work to increase the endowment of the museum she founded as well as that of the de Menil Foundation itself by soliciting funds from outside sources and encouraging gifts of art from other patrons. Her eclectic artistic tastes, combined with those of her husband, established one of the finest private art collections in the United States. Once the collection was made available for public viewing at the Menil Collection museum, she dedicated her efforts to funding additional research and improving public awareness of the collection's holdings—from its various antiquities to its contemporary artworks. Unwilling to ignore the pressing social concerns confronting her world, de Menil also devoted her fortune and her personal support to a variety of humanitarian and reform efforts.

Bibliography

Barnes, Susan J. *1948—The Rothko Chapel: An Act of Faith*. Houston, Tex.: The Rothko Chapel, 1989. A detailed examination of the design and creation of the Rothko Chapel as commissioned by Dominique de Menil and her husband. Explains the genesis of the fourteen paintings created by abstract expressionist painter Mark Rothko to decorate the walls of the ecumenical chapel, which was dedicated in Houston in 1971.

Bernier, Rosamond. "A Gift of Vision: On the Opening of Her New Museum, Dominique de Menil Reflects on the Houston House Where It All Began." *House & Garden* 159 (July, 1987): 121. An informative interview with de Menil that provides insights into her character and her interest in creating interiors that enhance the viewing of her art collections.

Glueck, Grace. "The Medici of Modern Art." *The New York Times Magazine*, May 18, 1986, pp. 28-46, 66, 106, 113. A collective profile of Dominique de Menil and her five children that discusses the family's history, their proclivity for art collecting, and their provision of charitable support for a variety of artistic endeavors. One of the best available sources of biographical information on Dominique de Menil.

Gregor, Katherine. "Menil Collection: The Power of Modesty." *ARTnews* 86 (September 1, 1987): 31. Although the author touches on the history of the de Menil family and their contributions to civic life in Houston, Texas, this article primarily focuses on the debut of the Menil Collection museum.

Jackler, Rosalind. "Philanthropist Fulfills Thirty-Year Dream in Multi-City Exhibit." *Houston Post*, December 17, 1992, p. C1. In a 1992 interview prompted by announcement of the seventh annual Carter-Menil Human Rights Prize, Dominique de Menil discusses her fascination with collecting and exhibiting art, particularly as exemplified by the commission and construction of the Rothko Chapel and the Menil Collection museum in Houston.

Papademetriou, Peter C. "The Responsive Box." *Progressive Architecture*, May, 1987, p. 87. A detailed discussion of the genesis of the Menil Collection museum that focuses primarily on the architecture of the building itself.

Ursula Burton

AGNES DE MILLE

Born: 1905; New York, New York
Died: October 7, 1993; New York, New York
Area of Achievement: Dance
Contribution: Agnes de Mille, a pioneer in modern dance, was the first to integrate dance into theatrical productions and to make it accessible to the general public.

Early Life

Agnes de Mille was born in 1905 in New York City into a family that was already deeply involved in the entertainment industry. Her father, William C. deMille, a playwright like his father before him, produced his first success at the age of twenty-five in collaboration with David Belasco. Her uncle was Cecil B. DeMille, the pioneering film producer. Anna George deMille, Agnes de Mille's mother, was the daughter of the political economist Henry George; following in her father's footsteps, she became an ardent Single-Taxer and a born crusader for various causes. The qualities of talent for the theater and crusading zeal became fused in Agnes and were controlling factors in her life.

In 1914, after one of his Broadway productions failed, William deMille accepted his brother Cecil's invitation to join him in Hollywood and try his hand in the fledgling motion picture business. Anna deMille dutifully packed up her daughters, Agnes and her sister Margaret, and followed her husband into what she considered the "primitive" land of the West. Although Agnes was disappointed that Hollywood did not contain the expected cowboys and Indians, it was this relocation that would be the shaping factor in her life.

Agnes was enrolled in the Hollywood School for Girls, where her best friends were the only two male pupils, Douglas Fairbanks, Jr., and Joel McCrea. Although she was a diligent student, Agnes most enjoyed her class in pantomime. She was convinced that since her family was in "the business," she would become an actress. To cater to this ambition, her father gave her a small role in his film *The Ragamuffin* in 1916. It was the following year, however, when the professional goals of Agnes de Mille took a marked turn as, awestruck, she watched a performance by the great ballerina Anna Pavlova.

During those years, dance was of no universal consequence; in fact, it suffered from universal indifference, perpetuated by a social taboo in which Agnes de Mille's father firmly believed. Ladies, he believed, simply did not dance. Coupled with her father's negation was the strict code of conduct and dress that her mother believed was appropriate for women of their social standing. Agnes continued to beg for ballet lessons but repeatedly was told no.

Fortunately for Agnes de Mille and for the world of the theater, providence intervened. Five years later, her sister Margaret, was diagnosed with fallen arches and the family physician recommended dance lessons as a means of strengthening her feet. Since Margaret was required to study dance, Agnes was allowed to do so as well, and both were enrolled in the Kosloff School. After her initial audition, Agnes was told that, at thirteen, she was probably too old to train but that she would be accepted if she agreed to work harder than most toward building resiliency.

Agnes knew that she had found her life's work, and she continued to train despite her father's continued objections. He knew better than to forbid his strong-willed daughter to enter the field, but he refused to support her work and did not attend a single recital or performance. At her parents' insistence, Agnes entered the University of California, one mile from her home, and was graduated cum laude with a degree in English. Her professors assured her that she had a talent for writing, but Agnes de Mille had other plans for her life.

Life's Work

The day after Agnes de Mille was graduated from college, her parents announced that they were divorcing. Agnes moved with her mother back to New York, where, with an allowance from her father and generous support from her mother, she continued to study ballet. She premiered as a dancer with Jacques Cartier in New York in 1928. Modest success, however, was not enough. It was her desire to expand traditional ballet into full-scale theater, but her financial support was insufficient to mount and produce such an event.

In an effort to gain further recognition, de Mille traveled to London, where she continued to study and helped to organize the London Ballet Company. When she returned to New York, the Depression was in full swing and entertainment funding had taken a backseat to basic survival. She made herself available for any type of work that involved theater, stating that she stopped short only of "jiggling on the sidewalk with a tambourine." In 1935, desperate for money, she tried giving lessons but found that she had no rapport with small children; many of her students complained of physical illness following a session with de Mille.

Finally, realizing that the situation in the United States was not going to change quickly, de Mille returned to London to work with Anthony Tudor and Hugh Laing, her longtime companions and partners. During that period, she gained some monetary success and a growing reputation as a dancer and choreographer. Her company toured Paris, Brussels, and Copenhagen, and she choreographed several films, including *I, Claudius* and *Romeo and Juliet* (1936). After she had spent six years in London, however, her work permit was not renewed. Europe was readying itself for war, and aliens were being sent home.

De Mille returned to New York. Using the funds she had accumulated in Europe, she studied with Martha Graham and in the process became her friend. Shortly after her return, however, she received a call that would change the direction of her life. The call was from a young man, Richard Pleasant, whom she had met several years earlier while he was running errands for a dance studio. Pleasant intended to mount a new international ballet company, Ballet Theater, and he wanted her to join him with the understanding that she would not dance—she would only choreograph.

Agnes de Mille worked with Ballet Theater for several years until the company ran into financial difficulty. Perhaps her most outstanding contribution during that time was *Black Ritual (Obeah)*, an exotic work with an African American cast. It marked the first use of African American ballerinas, who, until then, had been offered no market for their skill.

After leaving Ballet Theater, de Mille joined the newly formed Ballet Russe Company, and it was there that she established the criteria for the work that would occupy the balance of her life. In 1942, she designed and produced *Rodeo*, the first ballet ever created using traditional American themes, which featured music by Aaron Copland. The irony of working with primarily Russian dancers did not occur to her as she forced them to emulate the actions of bucking broncos and bareback riders, using nothing but their own torsos and pantomime. The production debuted at the Metropolitan Opera House on October 16, 1942, and received nineteen curtain calls.

From that point, the name Agnes de Mille became firmly implanted in the annals of American choreography. After fifteen years of concentrated endeavor, she was, at last, an "overnight success."

In the years that followed, de Mille became as much at home on Broadway as she was at the Metropolitan, and she worked on such productions as *Carousel, Brigadoon,* and *Gentlemen Prefer Blondes*. Through her, dance was integrated into the play to move the action forward, instead of functioning as an intrusive appendage. She won Tony Awards for her work in *Brigadoon* in 1947 and for *Kwamina* in 1962. Although her favorite was *Paint Your Wagon*, she is best known for her work in *Oklahoma!*, which debuted in March, 1943. During this period, she continued to create formal ballets, including *Three Virgins and a Devil, The Informer,* and *Fall River Legend*, a psychological study of Lizzie Borden. Many of these works were created for and premiered by the American Ballet Theater.

De Mille became an articulate advocate of federal support for the arts and served on the first board of the National Endowment for the Arts. Among her most prestigious honors were being named to the Theater Hall of Fame in 1973, receiving the National Medal of Arts in 1986, and being awarded a Kennedy Center Honor, the highest national recognition in the performing arts, in 1980.

In addition to having a career as a dancer, a choreographer, and an activist, Agnes de Mille also wrote fourteen books about dance, art, and her life. She placed the last one in her agent's hands a few days before her death. Her literary style is lively, personable, engaging, and honest. Among her works are three volumes of autobiography—*Dance to the Piper* (1952), *And Promenade Home* (1958), and *Speak to Me, Dance with Me* (1973)—as well as the definitive volume *To a Young Dancer* (1962).

In 1975, Agnes de Mille was disabled by a cerebral hemorrhage, but through rehabilitative therapy, willpower, and her unquenchable drive to survive, she recovered. She continued to work from a wheelchair or propped up in her bed. Having learned to write with her left hand, she penned another book, *Reprieve* (1981), about her illness. A mere fourteen months after her stroke, she received a standing ovation at the New York State Theatre during the premiere of her bicentennial celebration piece *Texas Fourth*.

On October 7, 1993, a second stroke ended the stellar career of Agnes de Mille, then eighty-eight, only a few days after she was honored by the Tony Awards on the fiftieth anniversary of *Oklahoma!*

Summary
Agnes de Mille broke new ground in dance in multiple ways. She was the first choreographer to use American folk themes extensively in her work, making dance more accessible to the general public. Consequently, she was also the first to produce a ballet that was truly American in spirit and style. She used humor in her pieces and was told she had a natural gift for comedy. She created human characters that were warm, witty, and often irreverent, and she insisted that her dancers portray their characters with honesty and vitality. Through her, the dance finally reached and conquered Broadway. She discarded the lyrical and the choreographed for what was theatrical or dramatic, thereby integrating dance into the script. Described as blunt, critical, and tenacious, Agnes de Mille drew on her own indefatigable spirit, rather than on the success of her family name, to revolutionize musical theater by incorporating into it elements of folk dancing and classical ballet.

Bibliography
Amberg, George. *Ballet in America.* New York: Duell, Sloan, Pearce, 1949. This book is an in-depth historical view of ballet from the early nineteenth century through musical comedy. It includes extensive information on the Ballet Russe and Ballet Theater and de Mille's involvement in both. Also included are a chronology and selected ballet repertories.
Anderson, Jack. *Dance.* New York: Newsweek Books, 1974. A brief overview of ballet history from its origins through the modern period. Includes biographical information on dancers, including de Mille, and a selected bibliography.
Balanchine, George. *Balanchine's New Complete Stories of the Great Ballets.* Edited by Francis Mason. Garden City, N.Y.: Doubleday, 1968. Written by one of the great masters of dance, this work includes plot summaries, brief historical information, and a chronology of significant events in ballet history. There is an annotated list of recordings as well as a selected bibliography.
De Mille, Agnes. *Dance to the Piper.* Boston: Little, Brown, 1952. The first volume of de Mille's autobiography, this work covers the period from her departure from New York to live in Hollywood through the "lean" years to the success of *Rodeo* and the launching of her career.
Kraus, Richard. *History of the Dance in Art and Education.* Englewood Cliffs, N.J.: Prentice-Hall, 1969. A historical overview of dance, including information on its meaning and purpose, beginning with primitive cultures and continuing through religious ceremonies to modern dance. Information is included on integrating dance into an educational curriculum.
Lloyd, Margaret. *The Borzoi Book of Modern Dance.* New York: Dance Horizons, 1949. This overview of modern dance includes thumbnail sketches of many of the

originators and innovators in the movement. It incorporates information on the changes in perception of dance from formal classical ballet to the humanizing of dance as an integral part of the theater.

Joyce Duncan

FRANCES DENSMORE

Born: May 21, 1867; Red Wing, Minnesota
Died: June 5, 1957; Red Wing, Minnesota
Area of Achievement: Anthropology
Contribution: A pioneer ethnomusicologist who studied American Indian music, Densmore collected several thousand Indian songs by means of recordings and transcriptions.

Early Life

Frances Theresa Densmore was one of two children of Benjamin and Sarah Densmore of Red Wing, Minnesota. Despite the fact that they were relative newcomers to the small town in southeastern Minnesota—Densmore's paternal grandfather, Judge Orrin Densmore, arrived in 1857 from New York via Wisconsin—the family was prominent. Densmore's father was a civil engineer who, with his brother, founded the Red Wing Iron Works.

The Densmores were a musical family, and Frances enjoyed the benefits of a rigorous musical education. After completing public school, she studied piano, organ, and harmony at the prestigious Oberlin College in Ohio. Densmore spent two years in Boston between 1888 and 1890 studying piano with German pianist Karl Baermann and counterpoint with Harvard professor John Knowles Paine. She credited attendance at concerts of the Boston Symphony Orchestra with broadening and deepening her musical appreciation. In 1890, she returned to Minnesota to settle in St. Paul, teaching music and lecturing on musicology while also serving as a choir director and organist.

Densmore's curiosity about American Indians was piqued by the Sioux whom she had met as a child in Red Wing. She had been fascinated by the music she heard emanating from a local Sioux encampment. During her adult years, the principal influence on Densmore was anthropologist Alice Cunningham Fletcher, whose pathbreaking *A Study of Omaha Music* was published in 1893. A year or two prior to the publication of that work, Densmore was alerted to Fletcher's research by Fletcher's transcriptionist, John C. Fillmore, director of the Milwaukee School of Music. Because Fillmore perceived an inherent harmony in Indian music, he had composed piano accompaniments to Fletcher's melodies. Densmore traveled to Milwaukee, where she learned Fillmore's technique. Her earliest work reflects his theories.

With Fillmore's encouragement, Densmore wrote to Fletcher concerning her own interest in studying Indian music; Fletcher's gracious response encouraged Densmore to proceed. For nearly a decade afterward, Densmore systematically read American Indian ethnography and traveled to expositions and fairs listening to Indian music. In 1895, she began lecturing on Indian music using examples from Fletcher's study. During her years of ethnographic preparation, Densmore functioned as a professional musician by performing concerts, teaching piano, and lecturing on musical subjects in Minnesota and neighboring states. In 1898, she furthered her musical education, traveling to Chicago to study piano with the renowned pianist and composer Leopold Godowsky.

Life's Work

Following several years of preparatory reading and concomitant lecturing on Indian music, Frances Densmore in 1901 transcribed her first song from a Sioux woman living near Red Wing. Aided by her acute sense of relative pitch, Densmore on several further occasions transcribed songs without the use of recording equipment. In 1904, for example, she attended a St. Louis exhibition where she requested a song from the renowned Apache warrior Geronimo. When he refused, she surreptitiously transcribed one he absentmindedly sang while fashioning a new arrow.

Accompanied and assisted by her sister Margaret, who aided her throughout her career, Densmore embarked on her first field trip in 1905, a visit to the Chippewa on a Minnesota reservation. She was delighted by their music and its accompanying ceremonies. Two years later, with borrowed recording equipment, she attended the annual Chippewa White Earth Celebration, where she met many of her original informants. Densmore forwarded the songs she recorded at this celebration to the Smithsonian Institution, where the Chief of the Bureau of American Ethnology, William H. Holmes, greeted her work enthusiastically. Holmes allotted her $150 for the recording of Indian songs, a sum she used to purchase the best available recording equipment, an Edison Home phonograph, thus inaugurating Densmore's lifelong association with the Smithsonian Institution.

Early in 1908, Densmore traveled to Washington to deliver her first report to the Smithsonian Institution. The Smithsonian paid her an additional $300 and included her findings in the Institution's annual report. During her stay in Washington, the Anthropological Society, forerunner to the American Anthropology Association, invited her to present a lecture on Indian music.

Densmore's first book, *Chippewa Music*, in which she described Indian songs in their cultural context, appeared in 1910. Although her original interest was entirely musical, Densmore shrewdly realized that song was a component of culture which could not be properly analyzed if viewed out of context. All of her works—notably, her early *Chippewa Music* (1910), and *Chippewa Music—II* (1913)—are consequently rich in ethnographic detail. She transcribed melodies, performed interviews, and provided analyses of the melodies' functions within culture. Densmore also collected American Indian musical instruments, herbs, and other paraphernalia associated with healing songs.

Initially, Densmore had subscribed to Fillmore's theory of latent harmony, in which notes are organized around a central keynote and the third is the fundamental harmonic unit. In transcribing melodies, Fillmore added accompaniments that he believed corresponded to the harmony latent in Indian songs. Although Densmore initially experimented with harmonization, in *Chippewa Music*, she presented her songs as melody sans accompaniment. In *Chippewa Music—II*, she openly questioned the validity of latent harmony in Indian music. If harmony existed at all, she believed, it was in a different and perhaps more complex form. As she studied more Indian tribes, Densmore began identifying harmonic intervals other than the third. She determined, for example, that the interval of a fourth frequently occurred among Pacific Northwest tribes.

Although Densmore transcribed songs in traditional Western notation, which recognizes no interval smaller than a half step, she also explored deviations from the Western scale. Working with psychologist Carl Seashore, Densmore devised a series of tests of Indian pitch discrimination which convinced her that Indians intentionally sang non-Western intervals. She therefore experimented with a graphic form of notation, although she intended it as an adjunct to, not as a replacement for, traditional Western notation.

Until her death at the age of ninety, Densmore maintained her association with the Smithsonian Bureau of Ethnology, first as a research associate, then as a special researcher in American Indian music, and finally as a collaborator. Although her work was primarily supported by the $3,000 grant awarded her annually, she also received funding from the National Research Council, the University of Minnesota, and Southern California's Southwest Museum, which between 1935 and 1938 sponsored her research among several southwest Indian tribes. In 1954, she worked as a consultant and lecturer at the University of Florida, during which time she made field trips among the Seminole Indians—work she began at age eighty-seven.

In 1940, because the Smithsonian lacked funding for the preservation of her original fragile cylinders, Densmore's collection of 3,523 songs and their transcriptions was accessioned by the National Archives. There, a generous private grant of $30,000 funded the transfer of her recordings to more permanent musical disks. Between 1940 and 1942 Densmore acted as a consultant for the archives, preparing a handbook for her collection which was representative of her fieldwork between 1907 and 1940. In 1943, the collection was transferred to the Archive of American Folksong at the Library of Congress, and Densmore was appointed to prepare ten albums for popular distribution, seven of which were completed before her death. The Smithsonian-Densmore collection of American Indian music constitutes Densmore's finest contribution to ethnomusicology. Aided by her discerning selection of aging, musically reliable members of the tribe, Densmore preserved music that was comparatively uncontaminated by Western contact but that, without her efforts, would have been irretrievably lost.

Although she was untrained in ethnography, Densmore was a prolific writer who published more than twenty books and one hundred articles about Indian music, for which she received wide professional recognition. In 1924, Oberlin awarded her an honorary master's degree, and in 1940, Macalester College bestowed on her an honorary doctorate; that same year, the National Association of American Composers and Conductors commended her with its Award of Merit. In 1952, Densmore received a congressional tribute. In addition, she maintained several professional affiliations and supported the development of the American Society for Ethnomusicology, serving as its vice president in 1956.

Summary

Frances Densmore's most singular achievement was the salvaging of a vast collection of Indian songs that otherwise might have been lost. Although she experimented with new technology as it became available, her primitive recording equipment was cumbersome and of limited use. Nevertheless, she recorded several thousand melodies during her life's work among a vast range of Indian tribes. The Smithsonian-Densmore collection remains a principal source of Indian music and a testimonial to her rigorous recording techniques. In addition, her rapport with Indians and her genuine interest in their culture enabled her to preserve ethnographic detail as well as to smooth the way for future researchers.

Although her ethnographic descriptions have been superseded by more rigorous scholarship, her studies are still respected by those ethnomusicologists best able to appreciate the theoretical foundations of her analyses.

Like many of her female contemporaries, including Alice Fletcher, Densmore functioned outside the male academic system. Yet she and her several female colleagues met with less resistance in performing their work than did later female anthropologists. Opposition to women was a function of the twentieth century professionalization of anthropology when female anthropologists encountered the barriers confronting all women who entered professions. Prior to professionalization, enlightened men sometimes recruited women or at least did not oppose them in their research. In 1899, for example, the Washington Anthropological Society invited members of the Women's Anthropological Association to join them, and in 1903, Alice Fletcher served a term as president. Nevertheless, the barriers to women in early twentieth century America were inhibiting to the vast majority of American women. Frances Densmore was a remarkably adept, prolific professional woman in one of the few fields that were not aggressively inimical to female members.

Bibliography

Archabal, Nina Marchetti. "Frances Densmore: Pioneer in the Study of American Indian Music." In *Women of Minnesota: Selected Biographical Essays*, edited by Barbara Stuhler and Gretchen Kreuter. St. Paul: Minnesota Historical Society Press, 1977. This, the most extensive analysis of Densmore's work, is particularly useful because it is written by a musician and therefore deals with musical as well as ethnographic information. Contains citations but no bibliography.

Frisbie, Charlotte J. "Frances Theresa Densmore." In *Women Anthropologists: A Biographical Dictionary*, edited by Ute Gacs et al. New York: Greenwood Press, 1988. A thorough yet concise biography of Densmore that lists her many achievements and publications. Contains a bibliography of primary and secondary sources.

Hofmann, Charles, ed. *Frances Densmore and American Indian Music: A Memorial Volume*. New York: Museum of the American Indian, Heye Foundation, 1968. Hofmann's collection of Densmore's writings contains valuable autobiographical material. Hofmann also included Densmore's *The Study of Indian Music*, originally published in the *Smithsonian Annual Report for 1941*, in which she describes in detail her techniques for collecting Indian songs as well as the limitations imposed by her primitive recording equipment.

——————. "Frances Densmore and the Music of the American Indian." *The Journal of American Folklore* 59 (1946): 45-50. Hofmann, who also compiled Densmore's papers, provides a brief biography of Densmore and describes her work.

Lurie, Nancy Ostreich. "Women in Early American Anthropology." In *Pioneers of American Anthropology: The Uses of Biography*, edited by June Helm. Seattle: University of Washington Press, 1966. Densmore's life is examined within the context of the early—all born prior to 1885—women contributors to anthropology. Densmore's forerunner and influence Alice Cunningham Fletcher is also described.

Mary E. Virginia

EMILY DICKINSON

Born: December 10, 1830; Amherst, Massachusetts
Died: May 15, 1886; Amherst, Massachusetts
Area of Achievement: Poetry
Contribution: Rejecting the social and literary conventions of her patriarchal society, Emily Dickinson became one of America's greatest poets.

Early Life

Emily Elizabeth Dickinson was born on December 10, 1830, in her father's home in Amherst, Massachusetts. The Dickinsons had played prominent roles in the town's history. In 1745, Nathan Dickinson had led a group of settlers to found the village of Amherst, and in 1821 his grandson (the poet's grandfather) Samuel Fowler Dickinson played a key role in the founding of Amherst College, the institution responsible for turning the farming village of Amherst into one of Massachusetts' cultural centers. Samuel's eldest son, the attorney Edward Dickinson, followed in the footsteps of his forebears, involving himself heavily in the town's government and becoming the treasurer of Amherst College in 1835. Edward Dickinson is important for more than his civic contributions to the town of Amherst. On May 6, 1828, he married Emily Norcross from the nearby village of Monson, and she bore three children—Austin, Emily, and Lavinia.

What information exists about Emily Dickinson's youth reveals that she was precocious, gregarious, and fun-loving. She enjoyed the several trips she took, and she often regretted that there was not enough time in a day to visit all the people she wanted to see. Living at a time when even the common cold could kill, Dickinson early in life experienced the deaths of many neighbors and several close friends; these experiences explain, in part, her later poetic explorations of death. She also lived through a time of intense religious revivals. As she herself was very aware, she alone of her family members and friends "[stood] in rebellion" and refused to give in to the revival fever.

At a time when many girls of Dickinson's social class received only a primary education, she attended Amherst Academy, the most respected secondary facility in the area. Entering on September 7, 1840, she studied such subjects as mental philosophy, geology, geography, grammar, natural history, physiology, and composition, most of which she thoroughly enjoyed. Amherst Academy not only provided courses on the cutting edge taught by attentive teachers but also sponsored lectures by published scholars such as Edward Hitchcock, whose eloquent addresses on natural science and religion are often counted as important influences on the burgeoning poet.

On September 30, 1847, Dickinson began her studies at Mount Holyoke College, founded as Mount Holyoke Female Seminary in 1836 by Mary Lyon, a protégé of Edward Hitchcock. For reasons that are not entirely clear, Dickinson withdrew after only two terms, thus signaling the end of her formal education. A few months before her eighteenth birthday, Emily Dickinson returned to her "own dear home."

Life's Work

It is not known when Emily Dickinson first earnestly attempted poetry. As early as March of 1853, she wrote to her brother Austin that she had been in the "habit" of writing poems. Certainly she was writing steadily in the late 1850's; in 1858, she began to gather her poetry into little volumes (variously called fascicles, volumes, or packets). By closely analyzing these manuscript books, scholars have pieced together Dickinson's methods for what many consider to be the most incredible instance of self-publishing in literary history. After jotting a verse down on whatever piece of paper lay at hand (the back of a used envelope, for example), Dickinson usually reworked the poem numerous times. Next, she copied it in ink onto a folded sheet of stationer's paper. She stacked such poems several pieces high, piercing two holes in the left margin with a darning needle threaded with cotton string, which she then tied into a bow.

Although they probably did not know about the fascicles, two people were especially important to Dickinson's poetic vocation. Thomas Wentworth Higginson, essayist with *The Atlantic Monthly*, received a letter dated April 15, 1862, from Dickinson asking if the four poems she had enclosed were "alive," thus beginning a correspondence and friendship that lasted until the poet's death. Though Dickinson continued to send poems (100 in all), apparently appreciating Higginson's comments, she never took any of his well-intended but conventional advice (for example, that she alter her "spasmodic" meter). It is likely that she did heed the advice of her sister-in-law Susan Gilbert Dickinson, to whom the poet sent at least 400 poems and letters during their thirty-year relationship. Their exchange of notes about "Safe in their Alabaster Chambers—" (#216) reveals that at least once Dickinson revised at someone's suggestion.

Generally, though, Dickinson created alone, and always at home. A point of contention in Dickinson scholarship is the fact that after about 1860, Dickinson refused to leave her house or to accept most visitors. There is nothing conclusive in her letters explaining this phenomenon. For many critics, however, her opus is explanation enough. While in the years between 1858 and 1861 Dickinson crafted between 52 and 94 poems a year (an accomplishment in itself), in 1862 she wrote an astounding 366 poems. These include, for example, "The Soul selects her own Society—" (#303), "After great pain, a formal feeling comes—" (#341), and "Much Madness is divinest Sense—" (#435). In 1863, she wrote 141 poems; in 1864, 174; in 1865, 85; and in 1866, 36. These numbers seem even more remarkable when it is noted that there are also extant 1,050 letters from this poet. Dickinson continued writing after 1867, though she slowed her pace to no more than 50 poems per year.

To create under such intense conditions while also keeping up with household duties is amazing. Clearly, Dickinson's retreat was a strategy, a planned refusal to let anything stop her from writing, and thus a rebellion against the social conventions of her day. In mid-nineteenth century America, very few avenues were open to women: They could marry and have children, they could become missionaries, or they could teach. A few successful women writers were familiar to Dickinson, such as Helen

Hunt Jackson and Emily Fowler Ford, but, unlike Dickinson, both of these women also married. Furthermore, Dickinson rebelled against the conventions of publication. After seeing the editing that her poem "A narrow Fellow in the Grass" (#986) received when it was published without her consent, Dickinson knew that the time for her poetry had not yet come. In a letter to Higginson, she pointed out that in conventionalizing the poem, editors had robbed it of its power and meaning. Dickinson wanted to create, but she chose not to take her poetic wares to market, especially a market that could not appreciate her gift. As many critics have noted, her strategic retreat from the marketplace and from the social conventions of her day was an incredible act of nonconformity.

Dickinson had the admiration of those close to her, including the three people responsible for most of the dozen poems published during her lifetime: Samuel Bowles and Josiah Holland, editors of the *Springfield Republican*, and Helen Hunt Jackson (who wanted to be Dickinson's literary executor). Despite their interest, Dickinson chose to secrete her trove of poems for a future audience. After refusing for fifty-five years to publicize her talent, Dickinson died in 1886 from complications of Bright's disease.

As was customary in nineteenth century America, she left instructions for her correspondence to be destroyed. As the story goes, Lavinia was in the midst of carrying out her sister's request when she discovered a locked wooden box. In it she discovered forty volumes of untitled poems, fifteen gatherings ready for binding, and hundreds of loose poems in various draft states. Immediately, Lavinia determined to see Emily's volumes published, so she requested the assistance of the two most powerful people she knew. Significantly, both of these individuals were women. After waiting for two years for Susan Dickinson to do something with the poems she had lent her, the frustrated Lavinia turned to Mabel Loomis Todd, who was consequently responsible for the first edition of Dickinson's poetry.

Todd and Higginson (whom Todd persuaded to coedit Dickinson's poems) published two well-received editions (*Poems*, 1890, and *Poems: Second Series*, 1891), and Todd later published one on her own (*Poems: Third Series*, 1896). Although well-intentioned, the two editors made significant changes in Dickinson's poetry. They conventionalized her lines, regularizing her syntax, punctuation, and meter, even changing words deemed too eccentric, and they arranged her unconventional verse under quite conventional headings such as "Love" and "Nature." Not until 1955, when Thomas H. Johnson published his three-volume *The Poems of Emily Dickinson*, was there an attempt to gather all known poems authored by Dickinson and publish them as the poet had written them. This text was groundbreaking because it revealed in one edition the incredible rebellion against convention that Emily Dickinson had waged.

Summary

For decades, biographers and critics focused especially on one aspect of Emily Dickinson's rebellion, her withdrawal from society. Study after study sought to discover what had gone wrong with Dickinson—who might have broken her heart and driven her to seclusion and poetics. In the 1980's, the work of feminist scholars postulated that Dickinson, living in a patriarchal society and faced with male-determined conventions, made the genre of poetry her own. Many literary historians have come to accept this understanding of Dickinson's literary activity.

By eschewing the accepted conventions of poetry, Dickinson created a poetry and a language of her own. Although she enjoyed reading contemporary poetry, she found no models among the most popular poets, such as Henry Wadsworth Longfellow, James Russell Lowell, John Greenleaf Whittier (the "Fireside Poets") and Lydia Huntley Sigourney (whose poetry represents the usual type of poetry written by women at the time). Nevertheless, Dickinson continued to write what she herself could easily see was a startling, revolutionary poetry. Clearly beyond its time, Dickinson's handling of language laid the groundwork for the experimentations of later modern poets. By appropriating the images of her Puritan ancestors and even the language of the Bible, Dickinson forged a path to a poetry that spoke from a woman's experience without relying on male strategies. In this process, Dickinson achieved a wrenching away of patriarchal language, infusing it with terms such as "bonnet" and "broom" and with a complexity and richness of syntax, music, and connotation uniquely her own. Critics have underscored the fact that Dickinson challenged the conventions not only of a genre but also of her time.

Bibliography
Dickinson, Emily. *The Complete Poems of Emily Dickinson.* Edited by Thomas H. Johnson. Boston: Little, Brown, 1960. This edition is a condensed reading version of the definitive three-volume variorum edition. It arranges the poems by approximate chronological order and is the most manageable way to see all extant poems of Dickinson.
——————. *The Letters of Emily Dickinson.* 3 vols. Edited by Thomas H. Johnson and Theodora Ward. Cambridge, Mass.: The Belknap Press of Harvard University Press, 1958. This collection of letters, though bulky, is an important primary source. Because it is arranged chronologically with introductions to groupings of years, even a casual reading will be beneficial.
Duchac, Joseph. *The Poems of Emily Dickinson: An Annotated Guide to Commentary Published in English, 1978-1989.* New York: Macmillan, 1993. This annotated bibliography is organized by poem and is an easy and helpful reference tool for those who wish to read critical interpretations of particular poems.
Ferlazzo, Paul. *Emily Dickinson.* Boston: Twayne, 1976. Written for beginning Dickinson students, this work is a good general introduction to Dickinson's life and poetry.
Juhasz, Suzanne, ed. *Feminist Critics Read Emily Dickinson.* Bloomington: Indiana University Press, 1983. This collection of essays by some of the most respected feminist Dickinson scholars is prefaced by Juhasz's article that briefly traces the history of recent trends in the interpretation of Dickinson's poetry and life and is,

thus, a good introduction for beginning students of Dickinson.

Wolff, Cynthia Griffin. *Emily Dickinson.* New York: Alfred A. Knopf, 1986. This critical biography makes use of past biographies and is much more manageable and accessible. Also, the bibliography is extensive and the index helpful.

Anna Dunlap

MARLENE DIETRICH

Born: December 27, 1901; Berlin, Germany
Died: May 6, 1992; Paris, France
Area of Achievement: Film
Contribution: Never a great actress, Marlene Dietrich established herself worldwide in a career that began in the infancy of the film industry, largely on the strength of her image as the modern femme fatale, glamorous, self-confident, erotic, and independent.

Early Life

In 1907, when her father suddenly died from a heart attack after being thrown from a horse, Maria Magdalena Dietrich—or Leni, as she was then known—was enrolled in the Auguste-Victoria School for Girls in the Nürnbergstrasse, Berlin. There she remained for the next dozen years while her widowed mother remarried (to Eduard von Losch, a colonel in the Royal Grenadiers) and Germany's Wilhelmian capital moved ever closer to the Great War. For Leni and her older sister Leisel (Elisabeth), it was a time of rigorous but not unpleasant routine, a time to take music lessons, to learn French and English, and to practice the deportment expected of an officer's daughter in a bustling city envied by much of Europe for its prosperity, military spit and polish, and wide variety of entertainment.

When the war came, things changed quickly. The holiday mood that had greeted its outbreak by a confident nation vanished as the number of German casualties soared. Food rationing, shortages of every kind, and growing lists of killed and wounded dominated everyday life. In school, the girls knitted gloves, sweaters, and scarves for the troops at the front. Leni's favorite teacher, Marguerite Bréguand, a young woman with whom she had eagerly practiced her French, was now gone. Indeed, the speaking of French and English had come to be perceived as almost treasonous.

Classmates appeared in the cold and gloomy schoolrooms wearing new black bands on the sleeves of their heavy sweaters, indicating the deaths of male relatives. Leni wore one, too, when, in 1918, her stepfather died in Russia.

Life's Work

That same year, World War I ended. Leni Dietrich had not missed her second father, a remote figure. Instead, she had enjoyed the additional freedom won at his departure and the company of women: Her sister, mother, aunt, and grandmother. For the remainder of her life, she had mixed feelings about men, often preferring those in distress, but she treasured relationships with—including romantic attachments to—those of her own sex.

In Berlin, unemployment and inflation raged. Youthful prostitutes haunted street corners. The urge to forget found expression in the new lifestyles of the jazz age, breeding excesses of every kind. Yet Leni—now calling herself "Marlene" (an elision of Maria and Magdalene), found the Roaring Twenties exhilarating. A new name, a new city, new habits—such as smoking and wearing men's attire—and a new life seemed to suit her. Photographs from these years show not the Dietrich of prominent cheekbones with heavily lidded eyes, but a plump, not-very-tall flapper with bobbed hair, cloche hats, and a tiny red mouth.

Marlene enrolled in drama school and auditioned for whatever parts were available at Berlin's theaters and new film studios. In 1922, she landed her first role in a forgotten silent film, *Der kleine Napoleon* (1923; little Napoleon). The next year saw her in *Tragödie der Liebe* (1923; *Tragedy of Love*, 1923) starring Emil Jannings, a widely known actor of stage and screen. On that set, she met Rudolf Sieber, whom she married on May 17, 1923. Sieber, the father of her only child, Maria, born on December 13, 1924, remained her husband until his death in the United States in 1976. Their relationship, which was exemplary in many ways, did not long include marital fidelity. Both turned to other sexual partners; Marlene acquired scores of them in her long life, a practice that was only whispered about during her years of fame.

Marlene appeared briefly in a number of films and plays until 1930, when she found herself sharing the screen again with Emil Jannings in the German-language film *Der blaue Engel* (*The Blue Angel*, 1931). *The Blue Angel* was the brainchild of Josef von Sternberg. While the "von" was bogus, the man decidedly was not. His discovery of Marlene and hers of him has the drama of the Pygmalion myth, for like Pygmalion, who turned his statue into a living woman, Sternberg turned a pudgy starlet into Marlene Dietrich—while falling in love with her. *The Blue Angel* tells the story of a pompous teacher who is undone by a cabaret temptress who shows lots of black silk-clad leg and sings in a smoky contralto. On the strength of *The Blue Angel*'s European success and von Sternberg's recommendations, Paramount Pictures beckoned, believing that Dietrich could be an appropriate competitor for Metro-Goldwyn-Mayer's smoldering Swedish beauty Greta Garbo.

The 1930's witnessed the creation of the Dietrich legend, the fabulous American film star of Hollywood's golden age. Earning enormous sums in the Depression (in 1936, she was the highest-paid woman in the world), photographed nightly at tables with several leading men—often her lovers—Dietrich lived the romantic existence others dreamed about. Her first American film, *Morocco* (1930), with Gary Cooper, was a smash. Von Sternberg's lighting created a hollow-cheeked mystery woman who follows her legionnaire into the desert, a creature who is self-willed, passionate, true to her own code, and somehow more human than Garbo. After *Dishonored* (1931), Dietrich returned to Germany to retrieve her daughter—though not her husband—and an old roommate (and lover), Gerda Hubner.

Her return to the United States saw a retroactive suit filed against her by von Sternberg's former wife, but the presence of her six-year-old daughter and ultimately her husband in July of 1931 silenced the wagging tongues of Americans who were incapable of conceiving family situations as bizarre as those in which Dietrich and Rudi Sieber regularly found themselves.

Near the end of the decade, however, Dietrich saw her popularity in serious decline: One trade publication called her "box office poison." Dreadful films such as *The*

Scarlet Empress (1934), *The Garden of Allah* (1936), *Knight Without Armor* (1936), and *Angel* (1937) were partially responsible, but new audiences were no longer satisfied with the escapist kitsch that Depression filmgoers had sought, and techniques in lighting and cinematography led away from the make-believe of earlier years.

In 1939, after ending a romance with film star Douglas Fairbanks, Jr., to begin a more intense one with the German writer Erich Maria Remarque, Dietrich received the offer of a role in a Western with Jimmy Stewart. *Destry Rides Again* (1939) proved to be a hit, and it put Dietrich's career back on track. Her next film was *Seven Sinners* (1940), the first of three with John Wayne.

In the 1940's, she engineered another headline romance, this time with Jean Gabin, the homesick French refugee actor, whom she mothered—as she often did her men—with home-cooked pot au feu. In 1944, she broke off acting to entertain troops and make propaganda broadcasts for the Allies, for which activities she accumulated medals and citations. America's youngest general, James M. Gavin, was smitten with her, to the distress of Jean Gabin, with whom she filmed the dreary *Martin Roumaganic* (1946). *A Foreign Affair* (1948), directed by German émigré Billy Wilder, was, in contrast, a triumph. In it, she projected what she had become, the woman who has seen it all and survived, though at the expense of a few illusions—"Illusions" was also the memorable Frederick Hollander song she sang in the film.

In the 1950's, Dietrich made fewer films than she had in her heyday. She interested herself in her daughter's family while continuing to form new intimate relationships with both men and women, most notably with actor Yul Brynner (who was twenty years younger than she) and singer Frank Sinatra.

When Las Vegas came into prominence, she joined high-paid celebrities there. Audiences took shocked notice of her gown, all but transparent to the waist, which soon became a trademark—proof that her famous figure was impervious to age. Few suspected that its careful construction hid a special elasticized foundation. The stage act she had introduced in troop shows grew ever more polished in Europe, South America, and eventually Israel, South Africa, and the Soviet Union. In 1959, with great courage, she returned to a Germany that had not completely forgiven her for her wartime hostility. At that time, she conducted a passionate affair with her musical director Burt Bacharach, who was almost thirty years her junior.

World tours continued for another seventeen years while Dietrich grew more obsessed with her appearance, forbidding photographs and becoming increasingly intractable. Her makeup rituals consumed hours as she attempted to disguise her age. In 1976, after her husband's death, she retreated to her Paris apartment, where she slowly cut herself off from her remaining friends. A drinking problem that began late in her life grew more severe, and her last years were mostly spent bedridden in a cluttered apartment until her death at age ninety-one on May 6, 1992.

Summary

When the biography *Marlene Dietrich* appeared in 1992, readers found it a shocking indictment, but in accusing her mother of each of the Seven Deadly Sins—and then some—author Maria Riva only made more apparent how completely Dietrich's admirers had accepted the legend that the star had created. That the legend was less than true made little difference, since actresses are ultimately judged by how well they play their roles.

If her generosity was limited, so be it. She seemed to lavish her wealth on others. If she were mean-spirited and dishonest, Americans had no knowledge of it. They saw instead a woman who had frequented the Stork Club entertaining soldiers in muddy fields. Dietrich appeared to be earthy, not lewd; passionate, not conniving; loving, not thoughtless. She seemed to be beautiful, sexy, and vulnerable. She had wit, spoke three languages, and fascinated both men and women. She did it "her way" long before her lover Frank Sinatra made those words famous.

Bibliography
Bach, Steven. *Marlene Dietrich: Life and Legend*. New York: William Morrow, 1992. A bulky, richly illustrated biography, well researched and informative—written from the perspective of an admirer. Bach conveys the impression—shared by many—that Dietrich was able to make individuals and audiences alike feel as if they were alone with her. The book stresses her performing audacity and her use of sex as both a weapon of control and a reward for good behavior in personal relations. There is much interesting analysis of the symbiosis of von Sternberg and Dietrich, with Dietrich's role emerging larger than her mentor's; furthermore, Bach deals successfully with the problem of Dietrich's zigzagging from the practical and down-to-earth to the wildly romantic.
Dietrich, Marlene. *Marlene*. Translated by Salvator Attanasio. New York: Grove Press, 1989. Totally unreliable in every possible way, this so-called autobiography is a fairly tale meant to perpetuate the Dietrich legend. Dietrich leaves out far more than she tells, changing events to suit herself and trimming casts of characters for dramatic effect. Her sister vanishes, her two fathers become one, and her husband barely surfaces. She does, however, stress those moments and events that most affected her, which may make this book valuable to the student of her life.
Higham, Charles. *Marlene: The Life of Marlene Dietrich*. New York: W. W. Norton, 1977. This work is outdated, but Higham shows great sensitivity in presenting the public Dietrich. Appreciative and gentle, the book is neither sentimental nor naïve.
Riva, Maria. *Marlene Dietrich*. New York: Alfred A. Knopf, 1993. This is an expansive, bitter biography in the vein of *Mommie Dearest* (1978), film star Joan Crawford's daughter's searing indictment of her mother. Dietrich's only child can forgive neither her mother nor her father. Although Riva doubtless exaggerates Dietrich's failings, the book has a ring of truth to it and is based on documents denied to others. Contains numerous pictures but lacks an index.
Spoto, Donald. *Blue Angel: The Life of Marlene Dietrich*. New York: Doubleday, 1992. This biography was written during Dietrich's last years in lonesome Parisian exile, when gossip and celebrity memoirs had begun to explode her myth and her indiscreet telephone calls contributed to the destruction. Spoto's wide knowledge

of Hollywood's public and private lives, together with his technical grasp of the film business and interest in motion pictures, makes the book especially rewarding. Although Berlin escapes him slightly (as it does Higham and Riva, who hates it as a symbol of her mother), Spoto has the advantage of having studied the émigré mentality in scores of other film figures.

James E. Devlin

DOROTHEA DIX

Born: April 4, 1802; Hampden, Maine (then part of Massachusetts)
Died: July 17, 1887; Trenton, New Jersey
Area of Achievement: Social reform
Contribution: A crusader for the rights of the mentally ill, Dix devoted her life to establishing psychiatric hospitals to provide proper care for those with mental and emotional problems.

Early Life

Dorothea Lynde Dix had a difficult childhood. Her father married, by his family's standards, below his station. Since married students were not accepted at Harvard, where he was studying at the time, he was sent to manage family holdings in Maine—nothing less than the frontier in the early nineteenth century. Never a financial success, he did win some notice as a traveling Methodist preacher and a writer of tracts. Thus, Dorothea was often without her father, and unfortunately, her mother was often too ill to give her the attention that young children require.

Dorothea's happiest memories of her solitary childhood revolved around visits to her paternal grandparents in Boston. Her grandfather, a successful if curmudgeonly physician, and grandmother provided a warm welcome. Dorothea's first exposure to public service came from watching her grandfather practice medicine. She had few playmates her own age and was four years older than her nearest sibling. At least one biographer believes that isolation from children and involvement with adults led to a high degree of self-interest and blocked the development of personal emotional commitment. In any case, she never married, and most, though not all, of her friendships were with people involved in her charitable endeavors.

At about twelve, unhappy at home, she began to live permanently with her then-widowed grandmother. To her dismay, her grandmother insisted on both academic and social discipline, and Dorothea's sense of rejection was actually worsened. After two years, she was sent off to live with a great-aunt, where she finally found a congenial home. Although still a teenager, she was allowed to open a school for small children, which she ran successfully for three years before returning to Boston. Two years later, in 1821, she opened a school for girls. Education for women was unusual—public schools accepted girls only for the few months when many boys were out for agricultural labor—and even more unusual was Dix's insistence on including natural science in the curriculum. Dorothea Dix proved to be a gifted teacher, and she seemed to have found her life's work. In a gesture that was a harbinger of her future, she added a program for poor girls who otherwise had no opportunity for schooling.

Ill health—apparently tuberculosis—and the collapse of a romance with her cousin resulted in a new direction for Dix. While recovering her strength in the mid-1820's, she became interested in Unitarianism and the ideas of William Ellery Channing. This Christian sect's emphasis on the goodness of humanity and the obligation to serve it would inspire her for the rest of her life. A new attempt to run a school, however, led to her complete collapse in 1836 and her doctor's orders never to teach again.

Life's Work

While recuperating, Dorothea Dix visited England. During her two-year stay with the William Rathbone family, she met a variety of intellectuals and reformers. When she returned to the United States, she found that the deaths of her mother and grandmother had left her financially independent. She spent several years seeking some focus for her life. Then, in 1841, she was asked to teach Sunday School for women at the East Cambridge Jail. She found the innocent and guilty, young and old, sane and insane crowded into the same miserable, unheated facility. Those regarded as insane were often chained or otherwise restrained. Her discussions with humanitarians such as George Emerson, who would become a longtime friend, led her to understand that conditions in East Cambridge Jail were, if anything, better than those in most jails. There was virtually no distinction made between mental illness and retardation, and in the entire country there were only about 2,500 beds specifically for those with emotional problems. Dix quickly had a sense that she had come upon something important that needed doing.

Dix's first move was to demand and get heat for the insane in the East Cambridge Jail. Then, after talking with other reformers, including Samuel Howe and Charles Sumner (later a radical Republican leader during Reconstruction), she began a survey of facilities for the insane in Massachusetts. Although the McLean Psychiatric Hospital was relatively progressive, most of the mentally ill were kept in local poorhouses, workhouses, and jails. She visited every one. Conditions were horrendous. Patients were often locked in dirty stalls, sometimes for years, and many were chained to the floor. Many were virtually naked, and physical restraint was virtually universal. She also found time to discuss treatment with the best doctors, finding that much more humane treatment was being successfully used in leading hospitals in Europe and a few in the United States. More common in America were strong sedatives to induce quiescence and the application of shocks, such as surprise dousings with ice water, to bring individuals back to reality.

After eighteen months, Dix prepared a petition to the Massachusetts legislature. The petition stated psychiatric facilities should provide for physical health and comfort (she would later expand this to prisons) and seek, with kindness and support, to cure diseased minds. When it was published, this document at first produced embarrassment and denial and then attacks upon the author. Her friends—Howe, Sumner, and others—rushed to defend her. She had her first victory when a bill providing for more and better accommodations for the mentally ill was passed. Her career was beginning to take shape.

Her initial investigations had occasionally taken Dix outside Massachusetts, where she found conditions to be generally worse than in her home state. From the mid-1840's to the mid-1850's, she traveled many thousands of miles around the United States and Canada, finding and exposing the suffering of the indigent insane. Although she did not travel to the far West (she did work in Texas), Dix visited almost every one of the thirty-one states of that era. She developed an investigative technique in which, by means of simple persistence and will, she forced her way into every facility where the insane were kept. There followed dramatic revelations of suffering and abuse that shamed all but the most hardened and/or fiscally conservative. Finally, she launched a petition to the legislature for the necessary funds and regulations to ensure improved care. She found the inevitable compromises necessary in any political campaign frustrating, but she settled for whatever state legislatures would fund and began again.

Results varied. New Jersey and Pennsylvania established state psychiatric hospitals as a result of her efforts. New York, however, rejected her call for six hospitals and only expanded the beds available in an existing facility. In 1845, with the help of Horace Mann and George Emerson, Dix expanded her efforts to prison reform and published a manual on that subject. Proper care for the mentally ill, however, remained her main focus.

From 1845 to 1846, Dix worked in Kentucky, Tennessee, Louisiana, Alabama, Georgia, and Arkansas, and she was working her way up the Mississippi when, in September, she collapsed in Columbus, Ohio. By December, she was sufficiently recovered to resume traveling, and in January, 1847, she presented a petition to the Illinois legislature, which resulted in the passage of a bill creating a psychiatric hospital. Later that year and in the following year, she had similar successes in Tennessee and North Carolina. Her fame was growing enormously, as were the respect and love with which Americans regarded her. One of the greatest marks of the latter came in 1863, when Confederate troops invading Pennsylvania stopped a train on which Dix was riding. A North Carolina officer recognized her, and the train was released to continue on its way. Not even the passions of Civil War could change people's feelings about Dorothea Dix.

Despite local successes—between 1844 and 1854 she persuaded eleven states to open hospitals—Dix recognized by the late 1840's that only a national effort would resolve the problems of the insane. No more than one-fourth of those needing care got it. She began to push for a federal effort, suggesting that 5 million acres of public land be committed to set up a fund to provide care for insane, epileptic, and mentally impaired Americans. A bill to this effect was introduced in Congress in 1848. Dix was provided with a small office in Washington from which to lobby. Questions about cost and constitutionality blocked the various versions of the bill until 1854, when, to her joy, it passed both houses. Her exultation was brief, however, for President Franklin Pierce vetoed the bill on the grounds that Congress had no authority to make such grants outside the District of Columbia. It was the final blow—the effort was abandoned.

Exhausted and ill, Dix planned to renew efforts in individual states, but friends and doctors persuaded her to rest. She visited friends in England, and within two weeks she was involved in efforts to reform psychiatric care there. She went so far as to go personally to the home secretary, Sir George Grey, to argue for improvements in

Scotland. Before she left, a Royal Commission to investigate the problem was in the works. She also helped to sustain a reform effort in the Channel Islands before touring the Continent, where she visited hospitals, asylums, and jails, exposing problems and demanding change. The force of her personality seems to have made her irresistible; even Pope Pius IX was forced to initiate improvements in the Vatican's handling of the mentally ill.

Her return to the United States in 1856 brought a large number of requests for aid. She was soon traveling again, seeking various reforms and funding. In the winter of 1859 alone, she asked state legislatures for a third of a million dollars, and in 1860, she got large appropriations for hospitals in South Carolina and Tennessee. The outbreak of the Civil War brought reform work to a halt, and Dix promptly volunteered her services. Appointed superintendent of United States Army Nurses, she spent four years of very hard work developing the Medical Bureau from a service set up for an army of ten thousand to one that could handle more than that many casualties from one battle. Unfortunately, she was too straitlaced at age sixty to cope with the rough-and-tumble style of the military. Her New England Puritanism showed in her tendency to think that an army doctor who had had a few drinks should be dishonorably discharged. Although her work in ensuring the provision of nurses and medical supplies at the beginning of the war was of great importance, in 1863 her authority was quietly reduced, to her bitter disappointment. After the war, Dix spent another fifteen years traveling as the advocate of the insane. Worn out in 1881, she retired to the hospital (the first created by her efforts) in Trenton, New Jersey, where she lived until her death in 1887.

Summary

Dorothea Dix's importance can be seen from simple statistics. In 1843, the United States had thirteen institutions for the mentally ill; in 1880, it had 123. Of the latter, 75 were state-owned, and Dix had been a key factor in the founding of 32 of them. She had also been able to get a number of training schools for the retarded established, and specialized training for psychiatric nurses had begun.

More important, the lives of many unfortunate people had been made easier thanks to her efforts. The idea that the insane, even if poor, deserved humane care and treatment intended to help them recover had been established in the United States. Dix's efforts began a process that has continued throughout the twentieth century and has left the United States a world leader in the treatment of mental illness.

Bibliography

Dain, Norman. *Concepts of Insanity in the United States, 1789-1865*. New Brunswick, N.J.: Rutgers University, 1964. A useful description of attitudes and problems that Dix had to confront during her career.

Dix, Dorothea. *On Behalf of the Insane Poor: Selected Reports*. New York: Arno Press, 1971. A valuable source of Dix's ideas and opinions expressed in her own words. Her eloquence and passion shine through.

Marshall, Helen. *Dorothea Dix: Forgotten Samaritan*. Chapel Hill: University of North Carolina Press, 1937. Although it is sometimes overly sympathetic to its subject, this is a solid and well-written biography.

Snyder, Charles M., ed. *The Lady and the President: The Letters of Dorothea Dix and Millard Fillmore*. Lexington: University Press of Kentucky, 1975. Provides interesting insights into one period of the life of Dorothea Dix.

Tiffany, Francis. *Life of Dorothea Lynde Dix*. Boston: Houghton Mifflin, 1890. Although it is dated and overly kind to Dix, this biography is reasonably good for its era.

Tuke, Daniel. *The Insane in the United States and Canada*. London: M. K. Lewis, 1885. This contemporary description of the problems Dix tried to solve gives a valuable perspective of the situation. It is very useful for modern students trying to achieve an understanding of her work.

Wilson, Dorothy Clarke. *Stranger and Traveler: The Story of Dorothea Dix, American Reformer*. Boston: Little, Brown, 1975. This relatively superficial biography emphasizes Dix's role as a woman who achieved much against great odds. A bibliography and many illustrations are included.

Fred R. van Hartesveldt

ELIZABETH DOLE

Born: July 29, 1936; Salisbury, North Carolina

Area of Achievement: Government and politics
Contribution: A dedicated government official, Elizabeth Dole served five American presidents in cabinet and other appointed positions.

Early Life

Mary Elizabeth Hanford was the younger of John and Mary Cathey Hanford's two children. Her brother, John, was thirteen years her senior. Elizabeth's first name was not used, and she often called herself "Liddy" as a toddler because it was easier to pronounce. Liddy's father operated a successful wholesale floral business in Salisbury. Her mother gave up plans to study at the Juilliard School of Music to marry John Hanford. Cora Alexander Cathey, Liddy's maternal grandmother, influenced her greatly. Liddy admired her grandmother's positive attitude, selflessness, and strong faith.

Elizabeth's education began at Wiley and Boyston Schools in Salisbury and continued at Duke University and Harvard. She was an excellent student and was involved in many activities. She was a leader at an early age, and her classmates elected her president of the Third Grade Bird Club. She later started a Junior Book Club and named herself president. Liddy also wrote award-winning essays. For one, she received a trophy from the United Daughters of the Confederacy. In high school, she was involved in drama, the National Honor Society, and student government. Despite her campaign manager's attempts to compare her to Queen Elizabeth, Liddy lost an election for high-school class president.

In fall, 1954, Elizabeth decided to attend Duke University, where she majored in political science. In 1957, she was elected president of the Women's Student Government Association and was asked to join the White Duchy, an elite society that accepted only seven new members annually. Elizabeth graduated with honors from Duke in 1958 after being selected for membership in Phi Beta Kappa, a prestigious honor society for top students, and being named Leader of the Year.

After her graduation, Elizabeth rejected her brother's offer of a job in the family business. In fall, 1958, she began a job at the Harvard Law School library and enrolled in a master's degree program in education and government at Harvard in 1959.

In summer, 1960, Elizabeth worked in the office of B. Everett Jordan, a senator from North Carolina. While working for Jordan, she networked with women in government, including Maine's Senator Margaret Chase Smith. Smith urged Hanford to earn a law degree. Elizabeth participated in her first national political campaign in 1960. She was a greeter in a whistle-stop campaign for vice presidential nominee Lyndon Baines Johnson.

In fall, 1960, Elizabeth took Margaret Chase Smith's advice and began law school at Harvard, despite her mother's concern and discouragement from her brother. Their

initial resistance notwithstanding, Elizabeth's family eventually supported her decision. Besides grueling academic work, Elizabeth and the twenty-three other women
in the 1965 Harvard Law School class of 550 endured a hostile environment. Some
professors either refused to call on them or publicly embarrassed them.

Life's Work

After earning her law degree, Elizabeth Hanford moved to Washington, D.C.,
passed the bar exam for the District of Columbia in 1966, and obtained an entry
position in the Department of Health, Education, and Welfare. When that job ended,
she became a public defender, practicing law in Washington, D.C., from 1967 to 1968.

For the next six years, Elizabeth held several executive branch positions dealing
with consumer interests. Under the Lyndon Johnson administration, she became a
consumer advocate. When Richard M. Nixon became president, many Johnson
appointees resigned, but Elizabeth stayed. Her new boss, Virginia Knauer, a Nixon
appointee, became her mentor.

In the early 1970's, Elizabeth began to receive rewards. She was named Washington's Outstanding Young Woman of the Year in 1970, and she received the Arthur S.
Flemming Award for outstanding government service in 1972.

In 1972, Virginia Knauer urged Elizabeth to help her lobby Senator Robert Dole,
head of the Republican party, to include a consumerism plank in the party's platform.
Bob and Elizabeth were impressed with each other when they first met, but Bob
waited several months to call Elizabeth, reportedly concerned about their thirteen-
year age difference. The two had much in common and enjoyed being together.
Because of their demanding work schedules, theirs was often a telephone courtship.

Besides introducing Elizabeth to Bob, Knauer urged Nixon to nominate Elizabeth
to fill a Federal Trade Commission (FTC) vacancy. Nixon agreed, but the director of
the Senate committee that needed to confirm Elizabeth did not. Elizabeth asked the
director what she needed to do to earn his support. He told her to get endorsements
from consumer advocates, which she did.

Elizabeth was confirmed as a commissioner on December 3, 1973. At the FTC,
Elizabeth worked on many projects, some of which benefited women. The FTC
investigated misleading claims about nursing home care and vigorously enforced the
Equal Credit Opportunity Act, which was designed to help widowed or divorced
women get credit. In 1975, Elizabeth helped start Executive Women in Government,
a network intended to aid women's career advancement.

By fall, 1975, Bob and Elizabeth were serious about their relationship. They were
married on December 6, 1975. Because of their high-profile positions, they were
labeled a "power couple," a term that Elizabeth disliked.

In 1979, Elizabeth resigned from the FTC to help Bob campaign for the Republican
presidential nomination. Feminists criticized her for this, as they would in 1987, when
she left a cabinet post for the same reason. Elizabeth disagreed with assessments made
by women's groups that her decision was a letdown to her gender. She wanted to
campaign for Bob and believed she should be free to make that choice.

Elizabeth chaired Voters for Reagan-Bush in the 1980 presidential campaign. In 1981, Ronald Reagan appointed Elizabeth assistant to the president for public liaison, a position she held until 1983. A longtime Equal Rights amendment proponent, Elizabeth was serving in an administration that opposed that amendment. With limited success, Elizabeth tried to convince women's groups that the Reagan Admin-istration would attack discrimination by urging governors to ban it in the states.

In January, 1983, Reagan named Elizabeth Dole secretary of transportation; she was to become the seventh woman to occupy a cabinet position. She was sworn in on February 7, 1983, and from then until October, 1987, she was in charge of more than 100,000 employees and a $27 billion budget. Her vita boasts that the United States had the best safety record in its history while she headed the Department of Transpor-tation (DOT). She was not, however, without critics. Some said that she irritated auto makers but pleased consumers. The Center for Auto Safety, however, accused Eliza-beth of caving in to car makers.

Elizabeth's major accomplishments at the DOT involved safety. She spearheaded a movement to raise the drinking age to twenty-one, backed random drug testing in public transportation, and improved traffic and air safety. While Elizabeth was the head of the DOT, the agency passed a rule requiring airbags or automatic safety belts in 1990 model cars unless two-thirds of the country's population lived in states with strict seat-belt laws. To reduce the number of rear bumper collisions, another rule required a rear, eye-level brake light beginning with 1986 models. Regarding airline safety, Elizabeth implemented tougher airport security and inspection measures and hired more federal marshals. She was criticized, however, for not developing a plan to cope with the aftermath of an earlier air traffic controllers' strike.

After the longest tenure of any secretary of transportation, Elizabeth resigned in 1987 to help Bob campaign for president. His unsuccessful bid did not diminish people's affection for Elizabeth Dole. In 1988, she received the Distinguished Alumni Award from Duke University and an award from the National Committee Against Drunk Driving. A Gallup poll named her one of the world's ten most admired women.

Newly elected President George Bush asked Elizabeth Dole to become secretary of labor. She accepted and was sworn in on January 30, 1989. This time she was in charge of 18,500 employees and a $31 billion budget.

At the Department of Labor, Dole's priorities included upgrading workforce quality, improving workplace safety, fighting discrimination, encouraging labor-management cooperation, and urging adoption of voluntary policies to help employ-ees balance work and family roles. Regarding the first priority, Dole's initiatives encouraged business to help at-risk youth develop basic skills. The Secretary's Committee on Achieving Necessary Skills was established to allow business, educa-tors, and labor to define human skills needed to make that transition successfully.

Regarding safety, the Occupational Safety and Health Administration, a Labor subagency, increased enforcement and raised penalties during Dole's tenure. More than two hundred additional inspectors were hired, and more construction industry inspections were scheduled.

Dole started a glass-ceiling initiative to move qualified women and minorities beyond mid-management levels. This program ensured that companies provided training and development opportunities and appropriate rewards to help women and minorities advance.

The settlement of the Pittston Coal Strike was gratifying to Elizabeth Dole. She appointed a skilled mediator to resolve the dispute and was pictured joining hands with labor and management representatives on New Year's Eve, 1989, when they agreed to end the strike.

Favoring voluntary policies that would help all employees excel on the job, Dole established an information clearing house on programs to break employment barriers. She wanted to convince companies that voluntary programs to assist workers with family responsibilities made good business sense.

In early 1990, the American Red Cross asked Dole to consider becoming its president, but she was not quite ready to leave her cabinet post. Later that year, she accepted the Red Cross position. The first Bush cabinet member to depart, she stepped down on November 23, 1990.

In 1990, Elizabeth Dole received more honors, this time from the labor movement. She received the Labor Management Award from the Work in America Institute and the Construction Person of the Year Award.

At the Red Cross, Dole revamped the blood collection system to increase the safety of the nation's blood supply. She modernized disaster relief services, improved financial accountability, and initiated a cultural-diversity program. To symbolize unity with the volunteers, Dole accepted no salary during her first year as Red Cross president. Her staff in that organization numbered nearly 30,000, and there were more than 1,500,000 volunteers.

Summary

Elizabeth Dole was the lone woman in President George Bush's cabinet. During her career, she faced obstacles, as have many employed women, but she viewed them as challenges and overcame them. Elizabeth advanced because she could pass through the narrow band of success as defined in 1987 by Morrison and Van Velsor in *Breaking the Glass Ceiling*. To fit through the narrow band, a woman must not be viewed as too stereotypically masculine or feminine. She must be firm and demanding but nonthreatening and able to put others at ease. Elizabeth Dole fits that description. Although women should not have to pass through a narrow band to succeed, in Dole's generation, it was a reality. Throughout her career, Elizabeth worked on issues that would benefit people. This was true from a 1960's assignment to organize a conference for the deaf to a 1990's task to oversee disaster relief. Related to her concern for people, improving safety, whether of consumer products, workplace conditions, or transportation systems, has been another of Dole's causes.

Elizabeth Dole is a positive role model for women in government service. Her leadership style, which includes empowerment, consensus building, teamwork, and self-competition, is appealing. A reformed perfectionist, she has tried to balance her life, and she is not afraid to support others' advancement.

She has worked for five presidents during the course of nearly twenty-five years, and her life has been one of service to her country and its people. Although she has denied interest in the presidency, Elizabeth Dole may yet serve her country in new and different ways.

Bibliography

Bartley, Diane. "Labor's Elizabeth Dole." *The Saturday Evening Post* 262 (May/June, 1990): 44-49. Briefly, Bartley reviews Dole's accomplishments as secretary of labor and gives information about her childhood and personal life.

Dole, Robert, and Elizabeth Dole. *The Doles: Unlimited Partners*. New York: Simon & Schuster, 1988. Elizabeth and Bob Dole alternated in the writing of this work. It describes Elizabeth's early background and work experiences through her stint as secretary of transportation.

Miller, James A. "Portrait: Elizabeth Dole." *Life* 6 (July, 1983): 21, 24, 28. A sketchy review of Dole's leadership style, childhood, and dual-career relationship, this article touches on her role as secretary of transportation.

Mulford, Carolyn. *Elizabeth Dole: Public Servant*. Hillside, N.J.: Enslow, 1992. This book examines Dole's life thoroughly from childhood through her position at the American Red Cross.

Weiss, Philip. "Charming Her Way to the White House." *The Washington Monthly* 19 (September, 1987): 29-43. Weiss attacks Dole's performance as secretary of trans-portation. He highlights her early life and role in a dual-career couple.

Margaret Foegen Karsten

HELEN GAHAGAN DOUGLAS

Born: November 25, 1900; Boonton, New Jersey
Died: June 28, 1980; New York, New York
Areas of Achievement: Theater and government and politics
Contribution: As a congresswoman from California and in her private life, Douglas was an outspoken advocate of civil liberties and opportunities for oppressed minorities.

Early Life

Mary Helen Gahagan (she was always called Helen) was born on November 25, 1900, in Boonton, New Jersey, where her parents briefly rented a home so that her father could supervise a construction project nearby. Her twin brothers had been born two years earlier, and a sister and brother would follow in 1902 and 1910. She grew up in Brooklyn, New York, in a comfortable household with strong-willed parents intent on imbuing their children with strong moral and educational ideals. Her father, Walter, was an engineer who founded his own construction company in 1899 and prospered from the outset. A graduate of the Massachusetts Institute of Technology, he read insatiably and filled the Gahagan house with shelves of books. Helen's mother Lillian had been reared on the Wisconsin frontier. She was a country schoolteacher before her marriage, and her beauty, optimistic outlook, and exquisite singing voice were inherited by her elder daughter.

Helen had the benefit of the accoutrements of affluence during her childhood. These included a summer home in Vermont, a family trip to Europe when she was twelve, accompanying her mother to the opera (which, ironically, Helen disliked intensely), and private schools. The first of these was the Berkeley School for Girls, which was located only a block from the Gahagans' home. It was at this school that her interest in acting blossomed under the direction of her drama teacher, Elizabeth Grimball. Her grades were mediocre in subjects unrelated to performing, but she studied intensely for a college preparatory school. She matriculated at Barnard College in New York in order to be close to the stage and her drama instructor.

She would spend only two years at Barnard College before her debut into the Broadway theatrical world. Her impressive performances in school productions and an Off-Broadway play led director William A. Brady, Jr., to cast her as the ingenue in *Dreams for Sale* in 1922. Over the extremely strong protests of her father, who insisted that she complete her education, Helen accepted.

She quickly became a star. Her generally favorable reviews led to contracts with Brady and other well-known producers and assured her a niche in the roster of leading ladies of the 1920's stage. Practically every new theatrical season brought a new role, and she toured the country in roles she established in New York. She was the subject of much press coverage, not only for her acting talent but also for her great beauty.

Gahagan's ambition to perform ultimately led in another direction. During the run of a New York play in 1926, she began to take vocal lessons from a Russian émigré,

Madame Sophia Cehanovska. For the next several years, Gahagan would devote time, money, and trips to Europe to the pursuit of performing operatic roles with leading companies, a pursuit that was never as successful as her Broadway acting career.

Helen's performance in the 1930-1931 Broadway production of *Tonight or Never* was important for a number of reasons. The play was her only collaboration with the legendary David Belasco (he would die during its run), her father died during the same run, and she married her costar, Melvyn Douglas. By the end of 1931, she had moved from New York to the West Coast, where Melvyn began his career in motion pictures. Except for some brief performing engagements, Helen would not live in New York again until after her immersion in and forced withdrawal from another career of a very different type.

Life's Work

The first task for Helen Gahagan Douglas and her husband, upon reaching California, was to establish a new way of life in new surroundings. Melvyn had a studio contract with Metro-Goldwyn-Mayer (MGM), and Helen was busy with singing lessons and performances on the West Coast stage in both acting and singing roles. Although Helen would have the opportunity to read dozens of film scripts in search of suitable parts, her efforts to find strong roles or to receive reasonable financial offers were stymied. She appeared in only one picture, *She* (1935), a film later considered a "classic" for its overblown production and acting rather than for any positive contributions to the cinematic arts.

The hectic pace of life on the dramatic and sound stages for the couple soon led both to seek a respite. They accomplished this by traveling around the world in 1933. A few months after their return home, Helen gave birth to their first child, Peter. A daughter, Mary Helen, would follow five years later. Helen continued her theatrical performances and vocal training, and the family settled into a new home built on three acres in the hills above the Hollywood Bowl.

Two significant events contributed to Helen's involvement in political causes. The first involved her awakening to conditions in Germany and Austria during a concert tour there in 1937. She ultimately canceled several engagements on the tour after encountering anti-Semitism directed against the pianist who was traveling with her. Although she was not Jewish, her husband Melvyn was, so she regarded these sentiments as a personal affront.

Back in California, she became involved in Democratic Party campaign activities in 1938. Her husband had joined in the statewide gubernatorial and congressional campaign efforts; at first, she merely accompanied him to meetings. After becoming acquainted with social and economic conditions firsthand, however, she began to take the lead in organizing efforts to assist migrant workers. As a result of their activities on behalf of California Democrats, the Douglases were invited to visit President and Mrs. Franklin D. Roosevelt in the White House in 1939. Helen was greatly impressed by Eleanor Roosevelt, who became something of a political mentor and role model for the actress.

Helen's intelligence and capacity for hard work, as well as her friendship with Eleanor Roosevelt, led to her rapid rise within the leadership of the Democratic Party in California. In 1940, she was selected as the state's Democratic National Committeewoman. In that capacity, she attended the Party's national convention, where she was an enthusiastic supporter of a third term for FDR. Following Roosevelt's reelection, she was appointed vice-chair and head of the Women's Division for the California state Democratic party. Her efforts for Southern California Democratic candidates in 1942 contributed to party successes there in spite of Republican victories throughout the rest of the state.

Helen's high visibility in state Democratic politics made her a natural choice for the congressional race in the Fourteenth District in 1944, when popular Congressman Thomas Ford announced his retirement. Although she did not live in the largely working-class district in central Los Angeles, she campaigned thoroughly there and won the nomination in the May primary. Prior to the general election, she delivered a principal address before the Democratic convention in Chicago, in which she reviewed the accomplishments of the Roosevelt administrations. In the fall campaign, she followed the lead of Democrats nationally in identifying her programs with FDR and the New Deal, a strategy that produced a narrow victory. She became only the third woman elected to Congress from California and the first who did not take over her seat from a deceased husband.

In Washington, D.C., Helen adhered to the same formula that had produced political success in California. She maintained a grueling schedule, largely eschewed social events, and applied her keen mind to the process of absorbing all available information on issues pending before Congress. Her legislative interests lay in two areas, one involving foreign affairs, the other domestic. She secured an appointment to the House Foreign Affairs Committee, which is usually an unimportant body, since only the Senate ratifies treaties. Nevertheless, with negotiations under way for the postwar international organization that became the United Nations, Helen believed that the House as well as the Senate would play an integral role in the increased nationwide commitment to internationalism. Membership on the Foreign Affairs Committee would provide a forum for activities designed to ensure world peace. In domestic affairs, Douglas' natural inclinations were bolstered by the makeup of her congressional district. She lent support throughout the postwar period to legislation benefiting organized labor and African Americans and other minorities.

Through her diligence, her charismatic appeal, and her high visibility in the press, Douglas became a leading figure in California politics. Following her second reelection, in 1948, her congressional seat seemed to be secure; she and her supporters now looked to a greater challenge—the seat in the U.S. Senate held by the conservative Democrat Sheridan Downey. Following the incumbent's withdrawal from the 1950 primary, Helen won the nomination in spite of vicious attacks on her internationalist position as being procommunist.

The smear tactics begun in the Democratic primary intensified in the general election, when Helen faced Congressman Richard Nixon. In an election that has since become famous for the infamous dirty tricks of the Nixon campaign, Helen Gahagan Douglas was removed from public office. In her autobiography some thirty years later, she wryly remarked: "There's not much to say about the 1950 campaign except that a man ran for the Senate who wanted to get there, and didn't care how."

Helen's life after politics was spent partly in the public eye, since she continued to speak in favor of causes such as world peace. She campaigned for Democratic presidential candidates Lyndon Johnson in 1964 and George McGovern in 1972. During the last three decades before her death from cancer in 1980, she was certainly not forgotten, but neither was she occupying her accustomed place in the limelight.

Summary

In a number of respects, Helen Gahagan Douglas had an enviable life and a great deal of good fortune. She became a famous actress almost overnight, not only because of her talent but also because of her great beauty. Capitalizing on her acting fame, she became a force in politics through intelligence and hard work. Although her fame boosted her political career at the outset, it eventually became a liability to Douglas as a politician seriously intent on pursuing an important agenda. She constantly downplayed her glamour in order to be taken seriously.

She was able, in the end, to use the press attention focused on her in order to advance an international and domestic social program that was liberal, enlightened, and forward-looking. She did not hesitate to challenge bigotry, isolationism, and red-baiting. Although her public service was cut short because of a malicious campaign against her in 1950, she stood as a symbol for other intelligent, forthright, public-spirited women and men to emulate.

Bibliography
Douglas, Helen Gahagan. *The Eleanor Roosevelt We Remember*. New York: Hill & Wang, 1963. In her autobiography, Helen Douglas clearly indicated that Eleanor Roosevelt was a major influence in her decision to become a political activist. This book, a tribute to Roosevelt, contains photographs from a variety of sources and an admiring text by Douglas.
——————. *A Full Life*. Garden City, N.Y.: Doubleday, 1982. An engaging autobiography in which the author thoroughly discusses her family life, stage experiences, and involvement in political affairs.
Douglas, Melvyn, and Tom Arthur. *See You at the Movies: The Autobiography of Melvyn Douglas*. Lanham, Md.: University Press of America, 1986. A posthumously published autobiography that focuses on the author's acting career and includes occasional anecdotes about his wife's careers and their marriage.
Morris, Roger. *Richard Milhous Nixon: The Rise of an American Politician*. New York: Henry Holt, 1990. Includes the fullest description and analysis of the 1950 Senate campaign in California; it is especially valuable for establishing the context of California politics. Morris covers the Douglas and Nixon primary campaigns as well as the general election.

Scobie, Ingrid Winther. *Center Stage: Helen Gahagan Douglas, a Life*. New York: Oxford University Press, 1992. A thorough biography by a professional historian who conducted research in manuscript and oral history collections around the country. Scobie also met with and interviewed Helen and Melvyn Douglas.

Richard G. Frederick

ISADORA DUNCAN

Born: May 26, 1877; San Francisco, California
Died: September 14, 1927; Nice, France
Area of Achievement: Dance
Contribution: Reacting against the strictures of classical ballet and the artificialities of other forms of dance, Duncan was a major innovator and one of the founders of modern dance. In her personal life, Duncan also endeavored to extend women's freedoms.

Early Life

Born in 1877 in San Francisco, Angela Isadora Duncan was the youngest of four children. Her father, Joseph Charles Duncan, was fifty years old and a divorced father of four other children when he married Mary Isadora (Dora) Gray in 1869. She was twenty. Joseph Duncan was a charming businessman who had achieved considerable financial success. In early October of 1877—at the time of baby Angela Isadora's christening—an illegal banking scheme in which Duncan was involved failed. Joseph Duncan disappeared, leaving bank records in chaos. Finally captured in February of 1878, he was tried four times, the first three resulting in hung juries. At his fourth trial he was acquitted. In the aftermath, Dora divorced Joseph Duncan, who remarried and moved to Los Angeles.

Dora stayed in the Oakland area, supporting the children by eking out a living as a music teacher. In her autobiography, *My Life* (1927), Isadora Duncan tells of a "good-looking," well-dressed man who appeared at the door and turned out to be her father. Subsequently, Joseph Duncan did provide a home for his former wife and children, but Isadora's childhood was largely fatherless.

At an early age, Isadora Duncan revolted against ballet lessons and developed an expressive style of dancing that relied on spontaneity and freedom of movement. This was basically the same approach she was to use in her mature work, freely interpreting the music of the great composers. Duncan's first public performances, in Chicago and New York, were as a dancer in other people's shows. In 1897, she traveled to London with Augustin Daly's theater company, returning to New York later that year. Subsequently, she quit the Daly company, and she and her family set off for England, where she eventually began to achieve recognition. In the British Museum, she and her brother Raymond studied the art of ancient Greece, convincing themselves that Isadora's use of dance rhythms was based on a classical model.

Her career began to gather momentum when she was invited to perform at private receptions, thanks in part to the patronage of well-known actress Mrs. Patrick Campbell. Dancing barefoot in a tunic, Duncan charmed her audiences, and soon she was performing to great acclaim in theaters and concert halls all over Europe.

Life's Work

Isadora Duncan rose from humble beginnings to international celebrity by being an independent-minded American. Her success in Europe was counterpointed by her defiance of traditional female roles. Her fame as a dancer was perhaps equaled by her notoriety as a woman who defied conventional mores. Duncan wanted to use dance as a form of self-expression to create a new way of living. Because most of her students were women, Duncan's identification of dance with freedom exerted a profound effect on women's roles.

To grasp Isadora Duncan's revolutionary attitude, it should be remembered that the world into which she was born was extremely conservative about exposing the human body and about women's roles. In her clothing, both the tuniclike Greek *chitons* in which she danced and the classical Greek garb she and her brother Raymond affected as street wear, Duncan shocked and fascinated audiences.

Contemporary accounts of her dancing, usually written by male dance critics, often mention her "scanty" or "flimsy" costumes, her bare legs and feet, and her scandalous behavior. Spectators who came to her performances expecting to be scandalized, however, more often than not went away deeply moved by Duncan's powerfully expressive dancing. Duncan was openly celebrating the relationship between body and emotions in a way she also acted out in her personal life.

A notorious free spirit, Duncan bore children out of wedlock by three different fathers. In *My Life*, she says that in her romance with stage designer Edward Gordon Craig, she felt an increasing tension between her art and her lover. Tempted to submerge her dancing in the tumultuous romance with Craig, Duncan bore her first child by him—a daughter, Deirdre—and, during her pregnancy, briefly left the stage.

Later, she had a son, Patrick, by Paris Singer, heir to the Singer Sewing Machine fortune. The wealthy Singer funded some of Duncan's projects, and even after their relationship was over, he continued to provide her with financial support. While Duncan was involved with Craig, and later, with Singer, both men were married to other women by whom they already had children. This fact contributed to the scandalous air surrounding Duncan's behavior.

In 1905, Duncan made a controversial visit to Russia, where she danced to great acclaim and came to the attention of Sergei Diaghilev, a critic and impresario who was to bring about an increased interest in ballet all over Europe. Although Duncan's methods and those of traditional ballet were at odds, she exerted a powerful influence on the development of modern dance as an expressive medium. Between Isadora Duncan and the Russian ballet, a new enthusiasm for dance caught fire.

All her life, Duncan was convinced that teaching children to express themselves freely through dance would revolutionize society. She started dance schools in Germany, France, Russia, and the United States. Because Duncan's method centered on freedom rather than on rigid technical rules, it proved to be difficult to pass on, and none of these schools survived. Only the first school, in Grunewald, Germany, produced students who stayed with Duncan and continued her work in her name.

The essence of Duncan's style was spontaneity, not form. Her great desire was to express emotion through movement. The word "joy" appears all through her autobiography, but Duncan wanted to express the whole range of human feeling, much as the great composers had done. Although a joyous freedom is the essence of her style, she was also capable of expressing much more.

Unfortunately, midway into her adult life, she experienced a tragedy which her dancing only partly helped to alleviate. In 1913, the car in which her two children and their nurse were riding rolled into the Seine River. All three were drowned. The following year a third child, a son fathered by a man she knew only briefly, died shortly after birth. At the same time, changing public tastes and turmoil in Europe were causing a diminished interest in Duncan's art.

Turning to the children of others, Duncan tried to found a school in France, but the beginning of World War I brought the project to a halt. Duncan's tours in South America and Europe during the war drew as much attention to her flamboyant life as to her dancing. After World War I, in 1920, Duncan was invited to found a school in Moscow, a challenge she accepted. Revolutionary herself in thought and deed, Duncan found the idea of revolutionary Russia attractive.

Although all her life Duncan criticized marriage, in 1922 she married Sergei Aleksandrovich Esenin, a poet seventeen years her junior. One practical reason for the marriage was that it enabled Duncan to take Esenin with her on a tour of the United States. In the United States, however, fear of the effects of the Russian Revolution was at a peak. Duncan and Esenin were suspected of being Bolshevik agents, and the dance tour was dogged by controversy.

At her performance at Symphony Hall in Boston, Duncan tried to introduce Esenin, but she was heckled and abused by members of the audience. She retorted in kind, and the performance ended in chaos. In the angry aftermath, Duncan left the United States, vowing never to return. She never did.

After they had spent several stormy years together, Esenin, drinking heavily and mentally unstable, separated from Duncan and returned to the Soviet Union, where he committed suicide in 1925. The stage was set for the tragic end of Duncan's own controversial life.

Isadora Duncan's death is sadly reminiscent of the accident that killed her children. Just as they had not traveled far from home before drowning in the Seine, Duncan herself had traveled only a few yards when her extravagant, trailing shawl became tangled around the axle of a sports car driven by a handsome young Italian with whom Duncan was flirting. The other end was around her neck. She was killed instantly.

Summary

In her attitudes toward women's roles and toward marriage, Isadora Duncan was deliberately iconoclastic. In her notions about self-expression and dance, she revolutionized attitudes toward the movements of the human body. Duncan was making something new in dance, expressing her inner life through dance as no one had done before.

Although Duncan failed to sustain the schools she hoped would fulfill her revolutionary vision, she did change the face of dance in several major ways. She is unquestionably one of the founders of contemporary dance. Moreover, her influence on classical ballet resulted in a loosening of form and an addition of lyricism to the work of more traditional choreographers.

Duncan did not simply dance to music; she integrated music and dance into a coherent whole. She battled criticism to make it acceptable to dance to music that was not written for dance, succeeding so well that pieces that were unthinkable as dance vehicles a hundred years ago are now the staples of ballet and modern dance practice rooms.

Six of Duncan's Grunewald students, sometimes known as the "Isadorables" or the Duncan Dancers, carried on her style. As time passed, however, interest in following Duncan's methods gradually faded. In the early 1990's, direct disciples of the Isadorables were making an effort to keep Duncan's style alive. What Duncan taught, however, was not slavish imitation of her style and techniques but an emotional expressiveness that freed the individual.

Bibliography

Blair, Fredrika. *Isadora*. New York: McGraw-Hill, 1986. The most complete biography, this work is accurate, readable, and well documented. Corrects the date of Duncan's birth based on Duncan's baptismal record. Of all the many books on Duncan, this is the best place to start. Contains a useful bibliography of relevant sources up to 1986.

Duncan, Isadora. *Isadora Speaks*. Edited by Franklin Rosemont. San Francisco: City Lights Books, 1981. Gathers together miscellaneous interviews, statements to the press, speeches, and other items hitherto buried in old periodicals. Includes Duncan's public statements about Esenin. Supplements *My Life* and *The Art of the Dance*.

_____ . *My Life*. New York: Liveright, 1955. Duncan's autobiography, finished just before her death. Not always reliable regarding facts, but emotionally revealing and entertaining.

_____ . *"Your Isadora": The Love Story of Isadora Duncan and Gordon Craig*. Edited by Francis Steegmuller. New York: Random House, 1974. Tells the story of Duncan's relationship with Edward Gordon Craig by assembling letters and commentary. Brings out the difficulties in both their personalities and reveals the tension between artistic goals and private passion.

Loewenthal, Lillian. *The Search for Isadora: The Legend and Legacy of Isadora Duncan*. Pennington, N.J.: Princeton Book, 1993. This volume re-creates Duncan's performances and documents her legacy. Follows the subsequent careers of the "Isadorables." Contains a helpful chronology.

Macdougall, Allan Ross. *Isadora: A Revolutionary in Art and Love*. New York: Thomas Nelson, 1960. Until Blair's book was published, this was the most complete biography of Duncan. Macdougall was Duncan's secretary and friend. Still worthwhile and readable, this work contains many minor factual inaccuracies and needs to be supplemented with more up-to-date information.

McVay, Gordon. *Isadora and Esenin*. Ann Arbor, Mich.: Ardis, 1980. A well-researched account of Duncan's relationship with Esenin, handled sympathetically. Blair directs readers to this book as a source of detailed information about Duncan's years with Esenin.

Seroff, Victor. *The Real Isadora*. New York: Dial, 1971. Seroff was a young Russian pianist who became Duncan's friend and lover in Paris after Esenin's death. Duncan confided in Seroff concerning her relationship with Esenin and revealed her emotional state near the end of her life.

Terry, Walter. *Isadora Duncan: Her Life, Her Art, Her Legacy*. New York: Dodd, Mead, 1964. A readable summary of the artistic impact of Duncan's dance theory and technique.

Thomas Lisk

KATHERINE DUNHAM

Born: June 22, 1909; Chicago, Illinois

Areas of Achievement: Dance, anthropology, and education

Contribution: Dunham, an ethnologist-choreographer-dancer, served as a catalyst and a creative force in theater and dance, translating cultural heritage through theater pieces. Her theories and techniques of movement are used by choreographers and dancers throughout the world.

Early Life

Katherine Dunham was born on June 22, 1909, to Fannie June Buckner, an assistant school principal of American Indian, French-Canadian, and African lineage, and Albert Millard Dunham, a man of Malagasy and Madagascar descent who was twenty years younger than his wife. The Dunhams lived in Glen Ellyn, Illinois, a white middle-class suburb. Katherine's mother, who had five children from a previous marriage, became ill with cancer soon after Katherine's birth and died when Katherine was four years old. Since the property holdings went to Fannie's adult children after her death, Albert Dunham was left with few financial resources with which to cope with the responsibility of rearing Katherine and her ten-year-old brother, Albert, Jr. Her father sold his tailoring business and became a traveling salesman, leaving the children in the care of his relatives. First, the children lived with his sister Lulu, a beautician; later, they stayed with an aunt and uncle who directed musical shows and brought Katherine into direct contact with show business people.

When her father remarried, Katherine and her family moved to Joliet, Illinois, where they operated a dry cleaning business. Her stepmother, Annette Poindexter, supported Katherine's love of dance and performing by sewing her costumes and by sending her to piano and ballet classes. As a young girl, Katherine belonged to the Terpsichorean Club, a dance club that introduced her to modern dance techniques developed by Jacques Dalcroze (eurythmics) and Rudolph von Laban (Labanotation). She applied her learning when she organized a cabaret performance night in a rented Elks Hall to raise money for the church. Katherine prepared the program, organized the singers, selected the music, choreographed the dances, and performed, activities that mirrored her adult life.

Because of continual conflicts with her father, Katherine and her stepmother left home when Albert, Jr., went off to college at the University of Chicago during the Great Depression. With her brother's help, Katherine found employment at a library, opened a dance studio that doubled as her apartment, and attended the University of Chicago. She studied modern dance and ballet, which led her to meet Ruth Page, the choreographer; Mark Turbyfill, the ballet instructor; and Nicholas Matsukas, cofounder of the Cube Theater, an interracial production company that included composer W. C. Handy, poet Langston Hughes, dramatist Ruth Attaway, sociologist St. Clair Drake, and performer Charles White. Dunham and Turbyfill formed a black dance group that debuted at the Beaux Arts Ball in 1931. In 1934, Dunham and her modern dance teacher, Ludmila Speranzeva, formed a company of seven women dancers for performances at the Chicago World's Fair. Katherine's performance with the Chicago Civic Opera increased the number of students in her dance company and led to an interview with the Rosenwald Foundation, since a prominent member of the audience was Mrs. Alfred Rosenwald Stern, who had been favorably impressed with Katherine's abilities on stage.

Life's Work

To prepare for a future that did not depend upon her deteriorating knees, Katherine Dunham turned her attention to anthropology. Earning her bachelor's, master's, and doctoral degrees from the University of Chicago, Dunham was influenced by Robert Redfield, an anthropologist of folk and peasant societies; Charles Johnson, a noted sociologist and member of the Rosenwald Foundation; and Erich Fromm, a psychoanalyst. Her thesis combined her love of dance with anthropology in a study of nonverbal communication through dance to ascertain the cultural traits and patterns of various peoples. With the help of her academic mentors, Dunham won a travel fellowship from the Julius Rosenwald Foundation to do anthropological field work in the West Indies. To prepare for her field work, she studied at Northwestern University with noted anthropologist Melville Herskovits, who taught her about West Indian customs, stratification, and social institutions; how to keep proper research records; and how to survive in a tropical climate. He also made contacts for her in the islands and within the social and political circles to which Dunham could turn in the future for financial and creative support.

In 1935, she did research among the Maroons of Accompong, Jamaica, which culminated in her book *Journey to Accompong* (1946). With the help of a Guggenheim Award in 1937, she investigated dance in Trinidad, Martinique, Jamaica, and Haiti. She continued her research in the field of dance and choreography as cultural and historical dimensions of African existence. Dunham believed that African and African diasporic cultures could be understood through motion, that dance was one of the African "survivalisms" of which scholars such as Herskovits spoke. Through her exposure of dances reflecting the African American experience, she made a major contribution to the theories of modern dance.

She returned to Chicago in 1938 and worked for the Work Progress Administration (WPA), developing the ballet *L'Ag'Ya*, based on a Martinique fighting dance that introduced a new body movement called the *Biguine*. In 1939, as the Federal Works Theater Project closed, she choreographed *Pins and Needles*, sponsored by the International Ladies Garment Workers Union, and helped organize her professional dance company to perform Brazilian songs and dances in the first color short by Warner Bros., *Carnival of Rhythm*. Dunham shared choreography responsibilities with George Balanchine for the musical *Cabin in the Sky*, on Broadway and on tour in 1940.

During these years with the Federal Theater Project, she worked with John Pratt, a white stage and costume designer. The interracial relationship upset coworkers and family, but she married John Pratt on July 10, 1941, in a private ceremony in Mexico. Later, they adopted an infant, Marie Christine, in Paris in 1948. During World War II, she made a film with comedian Eddie "Rochester" Anderson, *Star Spangled Rhythm* (1942). When her husband was stationed in Virginia, Dunham choreographed *Stormy Weather* (1943) and founded the Dunham School of Arts and Research in New York. The Dunham School of Cultural Arts combined ballet with dances from Caribbean, African, Spanish, Asian, and Central European sources and provided lectures on form and space, choreography, anthropology, languages, and acting from such teachers as Lee Strasberg, Jose Ferrer, Margaret Mead, and Irene Hawthorne. This technique for training dancers, the "Dunham technique," gained international acclaim, led to the development of schools throughout the world, and influenced dancers and actors such as Eartha Kitt, Marlon Brando, James Dean, Chita Rivera, Arthur Mitchell, Peter Gennaro, Rudi Genreich, and other famous performers, who were at one time members of Dunham's dance company. Eventually, her troupe became self-supporting through tours in Canada, Europe, Asia, and South America, and it became the first large troupe to appear in Las Vegas, where discrimination was a major problem for all traveling black entertainers. Their last performance took place in 1965 at the Apollo Theater in New York City.

Dunham fought racial discrimination throughout her life both in the United States and abroad. From 1939 to 1967, she toured the world visiting fifty-seven countries and learned about racial discrimination abroad. In her travels to Brazil, a country supposedly lacking color bars, she was refused accommodation at the Grande Hotel because of her color. Mediation and threats of lawsuits generally resolved the individual cases. During World War II, in Lexington, Kentucky, she canceled her appearances when management refused to change segregated seating practices. She had housing problems when she produced musical revues for clubs in the Hollywood strip, and she faced strikes by the lighting and stage crews of a St. Louis theater when she was allowed to live in a midtown white hotel during the show's tenure. On the eve of the Supreme Court's *Brown v. Topeka* decision, Cincinnati unions threatened the hotel where Dunham stayed in 1954 while her company appeared across the river in Covington, Kentucky. Her fight this time overturned the segregation law. Because of its theme of American lynchings, Dunham had to produce the ballet *Southland* outside the United States, in South America and in Paris.

During the 1940's and 1950's, Dunham appeared in Hollywood clubs; produced the musical revues *Tropics, Le Jazz "Hot,"* and *Bal Negre*; choreographed the musical *Windy City*; appeared in the film *Casbah*; and still managed to write. Her first book, *Journey to Accompong* (1946), was hailed as a beautiful anthropological account. While in Japan in 1958, she wrote an account of her early life, *Touch of Innocence* (1959).

The 1960's brought Dunham both personal and professional gratification. She returned to Broadway as a performer and choreographer in *Bamboche*, and she choreographed the film *Green Mansions* (1958) for director Mel Ferrer. She also developed *Ode to Taylor Jones*, to honor a black activist of the Civil Rights movement. In 1963, Katherine Dunham became the technical and cultural adviser to the president of Senegal, training the members of the Senegal National Ballet.

The 1960's also brought Dunham's influence to the campuses (Carbondale, Alton, Edwardsville, and East St. Louis) of Southern Illinois University (SIU). Her brother-in-law, Davis Pratt, a professor of design at the Carbondale campus, helped bring her in as the artist in residence of SIU's Fine Arts Department before her husband died in 1968. She established the Performing Arts Training Center (PATC) at the "mother campus" at Edwardsville, and she directs the Katherine Dunham Center for Performing Arts from the two-story Dunham home near the East St. Louis campus. Through integrated educational experiences in the arts, she worked with that city's young black militants in attempts to decrease alienation and violence and promote cultural pride and understanding, a process she called "socialization through the arts." Her interest extended to the elderly through Senior Citizens for the Performing Arts, a program enabling seniors to attend cultural events.

Dunham's efforts to meet the needs of the East St. Louis community will continue after her death, since her archives and costumes are housed in the Katherine Dunham Museum in East St. Louis. Videotapes of her master classes show Dunham reconstructing her dances and analyzing their meaning.

The decade also brought her many honors. In 1968, she received the Professional Achievement Award from The University of Chicago Alumni Association. In 1972, she choreographed *Aida* for the Metropolitan Opera Company. In 1974, she was inducted into the Black Filmmakers Hall of Fame in Oakland, California, and received a proclamation from the mayor of Detroit, Coleman Young. In 1979, she received the Albert Schweitzer Music Award at Carnegie Hall. In 1983, Dunham received the Kennedy Center Honors Award. She received the Scripps American Dance Festival Award in 1986. Dunham is a member of the American Guild of Musical Artists, the American Guild of Variety Artists, the American Federation of Radio Artists, Actors' Equity, the Negro Actors' Guild, the Women's Honorary Scientific Fraternity at the University of Chicago, and the Royal Society of Anthropologists in London.

Dunham has been honored by various international leaders. She keeps an altar to Yemanja in her home and practices vaudun, demonstrating the influence of Haiti on her life. She received the medal of the Chevalier of the Legion of Honor from Haitian President Dumarsais Estimé in 1948. In 1961, she became a Commander of the Legion of Honor of Haiti. In 1972, she received a Ribbon and Iron Cross and was named High Commander by Haitian President "Papa Doc" Duvalier. She received recognition at the Festival of Arts in Dakar in 1966 for her service to the president of Senegal, Leopold Senghor. In February of 1992, she conducted a forty-seven-day fast to show her support for changing U.S. policies toward refugees from Haiti.

Summary

Katherine Dunham's primary influence has been her research into and subsequent use of African-based rhythms and dance in her choreographed works: *Tropics* (1937), *Haitian Suite* (1937), *Island Songs* (1938), *Plantation Dances* (1940), *Bal Negre* (1948), *Afrique* (1949), *Spirituals* (1951), *Jazz Finale* (1955), and *Diamond Thief* (1962). Her analysis of dance and her role in understanding the African influence can be found in her scholarly and autobiographical works: *Journey to Accompong* (1946), *The Dances of Haiti* (1947), *A Touch of Innocence* (1959), *Island Possessed* (1969), and *Kasamance* (1974). The Dunham technique of "dance isolation" and the black dance style of movement has influenced students throughout the world.

Bibliography
Akinyemi, Omonike. "Dunham Speaks from the Heart." *Dance Magazine* 67 (January, 1993): 22-24. One of the best interviews with the dance legend, this piece includes Dunham's discussion of her life's work and her hopes for the future—especially her interest in the welfare of the Haitian people.
Aschenbrenner, Joyce. *Katherine Dunham: Reflections on the Social and Political Contexts of Afro-American Dance*. New York: CORD, 1981. Aschenbrenner stresses Dunham's influence on African American dance in its cultural and historical contexts with a special section that depicts and explains the Dunham technique. Photographs of performers and performances enhance the text. Her extensive bibliography includes works by and about Dunham and the social science fields in which Dunham worked.
Beckford, Ruth. *Katherine Dunham: A Biography*. New York: Marcel Dekker, 1979. Beckford, a colleague and former Dunham dancer, wrote this biography at Dunham's request to ensure Dunham's place in dance history. Written from the perspective of a trained dancer evaluating the importance of her mentor, the biography gives a personal look at Dunham's life, interests, and achievements. Many photographs from Dunham's personal collection enhance the narrative.
Biemiller, Ruth. *Dance: The Story of Katherine Dunham*. Garden City, N.Y.: Doubleday, 1969. Biemiller focuses mainly on Dunham's early personal life rather than her historical significance in this book for young readers.
Buckle, Richard. *Katherine Dunham: Her Dancers, Singers, Musicians*. London: Ballet, 1949. This is an assessment of Dunham's influences as a dance educator and mentor to dancers and performers throughout the years.
Clark, VeVe A., and Margaret B. Wilkerson, eds. *Kaiso! Katherine Dunham: An Anthology of Writings*. Berkeley: University of California Institute for the Study of Social Change, 1978. This collection of essays analyzes specific aspects of Dunham's career from the perspectives of different writers who have known or studied Dunham.
Harnan, Terry. *African Rhythm—American Dance: A Biography of Katherine Dunham*. New York: Alfred A. Knopf, 1974. This biography examines Dunham's linking of African dance and African cultural history in the Americas.
Lanker, Brian. *I Dream a World: Portraits of Black Women Who Changed America*. Edited by Barbara Summers. New York: Stewart, Tabori, & Chang, 1989. These

photographic essays include an examination of Dunham's philosophy about the African cultural connections in motion.

Dorothy C. Salem

ARIEL DURANT

Born: May 10, 1898; Proskurov, Russia
Died: October 25, 1981; Los Angeles, California
Areas of Achievement: Historiography and literature
Contribution: With her husband, Ariel Durant was the author of one of the twentieth century's most ambitious works on the history of civilization.

Early Life

Ariel Durant was born to a Jewish family in Proskurov, Russia, on May 10, 1898. She was named Chaya, Ida in English. Years later she became known as Ariel, given that name by Will Durant because she reminded him of Ariel in William Shakespeare's *The Tempest.* Her mother, Ethel Appel Kaufman, described by Ariel as proud and passionate, was the daughter of a rabbinical scholar. Joseph Kaufman, her father, was a less dynamic figure, a salesman in a clothing store. In 1900, he emigrated to the United States to improve his fortune. The family followed him there in 1901.

Joseph had not prospered in New York, resorting to selling newspapers. Soon pregnant with her seventh child, Ethel became estranged from her husband. Because of family hardship, including frequent moves from one East Side apartment to another and lack of attention from parents who both worked long hours, Ariel found little in the way of intellectual support for herself or her siblings. Although Ariel's education in the public schools was haphazard because of the family's many moves, this deficit was compensated somewhat by her experiences on the streets of New York, which provided a unique cosmopolitan education. In 1907, the tenuous security of Ariel's family life was disturbed. Dissatisfied with her domestic lot and inspired by various radical socialist and anarchist ideas popular among the immigrant community, Ariel's mother moved out, leaving the children's lives even less focused.

In 1912, at the age of fourteen, Ariel enrolled in the Ferrer Modern School, named after a Spanish radical. Her teacher was Will Durant. Durant, from a New England background, was born in 1885. Educated in Catholic schools, he had briefly studied to become a priest in order to please his mother, but was drawn to socialism and the secular world instead. Durant had been at the Ferrer school for two years when Ariel arrived.

She thought him somewhat ridiculous, being short and shy. Nevertheless, a bond quickly developed between the fourteen-year-old Ariel and the twenty-eight-year-old teacher. Passion and love quickly followed, and they were married on October 31, 1913, after Ariel rollerskated to the New York City Hall for their civil ceremony.

Life's Work

Ariel Kaufman had a thirst for knowledge before she met Will Durant; after their marriage, he continued to serve as her intellectual guide. When they married he was a graduate student in philosophy at Columbia University. He also wrote and spoke on radical social and political issues. In a short time, Will Durant developed a national reputation as a public speaker, traveling widely and frequently throughout the United States—a habit he continued for many decades. During the early years of their marriage, the couple lived in New York City, where Ariel was caught up in the dynamism of Greenwich Village. Max Eastman, founder and editor of *The Masses*, was a close friend, and Ariel posed nude for the artist Man Ray. Journalists, writers, artists, actors, and poets were part of their daily lives. The Durants' only child, Ethel, was born in 1919.

In 1922, Will Durant began writing a series of short studies of various philosophers, which were published in booklet form. Eventually these were collected as *The Story of Philosophy* in 1926. Surprisingly, it became a best-seller and provided the Durants with much of their income for many years. Even before that work was published, Ariel's prolific husband was writing and projecting numerous other works.

Although devoted to her husband, Ariel was restless being only the wife of a famous writer. Feeling neglected by her husband's full schedule, in 1926 she joined in establishing the Gypsy Tavern in Greenwich Village, a meeting place for artists, dancers, singers, and writers. Because the Gypsy Tavern served as an important intellectual and artistic outlet for Ariel, it caused friction and jealousy between husband and wife. In a letter written to her husband but never sent, she plaintively asked, "When will we be equals?"

Ariel was never able to establish an identity separate from Will. Still, she was more than simply a wife and mother. In 1927, she took part in a debate on the topic "The Modern Woman" with Fannie Hurst and others. As the only married woman on the panel, Ariel was prevailed upon to defend the occupation of the housewife, this in spite of her friendship with the radical Emma Goldman. Ariel had long been an inveterate reader and, often parted from Will, she frequently wrote to him about her latest perusings. The seeds were being planted for the future literary collaboration that would make her almost as famous as her husband.

As early as 1917 Will Durant had begun to consider the writing of a history of civilization. Objecting to the prevailing monographic technique that concentrated solely on one aspect of history, an approach which he called "shredded history," Will wished instead to write "integral history." This new project was not to be an abandonment of his interest in philosophy since, like others of his generation, he defined history as philosophy teaching by example. In 1930, the Durants began that integral history, planned originally for five volumes, with a research trip that took them to the Mediterranean, the Middle East, India, and the Far East. When the first volume, *The Story of Civilization: Our Oriental Heritage*, appeared in 1935, however, Will Durant was identified as the sole author.

Ariel's contribution to the early volumes of *The Story of Civilization* was in classifying and organizing the mountains of notes that Will accumulated for *Our Oriental Heritage* and *The Life of Greece* (1939). Although uncredited, hers was a significant task. She continued her own intellectual quest: In 1933, she gave several lectures in New York on "Women of the Great Salons," which included discussions on Madame de Staël and George Sand. In time the stories of famous and influential women were to be one of Ariel's contributions to *The Story of Civilization*.

Beginning in the mid-1930's, the Durants spent considerable time in Los Angeles. Because of his numerous lecture trips there, Will had become friends with such luminaries as Will Rogers and Charlie Chaplin. The Durants found Southern California an attractive contrast to the East Coast. The mild weather was important, but many intellectuals, such as Thomas Mann and Theodore Dreiser, were to be found there during those years. The Durants eventually made Los Angeles their permanent residence in 1943. *Caesar and Christ*, the third volume of their monumental series, appeared the following year.

After World War II, both Durants became involved in a movement to lessen the racial and religious tensions in the United States. Although Will was the key figure behind the "Declaration of Interdependence," Ariel took an active role, even discussing it on the radio. She began to travel extensively by herself, often to Mexico and Latin America. She also revisited New York City, a city whose urban excitement appealed to her after living in the hills above Hollywood.

The series' fourth volume, *The Age of Faith*, was published in 1950. Will Durant was still listed as the only author, but Ariel's contributions were increasingly important. Although she was still classifying and organizing, she was also supplementing and complementing his research. Will recognized her significance, referring to her as "my precious comrade." Before the volume was published, Ariel gave public talks about its contents, speaking knowledgeably about Muhammad, Maimonides, Charlemagne, Peter Abelard, and Dante. She had truly become Will's collaborator; as such, she was not uncritical of some of his decisions. She opposed his overwhelming focus upon the Italian nature of the Renaissance and his tolerance of the peccadilloes of many of the Renaissance popes in the next volume, *The Renaissance* (1953). It was Ariel who urged her husband to take seriously the aims of the Protestant Reformers; as a lapsed Catholic, Durant was more sympathetic to Erasmus than to Luther. Before *The Reformation*, the sixth volume, was published in 1957, Will wrote to Ariel that although "My hand moves the pen . . . the spirit is *ours*, and the work is a lifelong co-operation." This partnership was publicly recognized in 1961 in the seventh volume, *The Age of Reason Begins*, where Ariel and Will become the joint authors of *The Story of Civilization*.

France and England were Ariel's particular enthusiasms, and her temperament, imagination, and religious sensitivity complemented her husband's faith in reason and progress. He wrote about men, but she often wrote of the women who contributed to civilization. Volumes eight through ten were published during the 1960's: *The Age of Louis XIV* in 1963, *The Age of Voltaire* in 1965, and *Rousseau and Revolution* in 1967.

Generally, *The Story of Civilization* received favorable reviews. Many academic historians pointed out that the volumes contained no original research, a criticism that Will Durant fully accepted, and concentrated too much on the great men (and later women) of the time instead of considering underlying social and economic movements. Considering their length and academic content, they were extremely popular— *The Age of Louis XIV* was a Book-of-the-Month Club selection and sold 150,000 volumes. The Durants were awarded the Pulitzer Prize for *Rousseau and Revolution* and were elected to the Institute of Arts and Sciences. Ariel was chosen one of the five women of the year in 1965 by the *Los Angeles Times*. In 1969, she was awarded an honorary degree by the University of Akron.

The *Lessons of History* was published in 1968 and a survey of contemporary literature, *Interpretations of Life*, in 1970. The *Age of Napoleon*, the eleventh volume of *The Story of Civilization*, appeared in 1975. It, too, was a selection of the Book-of-the-Month Club. In January of 1977, they were both awarded the Presidential Medal of Freedom and their dual autobiography was published the same year. Ariel died on October 25, 1981, at the age of eighty-three. Will followed two weeks later, on November 7, at the age of ninety-six. Several days after his death, an editorial cartoon appeared in the *Los Angeles Times* featuring Ariel on roller skates welcoming Will to heaven.

Summary

Ariel Durant had a full life. A Jewish immigrant from Russia, she became one of the most famous woman writers of her era. She traveled extensively, knew many famous people in the arts and in politics, and her name appeared as the author of several widely known literary works. Toward the end of her life she received literary awards, honorary degrees, and other recognition.

She will be inevitably associated with her husband, Will Durant. Given her personality and ambition, she perhaps wanted an independent recognition of her own talents. Instead, she became her husband's literary assistant and toiled away in relative anonymity for many years. She had a significant impact on the focus and content of the multivolume *The Story of Civilization*. She was a critic, not merely a subordinate, and her own interests, in women, France, and England, were important influences, although it was only in volume eight that she received full title-page credit as a joint author. Even after her death, Ariel's accomplishments were subordinated to her husband's, particularly in their obituaries.

The immense popularity of the Durants' *The Story of Civilization* will probably not long outlive their own generation. Professional historians often criticized the volumes. Its glorification of the great men (and some women) of Western civilization has become unacceptable among those who prefer to focus upon the contributions of the common man and woman. Finally, in the late twentieth century few have either the time or the inclination to read the thousands and thousands of pages which comprise the completed work. Nevertheless, Ariel Durant's collaboration on this monumental work provided an outlet for her intellectual interests, and the volumes continue to provide important evidence of her significance as a historian in her own right.

Bibliography
Baker, John F. "Will and Ariel Durant." In *The Author Speaks: Selected PW Interviews, 1967-1976*. New York: R. R. Bowker, 1977. This joint interview with the Durants, which appeared in *Publishers Weekly* in 1975, provides insights into their

collaboration as historians and explains how they reconciled their divergent opinions during the course of their long authorial careers.

Durant, Will, and Ariel Durant. *A Dual Autobiography*. New York: Simon & Schuster, 1977. In this volume, the Durants tell the story of both their early lives and the years they spent together. Incorporating letters and other documents, it is a most valuable source.

Gershoy, Leo. "Radiance of the Sun-King Century." *The Saturday Review* 46 (September 21, 1963): 33-34. Gershoy, a prominent historian, praises the Durants for their ambition but finds their work a compilation of uneven and loosely connected essays, "some brilliant and engrossing, others . . . of indifferent worth."

Mellon, Stanley. "Historians and Others." *Yale Review* 53 (December, 1963): 291-294. Sympathetic to the aims of the Durants in their desire to write integrated history, the author faults them on their lack of historical methodology, being too willing to blindly trust other writers' findings.

Murphy, Cullen. "The Venerable Will." *The Atlantic* 256 (November, 1985): 22-23. Written several years after the Durants' deaths, the author writes a brief recapitulation of their literary accomplishments. Noting that the Book-of-the-Month Club sold 500,000 copies of *The Story of Civilization*, Murphy questioned how many people actually read the multivolume work.

Plumb, J. H. "Some Personalities on the Paths of History." *The New York Times Book Review*, September 15, 1963, sect. 7, p. 3. Plumb, an eminent English historian, was extremely critical of the Durants' volumes. Here he reviews *The Age of Louis XIV*, the first volume to which Ariel's name was included as author.

Eugene Larson

AMELIA EARHART

Born: July 24, 1897; Atchison, Kansas
Died: c. July 2, 1937; near Howland Island in the South Pacific
Area of Achievement: Aviation
Contribution: A pioneer in the field of aviation, Amelia Earhart proved that women had the ability and the endurance to contribute much to that budding and adventurous medium of travel.

Early Life

Amelia Mary Earhart was born on July 24, 1897, in a large wood and brick Victorian house located in Atchison, Kansas. The house was built in 1861, when Kansas became a state, by Amelia's maternal grandfather, Alfred E. Otis. Although Amelia's parents, Edwin Stanton Earhart and Amy Otis Earhart, lived twenty-two miles south, in Kansas City, her mother had returned to the Otis home for the birth of her first child.

Since Amelia attended school in Atchison, she spent much of her childhood at her grandparents' home, where her adventurous tomboy habits were restricted by the watchful eye of her Victorian grandmother. By the time she was seven, the traits that would one day carry Amelia Earhart far beyond the traditional feminine role were already evident.

Amelia lived with her parents and younger sister in Kansas City when school was not in session. Life there was very different from life in the household of her grandparents. Alfred Otis, a lawyer, U.S. District Court Judge, bank president, and chief warden of Trinity Episcopal Church, had not been pleased when his favorite daughter had married Edwin Earhart, the son of an Evangelical Lutheran minister. Although Edwin himself became a lawyer, he was never a financial success. In spite of the differences, Amelia was extremely happy in the less restricted home of her parents, and she idolized her father. In later years, however, the happy times in the Earhart home diminished as constant setbacks drove Edwin Earhart to the use of alcohol. Edwin and Amy Earhart divorced in 1924.

When Amelia was ten years old, her father was transferred to Des Moines, Iowa. The next summer, while visiting the Iowa State Fair, Amelia saw her first airplane. It was only five years after the Wright Brothers' flight at Kitty Hawk, and Amelia was not much impressed by what she saw at the fair.

By 1914, when Amelia Earhart was seventeen years old, family circumstances compelled her to begin taking control of her life and future. Becoming independent at a younger age than most girls of her generation enabled her to make decisions that helped determine her destiny.

Life's Work

Amelia's first significant encounter with an airplane came in 1918, when she was working in Toronto, Canada, as a nurse's aide treating wounded veterans of World

War I. While Amelia was attending an airshow with a friend, a pilot put his plane into a dive straight at the two young women. As expected, her friend hit the ground, but Amelia stood still. Later, she wrote, "I did not understand it at the time but I believe that little red airplane said something to me as it swished by." A short time later, Amelia had her first ride in an airplane and knew she had to fly.

In January, 1921, Earhart met Neta Snook, the woman who taught Amelia her basic piloting skills. In 1922, Earhart bought a yellow Kinner Canary biplane, in which she set her first record for women by rising to an altitude of fourteen thousand feet.

The fascination that Amelia Earhart had for airplanes became a passion in 1927, when she was asked by Captain H. H. Railey to become the first woman to fly across the Atlantic Ocean. That flight took place in 1928. Although Earhart was only a passenger with pilot Wilmer Stultz and mechanic Louis Gordon, she began to be identified by the public as a female Charles Lindbergh, whose Atlantic solo flight had been the previous year.

A few weeks before the 1928 flight, Earhart met George Palmer Putnam, of G. P. Putnam's Sons Publishing Company. Putnam knew Railey, who was planning the flight, and he was also the publisher and public relations agent for Lindbergh. The relationship between Earhart and Putnam led to their marriage in 1931, thirteen months after Putnam's first wife obtained a divorce.

In 1929, Earhart entered the first women's cross-country derby; she finished a disappointing third, but a short time later she set a women's speed record of 181 miles per hour. In 1931, she set an altitude record of 18,451 feet in an autogiro, a forerunner of the helicopter.

By 1932, Earhart was at the controls of her single-engine Lockheed Vega, in which, on the fifth anniversary of Lindbergh's flight, she became the first woman to fly solo across the Atlantic. Later in the same year, she broke the women's transcontinental nonstop speed record, only to break it again in 1933.

Amelia Earhart's 1935 adventures included becoming the first person to fly solo from Hawaii to California and from Los Angeles to Mexico City, and making a nonstop flight from Mexico City to Newark, New Jersey. With these accomplishments came international recognition, including receiving the Distinguished Flying Cross at a joint session of Congress and a White House meeting with President Franklin D. Roosevelt.

One additional adventure now began to dominate the life of Amelia Earhart: a flight around the world. In 1924, a group of army pilots had circled the world but for safety reasons had stayed close to land. Earhart's goal was a far more dangerous equatorial route, a trip that would total 29,000 miles. She indicated to several friends that this would be her last such adventurous flight.

In the book that Earhart had planned to entitle *World Flight* but is now called *Last Flight*, she describes her motives for this journey, which go far beyond pure adventure. She believed that the research and development of the aviation industry had neglected the effects of flight on personnel. She intended to make her trip a scientific journey, which can best be described in her own words:

I am interested in finding out whether one kind of food is better than another during flight; i.e., the effects of altitude on metabolism. Also . . . the rate at which fatigue is induced. . . . What will stratosphere flying do to creatures accustomed to the dense air of lower altitudes? Are men and women different in their reactions to air travel?

To obtain the type of airplane needed for this flight, Earhart secured the financial help of Purdue University, where she had been a career counselor for women. She now bought a $70,000 specially built twin-engine Lockheed Electra.

The flight itself would require many months of careful planning and the help of many people and organizations. George Putnam handled publicity and fund-raising. The U.S. government built an airstrip on a desolate speck in the South Pacific called Howland Island, and also provided diplomatic assistance. The airfield on Howland Island would be a critical refueling stop for the Lockheed Electra.

The first attempt to begin the world flight was a trip from Oakland, California, to Hawaii on March 17, 1937. A mishap in Hawaii forced a return to California for repairs to the plane. A second start was made on June 1, but changes in global weather patterns necessitated a reversal of the route; this time flying east to Miami, Florida. With Earhart was her navigator, Frederic Noonan.

The first 22,000 miles of the flight, through the Caribbean, South America, Africa, India, the Dutch East Indies, and Australia, ended at Lae, New Guinea, on June 30. The next leg, a flight of 2,556 miles to Howland Island, was the longest and most dangerous of the entire journey. The island is about 1,900 miles southwest of Hawaii and just north of the equator. To reach it from New Guinea would require fuel conservation and expert navigation. The airplane left Lae about mid-morning on July 1. By mid-morning the next day, July 2, 1937, the Lockheed Electra, Amelia Earhart, and Fred Noonan had disappeared.

Strong headwinds and overcast conditions had caused Earhart to miss Howland Island, and weak radio signals prevented significant help from the Coast Guard Cutter *Itasca*, which was waiting near the island. Earhart's last radio transmission, at 8:44 A.M., indicated uncertainty, a dwindling fuel supply, and obvious fear. Although President Franklin D. Roosevelt ordered one of the most intensive searches in U.S. history, covering more than 250,000 square miles of ocean and costing about $4 million, no trace of the airplane or its occupants was found.

Numerous theories have been proposed to solve the mystery of Amelia Earhart. The most likely scenario is that the plane simply ran out of gas and crashed at sea. More exciting theories range from capture by the Japanese to Earhart's secret return to the United States under an alias. To explain the search ordered by President Roosevelt, one writer believed that Earhart was actually on a secret government mission to spy on the Japanese. The only tangible evidence ever found was by Richard Gillespie on Nikumaroro, an uninhabited atoll south of Howland Island, in 1989. Among the items found are what could be a navigator's box from a Lockheed Electra and a heel and sole from a shoe similar to those worn by Amelia Earhart. These artifacts are interesting but inconclusive. The mystery of Amelia Earhart remains unsolved.

Summary

Although her aviation accomplishments are amazing, the impact of Amelia Earhart is far greater than a list of statistics would indicate. From a sledding incident at the age of seven to her last flight near her fortieth birthday, Earhart seemed determined to do things that were extraordinary for her generation. Her tremendous willpower opened doors not normally open to women. The career counseling position at Purdue gave Earhart the opportunity to help other girls with nontraditional interests. She believed that Purdue had a unique comprehension of this need. In *Last Flight*, Earhart discussed her desire to endow a machine shop for girls only, where they could work with motors, lathes, and other mechanical equipment. She also believed that traditional women should be taught how to make emergency household repairs.

Amelia Earhart entered the aviation industry in its infancy and played a major role in developing that industry from that first airplane she saw at the Iowa State Fair in 1908, which she described as "a thing of rusty wire and wood," to the plane that almost carried her around the world. With or without the mystery surrounding her last flight and death, Earhart had a major impact on the field of aviation. She has also had a continuing influence on increasing opportunities for women to pursue their individual goals in a male-dominated world.

Bibliography

Backus, Jean. *Letters from Amelia*. Boston: Beacon Press, 1982. An excellent overview of the life of Amelia Earhart, made up primarily of her own letters. The author stresses the more personal side of the subject, particularly her relationships with family and friends.

Earhart, Amelia. *Last Flight*. New York: Harcourt, Brace, 1937. Written by Earhart before and during her world flight, and arranged by her husband, George Putnam, after her disappearance, this book gives an intimate look at the motives that drove Amelia Earhart.

Goerner, Fred. *The Search for Amelia Earhart*. Garden City, N.Y.: Doubleday, 1966. This is one of many books that try to solve the mystery of Amelia Earhart. The author concludes that Amelia was captured by the Japanese while on a secret spy mission for the United States.

Klaas, Joe. *Amelia Earhart Lives*. New York: McGraw-Hill, 1970. Klaas develops the most fascinating, and least supported, theory of the Earhart mystery, asserting that Amelia secretly returned to the United States and lived for many years under an alias.

Loomis, Vincent. *Amelia Earhart: The Final Story*. New York: Random House, 1985. This author, like Goerner, believes that Earhart and Noonan were captured by the Japanese, but he does not claim that they were on a spy mission.

Lovell, Mary. *The Sound of Wings*. New York: St. Martin's Press, 1989. Lovell has written an excellent biography of Amelia Earhart. Much attention is given to Earhart's early years and to her relationship with George Putnam. Includes many photographs and letters.

Rich, Doris L. *Amelia Earhart*. Washington, D.C.: Smithsonian Institution Press, 1989. In this factual and detailed biography, the author gives a balanced coverage of the life, motives, and work of Amelia Earhart. Excellent reference notes are included.

Glenn L. Swygart

MARY BAKER EDDY

Born: July 16, 1821; Bow, New Hampshire
Died: December 3, 1910; Chestnut Hill, Massachusetts
Area of Achievement: Religion
Contribution: A deeply religious thinker, Mary Baker Eddy established the Church of Christ, Scientist—the first church movement to be founded in the United States by a woman.

Early Life

The youngest of six children, Mary Morse Baker was born in 1821 on her parents' farm in the township of Bow, New Hampshire. Her father, Mark Baker, was a respected farmer whose deep interest in theology prompted him to engage in serious religious debates with his neighbors. Mary's mother, Abigail Ambrose Baker, had grown up as the daughter of a prominent deacon of the Congregational church in nearby Pembroke and was known for her tender solicitude toward her family and neighbors. Both parents were devout members of the Congregational church; Mary was nurtured in their Calvinist faith and joined the church herself at the age of twelve.

As a young girl, Mary began her formal education in 1826. An intelligent, highly sensitive child, Mary suffered from ill health that frequently kept her at home. She became a diligent reader and an avid writer of poetry. Mary received individual instruction from her second brother, Albert, who served as a schoolmaster at Mary's school when he was twenty. Her brother's instruction provided Mary with an education well in advance of that commonly available to young women of the period, and she was introduced to the rudiments of Greek, Latin, and Hebrew as well as contemporary works of literature and philosophy.

In December of 1843, Mary Baker was married to Major George Washington Glover, a successful builder with business interests in the Carolinas. The newlyweds eventually settled in Wilmington, North Carolina. By June of 1844, George Glover's investments in building supplies for a project in Haiti were lost, and he was stricken with yellow fever. He died on June 27, forcing his pregnant and impoverished widow to return to her parents' home. Despite her dangerously poor health, Mary gave birth in September to a healthy son, whom she named George in honor of his late father. When Abigail Baker died in 1849, however, her daughter's grief and precarious health made further care for the boisterous young George Glover even more difficult. Mark Baker's second marriage less than one year later forced Mary and her son to leave the Baker house. Mary went to stay with her sister Abigail Tilton, but George Glover was placed in the care of Mary's former nurse. Mary was devastated by her separation from her son, but her family insisted that reuniting the two would further strain Mary's tenuous health.

In 1853, Mary was married to Dr. Daniel Patterson, a dentist who promised to provide a home for her and her son. That promise was never fulfilled, however, and Patterson's failings as a husband became increasingly evident. Mary's son moved with his foster parents to the West; they later told him that his mother had died. Mary's new husband was often absent in the course of his itinerant practice, and the couple found lodgings in various communities in New Hampshire. In the spring of 1862, while on commission to deliver state funds to Union sympathizers in the South, Patterson was taken prisoner by Confederate forces.

Barely able to care for herself, Mary sought relief from her persistent ill health at an institute in New Hampshire that promoted hydropathy, or the water cure. Finding little improvement during her visit, she traveled to Portland, Maine, to visit Phineas P. Quimby, a clock maker who had developed a reputation as a magnetic healer and hypnotist. After her first treatment at his office, Mary experienced a marked improvement in her health. In her enthusiasm to learn more about the methods Quimby used, she sought to reconcile Quimby's ideas with the spiritually based biblical healings with which she was so familiar.

Reunited with her husband in December of 1862 after his escape from prison, Mary returned to New Hampshire, where she experienced relapses of ill health. She sought relief by visiting Quimby at various times but could not discover a permanent cure for her illnesses. After Quimby's death in early January of 1866, Mary was seriously injured when she fell on an icy pavement in Lynn, Massachusetts, on February 1. Taken to a nearby house, she eventually regained consciousness sufficiently to convince her doctor and friends to move her to her lodgings in nearby Swampscott, where she was given little hope of recovery from the injuries to her head and spine. Visited by a clergyman on the Sunday after her accident, she asked to be left alone with her Bible. Turning to the ninth chapter of Matthew, she read the account of Jesus' healing of the man sick of the palsy (paralysis). Upon reading the story, she felt a profound change come over her and found that she was fully recovered from her injuries. Rising from her bed to dress and then greet the friends who waited outside her door, Mary astonished them with the rapidity and completeness of her healing, one that she credited to the power of God alone.

Life's Work

During the decade from 1866 to 1876, Mary Patterson's outward life seemed little improved, yet her conviction that she could discover the source of her healing experience inspired her to continue her study of the Bible. Her husband deserted her soon after her healing; they were divorced in 1873, and she resumed using the surname Glover.

Although her financial situation was precarious and she was still separated from her son, Mary realized that, at the age of forty-five, she was healthier than she had ever been in her entire life. For three years after her recovery, she dedicated herself solely to searching the Bible for answers to her questions regarding spiritual healing, withdrawing from social pursuits and her temperance movement activities in order to record the revelations she was gaining through her studies. She lived frugally in a series of boarding houses, began sharing her notes and interpretations of Bible passages with individuals who seemed receptive to her new ideas, and occasionally offered instruction in her healing methods in exchange for the cost of her room and board. A group of committed students eventually began to gather around her. In October of 1875, she managed to publish the first edition of her work, entitled *Science and Health*, with the financial assistance of some of her students.

It was in March of 1876 that Asa Gilbert Eddy, a native of Vermont who was ten years her junior and worked in Massachusetts as a salesman for the Singer Sewing Machine Company, became one of Mary's students. Asa Eddy, better known as Gilbert, became a successful healer. At a time when many of her most talented students were challenging her authority and attempting to undermine her teachings, Mary came to rely on Gilbert Eddy's sound judgment and his steady support of her leadership. The two were married on January 1, 1877.

Around this time, Mary Baker Eddy began revising *Science and Health*, adding five new chapters. This two-volume second edition was so rife with typographical errors that only the second volume was circulated. During this time, Eddy began to lecture weekly at the Baptist Tabernacle in Boston. The success of her public sermons led her to make a motion at a meeting of her students in 1879 that they organize a church; it was called the Church of Christ, Scientist. In Eddy's own words, the purpose of this church was "to commemorate the word and works of our Master, which should reinstate primitive Christianity and its lost element of healing." The new church was incorporated under a state charter, and Eddy was designated its president and appointed its first pastor. By the winter of 1879, Eddy and her husband had moved to rooms in Boston to be nearer to the growing church. She continued to teach new adult students about Christian Science, and the church established a Sunday school for the instruction of children in 1880. That same year, Eddy published the first of her many pamphlets: a sermon entitled *Christian Healing*. In an effort to give a more solid legal foundation to her classes, Eddy applied for a state charter in order to incorporate the Massachusetts Metaphysical College, a school dedicated to furthering the spread of her healing method by ensuring that students received unadulterated instruction directly from her.

Earlier, Mary Baker Eddy had begun revising and expanding *Science and Health* once again. The third edition of *Science and Health*, which appeared in 1881, was the first accurate edition of her writings to incorporate part of the treatise she used to instruct students in her classes. This publishing enterprise brought Eddy into contact with one of the leading printers of her day: John Wilson of the University Press in Cambridge, Massachusetts. Prospects for selling all one thousand copies of the third edition were not promising, but Wilson was convinced that Eddy would be able to finance the printing of her book through its sales. By 1882, the book had gone back to print for two additional editions of one thousand copies each.

Other publishing activities began. In April of 1883, Eddy published the first issue of *The Journal of Christian Science*. Originally a bimonthly periodical with articles designed to explore issues of interest to both newcomers and longtime students of Eddy's religion, the *Journal* was expanded to become a monthly publication and was one of the first authorized organs of the Christian Science church. A sixth edition of

Science and Health appeared in 1883; it was the first to contain Eddy's "Key to the Scriptures," a section initially consisting of a glossary with her metaphysical interpretations of biblical terms and concepts. By 1885, nine additional printings were made, bringing the total number of copies in circulation during the book's first ten years to 15,000.

The years following the publication of the sixth edition of *Science and Health* were prosperous ones, with many new students working to spread Christian Science and its healing practice throughout the United States. Nevertheless, several events occurred in the period from 1889 to 1892 that radically altered the structure and direction of the Christian Science church. Schisms among her students and the burdens resulting from those who increasingly relied on her personal leadership in all matters led Eddy to close her college at the height of its popularity and resign her post as pastor of the Boston church. Services continued to be conducted in Christian Science churches, but students voted to adjourn the activities of the National Christian Scientist Association for three years beginning in 1890. Withdrawing to a new home in Concord, New Hampshire, Eddy commenced work on a major revision of *Science and Health* to be published as the fiftieth edition in 1891.

September 23, 1892, marked the establishment of Eddy's newly reorganized church: the First Church of Christ, Scientist, in Boston, Massachusetts, also known as The Mother Church. She consulted with attorneys familiar with Massachusetts statutes in order to find a legal means to incorporate her church that would place its corporate government on a solid basis without encouraging undue attachment to her personal authority. The new charter provided a powerful centralized structure in the form of a five-member Board of Directors responsible for management of the church's affairs; it also fostered the practice of democratic self-government already established in the branch churches outside of Boston that were affiliated with the growing church movement. All members of these branches were invited to apply for concurrent membership in The Mother Church. Eddy was henceforth designated as the Discoverer and Founder of Christian Science. To her mind, this title expressed the scientific aspect of her work—emphasizing her role in formulating and articulating its religious teachings in much the same way that scientific laws and principles are formulated and articulated, but not created, by those who discover them.

In October of 1893, the building of the new church edifice was begun in Boston's Back Bay area, with the cornerstone of the church laid in May of 1894 and the first service held on December 30, 1894. Eddy took the unusual step of ordaining the Bible and *Science and Health*, rather than human ministers, as pastors of the church. When she published the *Manual of The Mother Church* in 1895, setting forth the rules by which the church was to be governed, she made provisions in its bylaws for the election of lay readers who would read texts from the Bible and from *Science and Health* relating to twenty-six topics she set forth. These texts were selected by a special committee; the resulting lesson sermons were studied daily by individual members and were read Sundays at Christian Science church services throughout the world. These changes were instituted by Eddy in order to avoid the adulteration of her teachings through personal preaching. In this way, she believed that the healing message contained in the Bible and in her book would speak directly to all who attended her church without the injection of personal opinion or conflicting interpretations.

In 1898, Eddy established a Board of Education to provide for the formal instruction of students in Christian Science by those who were approved to serve as teachers. She also established a Board of Lectureship to which practitioners (ordained healers within the church) and teachers of Christian Science were appointed. These lecturers were responsible for preparing and delivering public lectures on Christian Science in order to introduce and clarify its teachings to those unfamiliar with the religion. The Christian Science Publishing Society was created through a deed of trust and was charged with the responsibility for publishing and distributing *Science and Health* and Eddy's other books as well as *The Christian Science Journal* and the newly founded periodical, *The Christian Science Weekly* (renamed *The Christian Science Sentinel* in 1899). In 1902, Eddy completed work on her final major revision of *Science and Health*; it was the 226th edition of the book known as the Christian Science textbook.

Although she enjoyed the relative peace and seclusion of her New Hampshire estate, known as Pleasant View, Eddy faced bitter personal attacks in the popular press during early 1900's that threatened to undermine her church. These articles reflected the sensational "yellow journalism" of the period. Few pieces were more damaging than those published by Joseph Pulitzer, whose *New York World* newspaper claimed that Eddy was near death from cancer and that her alleged fortune of $15 million was being wrested from her control. Refusing to meet with Pulitzer's reporters, Eddy granted audience to representatives of several other leading newspapers and press associations. After answering three brief questions concerning her health, Eddy gave evidence of her well-being by departing to take her daily carriage ride.

Despite Eddy's efforts to disprove the rumors concerning her health, her son George was approached by the publishers of the *New York World* and was encouraged, on the basis of the paper's erroneous accounts of his mother's welfare, to begin legal proceedings to determine Eddy's mental competence and ability to conduct business affairs connected with her church. Although funded by Pulitzer's newspaper fortune, this lawsuit ultimately collapsed after a panel appointed to determine Eddy's competence held a one-hour interview and established that she was in full possession of her mental faculties.

Refusing to back down in the face of these personal attacks, Eddy was prompted to establish a trust for her property in order to preserve its orderly transfer to the church after her death. More important, Eddy was impelled to launch an enormous new undertaking: She directed the Trustees of the Publishing Society to establish a daily newspaper to be known as *The Christian Science Monitor*, which began publication in 1908. By bringing national and international events into clearer focus for its readers, *The Christian Science Monitor* would fulfill Eddy's vision of its purpose: to combat the apathy, indifference, and despair that were common responses to world affairs through its spiritually enlightened, problem-solving journalism.

Having witnessed the fruition of her long-cherished hopes, Eddy died quietly in her sleep on December 3, 1910.

Summary

Regardless of one's perspective on the validity of her religious beliefs, Mary Baker Eddy clearly led a remarkable life—one full of extraordinary success despite the prejudices that confronted her as a woman attempting to establish a spiritually minded religious movement during an age of rampant materialism. Novelist and humorist Mark Twain, who was one of Eddy's most outspoken critics, once remarked that she was "probably the most daring and masterful woman who has appeared on earth for centuries." A pragmatic and capable administrator who inspired her followers by her example of single-minded dedication, Eddy was equally comfortable in her role as a religious thinker—one who refused to compromise her conscience "to suit the general drift of thought" and was convinced of the importance of maintaining the intellectual and spiritual purity of her writings. Her church remains an active presence in the United States and throughout the world, and her book *Science and Health* was recognized by the Women's National Book Association in 1992 as one of seventy-five important works by "women whose words have changed the world."

Bibliography

Gottschalk, Stephen. *The Emergence of Christian Science in American Religious Life.* Berkeley: University of California Press, 1973. Although its examination of Christian Science from the perspective of intellectual history may make it less easily accessible to general readers, this work sets forth the distinctive contributions Christian Science has made to American theology and culture.

Orcutt, William Dana. *Mary Baker Eddy and Her Books.* Boston: Christian Science Publishing Society, 1950. Written by a distinguished bookmaker who worked closely with Eddy from 1897 to 1910 and helped design the oversize subscription edition of *Science and Health* that was released in 1941, this memoir provides an intriguing window on Eddy's career as an author.

Peel, Robert. *Mary Baker Eddy: The Years of Discovery.* New York: Holt, Rinehart and Winston, 1966.

——————. *Mary Baker Eddy: The Years of Trial.* New York: Holt, Rinehart and Winston, 1971.

——————. *Mary Baker Eddy: The Years of Authority.* New York: Holt, Rinehart and Winston, 1977. Written by a Harvard-educated scholar who had unprecedented access to church archival materials, this monumental three-volume biography remains the definitive work on Eddy's life. Although Peel was himself a Christian Scientist, his work gives evidence of his conscientious effort to provide "a straightforward, factual account free from either apologetics or polemics."

Thomas, Robert David. *"With Bleeding Footsteps": Mary Baker Eddy's Path to Religious Leadership.* New York: Alfred A. Knopf, 1994. Trained in the theories of psychoanalysis, Thomas brings this psychological perspective to bear on his study of Eddy's character and behavior. Despite his serious, scholarly approach, Thomas fails to provide a complete assessment of Eddy's significance as a religious leader and seems to fall short of bringing his subject fully alive. Nevertheless, this biography is useful as one of the few fair-minded studies of Eddy to have appeared since Peel's three-volume work, cited above.

Wendy Sacket

MARIAN WRIGHT EDELMAN

Born: June 6, 1939; Bennettsville, South Carolina

Areas of Achievement: Civil rights, education, and social reform
Contribution: Edelman created a lobbying organization dedicated to improving conditions for children in the United States.

Early Life
Marian Wright was born in Bennettsville, South Carolina, on June 6, 1939, to Arthur Jerome Wright and Maggie Leola Bowen Wright. Her father, a Baptist minister, said that "service is the rent we pay for living." Hence, helping others was the basic duty of all people and an essential part of her early family life. Her parents taught by example. They built a home for the elderly in which Marian cleaned and cooked. Her parents reared five of their own children and cared for twelve foster children over the years.

Marian's education emphasized international understanding. After she completed high school at Marlboro Training High School, she attended Spelman College in Atlanta, Georgia. During her junior year, she received a Merrill Scholarship to study at the University of Paris and at the University of Geneva during the academic year 1958-1959. In the summer of 1959, she participated in a student exchange study tour of East Germany, Poland, Czechoslovakia, and the Soviet Union. These experiences broadened her perspective on humanity. She returned to the United States unable to accept the indignities of segregation, under which she had grown up and lived.

In 1960, Marian received her bachelor's degree from Spelman College as the valedictorian of her class. During that same year, black college students were conducting sit-in demonstrations at college campuses throughout the South. Her own participation in a sit-in at Atlanta's city hall led her to be arrested along with fourteen other students. Marian's civil rights activism, coupled with her international experiences and her family's commitment to service, shaped her life. Instead of choosing to pursue graduate work in Russian studies and traveling abroad, she decided to become a lawyer and use the law to effect social change.

While she pursued higher education, she continued learning from other cultures through educational service. Her achievements led to her becoming a John Hay Whitney Fellow from 1960 to 1961 at Yale University. During the summer of 1962, she worked in Crossroads Africa, a work project in the Ivory Coast, West Africa. Wright eventually received a LL.B. degree from Yale University in 1963. With her law degree in hand, Wright was poised to launch her career as a civil rights attorney.

Life's Work
From 1963 to 1964, Marian Wright worked in New York City at the headquarters of the National Association for the Advancement of Colored People (NAACP), where she served as a staff attorney for the NAACP Legal Defense and Educational Fund.

Because the NAACP was working in cooperation with other civil rights groups on the Voter Education Project in Mississippi, Wright moved to Mississippi, where she became the first black woman to be admitted to the bar. Because she had to work with federal law, she also became a member of the bar in Washington, D.C., and in Massachusetts. From 1964 to 1968, she served as the director for the NAACP Legal Defense and Educational Fund in Jackson, Mississippi, where she successfully defended the Head Start Program from political attacks, helped to get student demonstrators out of jail, became involved in school desegregation issues, and risked injury and arrest in the process.

As part of her Head Start activities, Wright served on the board of the Child Development Group of Mississippi, a representative for one of the largest Head Start projects in the United States. Her advocacy for the poor of Mississippi led her to give testimony before the Senate and to work as a liaison between the Poor People's Campaign and Congress. In the course of this work, Wright came in contact with Peter Edelman, a Jewish lawyer who served as an assistant to Senator Robert F. Kennedy. Wright married Peter D. Edelman on July 14, 1968. Theirs was one of the first interracial marriages to take place in Virginia after the state's antimiscegenation laws had been declared unconstitutional. The couple eventually reared three sons: Joshua, Jonah, and Ezra.

In 1968, Marian Wright Edelman toured Eastern Europe, India, Israel, East Africa, and Southeast Asia. From 1968 to 1973, she served as coeditor with Ruby G. Martin of the Washington Research Project of the Southern Center for Public Policy, headquartered in Washington, D.C. The project used litigation to promote equal employment opportunity, monitored various federal programs in such areas as child care and school desegregation, and worked with community groups. This organization became the parent organization of the Children's Defense Fund, which became incorporated in 1973. In 1971, Edelman and her husband moved to Boston, from where she continued to travel regularly to Washington, D.C., as a partner of the Washington Research Project. She became a trustee of Yale University, the second woman to serve in this capacity in the university's 270-year history. She also served from 1971 to 1973 as director of the Harvard University Center for Law and Education, part of the Office of Economic Opportunity's legal services program. The organization emphasized reform in education through research and action related to the legal implications of educational policies.

In 1973, Edelman became a founder and the president of the Children's Defense Fund (CDF), an advocacy and public education association for children's issues that has become one of the best-known and best-connected of all lobbies, with an annual budget of $10 million and staff of more than 120. Soon, as the director of the nation's most effective organization for children's issues such as teen pregnancy, prenatal care, early childhood education, health services, child care, adoption, child labor, and child welfare, Edelman became known as "the children's crusader." Through the Children's Defense Fund, Edelman seeks to make it "un-American" for any child to grow up poor, lacking adequate health care, food, shelter, child care, or education.

In order to allow Edelman to spend more time at her organization's headquarters, she and her family returned to Washington, D.C., in 1979. As the spokesperson for the Children's Defense Fund, Edelman has avoided the politics of confrontation, choosing instead to forge alliances with other groups that seek to lessen the effects of poverty, injustice, inadequate health care, insufficient education, and family violence.

During the course of her tenure as director of the Children's Defense Fund, Edelman has testified about the human and public costs the United States would face if it continued to fail to provide adequate funds and resources to meet the needs of American children and families. Such problems became greater in the 1980's as increasing numbers of children and families faced poverty as a result of economic recession, structural change in the economy, stagnating wages, tax and budget policies that favored the well-to-do, lack of state enforcement of child support payments, and greater dependency on welfare by the growing number of female-headed households. Edelman uses statistics and personal testimony to demonstrate that children have become the poorest Americans and will become a permanent "underclass" if public policy fails to address the needs outlined by the Children's Defense Fund. Her passion is also mixed with optimism, since she not only stresses the problems but also provides remedies to build the broadest constituency to protect the children and alleviate poverty through education, legislation, and welfare reform.

Edelman has been a member of numerous committees addressing social, educational, and public policy, such as the advisory council of Martin Luther King, Jr., Memorial Library, the advisory board of Hampshire College, the Presidential Committee on Missing in Action (1977), the Presidential Committee on International Year of the Child (1979), and the United Nations International Children's Emergency Fund (UNICEF). She has also served on many boards of directors, such as those of the Eleanor Roosevelt Institute, the Carnegie Council on Children (1972-1977), and the Martin Luther King, Jr., Memorial Center. She has served as trustee for the March of Dimes, the Joint Center for Political Science, the Yale University Corporation (1971-1977), and the Aetna Center. In 1980, she became the chair of the Spelman College Board of Trustees, becoming the first African American and the second woman to serve in that role. Through the years, Edelman has worked closely with First Lady Hillary Rodham Clinton, a friend since 1969 and former staff attorney for the Children's Defense Fund. After the election of Bill Clinton as president, Edelman consulted with the First Lady on national health care issues and legislation but indicated that she did not want any administrative appointment.

Her outstanding contributions have been recognized with many awards. Edelman has been the recipient of sixty-eight honorary degrees from such institutions as Smith College, Columbia University, Swarthmore College, Rutgers University, Georgetown University, and Yale University. Named one of the Outstanding Young Women of America in 1966, Edelman has continued to be awarded for her outstanding achievements. She has received the *Mademoiselle* magazine award (1965), the Louise Waterman Wise Award (1970), the National Leadership award from the National Women's Political Caucus (1980), the Black Women's Forum award (1980), and the

Eliot Award of the American Public Health Association (1987). She was named a MacArthur Foundation Fellow in 1985. Edelman has also been honored with the Albert Schweitzer Humanitarian prize from The Johns Hopkins University (1987), the Hubert Humphrey Civil Rights award, and the AFL-CIO award (1989). In 1991, the Jackie Robinson Foundation recognized her decency and dedication to working on the behalf of children.

Summary

As a result of her leadership in shaping programs and legislation to improve life for American children, Marian Wright Edelman has become the nation's most effective lobbyist for the young. She continues to argue that present conditions must be changed in order to provide a better environment for the development of the nation's future leaders. In the course of her work, she has also contributed significantly to the efforts to obtain equal rights for all citizens, particularly African Americans and women.

Bibliography

Atkins, Norman. "Marian Wright Edelman." *Rolling Stone*, December 10, 1992, 126-130. This interview provides insights into the personality behind Edelman's public career.

Bouton, Katherine. "Marian Wright Edelman." *Ms.* 16 (July/August, 1987): 98-100. The author describes Edelman's attempts to juggle career and family while conducting the mission of the Children's Defense Fund.

Edelman, Marian Wright. *Families in Peril: An Agenda for Social Change.* Cambridge, Mass.: Harvard University Press, 1987. This book compares the status of black and white children and families in America. It discusses problems resulting from inadequate attention and a lack of public policies and programs to deal with these issues.

_____ . *The Measure of Our Success: A Letter to My Children and Yours.* Boston: Beacon Press, 1992. Edelman presents a blend of personal advice, homilies, and analysis of experiences in this work, which spent several weeks on the best-seller lists.

Kaus, Mickey. "The Godmother." *The New Republic* 208 (February 15, 1993): 21-25. This article provides a critical look at some of the basic arguments put forth by Edelman during her leadership of the Children's Defense Fund.

Dorothy C. Salem

GERTRUDE EDERLE

Born: October 23, 1906; New York, New York

Area of Achievement: Sports
Contribution: An American swimmer, Ederle became the first woman to swim across the English Channel, breaking the time record of the fastest man by one hour and fifty-nine minutes.

Early Life

Gertrude Caroline Ederle was born to a German immigrant family on October 23, 1906, in New York City. Her father, Henry J. Ederle, was a successful butcher who owned the Ederle Brothers Meat Market on upper Amsterdam Avenue. Her mother, Gertrude Haverstroh Ederle, was a homemaker who reared six children.

It was Trudy's mother who taught her to swim. At their summer cottage in Atlantic Highlands, New Jersey, her mother tied a rope around Trudy and let her down into the water. Dangling from the end of the rope, Trudy learned to dog paddle; within three days, she had learned to swim. Three years later Mrs. Ederle took Trudy and her five brothers and sisters to a swimming exhibition at the Highlands. It was there that Trudy decided she wanted to swim like the experts.

A mere four years after her mother taught her to swim, Trudy set an eight-hundred-yard freestyle record with a time of thirteen minutes and nineteen seconds. By the age of twelve, Trudy was the youngest person to break a nonmechanical world record.

After one year of courses, Trudy dropped out of high school. At about the same time, Charlotte Epstein of the Women's Swimming Association of New York had convinced the Amateur Athletic Union to register female swimmers and sponsor meets. Trudy's older sister, Margaret, encouraged her to swim for the association, and there Trudy received her early training and coaching.

At the age of fourteen, Trudy first demonstrated her long-distance swimming prowess by defeating fifty-one other women in a three and one-half mile international race from Manhattan Beach to Brighton Beach. By the age of seventeen, Trudy held eighteen world swimming records and was a member of the United States Olympic swimming team. During the 1924 Olympic Games in Paris, Trudy won a gold and two bronze medals in the five racing events open to women. The following year, Trudy swam the twenty-one mile distance from the Battery in lower Manhattan to Sandy Hook, New Jersey, in seven hours and eleven minutes, bettering the men's record. By this time, Trudy held twenty-nine national and world records.

Life's Work

With funding from the Women's Swimming Association, Gertrude Ederle first attempted to swim the English Channel on August 18, 1925. Eight hours and forty-six minutes in the water, with only six miles to go, a wave engulfed her, and she stopped to spit out the salt water. Her trainer thought that she was collapsing and called to a man swimming alongside her to grab her. He did, thus disqualifying her. Although Ederle said, "I could have gone on," there was no fame in defeat.

Many men and some women had tried to swim the English Channel, but the passage proved to be too severe. The existence of crosscurrents, heavy tides, and choppy waves made the English Channel a treacherous body of water. Until 1926, only five men had successfully made the swim. Of the five fastest times recorded, Enrique Tiraboschi of Argentina held the first position with the time of sixteen hours and thirty-three minutes.

Ederle's second attempt to swim the Channel would require funding, and the Women's Swimming Association simply did not have adequate resources to sponsor her swim. After learning of Ederle's situation, Captain Patterson, a newspaper publisher, agreed to provide the necessary funds, knowing that if Ederle was successful, he would have the exclusive story and the lead on every other newspaper in the country. Signing the contract for her expenses and a modest salary was something Trudy would have to give serious consideration. Once she signed the contract she would be upgraded to a professional status, and therefore, ineligible to participate in future amateur competition. With determination on her side, Ederle signed the contract.

Accompanied by her father, her sister Margaret, and her trainer, Thomas W. Burgess in a tug boat, Gertrude Ederle once again attempted to swim the English Channel. With a promise from her father that she would not be pulled out of the water unless she asked, Ederle began her swim at 7:08 A.M. on the morning of August 6, 1926. The odds were three-to-one that she would fail.

The sea was fairly calm when she began her swim. By mid-morning, however, rain began to fall; by afternoon, a change of tide brought increasing wind and currents, turning the channel into rough waters. After twelve hours of swimming, the winds reached gale proportions, and her trainer told her that she must come out of the water. Ederle simply asked, "What for?" She continued to swim the Channel using the American crawl stroke. Fourteen hours and thirty-one minutes after she began, Ederle walked ashore at Kingsdown on the Dover coast at 9:35 P.M., becoming the first woman to swim across the English Channel successfully. While the heavy sea had forced her to swim thirty-five miles to cover the twenty-one mile distance, Ederle swam from Cape Gris-Nez, France, to Dover, England, and broke the time record of the fastest man by one hour and fifty-nine minutes. The moment she completed her swim, she became the most famous and talked about woman in the world.

Ederle returned to New York to a heroine's welcome. The whistle-cord of every steamship in New York Harbor was tied down, sirens were sounded, and airplanes overhead dropped flowers. After stepping off the Berengaria liner, Trudy rode in a motorcade up lower Broadway, passing under the fall of ticker tape. On her route an enthusiastic crowd of two million people rushed to touch the car in which she rode. Never before had there been such a welcome for a sports hero. To newspaper reporters she simply said, "I knew I could do it. I knew I would, and I did."

After a day of being greeted and dined by everyone who was anyone in the city,

Ederle received her scroll of honor from the mayor of New York. The text of the scroll in part read, "to you for the indomitable courage, the skillful grace, the tremendous athletic prowess, which enabled you to be the first girl in the world to swim the English Channel." It was then that she stated, "It was for my flag that I swam and to know that I could bring home the honors, and my mind was made up to do it." At the end of her day of public adoration, yet another welcome awaited her on the west side of town. As neighbors and friends prepared for the homecoming of "Trudy, Queen of the Seas," thousands stood in front of her house, on adjoining roofs, and in windows to welcome her back to her neighborhood.

The day after the news of her return home, promoters, manufacturers, and motion picture producers lined up to solicit endorsements of every kind. Dudley Field Malone, her legal counsel, stated that the offers totaled $900,000. The offers included a contract paying $125,000 for a twenty-week appearance on the stage, and another for a forty-week theatrical offer. For the first time, riches were offered to a swimmer.

Ederle eventually signed a contract with the William Morris Agency to tour for two years in vaudeville as a swimmer. She costarred with Bebe Daniels in the film *Swim, Girl, Swim*. Unfortunately, Ederle's fame did not last, and the pressure of public life proved hard to endure. Her record as the only woman to swim across the English Channel successfully lasted less than a month when Amelia Gade Corson successfully crossed the Channel on August 29. Ederle's record time was broken when a German man named Vierkoetter swam the Channel in twelve hours and forty-three minutes. Her hearing, which was impaired since childhood and was further damaged by her Channel swim, eventually deteriorated into deafness. Ederle suffered a fall in 1933 that injured her spine; she was forced to wear casts for almost four years. Nineteen neurologists said she would never walk again.

With the same determination with which she swam the English Channel, Ederle recovered from her injury and appeared in Billy Rose's Aquacade at the New York's World Fair in 1939. Like thousands of other American women, she was employed in an aircraft plant during World War II. After the war, however, her dreams of becoming a swimming instructor were deterred by her deafness. Ederle overcame this obstacle by using it to her advantage and focusing her talents on teaching deaf children to swim. In 1965, she was one of the first twenty-one inductees into the international Swimming Hall of Fame.

Summary

On the very day Gertrude Ederle successfully swam the English Channel, a London newspaper ran a front-page editorial which argued that her previous failure to swim the Channel proved the athletic inferiority of women and the uselessness of competitive athletics for women. This was, however, not an unusual theme for the time. Experts in a variety of fields had long argued that strenuous activities for women could lead to problems in childbearing or the development of bulging muscles, and it was not until the late nineteenth century that women participated in competitive sports. Even still, appropriate sports and proper competitive levels were to be maintained so as not to compromise the traditional image of the woman which included traits of passivity and cooperation. No doubt Ederle helped lay to rest the notion that a competitive female athlete was an impossibility.

Ederle was among the first real sports heroines to prove that women were not physically inferior or incapable of strenuous activity. Her record-breaking times, beginning with the twenty-one mile race from the Battery to Sandy Hook and ending with her Channel swim, clearly proved that women were not physically inferior to men. With determination and hard work, she illustrated the potential for women who practiced hard and maintained their dedication. Her twenty-nine national and world records demonstrated that women were fully capable of achieving great prowess in competitive sports. The accomplishments of Gertrude Ederle will always serve as evidence for the endless possibilities for women in sport.

Bibliography
Butler, Hal. *Sports Heroes Who Wouldn't Quit.* New York: Julian Messner, 1973. Butler presents the stories of fifteen individuals who overcame seemingly hopeless odds to become acclaimed athletes. Included among these profiles is a somewhat brief sketch on Gertrude Ederle that mentions the lingering anti-German prejudice she encountered during the post-World War I period as well as the adversity she faced because of her gender.
Gallico, Paul. *The Golden People.* New York: Doubleday, 1965. A former sports editor for the *New York Daily News* who became a popular children's book author, Gallico draws on both of these backgrounds to create this account of various figures in American sports. He includes a profile of Ederle that covers her record-breaking swim, her impressive homecoming, and the personal turmoil that confronted her in later years.
Guttmann, Allen. *Women's Sports: A History.* New York: Columbia University Press, 1991. Guttmann, a noted sports historian and author of *The Olympics: A History of the Modern Games* (1992), traces the development of women's sports throughout the ages. Although Ederle receives only a brief mention, this source provides an excellent context for understanding women's participation in sports.
Lamparski, Richard. *Whatever Became of . . . ?* New York: Crown, 1967. Designed to provide readers with information on the subsequent careers of individuals who are no longer in the spotlight, this book includes an informative profile of Gertrude Ederle and her life after her record-setting swim across the English Channel.
Woolum, Janet. *Outstanding Women Athletes: Who They Are and How They Influenced American Sports.* Phoenix, Ariz.: Oryx Press, 1992. A thoroughly researched collection of sports biographies that includes a sketch on Ederle. Provides a relatively balanced account, with information on Ederle's early Olympic career, her Channel swim, her career as a celebrity, and her post-retirement work with deaf swimmers. Places Ederle's accomplishments within the context of women's sports during the 1920's and 1930's.

N. Jane McCandless

AMY EILBERG

Born: October 12, 1954; Philadelphia, Pennsylvania

Area of Achievement: Religion
Contribution: The first woman to be ordained as a rabbi in the Conservative branch of Judaism, Amy Eilberg has served as a chaplain at Methodist Hospital of Indiana in Indianapolis and as a community rabbi for the Jewish Welfare Federation and at the Jewish Healing Center in San Francisco, California.

Early Life

Amy Eilberg, the daughter of Joshua and Gladys Eilberg, was born and reared in Philadelphia, Pennsylvania, in a family that she has described as "Jewish culturally and philosophically down to our guts in every way." Her father, a lawyer and former Democratic congressman, and her mother, a social worker, involved Amy from an early age in causes ranging from the punishment of Nazi war criminals to the plight of Jews living in the Soviet Union. Her maternal grandmother, living in the Soviet Union after World War I, recalled begging Soviet authorities to spare her husband during one of the many pogroms suffered by the Jewish population. While still a teenager, Amy traveled to the Soviet Union to visit Jews there who had been denied permission to emigrate to Israel.

Eilberg's deep respect for the cultural and religious traditions of Judaism were awakened early. While involved in a summer program with the United Synagogue Youth when she was only fourteen, Amy rigorously observed traditional Jewish prayer and dietary regulations. She discovered during this experience what she called "the sense of connectedness with the faith community, both of the past and of the future, and the community of Jews around the world, with whom I have something in common." After returning home, Amy insisted on adhering to kosher dietary regulations, and her parents, impressed by her sincerity, agreed to make their household completely kosher.

While in high school, Eilberg played the flute in the orchestra and excelled as a member of the debating society. At an age when most of her peers showed little interest in spiritual matters, Amy remained dedicated to her religious principles. She lobbied unsuccessfully to have the senior prom moved from Friday night to another night so that students who were observing the sabbath (which begins on Friday at sundown) could attend without compromising their religious beliefs.

Life's Work

Amy Eilberg entered Brandeis University in 1972, already determined to pursue a career in Jewish education. After graduating from Brandeis summa cum laude in 1976 with a degree in Near Eastern and Judaic studies, she entered the Jewish Theological Seminary in New York to study the Talmud, an enormous body of literature dating from ancient times up through the fifth century that deals with all facets of Jewish law.

Eilberg entered the seminary with the desire to serve as a rabbi, but in 1976 women were not allowed to enter the program in rabbinical ordination. Undeterred, Amy completed a master's degree in Talmud in 1978 and spent a year teaching in Israel (a step required of all Conservative Jews seeking ordination). Eilberg remained hopeful that women would be allowed to pursue ordination at some point in the near future.

In 1979, after a year of debate on the issue of ordination of women, the faculty of Jewish Theological Seminary voted to suspend consideration of this emotional and divisive issue indefinitely. Amy despaired that "it would be a generation until the vote would come up again," but she nevertheless returned to the seminary the following year to resume Talmudic studies, eventually completing all the course work required for a Ph.D. She recalled, "I fantasized about taking all the courses, getting them onto my transcript and one day knocking at the chancellor's door and saying, 'Look at this transcript; what are you going to do now?'"

Later, after what she remembered as "a period of soul-searching," she decided to attend Smith University to study social work, hoping to flesh out her scholastic achievements with professional training in helping others. She called her decision "putting together my own kind of rabbinic training program," and she continued to study the Talmud while working toward a master's degree in social work, which she completed in 1984. During her last year at Smith, the faculty of Jewish Theological Seminary voted to accept women as rabbinical students during the following academic year.

Eilberg was elated by the decision, but she faced a difficult personal decision. Although she lacked only one year of study to complete the qualifications for ordination, Amy had married Rabbi Howard Schwartz and was living with him in Providence, Rhode Island, while he completed his Ph.D. In the fall of 1984, Eilberg moved into the dormitory at the seminary and began concentrated and single-minded study to complete the requirements for ordination, traveling to Rhode Island every Friday afternoon to see her husband. In January of 1985, Schwartz accepted a position as assistant professor of religion at Indiana University in Bloomington, and for several months, Eilberg recalled, they "saw each other every few weeks."

On May 12, 1985, Eilberg received her degree from Jewish Theological Seminary and was ordained as the first woman rabbi in the one-hundred-year history of the Conservative branch of Judaism. She expressed relief that "the years of struggle, of pain and of exclusion are at an end," and stated her hope that "our movement faces a new beginning, a new era of equality and vitality, and a beginning of a healing process that will bring us all to a new kind of unity, in which all may be included and to which all must contribute."

The Conservative branch of Judaism, which ordained Eilberg, stands between two other dominant groups. Differences between these forms of Judaic practice revolve primarily around different interpretations of *halacha*, or traditional Jewish law, as it has evolved through the centuries. The most traditional wing of Judaism is the Orthodox, which views *halacha* as authoritative and essentially unchanging and is most resistant to religious trends allowing women a greater role in Jewish worship and leadership. The most flexible branch of Judaism includes the Reform and Reconstructionist movements, which have been ordaining women since 1973. The Conservative faith has historically tried to strike a balance between the other movements by considering the *halacha* to be authoritative while acknowledging that interpretations of Jewish law can change over time to accommodate the realities of a changing world.

The decision to admit women to professional rabbinical bodies was not an easy one for the Conservative movement. Admission of women into the Rabbinical Assembly, the professional rabbinical body that governs the Conservative movement, required an amendment to the constitution of the Rabbinical Assembly. The two-thirds majority required for the constitutional amendment was obtained in 1985 through a mail ballot in which 70 percent expressed approval for the change. Soon after the results were announced, however, members of the assembly who opposed the change charged the assembly with using "parliamentary finesse" to force through a measure that almost certainly would have failed if the issue had been broached on the floor of the Rabbinical Assembly's annual convention. They warned that the change could become a point of division within the Conservative branch of Judaism.

At her ordination in May of 1985, Eilberg expressed relief: "The long vigil is over, and the wait was fully justified." She expressed the hope that other women would soon follow her into a leadership role in the Conservative faith. "I feel very excited, very proud," she commented to the press, "not just for myself but for all women. As of today, Jewish women need never again feel that their gender is a barrier to their full participation in Jewish life." She also acknowledged, however, that the changes that allowed her the opportunity to be ordained did not come without a price, quoting Rabbi Nehuniah ben Hakeneh, who entered a house of study saying "I pray no harm will come about because of me."

After her ordination, Eilberg accepted positions as chaplain at Methodist Hospital in Indianapolis and as community rabbi at the Jewish Welfare Federation there. She later moved to San Francisco, where she continued her work at the Jewish Healing Center. Since her ordination, Eilberg has encouraged dialogue on two fronts: gender-specific language in the Jewish tradition and modern medical ethics in Judaism. Her activity in the conflict over the language of prayer stems from her strong commitment to feminism. She has enthusiastically acknowledged the creation of new rituals and ceremonies by women, calling them a "marvelously positive phenomenon," and has expressed the hope that "women will have to open up the old books and enter into a new relationship with them, with love, but also with the courage to ask hard questions."

As a social worker, Eilberg has also brought unique insights into the growing need for Jewish leaders to address controversial, modern issues in medical ethics. She has expressed particular concern over issues such as surrogate motherhood, AIDS, and what she has called "the fundamental question of how a life-affirming tradition responds to the artificial prolongation of dying." She has shown herself to be highly critical of sexist, fundamentalist tendencies within Judaism which "equate Judaism with Orthodoxy" and fail to provide rational answers to current controversies.

Summary
   Amy Eilberg has modestly called her own ordination as Conservative Judaism's first woman rabbi "serendipitous," but her sincerity and dedication make her a truly outstanding example among religious leaders of both genders and of all faiths. She has paved the way for other women within Conservative Judaism who will take a leading role in that denomination. Her outspoken views on contemporary problems, tempered by her desire to maintain the traditional values of Judaism, have ensured that other women rabbis will be respected but will not be ignored.
   Eilberg's determination to combine scholarship with public service has given her an opportunity to help her parishioners both personally and organizationally. She is helping to redefine the role of Judaic rabbis within the community while integrating a traditional faith with the modern feminist movement. Through single-minded pursuit of her goals, Eilberg has set a shining example for all women who are blazing trails within professions that have heretofore been reserved for men.

Bibliography
"Amy Eilberg Will Be Conservative Judaism's First Woman Rabbi." *People Weekly* 23 (April 29, 1985): 50-51. This article contains a brief sketch of Eilberg's early life and education in preparation for a rabbinical career.
Cantor, Aviva. "Rabbi Eilberg." *Ms.* 14 (December, 1985): 45-46. This brief article contains a lively and interesting sketch of Eilberg's early life and the educational process she undertook to prepare herself for a career as a rabbi.
Eilberg, Amy. "Modern Medicine and Jewish Ethics; Jewish Values in Bioethics." *Journal of the American Medical Association* 258 (November 20, 1987): 2768-2769. In this review of two books, Eilberg encourages Jewish scholars to address such timely topics as "surrogate motherhood or treatment of the acquired immunodeficiency syndrome" and criticizes the tendency of modern thinkers to "equate Judaism with Orthodoxy," and thus to remain mired in "androcentric" interpretations.
"End of a Vigil." *Time* 125 (February 25, 1985): 61. This brief news release chronicles Eilberg's reaction to the ruling of the Rabbinical Assembly to admit both men and women who have completed rabbinical training to full membership.
Evory, Ann, and Peter M. Gareffa, eds. *Contemporary Newsmakers, 1985 Cumulation*. Detroit: Gale Research, 1986. This reference book contains a brief sketch of Eilberg's early life and ordination.
Goldman, Ari L. "Ten-Year Dream of Being a Rabbi Coming True for a Woman." *The New York Times*, February 17, 1985, p. A40. In addition to detailing Eilberg's ordination, this article contains useful insights into the struggles going on within the various Judaic movements to deal with the role of women in Jewish faith and religious practice.

Kimberly K. Estep

GERTRUDE BELLE ELION

Born: January 23, 1918; New York, New York

Area of Achievement: Biochemistry
Contribution: Elion developed new drugs for many serious diseases, including leukemia, herpes, and malaria, by carefully exploiting differences between normal and abnormal cells. She is one of very few women scientists to win a Nobel Prize or to hold a senior position at a major pharmaceutical firm.

Early Life
On January 23, 1918, Gertrude Belle Elion was born to Robert Elion and Bertha Cohen Elion. Her brother, Herbert, was born six years later. Robert Elion, who immigrated from Lithuania when he was twelve years old, was a successful dentist and real estate investor. Bertha Elion, who immigrated from Russia as a teenager, was a homemaker who valued education for her children very highly. Gertrude Belle Elion was also strongly influenced by her grandfather, who came from Russia to New York when Gertrude was three years old.

Gertrude, known by her nickname "Trudy," was an excellent student in all her subjects. By junior high, she had been skipped two years ahead of her classmates. She remained undecided regarding a career, however, until her beloved grandfather died of stomach cancer when she was fifteen years old. As she witnessed his painful decline, Trudy resolved to dedicate her life to fighting cancer.

Trudy's plans to attend college were threatened, however, when her father lost his money in the stock market crash in October of 1929. Luckily, Trudy was able to enroll in Hunter College, one of the New York City colleges that offered free tuition to students with good grades. She decided that the best way to equip herself in the battle against cancer was to study chemistry. At the age of nineteen, Trudy was graduated Phi Beta Kappa from Hunter College with a B.A. in chemistry. Trudy also became engaged to a statistician studying at City College, at about this time. Before the marriage could take place, her husband-to-be died of a strep infection to his heart valves. His early death strengthened Trudy's resolve to fight illness as a scientist. She would never think seriously about marriage again.

Armed with a college degree and outstanding credentials, Trudy set out to find a job as a chemist. Very quickly, she discovered that no one wanted to hire a woman chemist. At several of the laboratories where she interviewed, she was told that her presence would distract the men. This experience discouraged Trudy so much that she enrolled in secretarial school. Luckily, it was only a few weeks before she heard of an opportunity to teach biochemistry to nursing students. After the one-semester course ended, a friend offered Trudy a job in his laboratory. Slowly, Trudy was able to continue working toward her goals. She began graduate school at New York University and graduated summa cum laude with a master's degree in 1941.

This time, Trudy met with more success when she looked for a job. The Quaker

Maid Company hired her as a quality control chemist. In its food laboratory, Trudy checked fruit for mold and vanilla beans for freshness. This work grew tedious after a year, and when Trudy heard of an opening for a research chemist at Johnson & Johnson, she grabbed it. Six months later, her division was closed. Once again Elion was obliged to look for work.

Life's Work

This time, Gertrude Elion's job hunt was made easier by the start of World War II. As men were recruited to fight the war, women were recruited to fill the jobs they left behind. Opportunities were suddenly available for Elion and many other women.

On June 14, 1944, biochemist George H. Hitchings hired Elion to work in his laboratory as a research chemist at Wellcome Research Laboratories, a division of Burroughs Wellcome, in Tuckahoe, New York. It was an auspicious moment. Hitchings, who was thirteen years older than Elion, would remain her boss until his retirement. Together, they would discover new drugs and write scientific papers reporting their results. Together, they would be promoted up through the ranks of the company. It was a unique and fruitful relationship. Hitchings and Elion worked as true collaborators, but until they both received the 1988 Nobel Prize in Physiology or Medicine, Hitchings was typically regarded as the senior partner.

Although she had a secure job and interesting work, Elion still wished to continue her education. She knew that a Ph.D. would be necessary if she were to secure a place in the top ranks of science. She enrolled in the Brooklyn Polytechnic Institute (now Polytechnic University), the only university that offered night classes in chemistry. For two grueling years, she commuted to Brooklyn after work. Slowly but surely she moved toward her goal. One day, the dean of the school called her into his office and told her that she had to show a serious commitment to her studies by attending school full-time and quitting work. For Elion, this was impossible. Reluctantly, and with many misgivings, she surrendered her hopes of earning a Ph.D.

Elion and Hitchings based their approach to creating new drugs on their knowledge of how the body works when it is attacked by cancer or harmful bacteria. By carefully studying the differences between cancer cells and normal cells, for example, they hoped to find a drug that would destroy the cancer without harming the rest of the body. In the 1940's, this was a novel approach to drug discovery. It was far more typical for scientists in pharmaceutical companies simply to screen hundreds or thousands of compounds at random in order to find an effective one. The basic research in cellular metabolism done by Elion and Hitchings made them much more like scientists in academia. They never lost sight, however, of the practical reason for their work. Their goal was finding cures for some of the world's most deadly diseases.

In 1951, Elion developed a drug for childhood leukemia, a disease that typically killed its victims within a few months. Treatment with 6-mercaptopurine (6-MP), the drug developed by Elion, lengthened life expectancy after diagnosis to one year. Soon, the use of 6-MP, in combination with other treatments, made it possible to cure childhood leukemia. The success of 6-MP exhilarated Elion. To take people suffering from serious, life-threatening illnesses and make them better was her most valued reward as a chemist. Years later, when she was asked for her reaction to the Nobel Prize, she replied that the prize was very nice, of course, but curing people was her real goal. Her uncertainty about whether to choose her job over her Ph.D. also disappeared when 6-MP proved to be such an important and useful drug.

Elion and Hitchings began looking for other diseases that 6-MP might cure. They also learned everything they could about 6-MP to understand why it worked and how it could be modified. Leveraging the knowledge they had to gain even more knowledge about the body's reaction to drugs was also part of the team's strategy. Their creativity was rewarded by the discovery of more valuable pharmaceuticals. During the 1950's and 1960's, Elion, Hitchings, and other scientists learned that 6-MP could be used to suppress the immune system. This made the transplanting of organs from one unrelated person to another possible. A derivative of 6-MP known as azathioprine (trade name Imuran) prevented kidney rejection. It also worked against rheumatoid arthritis. Other drugs that Elion and Hitchings discovered included treatments for gout (allopurinol, trade name Zyloprim), malaria (pyrimethamine, trade names Daraprim and Fansidar), and infections of the urinary or respiratory tracts (trimethoprim, trade names Bactrim and Septra).

Wellcome Research Laboratories was relocated to Research Triangle Park, North Carolina, in 1970. Elion was now head of the department of experimental therapy, a position she moved into after Hitchings was promoted to vice president of research. The move meant that Elion's department would expand but also meant saying goodbye to many of her female technicians. Their husbands' jobs, their children's schools, and other family obligations forced them to remain in New York.

Elion's laboratories were now concentrating on drugs that fought viruses. The strategy, however, remained the same: find a way to dismantle the virus life cycle without interfering with the metabolism of healthy cells. At that time, in the late 1960's and early 1970's, very few labs were doing antiviral work. When Elion and her colleagues discovered a successful antiviral agent, acyclovir (trade name Zovirax), that worked against herpes, shingles, and chicken pox, interest in antiviral agents increased dramatically. Acyclovir became one of Burroughs Wellcome's most profitable drugs.

The surge of interest in antiviral agents, led by Elion's team, coincided with the discovery of the human immunodeficiency virus (HIV) and acquired immunodeficiency syndrome (AIDS). Around the world, scientists began looking for a cure for this deadly virus. The first drug approved for AIDS, known as azidothymidine (AZT), was discovered in 1984 by Wellcome Research researchers trained by Elion and Hitchings. Trimethoprim, the drug discovered by Elion years earlier, is also used to treat pneumocystis carinii pneumonia, the leading killer of people with AIDS.

Elion retired in 1983 as scientist emeritus at Wellcome Research Laboratories. Freed from daily responsibilities, she served as president of the American Association for Cancer Research and as a member of the National Cancer Advisory Board. She also became a research professor of medicine and pharmacology at Duke University.

In 1988, the Nobel Prize for Physiology or Medicine was jointly awarded to Elion, Hitchings, and British biochemist Sir James Black. Elion's award demonstrated once and for all that her collaboration with Hitchings was as an equal partner, equally talented and equally responsible for the drug discoveries.

Summary

Few scientists who have received the Nobel Prize have worked in industry, have lacked the Ph.D., or have been women. Gertrude Elion's notable career as a scientist and her Nobel Prize helped to shatter stereotypes about the function of women in science as mere technicians and assistants. As head of experimental therapy at Wellcome Research Laboratories, Elion also demonstrated that a woman could rise through the ranks at a major pharmaceutical firm. Although the drugs she discovered have cured countless individuals, her most outstanding legacy will be the method of research that she and Hitchings pioneered. By introducing rational drug design based upon an understanding of cellular metabolism, Elion and Hitchings made an enormously important scientific advance. For this they were awarded the Nobel Prize. Elion has said that she never found it necessary to have women as role models. Her heroes were scientists. Nevertheless, after her retirement, Elion spoke in schools to encourage young girls to pursue careers in science, presenting herself as an example of a successful woman scientist.

Bibliography

Altman, Lawrence K. "Three Drug Pioneers Win Nobel in Medicine." *The New York Times*, October 18, 1988, pp. A1, C16. In this newspaper story announcing the awarding of the 1988 Nobel Prize, Elion's work is described in some detail, along with the contributions of George H. Hitchings and Sir James Black.

Bouton, Katherine. "The Nobel Pair." *The New York Times Magazine*, January 29, 1989, 28. This profile of Elion and Hitchings' working relationship was written shortly after the Nobel Prize was awarded. The article makes an effort to show that their relationship is cordial yet somewhat strained.

Holloway, Marguerite. "The Satisfaction of Delayed Gratification." *Scientific American* 265, no. 4 (October, 1991): 40-44. This is a very readable article, full of anecdotes and quotes. It is organized around the theme of Elion's persistence.

McGrayne, Sharon Bertsch. *Nobel Prize Women in Science: Their Lives, Struggles, and Momentous Discoveries*. New York: Carol Publishing Group, 1993. This book describes the lives of fourteen women scientists, including Elion, who either won the Nobel Prize or came close to winning it. Elion's individual struggle as a woman scientist is placed here within the larger context of the historical role of women in science. In the bibliography on Elion, only two sources are cited.

McGuire, Paula, ed. *Nobel Prize Winners Supplement: 1987-1991*. New York: H. W. Wilson, 1992. An easily available source with a short, comprehensive summary of Elion's career. The bibliography includes only periodical articles and entries in various *Who's Who* editions.

St. Pierre, Stephanie. *Gertrude Elion.* Vero Beach, Fla.: Rourke, 1993. Although it is written for children, this book contains useful information about Elion's life and work.

Elizabeth L. Marshall

LINDA ELLERBEE

Born: August 15, 1944; Bryan, Texas

Area of Achievement: Broadcast journalism
Contribution: As a broadcast journalist and author, Ellerbee gained distinction for her direct, witty, and intelligent approach to writing and delivering the news.

Early Life
Linda Ellerbee was born Linda Jane Smith on August 15, 1944, in Bryan, Texas. The only child of Lonnie Ray Smith, the vice president of an insurance company, and Hallie Mainer Smith, a homemaker, Linda Jane was four when her family relocated to Houston.

A tomboyish loner, Linda was educated in the public schools and spent much of her free time reading. Her mother, possessing unfulfilled ambitions of her own, encouraged her daughter to grow intellectually. Linda displayed talent in art and writing; in high school, she won several awards for her paintings.

In 1962, Linda enrolled at Vanderbilt University in Nashville, Tennessee, intending to major in history. While there she won an essay contest sponsored by the United Methodist Church, entitling her to a summer's study in Bolivia. Writing came easily to Linda, but she was a noncommittal student. After marrying her college sweetheart Mac Smith, she dropped out of Vanderbilt in 1964.

Moving to Chicago, Linda worked as a bookkeeper, a writer for a trade magazine, and a disc jockey while her husband attended graduate school. Following their divorce in 1966, she worked as program director for a small radio station in San Jose, California, before moving back to Houston to assist her ailing mother.

Linda met and married the father of her two children, Van Veselka, in 1968. Her daughter Vanessa was born in 1969, and son Joshua came soon after the family relocated to Juneau, Alaska, where they lived in a commune. The demise of her second marriage, according to Linda, was a catalyst for the ambition that led to her subsequent professional success. Finding herself with two children to support she plunged ahead, forging the path that led to her career as a journalist.

Life's Work
Linda Veselka remained in Alaska for a year, working for a local radio station and writing speeches for Terry Miller, the majority leader of the Alaska state senate. Longing to return to Texas, she contacted dozens of radio stations and newspapers in 1972, hoping for a reply. The Associated Press (AP) bureau in Dallas contacted her, offering to test her to determine if she was qualified to write news.

Undaunted by her own inexperience and lack of a degree, Linda hastily devoured a few secondhand college textbooks on basic journalism to prepare for the test. She did well enough to convince the AP to hire her to write news stories for radio and television. Six months passed before she triggered an incident that not only cost her

her job but also transformed her into a local celebrity.

One evening Linda wrote a long and chatty letter to a friend back in Alaska. In it she criticized her boss, two local newspapers, the Dallas city council, the Vietnam War, and someone she was currently dating. Hitting the button on the AP computer to print out a single copy, she inadvertently pushed another button as well and the computer sent her letter out over the AP wire in four states. She was promptly fired.

The embarrassing incident, referred to later as "the Letter," not only brought Linda regional notoriety and some job offers but also illuminated her signature style of journalism. Dick John, the news director of CBS affiliate KHOU-TV in Houston, recognized Linda's humorous and pointed writing and hired her as a television reporter.

Linda learned quickly and within ten months came to the attention of Eric Ober, the assistant news director of WCBS-TV, the CBS flagship station in New York City. She was offered the position of general assignment reporter and accepted, with the encouragement of her third husband Tom Ellerbee, a Houston architect whom she had recently wed. Although the marriage did not survive her first year at the New York station, Linda Ellerbee toiled on for three years, covering the inevitable strikes, homicides, fires, and riots encountered on the 3 P.M. to midnight shift.

In 1975, Ellerbee began her eleven-year affiliation with NBC News. From 1976 to 1978, she covered the House of Representatives for the NBC Washington bureau. Her work caught the eye of Reuven Frank, an executive producer of NBC News who offered her a chance to coanchor a network news program. The offer coincided with the end of her two-year marriage to journalist John David Klein.

Coanchoring *NBC News Weekend* with Lloyd Dobyns, Ellerbee learned, under the tutelage of Reuven Frank, to construct a story around the accompanying visual images. Despite kudos for its literate approach to the news, the show was canceled in the spring of 1979 because of poor ratings. Afterward Ellerbee became the New York correspondent for the *NBC Nightly News* for the next three years.

When Reuven Frank became president of NBC in 1982, he immediately created an opportunity to reunite the praiseworthy team of Ellerbee and Dobyns. *NBC News Overnight* debuted in July of 1982. Airing live five nights a week from 1:30 to 2:30 A.M., the show gave its anchors license to present the news any way they wished, or, as Ellerbee put it, network executives "gave the inmates a chance to run the asylum." Using news reports from foreign news services, network correspondents who wanted their stories presented uncut, and even contributions submitted by reporters from NBC's local affiliates, the show was widely lauded and developed a loyal following of some two million late night viewers.

Devoted fans were unfazed when Dobyns went on to another position and was succeeded by Bill Schechner. The consistent quality of the program was praised by one reviewer for its commitment to emphasizing "the reporting and interpreting skills of its anchors and correspondents instead of flashy graphics or stagy on-camera confrontations." Despite a sea of protests, the program was canceled at the end of 1983 for economic reasons. Shortly thereafter, the program earned the Alfred I.

DuPont-Columbia University Award, the highest prize in broadcast journalism.

Deeply disappointed by the cancellation but happy to have been a seminal part of such an innovative news program, Ellerbee went on to coanchor *Summer Sunday* with Andrea Mitchell. Another experimental news program and the first ever to feature two women as coanchors, *Summer Sunday* was broadcast from various outdoor locations around the country and ran opposite the CBS network's highly successful *60 Minutes*. Marred by technical glitches, *Summer Sunday* limped along and eventually completed an unremarkable nine-week run.

Ellerbee's last assignment at NBC was a weekly five-minute feature for the *Today* show called "T.G.I.F." (Thank God It's Friday). The assignment gave Ellerbee the opportunity to reprise her trademark reporting formula in microcosm. Mining over-looked stories from a wide variety of sources, Ellerbee plied her style of wry, succinct narration. During this period, she also penned the best-selling book, *And So It Goes* (1986). The book's title was taken from the stock phrase with which Ellerbee concluded every broadcast. Ellerbee provided her readers with a humorous and outspoken memoir chronicling her years in television news.

Ellerbee left NBC in 1976 in the wake of a forty percent reduction of her salary and corporate murmuring that she needed to slim down (she had gained twenty pounds). Both CBS and ABC vied for her services. ABC won, promising her greater creative freedom and more money than she received at NBC.

Ellerbee revived her "T.G.I.F." spots for *Good Morning America*. She also coan-chored *Our World*, an ABC News prime-time series about recent historical events. Ellerbee described it as a "video scrapbook of a particular time." Airing opposite NBC's hit series *The Cosby Show*, *Our World* lasted a mere season.

Angry and disappointed that there did not seem to be a place for her vision of journalism in network television, Ellerbee quit ABC. She had long dreamed of starting an independent production company. In 1988, along with her partner Rolfe Tessem, a television director, Ellerbee created Lucky Duck Productions. With her unwavering faith in the intelligence of television viewers and a desire to see television fulfill its potential for greatness, Ellerbee and her creative team began marketing innovative programming to PBS and various cable networks, including Nickelodeon. Ellerbee's venture was a resounding success. Her Nickelodeon special on AIDS with Magic Johnson won the CableACE award for best news program in 1992. After launching a weekly news show for children on Nickelodeon called *Nick News W/5*, Ellerbee not only attracted a new viewing audience but also earned the prestigious DuPont award for her efforts to inform and educate kids.

Ellerbee dabbled in other enterprises at this time, both of which were considered by some to be unusual pursuits for a television journalist. Not long after leaving network television Ellerbee was asked to write a syndicated newspaper column for King Features. Although a move from broadcast to print journalism is atypical, Ellerbee gladly accepted, ever eager for a forum to air her views. Then in 1989 she agreed to do a commercial for Maxwell House. In her second autobiographical book, *Move On* (1991), Ellerbee explained that she pitched for Maxwell House to save

Lucky Duck Productions. Citing the "chicanery" of an employee and her own lack of business acumen, Ellerbee admitted that Lucky Duck had lost a considerable amount of money. Although she was widely criticized for doing the commercials, Ellerbee harbored no regrets since they enabled her to save her company.

Ellerbee's personal life has had its share of difficulty as well. A survivor of four divorces and rehabilitation for alcoholism at the Betty Ford Center, Linda Ellerbee was diagnosed with breast cancer in 1992. After the diagnosis, Ellerbee underwent a double mastectomy and extensive chemotherapy at a Boston hospital. She suffered all the grueling side effects of that treatment; by September of 1993, her doctors proclaimed her cancer-free.

Grateful for her health and sobriety, her grown children, and a stable relationship with Tessem, Ellerbee has continued to produce projects that are meaningful to her. In 1993, she created a special for ABC television called *The Other Epidemic: What Every Woman Needs to Know About Breast Cancer*; she also had a project in the works about women and alcoholism.

Summary

Linda Ellerbee vaulted into the world of journalism in an era when a disproportionate number of female television reporters were, as she put it, "pretty, pearl-wearing vacant-headed paper dolls—the kind of women you swear blow-dry their teeth." Her own literate and irreverent approach combined with her indifference to image has continued to distinguish her from the mainstream of television journalism.

Ellerbee came of age in the 1960's. Her loyalty to the era's philosophy is evident not only in her own personal style—as a fan of rock 'n' roll, blue jeans, and sneakers—but also in her professional bent. Ellerbee is noted for her fierce independence, her unflinching ability to "tell it like it is" (or at least as she sees it), and her distrust of the status quo. Her distinctive personality even provided inspiration for Candice Bergen's character in CBS television's situation comedy, *Murphy Brown*.

Ellerbee's feisty determination helped her overcome her limited college education, the dearth of appropriate recognition for her talent by the major networks, and many personal crises. Despite the obstacles, she has held onto her vision of what television journalism ought to be and has carved out her own path in order to reach her goals.

Bibliography

Ellerbee, Linda. *"And So It Goes": Adventures in Television*. New York: G. P. Putnam's Sons, 1986. An amusing memoir chronicling Ellerbee's early years in television news.

————— . *Move On: Adventures in the Real World*. New York: G. P. Putnam's Sons, 1991. Ellerbee's second book continues the saga of her life in journalism but reveals more of her personal story, past and present.

Goodman, Mark, and Toby Kahn. "Life Force." *People* 40 (September 20, 1993): 59-60. A brief report on Ellerbee's battle with breast cancer and her successful independent productions for Nickelodeon.

Persons, Lauren, and Seth Guinals. "TV's Lucky Duck." *National Geographic World*, no. 212 (April, 1993): 7-9. An interview with Ellerbee providing information of interest to the young fans of her news programs on the Nickelodeon cable channel. Although clearly addressed to a juvenile audience, this article is noteworthy for its timely inclusion of amusing anecdotes and details from Ellerbee's career through the early 1990's.

"Surviving Breast Cancer." *McCall's* 121 (October, 1993): 110-123. Linda Ellerbee is one of nine survivors of breast cancer who are profiled in this article. Ellerbee and the others explain the variety of treatment options available to women as of 1993 and debunk the myths surrounding the disease.

Waters, Harry F. "Ellerbee Takes on the 'World.'" *Newsweek* 108 (September 29, 1986): 60. An article recounting Ellerbee's leap from NBC to ABC's prime-time program, *Our World*. Provides some background details on her career in broadcast journalism.

Kim Dickson Rogers

DIANE ENGLISH

Born: 1948; Buffalo, New York

Area of Achievement: Television

Contribution: A gifted writer and innovative television producer, English has created several television series that have featured strong roles for women, explored social and political issues, and aided the cause of women working within the television industry.

Early Life

Diane English was born in 1948, to a middle-class family in Buffalo, New York. Ann English, her mother, was a homemaker and nightclub singer; Richard English, her father, was an electrical engineer with a drinking problem. His alcoholism created an unhappy home situation for his wife, daughter Diane, and son Rick. When Diane and Rick reached their teens, their mother divorced their father and remarried. English later described the strain and insecurity she experienced in her childhood as instrumental in developing her skill as a writer of comedy—the unhappiness became the source of the comic material.

English's feelings of insecurity also may have fueled her success in high school, where she demonstrated her competitive drive to excel, to be recognized for not only her academic achievements but also for her athletic ability and leadership as captain of the school volleyball team and her involvement in other extracurricular activities. Her position as editor of her high school newspaper also reflected her writing skills, organizational abilities, and ambition.

With her mother's support, English decided to become a playwright. During her undergraduate years at Buffalo State College, however, she changed her mind and majored in education with a minor in theater. After graduating from college in 1970, she secured a teaching position at an inner-city public school, where she became discouraged by the system and her situation. Fortunately, one of her writing instructors urged her to go to New York City and resume her writing for the theater. After a short stint as a poorly paid theater publicist, English landed a secretary's position with WNET, the New York City public television station. Her ambition and talent were rewarded, and she eventually became the associate director of WNET's Television Laboratory, where she soon had the opportunity to use her writing talent. Assigned to draft a script for a television adaptation of Ursula K. Le Guin's *The Lathe of Heaven*, a science fiction novel, English prepared a screenplay that won her a nomination for a Writers Guild Award.

While she worked at WNET, English met her future husband Joel Shukovsky, owner of an advertising agency. With his graphic arts background, Shukovsky was a perfect complement to her verbal skills. Eventually, English also achieved success as a television columnist for *Vogue*. Envisioning a partnership forged from her critical skills and writing talent combined with her husband's visual gifts, English confirmed her belief that her future, and that of her husband, was in Hollywood, the creative center of television. While her husband learned all he could about the television industry, she worked on writing more television scripts.

Life's Work

After three of Diane English's nine television scripts were produced, CBS television executives offered her the opportunity in 1985 to create and produce *Foley Square*, a comedy series set in Manhattan featuring a female district attorney as its protagonist. This first series aired from December of 1985 through July of 1986. Executives at Warner Bros. apparently liked her work because after *Foley Square* was canceled, the company offered to make her the executive producer of *My Sister Sam*, a new comedy series to be produced for CBS. The show featured Pam Dawber as Samantha "Sam" Russell, a free-lance commercial photographer whose teenage sister comes to live with her in San Francisco. Many of the episodes focused on Sam's attempts to juggle her commitments as a single career woman with her responsibilities as a substitute parent. Outlasting *Foley Square*, *My Sister Sam* received mixed critical response, but was popular enough with viewers to last for two seasons before it, too, was canceled in 1988.

English, however, had established that she had a flair for comedy, particularly when it featured strong women characters. After being assigned two series, she created her own series, which Warner Bros. turned down; but they and CBS did finally accept her *Murphy Brown* concept, though not without some reservations. As drawn by English, Murphy is a workaholic television newsperson who is bright, courageous, candid, even occasionally rude; she is also a recovering alcoholic, a single mother, and the epitome of the liberated woman of the 1980's.

The show, which starred Candice Bergen in the title role, first aired in November of 1988 and won high praise from the critics, though audience response was initially mediocre. At the end of its first season it ranked only thirty-sixth in the ratings, but due in part to continued critical acclaim, it rose steadily in the ratings as it garnered several prestigious awards. By the time it reached the number three ranking, some four years later, it had won fifteen Emmy awards, two of them for best comedy series. In 1991 alone *Murphy Brown* won the George Foster Peabody Award and the award from the Television Critics Association for best comedy series. English herself won an Emmy for outstanding writing in a comedy series.

Murphy Brown was a rarity in popular situation comedies because it was an intelligent series about bright but funny characters confronting "real" problems. Bergen's performance was such that she and Murphy Brown seemed one, and her success paved the way for several lucrative endorsements. In broadcast journalism, one of the last bastions of male chauvinism, Murphy Brown succeeded by utilizing so-called "masculine" characteristics (assertiveness, self-confidence) while remaining quintessentially feminine. English's creation was a 1980's woman "who had it all," or at least most of it. In 1991, English decided to round out Murphy's life by adding single motherhood to her career, thereby adding openness and commitment to a character accustomed to keeping colleagues and friends at an emotional distance.

While single motherhood was a controversial topic, even for a show known for its treatment of topical political issues, Murphy's decision to reject marriage proposals from two suitors and bear an illegitimate child became a national issue when in May, 1992, Vice President Dan Quayle condemned her actions. Positing the prime importance of what he termed "family values," Quayle spoke out against alternative lifestyles and diminishing the importance of fathers. English responded to Quayle's comments, which she regarded as a personal attack on herself and her family, and used the occasion to point out that his objections to single motherhood made abortion a necessary option for women. The furor continued when at the Emmy Awards in late summer English, Bergen, and other industry members derided Quayle and the Bush Administration. When the first episode of the 1992-1993 season, appropriately entitled "Murphy's Revenge," aired, *Murphy Brown* received extremely high ratings; the seventy million viewers comprised the largest audience for any regularly scheduled television show since November, 1990.

Before the season began, however, English had severed her official connection with the show (though she was still credited as its creator and kept in touch with the writers) and started, with her husband, Shukovsky English Entertainment, an independent production company. CBS contracted with the company to produce some new series with English as creator and executive producer. *Love and War*, starring Jay Thomas and Susan Dey, was the first series to air, and its debut in 1992 was moderately successful. The series, featuring a male-female "Odd Couple" comprising a sophisticated career woman in the restaurant business and an uncultured newspaper columnist, focused on another woman's attempts to "have it all"—career and a successful relationship. Although certain concerns about Dey's ability to fit in the show's comedic ensemble led to Dey's replacement in the second season by former *Designing Women* star Annie Potts, the basic format of *Love and War* remained unchanged.

Known as a tough negotiator (CBS was not enthusiastic about casting Bergen as Murphy Brown), English has also been criticized for her replacing of technicians on the set of *Love and War*. The action was taken to check the organizing efforts of the International Alliance of Stage Employees. Although the National Labor Relations Board rejected the union's claims, the episode is at odds with the liberal stance associated with English. She has received several awards, however, that attest her commitment to working women: the National Commission on Working Women Commissioner's Award (1992), the American Women in Radio and Television Genie Award (1990), and, significantly, the Feminist of the Year Award (given by the Feminist Majority Foundation in 1992). She enjoys the respect of the industry and is touted as a likely choice as the first woman to direct a network's entertainment division. Appealing as that prospect is, English seems intent on developing, with her husband, a television company on approximately one hundred acres in Malibu, where they live. The lucrative contract Shukovsky English Entertainment has with CBS for the development of several new series suggests that English will continue to play an influential role in television.

Summary

Diane English brought a new dimension to television situation comedies. While previous series had featured outstanding female comics (Lucille Ball, Roseanne Barr) or actresses with strong ensemble casts (Mary Tyler Moore), *Murphy Brown* was the first series to feature a strong career woman and to treat controversial issues, such as homelessness, single motherhood, and environmental protection, in a sophisticated comic manner. Moreover, the Murphy Brown character served as a positive role model for many young women intent on making a career for themselves in an essentially male domain complete with "glass ceilings." Murphy competed and succeeded; she was as "assertive" as her male rivals without falling into the neurotic "aggressive" behavior the media often associate with career women, who are usually portrayed as cold, calculating, and ruthless (*Working Girl*) or obsessed and psychotic (*Fatal Attraction*).

In her handling of the single motherhood issue, English, who had the support of CBS, was not intimidated by the Bush Administration or the fundamentalist politics of the Moral Majority. At a time when there was a considerable backlash against the women's movement, *Murphy Brown* alone demonstrated that working women were not incompatible with American families. English seems to have a special flair for using a comic scalpel to probe women's issues and to cure them with healthy doses of laughter. Her efforts have done much to redress the gender imbalance in television programming. Approximately 25 percent of television writers during the early 1990's were women; and English and Linda Bloodworth-Thomason, creator of the popular series *Designing Women* and *Evening Shade*, controlled two-and-a-half hours of prime-time television.

Bibliography

DeVries, Hilary. "Laughing off the Recession." *The New York Times Magazine*, June 3, 1993, pp. 18-21, 24, 26. The most thorough essay on English's life, career, work habits, and plans for the future. DeVries begins with a description of English's writing team editing an episode of *Love and War*, a recession-era comedy about the differences between men and women, but moves to other matters, including English's union problems, her desire to "control," her feminism, her plans for developing a 100-acre studio in Malibu, and the growing importance and power of women producers in television.
"Diane English." *People Weekly* 38 (December 28, 1992-January 4, 1993): 69. Unsigned article comments on English's ironic role as the standard bearer for single mothers in America since she herself is childless. Makes an interesting and informative contrast between CBS's 1969 cancellation of the *Smothers Brothers Comedy Hour*, also anti-administration, and CBS's support for English and *Murphy Brown*.
Morgenson, Gretchen. "Not with My Money You Don't." *Forbes* 150 (November 23, 1992): 47. A scathing indictment of English's troubles with the International Alliance of Stage Employees, a union which unsuccessfully attempted to organize

the lower-paid technicians who worked on the series *Love and War*. Morgenson implies that the highly paid and politically liberal English acted hypocritically in replacing her original technicians, who did not receive health and pension benefits from her company.

Price, Susan. "Diane English: Prime-Time Power." *Ladies' Home Journal* 108 (June, 1991): 64. Price focuses on English's ambition and drive, beginning with the production of her play at the New London Playhouse in New Hampshire when she was only twenty through *Foley Square*, "a critically acclaimed flop," to *Murphy Brown*, the series which established her as a power in the industry and a likely candidate to head a network's entertainment division.

"The Real Murphy Brown Hears Her Clock Tick." *People Weekly* 35 (Spring, 1991): 63-64. Examines the parallels between English and the Murphy Brown character and finds that both reached the top, then realized they had paid a price, family; but Murphy Brown, unlike her creator, becomes a mother. The article also concerns English's early days at WNET and her working relations with male writers.

Thomas L. Erskine

588

NORA EPHRON

Born: May 19, 1941; New York, New York

Areas of Achievement: Journalism and film
Contribution: Known for her critical, comedic observations in magazine writing and films, Ephron is one of Hollywood's most successful screenwriters and directors.

Early Life

Nora Ephron was born in New York City on May 19, 1941, the eldest of four daughters of screenwriters Henry Ephron and Phoebe Wolkind Ephron. Henry, whose plays had not been produced, worked in the New York theater as stage manager for playwright George S. Kaufman and director Moss Hart.

When Nora was born, Phoebe rejected full-time motherhood, and Phoebe and Henry began their lifelong collaboration. The Ephrons' play *Three's a Family* focused its comedy on the addition of a baby to a household. The play was produced on Broadway, winning the Ephrons a motion picture contract with Twentieth Century-Fox. In 1944, they moved to Hollywood with daughter Nora.

Phoebe and Henry collaborated on screenplays for films such as *The Desk Set* (1957) and *Carousel* (1956). The Ephron family was close-knit; dinner had a talk show atmosphere, and the four children competed for attention by telling amusing anecdotes about their daily activities or arguing about politics. The children were encouraged to be interesting and amusing, and three of the four daughters became writers.

Nora Ephron cites her mother as a role model, a working mother in an era when most women were housewives. Phoebe passed on the Ephron philosophy of life and art: to use one's experiences as a basis for writing. Like her parents, Nora often collaborated in her screenwriting, once with her sister Delia Ephron. Her three marriages have been to writers.

Nora grew up in Beverly Hills, as part of an upper-middle-class Jewish milieu in the shadow of the film industry. At Beverly Hills High School, Nora edited the front page of the school newspaper, having discovered that she wanted to be a journalist at age thirteen. She also published news and sports stories in the *Los Angeles Times*. Her idol was satirist Dorothy Parker, the quintessential New York writer, and New York was her spiritual home.

In 1958, Nora entered Wellesley College in Massachusetts, and she was graduated in 1962. She later wrote that Wellesley taught women to restrain themselves, to be too polite. Nora's letters home from college became the basis for her parents' Broadway hit comedy *Take Her, She's Mine* (1961).

Life's Work

While in college, Nora Ephron worked one summer as a copy girl for CBS in New York. After being graduated, she was hired by *Newsweek* to work in the mail room and was eventually promoted to researcher. In 1963, she was hired as a general assignment reporter by the *New York Post*, writing short pieces. After two years, she was assigned her first series. Ephron values this period of honing her craft, of learning to condense and research thoroughly. She began to submit articles to magazines.

In 1968, Ephron left the *Post* to work full-time as a freelancer, writing profiles of celebrities. Ephron's authorial voice emerged as she used her barbed humor to make serious comments on a variety of popular culture topics: mass media, show business, the worlds of fashion and food, and popular novels. She defended her interest in popular culture by declaring it trivial but as much a part of her life as world politics.

In 1970, Ephron published a collection of articles, *Wallflower at the Orgy*. The title reflected what she called her journalistic detachment, meaning not objectivity (which she did not deem possible) but a sense of the absurdity of life that tended to make her a witness of events rather than a participant. She claims that it took years for her to use the word "I" in her writing.

Ephron makes use of her direct experience in a harrowing account of a beauty makeover. A piece on Helen Gurley Brown, editor of *Cosmopolitan* magazine, recounts Ephron's own experience of being edited by Brown. Her analysis of the cult popularity of writer Ayn Rand's *The Fountainhead* (1943) mentions her own adolescent fascination with the novel. Her interview with film director Mike Nichols is a conversation; Ephron is not the invisible interviewer.

In 1972, Ephron joined the staff of *Esquire* magazine as contributing editor, writing a column on women's issues for the male-oriented publication. Joining *New York* magazine in 1973, Ephron continued to write on women. Twenty-five of Ephron's columns for *Esquire* are collected in her book *Crazy Salad: Some Things About Women* (1975).

Ephron's essays here take a personal tone. The lead essay, "A Few Words About Breasts," describes her own experiences as an adolescent growing up in the American culture of the 1950's. Even in adulthood, her small breast size figured in competitive interactions with women as well as in relationships with men. For Ephron, observation of her personal experience became an avenue for reporting general cultural phenomena surrounding women. "Fantasies" poses the problem of the contradiction between feminist politics and a culturally induced desire to be dominated.

Ephron's observations of the political maneuverings of women's movement leaders at the 1976 Democratic Convention were criticized as a betrayal of the movement. In "Truth or Consequences," Ephron explores the tension she felt between her professional commitment as a journalist to report the truth and her political commitment as a feminist. She ultimately comes down on the side of truth-telling.

In essays such as "Vaginal Politics," on the women's medical self-help movement, and "On Consciousness-Raising," Ephron mounts a cautious critique of the movement's tendency to dissolve into personal narcissism.

Returning to *Esquire* in 1974 as senior editor, Ephron began a column on media; twenty-five of the resulting pieces are collected in *Scribble Scribble: Notes on the Media* (1978). Ephron criticizes editorial policies that degrade newspaper journalism into gossip. She also tackles off-beat media targets: conflicts of interest in food writing; authors of double-crostic puzzles; a Palm Beach, Florida, society paper; and an apartment newsletter. Her last piece, "Enough," ends the column by deploring the transformation of journalists into celebrities who, Ephron insists, should not be treated as more interesting than the stories they cover.

Ephron's second husband, Carl Bernstein, was himself a celebrity journalist who, with fellow investigative reporter, Bob Woodward, had broken the Watergate story that ended Richard Nixon's presidency. When *All the President's Men* was adapted for film, Bernstein and Ephron prepared a draft of the script, rewriting the original screenplay by writer William Goldman. Ephron claims that rewriting Goldman's script was like taking a course in screenwriting from a master.

Ephron's first credited script was for a film made for television, *Perfect Gentlemen* (1978), starring Lauren Bacall, about four women who break into a hotel safe. Her cinematic breakthrough was a collaborative script with writer Alice Arlen for *Silkwood* (1983). Directed by Mike Nichols, the film starred Meryl Streep as activist Karen Silkwood, who died on her way to a meeting with a reporter to expose criminal activities at the nuclear power plant where she worked. Critics noted the nonidealized depiction of the working-class heroine. Ephron and Arlen were nominated for an Academy Award for the screenplay.

In 1979, Ephron's marriage to Carl Bernstein broke up, and Ephron moved back to New York with her two sons. As a single parent, she wrote screenplays to support herself, including an uncredited draft of *Compromising Positions* (1983). Between screenplays, Ephron worked on a novel, *Heartburn* (1983), which is widely regarded as a *roman à clef* based on the breakup of her marriage. In the novel, Rachel Samstat, a cookbook author, discovers her husband, a political columnist, in an affair with a Washington socialite. The novel, which quirkily contained Rachel's recipes, was on *The New York Times* best-seller list for twenty-seven weeks.

Ephron adapted the screenplay for *Heartburn* (1986), which starred actors Meryl Streep and Jack Nicholson and was directed by Mike Nichols. Critics noted that the film did not retain the Jewishness of the milieu depicted in the novel.

Ephron received another Academy Award nomination and won the British Oscar for best screenplay for her script for the blockbuster comedy *When Harry Met Sally* (1989). Ephron based the character of Harry on conversations she had with director Rob Reiner and producer Andy Scheinman about their lives as single men. The romantic comedy that emerged starred Billy Crystal and Meg Ryan as friends who test their friendship through a sexual relationship.

With collaborator Alice Arlen, Ephron cowrote the screenplay for *Cookie* (1989), a comedy by director Susan Seidelman starring Peter Falk as a Brooklyn mobster. Cookie, the mobster's free-spirited daughter, reared by his mistress, becomes her father's getaway driver. Ephron and Arlen based the script on crime reporting by Ephron's third husband, writer Nicholas Pileggi. The two female characters are surprisingly tough women in conventional sexpot packaging.

Ephron's next screenplay was another comedy, *My Blue Heaven* (1990), directed by Herbert Ross and featuring comedians Steve Martin and Rick Moranis. Ephron participated in the casting when she convinced Martin to take the role of a Mafioso who is relocated to a small town by the Federal Witness Protection program. He had originally been slated to play the repressed FBI agent.

Ephron often commented on the lack of control that a screenwriter has over the finished product, noting that a film becomes the creation of the director and actors. In 1989, she signed a contract with Columbia Pictures to write and direct two films. *This Is My Life* (1992), Ephron's directorial debut, was cowritten with her sister Delia. Because of a change in studio ownership, the picture almost was not made; eventually, Twentieth Century-Fox agreed to finance the picture.

The script, adapted from a novel by Meg Wolitzer, follows the career of a stand-up comedian and single mother, played by Julie Kavner, and examines how that career affects the lives of her children. Ephron and her sister claim their childhood experience as a source, but Ephron also identifies closely with the plight of the working mother whose professional successes spell absence from children, citing balancing career and home as the quintessential problem of contemporary women.

Ephron's second film as director was the hit comedy *Sleepless in Seattle* (1993), released by Tri-Star Pictures. The screenplay, by Jeff Arch, David Ward, and Ephron, depicts the love story between a Seattle widower, played by Tom Hanks, and a Baltimore journalist, played by Meg Ryan, who hears the widower reveal his feelings on a radio talk show. The film was one of seven films that grossed more than $100,000,000 in 1993.

Summary

A best-selling novelist, magazine journalist, screenwriter, and film director, Nora Ephron has achieved extraordinary commercial success in a variety of competitive, male-dominated fields. Her authorial voice, which addresses serious issues comedically, has contributed to blockbuster films *When Harry Met Sally* and *Sleepless in Seattle* and has led to two Academy Award nominations for best screenplay *(Silkwood* and *When Harry Met Sally)*. Ephron is among the highest-paid screenwriters in Hollywood and is a highly successful director, known for her comedic portrayals of contemporary lifestyles and gender relations. Her women are strong but nonidealized constructions.

As a journalist, Ephron covered the women's movement with a critical voice that found much to defend as well as to criticize. She deplored what she feared was the movement's degeneration into personal narcissism and lack of humor, believing that humor might accomplish more than polemics.

Ephron covered popular culture at a time when it was not taken seriously as a topic for commentary. She used her interest in the popular and the everyday to explore the cultural worlds that women are expected to inhabit.

Bibliography
Ephron, Henry. *We Thought We Could Do Anything: The Life of Screenwriters Phoebe*

and Henry Ephron. New York: W. W. Norton, 1977. Ephron's father relates the story of his and his wife's lives and careers, including material on Nora's childhood and social life. The book contains Henry Ephron's occasional comments on Nora's adult sense of herself, as well as an epilogue by Nora Ephron in which she discusses her mother as a role model.

Ephron, Nora. *Crazy Salad: Some Things About Women.* New York: Alfred A. Knopf, 1975. This collection contains many autobiographical pieces, such as "A Few Words About Breasts," "Reunion," "Fantasies," and "On Never Having Been a Prom Queen."

——————. *Heartburn.* New York: Alfred A. Knopf, 1983. Ephron's novel is widely considered a *roman à clef* about the breakup of her marriage to Carl Bernstein.

Palmer, William J. *The Films of the Eighties: A Social History.* Carbondale: Southern Illinois University Press, 1993. With chapters such as "The Yuppie Texts" and "Neoconservative Feminist Texts," this social and political analysis covers films of the time period. Admiring *Silkwood* for its working-class and anti-corporate perspective and its accuracy, the author sees *Heartburn* as a yuppie film in which having a good job makes up for personal failings.

Walker, Nancy. "Ironic Autobiography: From *The Waterfall* to *The Handmaid's Tale.*" *Women's Studies* 15, nos. 1-3 (1988): 203-220. Walker analyzes Ephron's novel *Heartburn*, comparing it to novels by authors Margaret Atwood, Fay Weldon, and Margaret Drabble. Walker sees these novels as employing an ironic autobiographical approach in which a narrator presents a split self who comments on her own embeddedness in a feminine cultural system. The humor generated by this comedic irony undermines the authority of male-dominant definitions and becomes a means for the female characters to control their stories and ultimately their lives.

Allison Carter

LOUISE ERDRICH

Born: June 7, 1954; Little Falls, Minnesota

Area of Achievement: Literature
Contribution: A poet and novelist of Chippewa and German descent, Erdrich has become one of the most important authors writing Native American fiction in the late twentieth century.

Early Life

Louise Erdrich was born in Little Falls, Minnesota, across the Red River from Wahpeton, North Dakota, the small town that later served as a model for Erdrich's fictional town of Argus. Her father, Ralph Erdrich, was a German immigrant; her mother, Rita Journeau Erdrich, was a three-quarters Chippewa. Both her parents were employed by the Wahpeton Bureau of Indian Affairs boarding school. Louise grew up in Wahpeton, the oldest of seven children, and was exposed to the cultures of both her parents. Maintaining a close bond with her German Catholic grandmother, she was also on familiar ground with her extended Chippewa family on the Turtle Mountain reservation. Her maternal grandfather was a tribal chairman there, and the North Dakota plains reservation eventually became the setting for much of Louise's fiction.

Erdrich later claimed that she had never given serious attention to her Native American background while growing up, had never thought about "what was Native American and what wasn't." In 1972, she entered Dartmouth College in New Hampshire and majored in creative writing. Her parents had encouraged her interest in writing since her childhood, binding her stories into homemade books. At Dartmouth, she began to garner awards for her poetry and stories. After her graduation from Dartmouth she worked a variety of odd jobs, compiling a personal archive of experiences for use in her writing. While pursuing her M.A. at The Johns Hopkins University, which she earned in 1979, she composed many of the poems that would be collected in her first published book. *Jacklight* (1984) received critical praise, but it was her short stories, appearing in literary magazines, that produced a sense of anticipation among literary critics. "The World's Greatest Fisherman," set on the reservation and centering on the death of June Kashpaw, won first prize in the Nelson Algren fiction competition in 1982. Introducing the various members of the Kashpaw, Lamartine, and Nanapush families, this story became the starting place for a number of related novels reaching back in history as far as 1912.

Erdrich's marriage to Michael Dorris in 1981 coincided with her burgeoning interest in her Chippewa heritage. Dorris, who had been a professor in the Native American studies program at Dartmouth, shared Erdrich's writing ambitions and a similar ethnic background. He had previously adopted a son, whose struggle with fetal alcohol syndrome (FAS) led Dorris to write *The Broken Cord* (1989). Dorris adopted two more children; Erdrich adopted all three of Dorris' children, and together Erdrich and Dorris produced three more. In addition to rearing their large family, Erdrich and

Dorris have collaborated on all of their writing and have campaigned together against the increasing incidence of FAS.

Life's Work

When Louise Erdrich's *Love Medicine* first appeared in 1984, two of its stories had already been honored: "Scales," which was anthologized in *Best American Short Stories, 1983* (1983); and the 1982 Nelson Algren competition winner, "The World's Greatest Fisherman." "Saint Marie" was later selected for *Prize Stories 1985: The O. Henry Awards* (1985). Among the awards Erdrich received for *Love Medicine* are the National Book Critics Circle Award and the *Los Angeles Times* Award for Fiction. Erdrich was immediately hailed as an original and powerful talent, and her second novel, *The Beet Queen* (1986), confirmed her place among important contemporary authors.

Native American fiction began to rise with the cream of twentieth century American literature with the publication of N. Scott Momaday's *A House Made of Dawn* (1969). Readers, primed perhaps by the Magical Realism of Gabriel García Márquez and the "boom" writers of Latin America, appeared ready for the transcendent storytelling of such writers as Leslie Marmon Silko, James Welch, Gerald Vizenor, and Sherman Alexie. Silko's *Ceremony* (1977) and *Almanac of the Dead* (1991), and Vizenor's *Bearheart: The Heirship Chronicles* (1990; originally published as *Darkness in Saint Louis Bearheart*, 1978) not only appeared on best-seller lists but also demanded the attention of critics and scholars.

A distinctive yet difficult element of Erdrich's fiction for which she has been criticized is the apparent disjointedness of her narratives: cross-cutting points of view, circular plotting, jarring shifts in time. Casual, linear reading produces an impression of a beautifully written but incoherent patchwork of short stories. A more careful approach reveals a deliberate and artful weaving of tales, all related—some more distantly than others—but all essential to the whole.

While *Love Medicine* dealt with the extended family of the Kashpaws on the reservation, *The Beet Queen* told the somewhat more tightly plotted story of the Adares: siblings Mary and Karl (who, in one of the most memorable scenes in American literature, are left amid an expectant crowd as their mother unexpectedly flies away with a stunt pilot), and Karl's daughter Dot. Dot is the intersection at which the worlds of the white Adares and Erdrich's Chippewas overlap. Celestine, Karl's lover and Dot's mother, is half-sister to Russell Kashpaw; Gerry Nanapush is the adult Dot's lover.

Tracks appeared in 1988, continuing the histories of characters begun in the two previous works. The action in this novel is concentrated in the years 1912 through 1924, though its repercussions travel backward through *Love Medicine* and *The Beet Queen* (and forward through time), filling in crucial details and enriching the entire saga. A full, vibrant, and complex picture of the Matchimanito reservation, its inhabitants and neighbors, emerges; Erdrich brings into flower a mature and many-branched family tree. Nanapush and Pauline Puyat alternate their narratives, each revealing from strikingly different perspectives the life of Fleur Pillager, an alluring and mystical figure who calls Nanapush "uncle" and loves Eli Kashpaw. It is the descendants of Pillager, Nanapush, and Eli that people Erdrich's Matchimanito.

In 1993, Henry Holt issued an expanded edition of *Love Medicine* that included five new sections. Erdrich believed that the new stories belonged with the earlier work. Then in 1994, she released *The Bingo Palace*, bringing the latest generation of her characters to adulthood.

The web of characters Erdrich spins is dizzying in its complexity. An enthusiastic reader would be well advised to map out the relationships in order to appreciate fully the varying perspectives that characters have of one another. Lulu Nanapush Lamartine, for example, is the daughter of Fleur and Eli. She has eight children, each with a different father. She is also the love interest of her uncle Nector, rival to Marie Lazarre, and grandmother to Lipshaw Morrisey. She appears as an infant in *Tracks* and as a middle-aged woman in *The Bingo Palace*. Her son Gerry is the lover of both June Kashpaw (Lulu's half-sister) and Dot Adare. Gerry's son Lipshaw becomes the rival of his uncle Lymon (another of Lulu's sons).

It is easy to draw comparisons between Erdrich's fictional community and William Faulkner's Yoknapatawpha County. Erdrich herself has named Faulkner as an influence. Matchimanito is based on Turtle Mountain reservation, where Erdrich spent much of her youth; the off-reservation town of Argus is a re-creation of her hometown of Wahpeton. The complicated family network that binds her fiction into a comprehensive whole is certainly inspired by the author's own Chippewa relatives. Her familiarity with the more sinister aspects of Catholic mysticism and the dangers posed by its mingling with Indian superstition appears especially in the dark, twisted reasoning of Pauline, the fanatic nun and nemesis of Fleur.

The themes raised in Erdrich's fiction are universal: the value and potency of hope and love and the importance of home and family. The issues that illustrate these themes stem from the condition of Native Americans in the twentieth century. The reservation is a blighted residue left over from previous centuries of decline, a place of concentrated despair; yet it is also a community where ties among members are strong and the connection of its people to the land is ancient and sacred. Poverty, alcoholism, abandoned or distorted faith are balanced against self-worth, endurance, and love.

Erdrich's plots also involve a variety of contemporary issues, including the erosion of land rights; the education of children in both the government schools (in which Indian children endured forced assimilation and the attempted erasure of their own language and culture) and in the wilds; tribal politics; religious conflict; generational conflict; and intermarriage.

Summary

Louise Erdrich's contribution to the canon of Native American literature is an important one. In addition to giving expression to the trauma of the Chippewa experience, she has presented the lives of American Indians not as defeated but as determined and vital. She has also brought to the storytelling tradition a literary artistry that is both challenging and refreshingly original. Critical opinion, however, does not confine Erdrich to the narrow category of Indian writer. She is unquestionably among the most important novelists of the twentieth century.

In addition to her fiction she also published works of poetry and folktales, including *Baptism of Desire* (1989). A rewarding collaborative relationship with Michael Dorris resulted in other works of fiction, including *A Yellow Raft in Blue Water* (1987) and *The Crown of Columbus* (1991), as well as Dorris' autobiographical work *The Broken Cord*.

Erdrich and Dorris' campaign against fetal alcohol syndrome, which afflicts many reservation children because of the high rate of alcoholism among Native Americans, helped to draw the nation's attention to the dangerous effects of alcohol on fetuses. Legislation was eventually passed requiring the posting of warnings to pregnant women anywhere liquor is sold.

Bibliography
Owens, Louise. "Acts of Recovery: The American Indian Novel in the '80s." *Western American Literature* 1 (May 22, 1987): 53-57. Places Erdrich within a survey of Native American authors. Dated but useful.
Rainwater, Catherine. "Reading Between Worlds: Narrativity in the Fiction of Louise Erdrich." *American Literature* 62 (September, 1990): 405-422. Explores the thematic and chronological structure employed by Erdrich in her first three novels. Rainwater emphasizes the conflicting messages found in these narratives and discusses Erdrich's use of narative devices.
Sergi, Jennifer. "Storytelling: Tradition and Preservation in Louise Erdrich's *Tracks*." *World Literature Today* 66 (Spring, 1992): 279-283. Focusing on *Tracks*, this article discusses the ways in which Erdrich builds her multilayered narrative, drawing on the centrality of collective memory in tribal tradition.
Towery, Margie. "Continuity and Connection: Characters in Louise Erdrich's Fiction." *American Indian Culture and Research Journal* 16 (1992): 99-122. A welcome companion to Erdrich's Matchimanito novels. Towery provides a genealogy of the characters and discusses their lives and relations.
Wong, Hertha D. "An Interview with Louise Erdrich and Michael Dorris." *North Dakota Quarterly* 55 (Winter, 1987): 196-218. A comprehensive interview with Erdrich and her husband. The two discuss their collaborative methods, the origins of their fiction, and their academic activities as well as their personal lives.

Janet Alice Long

GLORIA ESTEFAN

Born: September 1, 1957; Havana, Cuba

Area of Achievement: Music
Contribution: A vocalist and songwriter, Gloria Estefan draws from her Cuban origins to attract popular audiences in the United States and Latin America.

Early Life

Gloria's youth was characterized by turmoil and uncertainty. Her father, José Manuel Fajardo, was a security officer for Fulgencio Batista, Cuba's controversial head of state, who was overthrown by Fidel Castro in 1959. Soon after Batista's downfall, Fajardo and his family fled to Miami, where he joined the effort to oust Castro. He participated in the ill-fated Bay of Pigs invasion and, after his release from imprisonment in Cuba, joined the United States Army to serve in Vietnam. He returned from combat with multiple sclerosis. Teenaged Gloria Fajardo and her mother cared for her fatally stricken father as his health deteriorated. Isolated from other teenagers, Gloria was sensitive, overweight, shy, and seemingly overwhelmed by the slow, painful demise of her father and the challenges of growing up in Miami's multicultural society.

Music was a private matter at first. She listened to the popular artists of the United States in the late 1960's and early 1970's—the Carpenters, for example—along with Cuban and other Latin music. To escape her loneliness in these years, Gloria retreated to her room, took up her guitar, and sang for hours. In a 1990 *Rolling Stone* interview, she recalled: "I wouldn't cry. I was afraid if I let go just a little bit, it would all go. I would sing for hours by myself. . . . It was my way of crying."

Family and neighbors provided her with friendly, if small, audiences, often at weddings, but in October of 1975 she ventured into a larger sphere. She auditioned for the Miami Latin Boys, a band that played for parties in the south Florida area. The organizer of the band, Emilio Estefan, heard her sing and quickly recognized the warmth and sincerity that underlay the strength in her voice. With Gloria as vocalist, the band changed its name to the Miami Sound Machine and began to acquire a larger following. A combination of diet and a busy schedule helped Gloria to shed excess weight and become a svelte, smooth dancer. Several months after she joined the band, she and Emilio began to date, and on September 1, 1978, the two were married.

Life's Work

Gloria Estefan rose to stardom as the lead vocalist for the Miami Sound Machine. Emilio quit his lucrative job with Bacardi, the rum manufacturer, in 1980 to work full time managing the group. The band's growing popularity soon brought a contract with Discos CBS International, and in 1984 CBS Records released Miami Sound Machine's first English-language album, *Eyes of Innocence*, for the mainstream audience in the United States. Emilio's energy and business acumen guided the band to lucrative concert tours and recording contracts. The Miami Sound Machine's knack for synthesizing Cuban music with other Latin rhythms and incorporating this mixture into the popular music of the United States produced a series of hits in their next albums: *Primitive Love* and *Let It Loose*. Gloria, Emilio, and the band constituted an unusual phenomenon in a highly competitive business—a band with Latin roots and a large following in Latin America that, at the same time, had a major impact in the United States. In a February, 1990, interview with the trade journal *Advertising Age*, Gloria described an example of their success in bringing Cuban music to the heartland of the United States. At a concert in Iowa, the audience responded to the band's rendition of its hit "Conga" by forming a dance line of 11,142 midwesterners, certainly one of the longest conga lines in history.

In 1987 and 1988, Estefan gained acclaim for her vocal performances, while the Miami Sound Machine faded into the background. The cumulative effects of her earlier hits came to a dramatic peak on a nationwide concert tour. Her mainstream romantic ballad "Anything for You" reached number one on the popular song charts, and the rapid growth of her concert audiences required a move from 5,000-seat auditoriums to those with a capacity of 30,000 or more. Yet this popularity was accompanied by tensions within the original Miami Sound Machine. The emphasis on mainstream American popular music dismayed Cuban-American band members Joe Galdo and Kiki Garcia. This issue and other problems led to the breakup of the Miami Sound Machine. Galdo and Garcia departed to pursue their own careers, leaving Gloria as the lead vocalist backed by a group of young musicians. Emilio, as at the beginning, remained in charge of business operations.

Gloria's success owed much to the work of her husband-manager. Emilio Estefan was the son of Lebanese immigrants who had settled in Santiago, Cuba. The family's business fell victim to Castro's socialization of the economy, and the Estefans moved to Spain. In 1968, young Emilio came to Miami. With little fluency in English, he found a menial mail delivery job at Bacardi, the rum manufacturer. Within twelve years, he rose to become head of the corporation's Latin American marketing operations. An aspiring musician as well as an energetic entrepreneur, Emilio used his spare time to organize the Miami Latin Boys. After Gloria joined the band, Emilio gave more of his time to the business side of its operations. In 1980, he left Bacardi to become full-time manager of the Miami Sound Machine; by the late 1980's, he was directing Gloria's career as an independent performer.

Emilio's support suddenly became even more essential on a cold, snowy night in March of 1990. The bus carrying their entourage to a concert in Syracuse had stopped because a truck had jackknifed across the road in front of them. Suddenly, another truck hit the Estefans' bus from behind, throwing Gloria violently onto the floor. The force of the crash cracked a vertebra in her spinal column. Emilio and their nine-year-old son, Nayib, suffered relatively minor injuries, but Gloria faced the possibility of paralysis. In spite of successful spinal surgery soon after the accident, her doctors as well as her fans were uncertain whether she could recover. After several months of physical therapy and an assiduous training regimen, she regained most of her mobility and began to make concert appearances again. Her voice was unaffected, and she continued to attract large audiences.

Gloria's recovery from her career-threatening injuries brought out a side of her character that many of her fans had only glimpsed before 1990. The quiet, reclusive teenager had grown into a popular singer who was also a highly professional song-writer and performer. The motivation and intensity that helped her through physical rehabilitation had been central in her rise to preeminence in the Miami Sound Machine. She had written many of her hit songs, including "Anything for You" and "Oye Mi Canto," and had cowritten "The Rhythm Is Gonna Get You" with Kiki Garcia. Even the departed Joe Galdo, a critic of the band's shift toward mainstream popular music, praised her devotion to hard work and her lack of egotism in a business notorious for the contentiousness of many self-centered stars.

By the mid-1980's, the three- to four-minute video productions for the nationwide Music Television (MTV) cable channel had become a standard part of the popular vocalist's work. Madonna, Sheena Easton, and other female singers relied on raunchy choreography, skimpy costumes, and other types of sex appeal in their videos. By contrast, Gloria's video productions seemed closer to the more reserved but no less alluring vocal and dance performances of Hollywood's golden age from the 1930's into the 1950's. She released several strong video performances in the late 1980's, including "The Rhythm Is Gonna Get You," "Bad Boy," and "Oye Mi Canto." A lengthier home video program, her post-accident "Coming out of the Dark," gained critical praise and a Telly Award for video excellence.

In 1993, Gloria turned to pre-Castro rural Cuba to draw from its traditional music, the guajiro, in a new album called *Mi Tierra*. Supported by Cuban musicians Juanito Marquez and Israel "Cachao" Lopez, she utilized the acoustic guitar and romantic Spanish lyrics typical of the 1930's and 1940's. Like Mexican American singer Linda Ronstadt in her 1987 album *Canciones de Mi Padre*, Gloria led her popular audience into an appreciation of earlier musical forms, closer to her own cultural roots.

Summary

Gloria Estefan's emergence as a popular performer is an important chapter in the long history of Cuban music in the United States. She became an integral part of this movement as she frequently tapped the deep reservoir of rhythms introduced by her predecessors: big band leader Xavier Cugat, who, from the 1920's to the 1950's, fused the rumba into the mainstream in Hollywood and New York; Desi Arnaz, who brought the conga drum and the conga line to popularity in the late 1930's; and Celia Cruz, who led in the dissemination of salsa, a mixture of Cuban folk and popular music with North American jazz.

Estefan's public image stands in contrast to the tendencies toward violence and vulgarity in American popular culture in the age of Music Television. Capable of rapid-fire vocalizations and high-energy dancing, Gloria is also sensual and romantic while avoiding the risqué gestures and near-pornography of other performers. Her frequent public appearances with Emilio and their son Nayib help to make her a rare symbol of family values in the popular music of the 1980's and 1990's.

Gloria Estefan has an exceptional talent for synthesizing Cuban and U.S popular music while holding large audiences in both Latin America and the United States. Although she is sometimes criticized for moving away from Cuban traditions, she manages to walk the narrow path that touches both sides of the Anglo-Latino cultural boundary. With her home base in south Florida, she personifies what Peruvian intellectual Mario Vargas Llosa has called the "Miami Model," in which Latinos and Anglos live and work together in relationships that evince more harmony than antagonism. In this larger sense, Estefan's musical career is representative of the melding of Latino and Anglo American cultures not only in south Florida but also on a much larger national and international scale.

Bibliography

Catalano, Grace. *Gloria Estefan*. New York: St. Martin's Press, 1991. A fast-paced biography with valuable insights on Gloria's early life and her creative blending of Latin and U.S. popular music. Includes a convenient discography and videography but no bibliography.

Cobb, Charles, Jr., and Maggie Steber. "Miami." *National Geographic* 181 (January, 1992): 86-113. Clear prose and color photographs emphasize the importance of the Cuban community in south Florida.

Estefan, Gloria, and Kathryn Casey. "My Miracle." *Ladies Home Journal* 107 (August, 1990): 99-100, 152-155. Estefan's account of the bus accident and her recovery.

Lannert, John. "Estefan's New Album Hits Close to Home." *Billboard* 105 (June 26, 1993): 1, 66, 75. A critic's assessment of *Mi Tierra*, including details on the composition and recording of the songs as well as the production and marketing for the United States, Latin America, and Europe.

McLane, Daisann. "The Power and the Gloria." *Rolling Stone*, June 14, 1990, pp. 72-76. An incisive account of the Estefans' rise to celebrity based on interviews and a firm grasp of the nuances of the popular music business.

Roberts, John Storm. *The Latin Tinge: The Impact of Latin American Music on the United States*. New York: Oxford University Press, 1979. A well-researched study that covers Cuban as well as Brazilian, Mexican, and other influences. Although it was written before Estefan's emergence, it provides excellent background material.

Stefoff, Rebecca. *Gloria Estefan*. New York: Chelsea House, 1991. This popular biography written primarily for juvenile readers includes some valuable information.

Vargas Llosa, Mario. "The Miami Model." *Commentary* 93 (February, 1992): 21-27. An analysis of the interactions of Latin American and Anglo American cultures in south Florida. Helpful in understanding the environment in which Estefan rose to prominence.

John A. Britton

CHRIS EVERT

Born: December 21, 1954; Fort Lauderdale, Florida

Area of Achievement: Sports
Contribution: Chris Evert burst upon the tennis scene in 1971 as the first of the modern teenage stars. During the two decades that followed, she became one of the great champions of the sport and one of the most popular players that tennis has ever known.

Early Life

Christine Marie Evert was born on December 21, 1954, in Fort Lauderdale, Florida, to James Evert, the manager of a tennis center, and Colette Evert. Chris was the second of their five children. All the Evert children learned to play tennis, but Chris displayed an aptitude for the game at an early age. Her parents, however, did not direct her toward a professional career in the sport. Jimmy Evert did teach his daughter the two-handed backhand stroke that became her trademark because young Chris lacked the strength to execute it with only one hand. From an early age, Chris stressed discipline and practicing to perfect her game.

She began to attract the attention of top tennis players when she was fifteen. In the autumn of 1970, at a small tournament in Charlotte, North Carolina, the Carolinas International Tennis Classic, Chris beat two top-ranked players. Her most notable triumph was over Margaret Smith Court, the number one woman player in the world, who had just won the Grand Slam the preceding year. The score was 7-6, 7-6. Chris lost to Nancy Richey in the final, but she was now a rising young star on the circuit.

During 1971, Chris continued to beat some top players in the tournaments that she entered. She won the Virginia Slims Masters in St. Petersburg, Florida, in April and then was selected for the American Wightman Cup team to compete against Great Britain. She won two matches and was named the most valuable player in the competition.

Her true emergence as an international star occurred at the United States Open at Forest Hills in late August. Though still just sixteen, she won her first-round match easily. Facing defeat and elimination in a second-round match against Mary Ann Eisel of the United States, Chris rallied from a match point against her in the second set to win in three exciting sets, 4-6, 7-6, 6-1. Chris captivated the crowd. She defeated two more players to reach the semifinals against Billie Jean King. King defeated her 6-3, 6-2 and went on to win the tournament. For the spectators there and for the national television audience, Chris Evert was the story of the United States Open in 1971. She became a celebrity player and remained popular during the two decades of her career that followed.

Life's Work

Chris Evert's career as a tennis star included so many victories and records that they cannot be easily summarized in a brief space. She entered thirty-four Grand Slam tournaments between 1971 and 1983 and made the semifinals in every one of them. From 1974 through 1986, she won at least one Grand Slam tournament every year. She was invincible on clay from August of 1973 through May of 1979, when she won 125 consecutive matches on her favorite surface. She was never ranked lower than fourth in the world throughout her career. She won 1,309 singles matches as against only 146 losses. In doubles, her record was 119 wins and 39 losses. Her career earnings totaled nearly $9 million.

She was especially dominant in the Grand Slam matches at the height of her career. Chris won the United States Open four years in a row between 1974 and 1978 and won individual titles there in 1980 and 1982. She won 101 matches at the Open, a record for both men and women. Her appeal to the New York crowds never faded, and it was appropriate that she played her last major professional match at that tournament in 1989.

The Australian Open was a tournament that Chris entered only five times. Yet she was a finalist in each of the tournaments, winning in 1982 and 1984. One of her victories came in 1982 against her friend and traditional rival Martina Navratilova, in a match that went three sets, 6-3, 2-6, 6-3. She outlasted Helena Sukova in the 1984 final, 6-7, 6-1, 6-3.

The red clay courts at Roland Garros Stadium for the French Open were a friendly surface for Chris Evert throughout her career. She won the tournament seven times, in 1974, 1975, 1979, 1980, 1983, 1985, and 1986. Her last two victories were at the expense of Martina Navratilova, and each one went the full three sets. In 1985, Chris triumphed 6-3, 6-7, 7-5, and a year later the score was 2-6, 6-3, 6-3.

Although Chris won Wimbledon three times, she did not excel in this tournament to the extent that she did in the French Open or U.S. Open. The grass court surface was less suited to her baseline game, and the spectators and press, which dubbed her the "Ice Maiden" early in her career, did not always appreciate the intense concentration that characterized her playing style. Despite these handicaps, she won her first Wimbledon title in 1974, two years after her first appearance in the tournament, with a victory over the Russian player Olga Morozova, 6-0, 6-4. Two years later, she triumphed again, defeating Evonne Goolagong Cawley, 6-3, 4-6, 6-1. Martina Navratilova defeated Chris twice in Wimbledon finals, in 1978 and 1979, and Evonne Goolagong Cawley also beat Chris in 1980. Evert won her third and last Wimbledon in 1981. She then lost three more finals to Martina, in 1982, 1984, and 1985.

Two rivalries with top players marked Chris Evert's long career. During the 1970's, she often met the great champion of women's tennis, Billie Jean King, in key matches of top tournaments. The rivalry that most affected Chris during the 1980's, however, was the contest she waged with Martina Navratilova for the top ranking in the women's game. In the cases of both Billie Jean and Martina, the difference in approach to the game gave these matches great charm. Both Billie Jean and Martina played an attacking style of serve-and-volley tennis. Chris's game, however, was built on her devastatingly accurate ground strokes hit from the baseline. Her most lethal weapon was her two-handed backhand, but her forehand, drop-shots, and lob were equally important in keeping her opponents off balance. Along with the excellent technical execution of her strokes, which good footwork and racquet preparation set up, she added tremendous concentration, discipline, anticipation, and tactical control of points to her game.

The challenge that Martina brought helped to prolong Chris's tennis career. Martina's dominance pushed Chris to add new dimensions, such as a greater use of net play, to her game. When she retired at the end of the 1989 season, her career of almost two decades was one of the longest and most memorable in the history of women's tennis.

Chris brought a personal charisma to tennis that has also been reflected in her life off the court. In 1974, she was engaged to the popular men's player Jimmy Connors. Their twin victory at Wimbledon made headlines as the "Love Double," but they ended their engagement later that year. In April of 1979, Chris married John Lloyd, a British tennis player. The strains of life on the professional tennis circuit took their toll, however, and their marriage ended in divorce in 1986. Since 1988, Chris has been married to Andy Mill, a former Olympic skier. They have a son, Alexander James, who was born in 1991.

Since her retirement in 1989, Chris has continued to have an active involvement with tennis. She sponsors an annual pro-celebrity charity tournament and participates in other fund-raising tennis programs. She has served as a television commentator for the French Open, Wimbledon, and the 1992 Barcelona Olympics. She has collaborated on two autobiographical books, and she is a contributing editor to a tennis magazine, writing articles on various aspects of how to play the game. She continues to be a leader in the Women's Tennis Association.

Summary

Chris Evert's impact on the game of women's tennis has been as significant as that of any other player in the history of her sport in the twentieth century. She became the most popular figure in women's tennis at the time of her rise to prominence in 1971, and she has sustained that level of acclaim ever since. Her disciplined, precise style of tennis attested her commitment and her determination on the court. As she wrote in her autobiography *Chrissie* (1982), "I love tennis, I love the competition, the sheer challenge of playing to perfection." At the same time, she was always dignified and sporting in her demeanor toward opponents. As a result, she was able to be feminine and athletic simultaneously.

Chris's professionalism and dedication have made her a leader in the development of women's tennis since the 1970's. She has done much for the Women's Tennis Association as an officer, but as a star player and celebrity she has helped to lift the game to heights of popularity in the United States it would not otherwise have attained. The Women's Sports Foundation named her the Greatest Woman Athlete of the preceding twenty-five years in 1985. Though now retired, she still remains the most recognizable women's tennis player in the United States. According to a poll taken by American Sports Data in 1991, she was the most widely known athlete in the nation. Her distinguished place in the history of American sports is secure.

Bibliography
Brown, Gene, ed. *The Complete Book of Tennis*. New York: Arno Press, 1980. A history of tennis based on accounts from *The New York Times*, this book offers a good survey of Chris Evert's major matches as she rose to international stardom during the 1970's.
Collins, Bud. *My Life with the Pros*. New York: E. P. Dutton, 1990. A very lively memoir by a reporter and broadcaster who covered Chris Evert throughout her career and who later worked with her as a commentator on televised tennis matches. A valuable source for the inside perspective on her impact as a tennis star.
Feinstein, John. *Hard Courts: Real Life on the Professional Tennis Tours*. New York: Villard Books, 1991. Though the subject of his book is the 1990 tennis year, Feinstein has much to say about Chris Evert's impact on the women's game.
King, Billie Jean, and Cynthia Starr. *We Have Come a Long Way: The Story of Women's Tennis*. New York: McGraw-Hill, 1988. An engaging history of the women's game written by one of Chris Evert's most famous rivals. King makes some perceptive remarks about the popular response to Chris and the reaction of her fellow women tennis players to Chris's stardom.
Lloyd, Chris Evert, with Neil Amdur. *Chrissie: My Own Story*. New York: Simon & Schuster, 1982. A forthright memoir of her tennis career up to 1982, with comments about the place of tennis in her family, her approach to the game, and how she dealt with her celebrity status.
Lloyd, Chris Evert, and John Lloyd, with Carol Thatcher. *Lloyd on Lloyd*. London: Willow Books, 1985. Written in England with her first husband, this book gives a vivid picture of Chris's life during the mid-1980's and shows how the marriage of two professional players affected their careers.
Lumpkin, Angela. *Women's Tennis: A Historical Documentary of the Players and Their Game*. Troy, N.Y.: Whitston, 1981. This overview of the role of women in tennis considers Chris Evert's effect on the game and provides references to many of the articles written about her during the 1970's.
Wade, Virginia, with Jean Rafferty. *Ladies of the Court: A Century of Women at Wimbledon*. New York: Atheneum, 1984. This survey of women at Wimbledon has a very good chapter on Chris Evert's victories in this prestigious championship.

Karen Gould

FANNIE MERRITT FARMER

Born: March 23, 1857; Boston, Massachusetts
Died: January 15, 1915; Boston, Massachusetts
Area of Achievement: Education
Contribution: Farmer was a teacher of cooking and food science. Her 1896 *Boston Cooking-School Cook Book* was the first modern cookbook with clear instructions stressing precise measurements.

Early Life

Fannie Merritt Farmer was born on March 23, 1857, in Boston, Massachusetts, and grew up in nearby Medford, Massachusetts. She was the eldest of the four daughters of J. Franklin Farmer, a master printer who owned his own print shop, and Mary Watson Merritt Farmer. Although they were not wealthy, the Farmers valued books and education and aspired to a genteel lifestyle. Fannie's three sisters all became teachers.

Fannie, the eldest and brightest, would have gone to college had she not become ill in her sixteenth year. She fell getting out of bed one morning and had no sensation in her legs; the malady was diagnosed as a stroke, but it may have been an attack of poliomyelitis. She was confined to her bed for months and remained an invalid for several years. She never regained the full use of her legs and always walked with a limp.

Her father's printing business did not thrive, and the family moved back to Boston, where there were relatives willing to board with them and share expenses. The household expanded to thirteen, including the husband and son of Fannie's sister Cora, the only one of the daughters to marry.

Fannie could do little to help the family finances until she was in her middle twenties, when she took a position as mother's helper in the household of a family friend, Mrs. Charles Shaw, who encouraged her interest in cooking. At the urging of Shaw and her parents, Fannie enrolled at the Boston Cooking School in 1887, an institution founded by the Women's Education Association of Boston in 1879 to train teachers of scientific cooking, as well as housewives seeking to expand their skills. Fannie did so well in the two-year teacher-training course that in 1891 she was kept on in the position of assistant principal. She became principal of the school in 1894 when the previous principal resigned.

Life's Work

Fannie Farmer's enthusiasm and teaching skills transformed the school, increasing the enrollment and influencing the cooking habits of thousands of households through her classes, her demonstration lectures, and her six cookbooks. Unlike other leaders of the late nineteenth century domestic science movement, who were primarily interested in transmitting newly discovered scientific and nutritional information to their pupils, she insisted that food should also look and taste delicious.

She did her work with zeal. Dressed in shoulder-to-ankle white aprons that set off her flashing blue eyes and red hair, she dominated the lecture platform, measuring and mixing neatly, and explaining each step of her procedure clearly and precisely. During the eight years she headed the school, the size of the teacher training classes doubled and attendance at her weekly demonstration lessons rose to more than three thousand a year. She set up eight special classes in invalid cookery for nursing students and was invited to lecture to fourth-year students at the Harvard Medical School. Demand for private lessons and invitations to lecture before women's groups grew steadily.

Early in her years at the school, she began to revise the text used in the school in order to make it useful as a general cookbook as well as for prospective teachers. Aiming at the middle-class household, then thought of as a family of six with no more than one servant, she condensed the lengthy expositions of the principles of nutrition and food chemistry that other domestic science reformers stressed. She presented clear recipes that she had tested and knew would work, with precise directions that even a novice could follow.

A brief exposition of scientific principles opened her new cookbook. The second chapter included three pages on how to build a fire in the cast-iron wood- or coal-burning stoves then in use. It went on to define cooking methods (boiling, baking, and so forth) and followed with clear instructions on such matters as "How to Bone a Bird" and "Ways of Preserving."

What Farmer stressed above all was precise measurement. Previous cookbooks might describe quantities in terms of a "handful," "butter the size of a walnut," or a "rounded" teaspoon. Legend has it that when showing Marcia Shaw, the daughter of her first employer, how to cook, Farmer was stumped when the child asked her how round was a rounded teaspoon. Now she had the answer. *"A tablespoonful is measured level, A teaspoonful is measured level,"* she wrote in a rare use of italics, and she insisted that the back of a knife be used to ensure that the leveling was accurate. Every recipe in all her books stressed this procedure, winning for her the title "Mother of Level Measurement."

Each of the original cookbook's thirty-nine chapters began with definitions of terms and explanations of the material to be covered. Before presenting the reader with any recipes for beef, she described the various cuts of beef and included a table of their nutritional qualities. A chapter of suggested menus, mostly for family dinners, closed the volume, but for the ambitious she included a description of how to plan a twelve-course formal dinner.

Farmer was proud of her cookbook, and she asked Little, Brown and Company, a leading Boston publisher, to bring it out, but the publisher thought that its success was so unlikely that they insisted that she pay all expenses and take the full financial risk. *The Boston Cooking-School Cook Book* (1896) exhausted its first printing of 3,000 copies in short order, and two other printings were needed the next year.

Four of her five other cookbooks elaborated on chapters in the 1896 book, putting in print material she used in her lectures and demonstrations. *Chafing Dish Possibilities* (1898) explained techniques that men and women could use at the dinner table to demonstrate advanced cooking skills. *Cooking for the Sick and Convalescent* (1904), which Farmer thought was her most important work, grew out of her own experience of invalidism as well as her lectures to medical students. She put the appearance and taste of food at the top of her list of basic principles for evaluating sickroom food; nutritive value and cost came last, the reverse of the order that most domestic science reformers would have used. *What to Have for Dinner; Containing Menus and the Recipes Necessary for their Preparation* (1905) and *Catering for Special Occasions, with Menus and Recipes* (1911) expanded on the final chapter of her 1896 cookbook with more elaborate recipes.

A *New Book of Cookery* (1912) covered the full range of cooking but was designed to supplement rather than replace the 1896 volume. The more than 800 recipes included much more elaborate variations, reflecting what Farmer had learned of the culinary ambitions of middle-class women as she improved and revised her lectures and demonstrations. The chapter on sandwiches, which was designed for afternoon tea parties, consisted of twenty-five recipes for fancy, finger-sized sandwiches.

In 1902, Farmer left the Boston Cooking School to open her own school. The successful Miss Farmer's School of Cooking expanded until she had four kitchens and ten assistants under her supervision. Her cookbooks made her nationally famous; demands for lectures to women's groups proliferated, and she was invited to tour the West Coast giving lectures and demonstrations. With the aid of her sister Cora Perkins, she wrote a monthly column for the *Women's Home Companion* from 1905 to 1915, answering questions and explaining recipes and menus.

In her fifties, she suffered two bouts of illness, again diagnosed as strokes, though they may have been recurrences of polio. They affected her legs but not her determination to continue her work. For the last two years of her life, she lectured from a wheelchair, giving what proved to be her final demonstration just ten days before her death.

Summary

Fannie Farmer never let her physical handicap deter her from achieving her goals. Through her school, her cooking demonstrations, and her cookbooks, she influenced the cooking habits of thousands, perhaps millions, of her fellow Americans and transformed the way in which cookbooks would be written.

The school survived her death until 1944, but much more significant was *The Boston Cooking-School Cook Book*, which, though she retained that title on three revisions—1906, 1912, and 1914—soon became popularly called the "Fannie Farmer Cookbook." During her lifetime, Little, Brown regularly issued annual printings of 50,000. More than four million copies were in print by the time the thirteenth edition appeared in 1990. The success of the book ensured that all future American cookbooks would resemble hers.

Farmer's way of cooking put the preparation of nutritious food that looked and tasted delicious within the capabilities of ordinary housekeepers and encouraged them to try more elaborate dishes. The clear directions and precise measurements of her carefully tested recipes made it easy for beginners, whether bachelors or newly married brides, to prepare successful meals. The imaginative variations and novelties for which she became famous in later life inspired people to attempt more creative cookery.

Although Farmer was one of many American men and women who used the findings of modern science to transform the American diet, she is the only one still widely remembered. Her powerful urge to teach Americans how to cook and eat better led her to invent the modern cookbook and transformed the way Americans cooked.

Bibliography
Bird, Caroline. *Enterprising Women.* New York: W. W. Norton, 1976. "Professionalizing Housework: Ellen Richards, Fannie Farmer, Alice Lakey" considers women who tried to apply science to housework and thus establish homemaking as a profession women could be proud to practice. Fannie Farmer is praised for bringing into the kitchen scientific standards that improved the taste and nutrition of the American diet.

Fordyce, Eleanor T. "Cookbooks of the 1800s." In *Dining in America, 1850-1900,* edited by Kathryn Grover. Amherst: University of Massachusetts Press, 1987. Traces the evolution of cookbooks as kitchens shifted from open-hearth cookery to cast-iron stoves, from the earliest printed in America in the eighteenth century to Fannie Farmer.

Shapiro, Laura. *Perfection Salad: Women and Cooking at the Turn of the Century.* New York: Farrar, Straus & Giroux, 1986. A critical account of the development of the fields of scientific cookery and home economics using primary source material, with a full bibliography. Chapter 5, "The Mother of Level Measurements," is the fullest account of Fannie Farmer in print.

Smallzried, Kathleen Ann. *The Everlasting Pleasure: Influences on America's Kitchens, Cooks, and Cookery from 1565 to the Year 2000.* New York: Appleton-Century-Crofts, 1956. Fannie Farmer is the heroine of chapter 27, "Uniformity," praised as the person who, more than any other, taught housewives to produce dependable cooking results through her insistence on precise measurement of ingredients.

Steele, Zelma. "Fannie Farmer and Her Cook Book." In *Lives to Remember,* edited by Leon Stein. New York: Arno Press, 1974. A highly favorable account of the life and work of Fannie Farmer, with anecdotes of her home life provided by her niece and nephew. Originally published as a magazine article in 1944.

Vare, Ethlie Ann, and Greg Ptacek. *Mothers of Invention: From the Bra to the Bomb—Forgotten Women and Their Unforgettable Ideas.* New York: William Morrow, 1988. A brief biography praises Fannie Farmer for overcoming her physical limitations and becoming a technological innovator as the inventor of the modern style of recipe writing.

Milton Berman

SARAH JANE FARMER

Born: July 22, 1847; Dover, New Hampshire
Died: November 23, 1916; Portsmouth, New Hampshire
Area of Achievement: Religion
Contribution: Founder of Greenacre summer conferences on comparative religion in Eliot, Maine, Farmer later established the first American Baha'i community there.

Early Life

Sarah Jane Farmer was born on July 22, 1847, to a family with solid New England roots. Her father, Moses Gerrish Farmer, was an inventor who developed several electrical devices (including the first incandescent light bulb in 1859, when Thomas Edison was only twelve years old) but never patented them, believing that inventions were given by God to be shared by all humankind. In the 1860's, Moses Farmer was made consulate to the United States Department of the Navy in Newport, Rhode Island. Moses was an avid scholar of Ralph Waldo Emerson and reared Sarah in the Transcendentalist tradition. Sarah's mother, Hannah Shapleigh Farmer, was a social activist and ardent abolitionist. The Farmer home was often used as a way station in the Underground Railroad, a secret network designed to help slaves escape out of the South. Sarah later recalled meeting many famous women through her mother's abolitionist and charitable work, including Sojourner Truth, Harriet Beecher Stowe, Harriet Tubman, and Clara Barton.

In 1882, Moses Farmer began showing signs of physical decline, probably as a result of multiple sclerosis. He resigned his post as U.S. Navy consulate and moved to Eliot, Maine, a sleepy farming community on the Piscataqua River, four miles from Portsmouth, New Hampshire. As the only surviving child, Sarah moved with her parents, although she recalled deep regret at leaving the thriving intellectual community at Newport for a more isolated and rural community. Sarah and her mother quickly became involved in charitable work in Eliot. Hannah Farmer opened Rosemary Cottage, a house for unwed mothers, that same year. Sarah began building a community library in Eliot. She persuaded eminent friends to donate books, and in 1887 and 1888 she sponsored summer fairs to raise money for the enterprise. The philanthropic work of the Farmers in Eliot earned them lasting esteem in the community.

Soon thereafter Sarah and four Eliot businessmen launched a plan to build a summer resort in Eliot. In 1889, the partners raised money to build Greenacre Inn, a multistory structure with room for one hundred guests. It became a popular summer vacation spot for Bostonians, but the resort was not an economic success. By 1892, it had to close for part of the summer because of lack of funds.

Life's Work

A turning point in Sarah Farmer's life occurred in the summer of 1893, when she attended the Parliament of Religions at the World's Columbian Exposition in Chicago.

Farmer was deeply impressed with the points of connection between the different religions of the world. She envisioned transforming the Greenacre resort into a summer conference devoted to bringing together lecturers from a variety of religious and philosophical traditions in order that "the points of contact might be found . . . the oneness of truth . . . the tearing down of walls of prejudice and superstition."

Farmer convinced her business partners to allow her to organize a summer lecture series around the Greenacre Inn resort. In July, 1894, the first Greenacre Institute was launched. Farmer insisted that participants in the conference adopt a comparative approach—no speaker was to debate or dispute with other speakers. Instead, she hoped that the Institute would create an inclusive and tolerant atmosphere. She also believed that the Institute should be open to anyone, and so refused to charge admission. As a result, many curious travelers and students, who could not afford to stay at the Greenacre Inn, attended the lectures and stayed in tents, which were soon scattered all over the resort's grounds. Local farmers rented rooms to visitors for a few dollars a week. Lectures were held in a huge tent, open to the summer breezes. In true Transcendentalist tradition, Farmer hoped that the Institute would give participants an opportunity to commune with nature as they searched for philosophical truth. Topics addressed in the Institute ranged from religion to philosophy, sociology, history, art, and literature. In later years, a music school was added.

In its early years, Greenacre was closely linked to the American Transcendentalist movement, of whom Benjamin Franklin Sanborn and Charles Malloy were the most famous surviving proponents. Sanborn and Malloy took a leading role in the Institute's early years, presenting lectures on the lives and works of Emerson and Henry David Thoreau. Early Greenacre Institutes attracted a great number of Bostonians, including many Harvard students. The Monsalvat School for Comparative Religions, founded as a separate part of Greenacre in 1896, quickly became the most famous wing of the Institute. It attracted speakers from all over the world who lectured on Hinduism, Zoroastrianism, Islam, Christianity, Taoism, Buddhism, and countless other religious traditions.

By 1897, the Institute had become a popular success. Contemporaries estimated that thousands of visitors crowded into Eliot, filling the Greenacre Inn and camp-grounds and prompting local businessmen to construct several houses near the inn to accommodate the overflow. The railroad line was extended to Eliot, and steamships brought loads of passengers up the Piscataqua River to Greenacre. Unfortunately, the venture did not prove to be a financial success. By 1899, the Institute was threatened by bankruptcy.

Exhausted by overwork and encroaching arteriosclerosis, Farmer found herself in failing health. In 1900, a friend paid the expenses for Farmer to embark on a cruise of the Mediterranean to regain her health. In her absence, the Institute was left in the hands of Dr. Lewis G. Janes, head of the Monsalvat School. Sanborn and Malloy were not invited to lecture, and the school's activities were reduced substantially.

Farmer's trip abroad took her to Persia, where she met Abdu'l-Baha, leader of the Baha'i faith, then in prison for his religious and political teachings. Sarah was deeply impressed with Abdu'l-Baha, whose teachings seemed to echo her desire for religious toleration and spiritual unity. The Baha'i religion had been founded in 1844 in Persia (modern Iran), and was based on the teachings of a prophet called Baha'u'llah, whom Baha'i followers believe to be the successor of prophets of earlier ages, such as Abraham, Jesus Christ, and Muhammad. The Baha'i is emphasize toleration, peace and cooperation. They hope to alleviate the great evils of the modern world by ending nationalist competition, economic inequality and prejudice. They believe their religion to be the culmination and perfection of various religions from all over the world, most directly out of the traditions of Judaism, Christianity, and Islam.

During the summer of 1901, Farmer introduced the study of Baha'i into the Monsalvat School curriculum. This decision provoked instant controversy. Sanborn and Malloy returned to Greenacre that summer, and the Transcendentalists and religious seekers split into two camps, living in grudging toleration of each other. Tension also arose between Farmer and Lewis Janes. Sarah desired to make the seminars on religion more free-form, in order to provide a more spontaneous and varied program, while Janes insisted that the specific program of speakers and dates used in previous years should be maintained.

Beginning in 1901, the school drew a large number of Baha'is from the United States and around the world. Many of the American Baha'is were quite wealthy, and they soon began exerting a strong influence over the school. In 1902, the Greenacre program was prefaced with the proclamation:

> Believing that the Revelation of Behá'u'lláh of Persia announced this great Day—the beginning of the Golden Age prophesied by all seers, and sung by poets—and finding that it provides a platform on which the members of all great religious bodies can stand together in love and harmony, each holding the form which best nourishes his individual life, the founder of Green Acre feels that its work in the Nineteenth Century was but the preparation for the greatest of all joys—the giving of the Message of Unity to all who are willing and ready to receive it, and who ask for it.

Janes had died in 1901 and was succeeded as director of the Monsalvat School by Dr. Fillmore Moore, who helped heal the misunderstandings of the previous year. Farmer arranged several lectures on the Baha'i faith, but Sanborn noted with relief that 1902 saw a decline in "wandering pundits from India and Persia," and the following year he wrote that "nearly all the foreigners who are attracted hither are either readers of Emerson or eager to read him." For the next several years, the Transcendentalists and the Baha'is managed to achieve an acceptable balance. Despite a strong emphasis on Baha'i teachings and a growing tendency towards disorganization, Emerson and Thoreau remained popular lecture topics at Greenacre up through 1910.

In 1910, Sarah Farmer fell gravely ill and was committed to an insane asylum in Portsmouth. She was completely unable to forestall the continuing friction between the Transcendentalists and the Baha'is on the Board of Trustees of Greenacre; by 1911, Sanborn and Malloy had ended their lecturing activities there. In 1912, Sanborn noted with alarm that Farmer's name was not even mentioned in the program sheet, and he began a campaign to prevent what he interpreted as the takeover of Farmer's property without her consent and the twisting of Greenacre's purpose into something Farmer had never wanted. He wrote and circulated articles, press releases, and correspondence to gather support on her behalf.

In 1913, an open dispute broke out between the Baha'i and non-Baha'i trustees of Greenacre. The Baha'is outvoted the other trustees and declared that henceforth Greenacre and the Monsalvat School would be strictly limited to the teachings of Baha'u'llah. Sanborn noted that by 1914, Sarah Farmer was terminally ill with arterial sclerosis and that her estate was being scavenged by those "who say they are her friends," who had reduced her to living off the charity of others. Farmer died of pneumonia and heart failure in 1916.

Summary

After Sarah Farmer's death, the Eliot Baha'i community published a short flyer on the history of Greenacre that reflected a much different interpretation of the events of 1900-1913. It portrayed an institute plagued with financial difficulties, which by 1899 "was near collapse." According to the Baha'i community, when Farmer met the Abdu'l-Baha she immediately recognized in him "the fulfillment of the hopes of all the religions" she had worked with, returning to Greenacre in 1901 with a new vision and setting about immediately to transform Greenacre into a Baha'i center. The Baha'i circular portrayed this transition as a spiritual and economic success.

Abdu'l-Baha visited Greenacre himself in 1912, where he lectured on the importance of concentrating on the real world, rather than on tradition or ideology. He proclaimed his desire to transform the Monsalvat School into "one of the great Baha'i universities of the future." This prophesy was soon carried out, due in part to what the Baha'is claimed to be the diversion of the Transcendentalists and other intellectual groups into other concerns. The Baha'i constitution adopted at the Institute in 1913 credited the Baha'is with reviving "the sagging fortunes of Green Acre." In 1928, Greenacre was incorporated as a Baha'i school.

There is some doubt that the Baha'i takeover of Greenacre truly met with Farmer's approval, going as it did against the ideal of religious pluralism upon which she set up the original Greenacre Institute. Farmer was responsible, however, for bringing the Baha'i faith to Greenacre, and she claimed herself as one of its converts. It is probable that Farmer found in the Baha'i faith's profession of the unity of all religious faiths an echo of her own religious convictions. Regardless of the disputes that occurred near the end of her life, modern followers of Baha'i teachings credit Sarah Jane Farmer as their American founder.

Bibliography
Cameron, Kenneth Walter, ed. *Transcendentalists in Transition.* Hartford, Conn.: Transcendental Books, 1980. Cameron traces the last years of the American Transcendentalist movement through the activities of Benjamin Franklin Sanborn

and Charles Malloy. He portrays Greenacre as the successor of the Concord School of Philosophy and, as such, the last center for the American Transcendentalist movement. His work is in large part a compilation of Sanborn's writings, correspondence and memoirs of Greenacre students, and reprints of Greenacre programs. He also includes a copy of a circular printed by the Baha'i community after the takeover, called "Greenacre an Intellectual Center Before Becoming Bahá'í School."

Gaver, Jessyca Russell. *The Bahá'í Faith: Dawn of a New Day.* New York: Hawthorn Books, 1967. Gaver gives a flattering, but easily understandable, description of the foundation and historical development of the Baha'i faith worldwide. She briefly describes Farmer and her work at Greenacre, depicting Farmer as "a true teacher of the Faith and a very wonderful person."

Ingersoll, Anna Josephine. *Greenacre on the Piscataqua.* New York: Alliance, 1900. This brief pamphlet gives a general description of the founding and early years of Greenacre. It is written in romantic and picturesque language and concentrates mostly on the scenery and atmosphere of Greenacre.

Miller, William McElwee. *What Is the Baha'i Faith?* Grand Rapids, Mich.: Wm. B. Eerdmans, 1977. A more scholarly treatment of the Baha'i faith which traces its roots in Islam, Miller's book, which is an abridgment of his book *The Baha'i Faith: Its History and Teachings* (1974), is brief enough to be accessible to the college reader.

Kimberly K. Estep

BEATRIX JONES FARRAND

Born: June 19, 1872; New York City
Died: February 27, 1959; Bar Harbor, Maine
Area of Achievement: Landscape architecture
Contribution: The first American woman landscape architect, Farrand was instrumental in the popularizing of a natural style of landscape design.

Early Life
Beatrix Cadwalader Jones was born on June 19, 1872, in New York City to a wealthy, socially prominent family. Her parents were Frederick Rhinelander Jones and Mary Cadwalader Rawle. They divorced by the time Beatrix was twelve. Her aunt was the novelist Edith Jones Wharton, a keen gardener with whom Beatrix had a close relationship.

Beatrix was the only child of divorced parents at a time when divorce was a social disgrace. The changed circumstances forced her mother to earn money creatively in ways acceptable to polite society. She became a part-time literary agent for her former sister-in-law Edith Wharton and organized charity projects that people in her social circles supported. As a result, Beatrix grew up with at least two examples of enterprising women who made socially acceptable professional places for themselves. Like all girls of her social circle, Beatrix was tutored at home and received no formal education of any kind. As part of her education, she traveled to Europe with members of her mother's and father's families.

At the age of twenty-one and not yet married, she realized that she needed to find a way to support herself. Through family connections, she had met Charles Sprague Sargent, the first director of the Boston Arnold Arboretum. After a social visit in the Sargent home in 1893, she expressed an interest in landscape gardening and began to study with Sargent. From him she learned botany, how to survey, and how to stake out a piece of ground. At that time, Sargent was laying out the grounds of the Arboretum with Frederick Law Olmsted. Consequently, Beatrix had an opportunity to observe some stages of the formation of a major project by the preeminent American landscape architect.

Beatrix was advised to travel widely to study gardens. For that purpose, she visited the Columbian Exposition grounds in Chicago, for which Olmsted had created the site plan. The year 1895 was spent studying gardens in Italy and England. The hedged and walled garden rooms at Sissinghurst in England became useful models for her career. While in England, she met Gertrude Jekyll, the leading figure in promoting the informal cottage garden style. Jekyll promoted the use of native plants and was well known for her use of harmonious plant color and arrangement. The lessons Beatrix Jones learned from Jekyll included the need to observe the difference in plant forms, to treat those forms as groups as well as use them against other plant forms, and never to treat a plant as a specimen to be looked at individually. The plant must fit the total scheme. Beatrix also visited the Penshurst estate gardens, where classical concepts were used which emphasized strong structure and geometric regularity in the garden layout. Both of these approaches, the classical and the more natural, governed her design philosophy throughout her career.

Life's Work

Beatrix Jones returned to New York City in 1895 and opened an office on the top floor of her mother's house. She immediately began to receive commissions to design gardens for private homes in the suburban New York City and New England area. Since these clients were from the same social background as Jones, she was an ideal choice. None of the gardens from these early years exist. Surviving plans and photographs, however, give some idea of her accomplishment. In these documents, it is possible to follow the evolution of her gardening design theory, based on what she observed in Europe. An experimental attitude can also be observed in Beatrix Jones's work.

Within three years, she was considered a nationally important figure in the field. In 1899, Jones, the only woman among eight men, helped to found the American Society of Landscape Architects, the first such professional group in this country.

The formative years of her career were over by about 1912, when she began to receive large-scale public commissions to design for college campuses. In 1916, she married Max Farrand, a professor of history at Yale University. It was also during this period that she began work on the two private commissions for which she is best known: Dumbarton Oaks in Washington, D.C. (1921-1947), and the Abby Aldrich Rockefeller garden at Seal Harbor, Maine (1926-1950). These gardens still exist, and Dumbarton Oaks is open to the public. During her long period of association with these gardens, Farrand acted as adviser on maintenance and designed changes.

The Rockefeller garden, a walled and regular formal garden, includes informal and harmonious flower plantings with a surrounding border of trees and shrubs to display a collection of oriental sculpture. Farrand made two subsequent major revisions. Dumbarton Oaks is a more complex work. The estate is a country house within the city of Washington, D.C., which was used as a home and a place for entertaining by a career diplomat and his wife, Mr. and Mrs. Robert Woods Bliss. At Dumbarton Oaks, Farrand worked out her philosophy for more formal gardens as individual hedged rooms near the house. The farther away they are from the house, the less formal the gardens are, until, at the bottom of the hilled site, naturalistic gardens, parklike in character, end along a stream. Working with constantly changing contours, Farrand skillfully constructed terraces, steps, and walkways that enhanced the experience of negotiating changing grades. When the property was given to Harvard University in the 1940's for a museum, research library, and public garden, Farrand made the changes necessary to turn a private garden into a public one.

In 1914, Farrand developed her own home, Reef Point, near Bar Harbor, Maine, and its extensive grounds, into an experimental garden with a horticulture research library. She and her husband had intended this to be a permanent research facility, but lacking funds to support it, Farrand dismantled it in 1955. Max Farrand helped to develop a collection of rare botany and horticulture volumes as well as books of a more functional nature.

The Princeton University campus was a design project of 1912, and until 1943, Farrand advised on design upkeep, changes, and enlargements. She performed in the same capacity of designer and long-term adviser for Yale University (1922-1945) and the University of Chicago (1929-1936). She provided designs for smaller campuses, such as Oberlin, Hamilton, Vassar, and Occidental College, but did not perform the long-term advisory role. The campus designs required trees, shrubs, walkways, and open lawns, capitalizing on terrain to create the naturalistic semirural atmosphere that became fashionable as campuses grew and were expanded from the time of the Civil War. At Princeton and Yale, where Farrand's designs are the most extensive, she began by designing plantings for residential colleges. Farrand invented the tree moat for these designs. The moat was a dry ditch close to a building planted with trees. The effect is an intimate romantic one. She also created tree and shrub nurseries on campus to provide cheaper plants for future needs and replacements. These nurseries also experimented with plant material to meet changing needs.

For Edith Wilson, the wife of President Woodrow Wilson, Farrand designed the lawns and gardens for the White House in Washington, D.C., between 1913 and 1916. There are, unfortunately, few drawings to reveal what the design was, and no other documentation exists.

Max Farrand became the first director of the Henry E. Huntington Library and Art Gallery in San Marino, California, in 1927. At the same time, Beatrix Farrand was offered the position of curator of the art collection. When she discovered that very little would be expected of her, she turned the offer down. Farrand designed the landscaping for the new Director's House on the Library grounds.

After 1927, Farrand maintained offices in New York City (the principal one), Reef Point, Maine, and San Marino. This arrangement meant traveling even more than she had done before. Initially, she hoped that enough commissions would develop in California to warrant a permanent move there. Not enough work developed, however, to justify giving up her established offices. Farrand did receive a commission to design a Humanities Garden for the California Institute of Technology in neighboring Pasadena, a design that is still structurally intact. She created a classical olive grove in a courtyard, which complemented the Mediterranean architecture of the campus. Clearly, she enjoyed the opportunity to experiment with plants that were new to her. From 1938 until her death in 1959, she acted as a consultant for the Santa Barbara Botanic Garden, working in tandem with another landscape designer, Lockwood De Forest. The two designers used naturalistic plantings and public walkways that emphasized the vistas. The site was on varied terrain, and Farrand's design concepts enhanced the change of grade with wide, easy-to-negotiate steps.

During the 1930's, Farrand landscaped an English estate, Dartington Hall in Devon. One of the owners was an American friend, Dorothy Elmhirst, who commissioned Farrand when she could not find a landscaper who was sympathetic to her wishes. The designs for the two-thousand-acre estate included roads, walks, terraces, lawns, varied flower beds, an outdoor theater, and wooded areas. She also made suggestions for the placement of several new buildings. The initial designs date from 1933, and Farrand advised on further plans until 1939 when war broke out.

Farrand continued to work for two decades, devoting her final years to the gardens of her own home, Reef Point, in Bar Harbor, Maine. She died in Bar Harbor on February 27, 1959.

Summary

Beatrix Jones Farrand is sometimes referred to as the American Gertrude Jekyll, which is not quite accurate. Landscape architects were, to some extent, divided into two theoretical groups: the naturalists and the formalists. Jekyll fell squarely into the naturalist camp. Farrand's great synthesizing skills, however, allowed her to pull these two divergent approaches together to produce landscape designs that were in keeping with the developing trends of the twentieth century. Her career spanned the early years of the profession in the United States, through two world wars and the Great Depression. She witnessed sweeping changes during these years which required her to scale back the size of her private commissions and forced her to move more into public ones. She produced an enduring style based on readily available material which could incorporate future changes. She maintained her belief in laying out a strong pattern in the garden plan, which was formed by shrubs and trees, and using that regular background for her harmonious flower choices and naturalistic plant material. This approach was always adapted to the particular site.

Farrand's gardens and campuses have been much admired ever since they were first constructed. Paradoxically, her name was not much known in the interval between her death and the 1970's, when popular interest in landscape gardening began a resurgence. Since that time, her influence has been strong.

Bibliography

Balmori, Diana, Diane Kostial McGuire, and Eleanor M. McPeck. *Beatrix Farrand's American Landscapes: Her Gardens and Campuses.* Sagaponack, N.Y.: Sagapress, 1985. This book confines its investigations to Farrand's American work in the public arena. It does, however, contain an appendix listing all her private American commissions. A short, thorough biography is included. The work complements an exhibition of material relating to Farrand's work.

McGuire, Diane Kostial, ed. *Beatrix Farrand's Plant Book for Dumbarton Oaks.* Washington, D.C.: Dumbarton Oaks, 1980. Contains "An Attempted Evocation of a Personality" by Mildred Bliss, the owner of Dumbarton Oaks, with whom Farrand worked over many years to create her largest, best-known, still surviving private commission, which is now open to the public.

McGuire, Diane Kostial, and Lois Fern, eds. *Beatrix Jones Farrand: Fifty Years of American Landscape Architecture.* Washington, D.C., Dumbarton Oaks, 1982. This comprehensive volume contains papers given at the eighth annual Dumbarton Oaks Colloquium on the History of Landscape Architecture. Each paper highlights a particular aspect of Farrand's life and career. A chapter on the large body of working papers and manuscripts left by Farrand is included.

Salon, Marlene. "Beatrix Jones Farrand, Pioneer in Gilt-Edged Gardens." *Landscape Architecture* 67 (1977): 69-77. A journal article outlining the types of designs Farrand produced for the homes of her wealthy clients. It does not include any material on the one non-American design in this group, Dartington Hall.

Ann Stewart Balakier

SUZANNE FARRELL

Born: August 16, 1945; Cincinnati, Ohio

Area of Achievement: Dance
Contribution: Farrell was a principal dancer in the New York City Ballet and an interpreter of and collaborator with choreographer George Balanchine.

Early Life
Born Roberta Sue Ficker, the third child of Robert and Donna Ficker, Suzanne Farrell began life surrounded by her mother and two sisters. Her father worked as a shipping foreman for a meat packing company, which involved being away several nights a week. Later, her parents were divorced. After the divorce, Farrell's mother worked the night shift, so that she would be available to her daughters after school and in the early evenings. In spite of her limited budget, she was dedicated to their getting the best dance and music lessons available in the Cincinnati area.

Farrell began serious ballet lessons at the age of nine at the Conservatory of Music in Cincinnati. At about the same time, the Ballet Russe came to town. It was the first time Farrell had ever seen a professional ballet company. She watched *The Nutcracker*, however, not from the audience but from the stage. A company member danced the lead role of Clara during the first act, but a child was needed to play Clara in the second act. The conservatory was called, and Suzanne Farrell was suggested. Her part consisted primarily of sitting on a red velvet cushion and watching the second act. Nevertheless, it was a beginning. Several years later, the Royal Ballet came to Cincinnati's Music Hall. Four mice were needed for a production of *Sleeping Beauty*. Again Farrell was among those chosen.

After her parents' divorce, Farrell's now all-female family moved directly across the street from the conservatory in Cincinnati. Living so close, she began to spend most of her spare time there. By the age of twelve, she knew that she wanted to be a dancer. Farrell and her mother understood that if she were to have a career in dance, Farrell would need to leave Cincinnati. When the National Ballet of Canada came to Louisville, Kentucky, she auditioned for admission to their school. She was accepted, but no scholarship was offered.

In 1958, the New York City Ballet came to Bloomington, Indiana, and Farrell, her mother, and her sisters attended. There she saw the kind of ballet that really thrilled her. A few weeks after Farrell had auditioned for the Canadian Ballet School, a talent scout from the school associated with New York City Ballet, the School of American Ballet, arrived in the area. The Ford Foundation had set up a dance scholarship program, and a member of New York City Ballet, Diana Adams, was responsible for screening applicants. She did not immediately offer Farrell a scholarship, however, because Farrell had not had as much formal training as had most other girls her age. This meant that her technical skills were deficient. Nevertheless, Adams saw in her other things that were important: movement quality and musicality. She suggested that

Farrell should come to New York for a second opinion.

With only the hope of a scholarship, the family moved to New York. At age fifteen, Suzanne Farrell auditioned for George Balanchine, the Russian-born choreographer and head of the School of American Ballet and the New York City Ballet. She won a full-tuition scholarship to the school and an additional grant to cover tuition at the Professional Children's School. A year later, she was invited to join the New York City Ballet.

Life's Work

Shortly after joining the company, Roberta Sue Ficker became Suzanne Farrell. She was in the eleventh grade but had less time than ever to study. She now attended the Rhodes School, where she could take three classes beginning at 8:00 A.M. before company classes began at 10:30 A.M. During performance season, she danced until 11:00 P.M. It was a grueling schedule.

In her first season she learned many new ballets. She was cast in her first demi-solo part, as one of the three Fates in Maurice Ravel's *La Valse*. In 1962, she danced in her first solo part as the Dark Angel in *Serenade*. This was the first ballet that Balanchine choreographed for American dancers on American soil. It is one of his most famous works and is considered a signature work of the New York City Ballet. Farrell was filling in for an injured dancer—something she would do many times. She had three days to learn her part.

The first ballet that was choreographed for Farrell was done by John Tarans in 1963. Called *Arcade*, it was danced to Igor Stravinsky's *Concerto for Piano and Wind Instruments*, which was one of Stravinsky's most atonal, complex pieces. She received a rave review in the *New York Herald Tribune* (April 10, 1963). Critic Walter Terry wrote:

> As for Miss Farrell, she is the ideal female figure for the present Balanchine period. In *Movements* ballerina elements—highlighted personality, gestural idiosyncrasies, projected glamour—are absent. Only the tool of dance image—the body—functions. This is not to say that Miss Farrell is unattractive. To the contrary she is beautiful. But here is the beauty of a body superbly trained so there is not an extra ounce of weight on it and so brilliantly disciplined that, say, a high-swing of the leg is not a trick but rather a command to action.

In 1963, at the age of seventeen, Farrell became a soloist. She danced in many lead roles. She was also still in high school, but the time demands of her career finally won out over school. Since it appeared that she would succeed as a dancer, her mother, with whom she still lived, agreed that she no longer needed to try to balance the requirements of scholarship and dance. Years later she received an honorary doctorate.

In little more than a year's time Farrell danced sixteen new ballets. In 1965, Balanchine choreographed an important new ballet for her, *Don Quixote*. He performed the lead role of Don Quixote, and she performed the role of Dulcinea. They appeared together on the cover of *Life* magazine.

During the next four years, Farrell danced in many Balanchine ballets and became very close to Balanchine, although by her own account the intimacy never became physical. In 1969, she married another company member, Paul Mejia. This angered Balanchine, and within months both Farrell and Mejia were unemployed. American companies did not want to hire them for fear of antagonizing Balanchine, whose ballets they wanted to perform.

After many months of little work and less sense of direction, Farrell and Mejia decided to buy a rundown cottage in the Adirondack Mountains, which they called Cedar Island. Shortly afterward, they were invited to join the Ballet du Vingtième Siècle (Ballet of the Twentieth Century), which was based in Brussels, Belgium. This company was wildly avant-garde and theatrical, with an emphasis on male dancers. Touring in America, the company received negative reviews from critics, but audience response was enthusiastic. Productions were consistently sold out. The company was, however, popular with critics and audiences alike in Paris.

Each year, Farrell and Mejia had the summer off, so they returned to their mountain home, which they gradually rebuilt. After four years, Balanchine was ready for Farrell to return to the New York City Ballet, so in 1975 she came back and danced for Balanchine again. Over the next few years, the New York City Ballet reached a new level of success, both artistic and financial. Balanchine choreographed eighteen ballets, and Farrell danced lead roles in many of them. In 1978, Balanchine suffered a mild heart attack.

When Farrell returned to the New York City Ballet, there had been no place for her husband. He became the artistic director of first the Ballet Guatemala, next the Chicago City Ballet, and later the Fort Worth Ballet. Despite their busy schedules, Farrell and Mejia continued to spend summers together at Cedar Island. In 1981, they opened a small summer dance camp for young students at which they both taught and cooked for the dancers.

Although Balanchine had recovered from his heart attack, another affliction began to bother him. It was not until a year after he died that his illness was diagnosed as Creutzfeldt-Jakob virus, a disease that afflicts the body's motor functions. In 1983, he died, and a dance era came to an end.

The New York City Ballet continued under the direction of Jerome Robbins and Peter Martins. Farrell also continued dancing, but before long she was suffering from a severely arthritic hip—death for a dancer. She continued dancing until it became impossible to continue. In 1987, she retired and underwent hip replacement surgery. Against all expectations, she recovered and danced with the New York City Ballet again before retiring from dancing a second time in 1989.

In March of 1989, she was well enough to be presented with the Lion's Award from the New York City Library. In late June, she received a Golden Plate Award from the Academy of Achievement, and later she was the recipient of an honorary doctorate in fine arts from Yale University.

In early 1988, Farrell danced in *Vienna Waltzes*. The *MacNeil-Lehrer News Hour* had been preparing a segment chronicling her surgery, recovery, and possible return to the stage. It was a triumphant moment for her, modern medicine, and the world of dance. Farrell was forty-two and was still dancing, but she was beginning to turn her creative energies toward teaching others. She traveled to Leningrad to stage two Balanchine ballets for the Kirov Ballet.

On November 26, 1989, Farrell retired from dancing. In her last performance she danced *Vienna Waltzes* and *Sophisticated Lady*, a ballet Peter Martins had choreographed for her. He came out of retirement to dance with her. To the tune of Duke Ellington's "Don't Get Around Much Anymore," they danced their last duet. At the end of the performance the audience showered the stage with one thousand dethorned white roses.

In 1990, Farrell wrote her autobiography, *Holding on to the Air*, with another New York City Ballet dancer, Toni Bentley. In this spellbinding story, she chronicles her own artistic, emotional, and spiritual journey and pays tribute to her dearly beloved teacher and friend George Balanchine.

Summary

Suzanne Farrell's impact on dance is inextricably bound together with that of George Balanchine. He was the choreographer—she, the interpreter of his work. Yet there was a quality of collaboration about their artistic partnership. Both loved to experiment, to test physical and aesthetic limits. Farrell inspired Balanchine, and she in turn loved to work for and with him. She was not his only principal female dancer, but she was a very important one during the last twenty years of his life.

Farrell also made an impact because of her arthritic hip. She proved that with modern medical hip-replacement surgery, even an aging ballerina can dance *en pointe* again. Ever pushing the limits, she refused to accept the word no. Finally, her autobiography is a powerful testimony to the joys of dance in general and of Balanchine-style ballet in particular.

Bibliography
Como, William. "Farrell on Farrell." Parts 1-3. *Dance Magazine* 59 (April-June, 1985). A series of interviews of Farrell by William Como with illustrations.
Farrell, Suzanne, with Toni Bentley. *Holding on to the Air: An Autobiography*. New York: Summit Books, 1990. A fascinating account of Farrell's life that discusses her relationship with Balanchine at length. Includes a partial listing of newspaper and magazine reviews.
Kirstein, Lincoln. *Thirty Years: Lincoln Kirstein's the New York City Ballet*. New York: Alfred A. Knopf, 1978. This book is a history of the New York City Ballet. Suzanne Farrell, as one of the organization's principal dancers, is discussed at various points.
Swope, Martha. *Suzanne Farrell*. New York: Dance Horizons, 1975. A short book about Farrell's career up to 1975. Accessible to the general reader.

Alice Ogden Bellis

DIANNE FEINSTEIN

Born: June 22, 1933; San Francisco, California

Area of Achievement: Government and politics
Contribution: In each of her elected offices from the presidency of the Board of Supervisors of San Francisco to U.S. Senator from California, Dianne Feinstein has been a pioneer, the first woman to hold that position.

Early Life
Dianne Goldman was born in San Francisco, California, on June 22, 1933, to Leon Goldman, a Jewish physician, and Betty Rosenburg Goldman, a Catholic woman of Russian descent. Dianne endured a difficult childhood that could have irreparably scarred her but instead left her resilient and strong. An alcoholic who was ill with a brain disorder that was not diagnosed until much later, Betty Goldman was frequently abusive toward her daughters, and Dianne assumed a protective role for her two younger sisters. Her father, a busy physician, was a sustaining force in Dianne's life as well as a highly respected member of the community. The poles of opposition that dominated Dianne's childhood were reflected in her concurrent attendance at temple services and the Convent of the Sacred Heart High School, where she was graduated in 1951.

One of the stabilizing forces during Dianne's youth was her uncle, Morris Goldman, who moved in with the family and introduced Dianne to the workings of government by taking her to meetings of the San Francisco Board of Supervisors. Often critical of the board's actions, he urged his niece to get an education and do the job better. She determined while still in high school to pursue a career in government service. In preparation, Dianne attended Stanford University. During her senior year, she served as vice president of the student body.

After graduating from Stanford with a bachelor's degree in history in 1955, Dianne accepted an internship in public affairs with the CORO Foundation and spent a year studying public policy. In her subsequent position as an administrative assistant for the California Industrial Welfare Commission, she met and married Jack Berman, a lawyer, but the marriage lasted less than three years. With her nine-month-old daughter, Katherine Anne, Dianne started anew. Governor Edmund S. Brown, having been impressed by Dianne when she was a high school friend of his daughter, sought her out to serve on the California Women's Board of Terms and Paroles, a position she held from 1960 until 1966.

Dianne's second marriage in 1962 to Bertram Feinstein provided stability in her personal life. Her second husband encouraged her continued involvement in public activities. Dianne Feinstein's interest in the justice system broadened with positions on the Committee on Adult Detention and the San Francisco Mayor's Commission on Crime. Her experiences in these jobs further prepared her to seek elected office.

Life's Work

Dianne Feinstein's election to the San Francisco Board of Supervisors in 1969 marked the beginning of her noteworthy career as an elected public official. As one of the first San Francisco politicians to use television extensively for campaigning, Feinstein received more votes than any other candidate for supervisor. Thus, she became president of the Board of Supervisors for 1970-1971, the first woman to serve in that position.

Despite Feinstein's popularity as a supervisor and as president of the Board— serving a second term as president from 1974 to 1975, and being reelected for a third term in 1978—life was not without its setbacks for her both professionally and personally. After losing two bids for mayor in 1971 and 1975 and coping with her husband's long bout with cancer and subsequent death in April of 1978, Feinstein was so emotionally bereft that she contemplated a full withdrawal from public life. Only hours after making such a pronouncement to reporters, however, Feinstein found herself acting mayor of San Francisco. The assassination of Mayor George Moscone and Supervisor Harvey Milk thrust Feinstein abruptly into the forefront of San Francisco government and placed her once again in a pioneering role as the first woman to serve as the city's mayor.

The dignity and poise with which she handled the crisis evoked strong support for Feinstein from her constituency. Running a city with as many diverse groups as San Francisco possessed was not easy. Feinstein prided herself in being a centrist, however, and immediately demonstrated her intention to be an activist mayor. She established such early priorities as reducing response time for police and firemen, revitalizing public transportation, and improving garbage pickup. To ensure the success of her endeavors, Feinstein raised taxes when necessary, leading some critics to label her as a "tax and spend" Democrat while others complained about her lack of a long-term plan.

Feinstein remained politically popular, winning her second full term as mayor with 80 percent of the vote. By law, however, she was unable to seek a third term and began exploring the possibility of running for governor of California. Although the office of mayor in San Francisco was nominally nonpartisan, Feinstein's allegiance to the Democratic party was widely known, and she had been seriously considered for the 1984 Democratic vice presidential nomination. Although Democratic challengers faced a difficult battle for the governorship (which had been dominated by Republicans), especially a candidate without a statewide political base or network of support, Feinstein believed that the time was right and committed herself to a campaign for California governor.

The early stages of Feinstein's campaign for the Democratic nomination for governor were fraught with problems in staffing. Feinstein was also troubled by physical problems that left her without adequate energy and forced her to undergo major surgery in July of 1989. Her opponent, California Attorney General John Van de Kamp, had pulled far ahead of her in the polls by late fall, and her campaign was so underfunded that her staff contemplated the possibility of her withdrawal. At that point, however, Feinstein responded by conferring with her staff to devise a strategy to revitalize her campaign. Her third husband, Richard C. Blum, an investment banker whom she had married in 1980, provided strong financial support for Feinstein's advertising campaign on television. The most effective commercial centered on her ability to handle crises, as illustrated through dramatic black and white footage of Feinstein's announcement of Moscone and Milk's deaths. This sympathetic portrayal of Feinstein's leadership ability was a major influence in her come-from-behind victory over Van de Kamp.

With the momentum of a strong primary victory, Feinstein moved into the general election against the Republican candidate, Senator Pete Wilson. The election was especially significant to both parties because the victor would oversee reapportionment of the seven new congressional districts that were to be created in California as a result of the increase in population measured by the 1990 census. Republicans were thus pouring in considerable money, and Feinstein again found herself confronting the difficulties of raising money and reaching voters statewide.

In addition to promoting government reform, Feinstein campaigned on issues related to the environment and abortion rights. Although Feinstein had identified herself as unequivocally pro-choice in the primary, most feminist leaders, including the state chapter of NOW, had endorsed her opponent, Van de Kamp. Even in the general election, feminist supporters were unenthusiastic, and some analysts suggested that her lack of ties to women's groups ultimately cost Feinstein the election.

Once again, the Feinstein campaign relied heavily on television advertising and centered on the slogan "tough but caring." During the last weeks of campaigning, the race became extremely close, but Feinstein eventually lost by 3.46 percent of the vote. Campaign manager Bill Carrick attributed the loss to a failure to produce commercials that attracted voters, citing the difficulty of presenting a woman candidate as tough enough for the job without creating a sense of hardness that alienates voters.

Undaunted by the loss, however, Feinstein proclaimed that public service had been and would continue to be her life. Indeed, she moved almost immediately into a campaign for the Senate, announcing in early 1991 her intention to run in the 1992 election for Pete Wilson's former seat, then being filled by Wilson's appointee, Republican John Seymour. Some political analysts questioned Feinstein's decision to run for the remaining two-year term rather than for the full six-year term to succeed retiring Senator Alan Cranston. Although Feinstein may have hoped to preempt the Democratic field with her early move and avoid an expensive primary campaign, that did not occur, and state controller Gray Davis provided strong opposition.

Because she had proved herself a viable statewide candidate in the 1990 race for governor, however, Dianne Feinstein found fund-raising easier and she had to rely less on her husband for campaign financing. Nevertheless, the issue of finances plagued the early part of her campaign when the California Fair Political Practices Commission filed an $8 million suit for campaign reporting violations in her race for governor. The suit was eventually settled for $190,000 with both sides agreeing that unintentional errors in bookkeeping and reporting had occurred.

Following a decisive victory in the Democratic primary, Feinstein entered the general election alongside noted feminist politician, Barbara Boxer, who had won the Democratic nomination for the second Senate seat. Feinstein's male Republican opponent was John Seymour, who was known for his support of feminist causes over the years. As a result, Feinstein, who had generally not emphasized women's issues in previous campaigns, began aggressively stressing such feminist issues as abortion rights, family leave, child support, and domestic violence. A prominent campaign phrase also played on the fact that only two members of the U.S. Senate were women: "Two percent may be okay for milk, but it isn't for the U.S. Senate."

When critics complained about her record on women's issues while she was mayor, Feinstein admitted she had been wrong in refusing to sign a 1983 resolution commemorating the tenth anniversary of *Roe vs. Wade*, but noted she had consistently been pro-choice. She also defended her veto of a comparable worth plan in 1985 by arguing that it was inadequate and by emphasizing that she had written a better proposal which passed the following year.

With her subsequent election to the Senate, Feinstein again broke new ground. She and Boxer became the first female senators from California, the first Jewish senators from the state, and the first all-female delegation to the U.S. Senate. Analysts indicate that major factors in Feinstein's victory were her plan for improving the economy (especially reducing military spending in order to increase funding for environmental protection projects), the desire to initiate change in Washington, the anger over the Senate's treatment of Anita Hill during the confirmation hearings of Clarence Thomas to the U.S. Supreme Court, and the related desire to see more women in the Senate. In 1994, she easily won her primary campaign for reelection, but faced stiff competition and numerous negative campaign advertisements from her Republican challenger, Michael Huffington.

Summary

In many respects, Dianne Feinstein's life has been one exploring new territory for women. In each of her elected positions, she has been the first woman to hold that office, a situation often fraught with difficulties. Feinstein has acknowledged feeling that she is constantly being tested because of being "first," yet she has successfully met the challenges in each position. Having begun her quest for political office prior to the full flowering of the feminist movement, Feinstein established her position in the world of politics independent of women's groups and without a feminist agenda. Subsequently, however, she embraced women's causes and made them a significant part of her life's goal, to contribute to humankind through government service.

Bibliography

Leavitt, Judith A. *American Women Managers and Administrators*. Westport, Conn.: Greenwood Press, 1985. Provides brief but basic biographical data through Feinstein's career as mayor of San Francisco.
Morris, Celia. *Storming the Statehouse: Running for Governor with Ann Richards and*

Dianne Feinstein. New York: Charles Scribner's Sons, 1992. The most valuable source of information available on Feinstein. Although the work focuses on her unsuccessful bid for governor in 1990 (in contrast to Richards' successful bid), it also presents essential biographical details of her earlier personal and professional life.

Stall, Bill. "Battle with Wilson Left Feinstein Tougher, Quicker." *Los Angeles Times,* April 28, 1992, p. A1. A good analysis of the Feinstein campaign for Senate.

Wilkinson, Tracy. "Senate Races Offer Stark Contrasts on World Affairs." *Los Angeles Times,* September 20, 1992, p. A3. Provides Feinstein's views on major issues during her campaign for Senate.

Witt, Linda, Karen M. Paget, and Glenna Matthews. *Running as a Woman: Gender and Power in American Politics.* New York: Free Press, 1993. A journalist, a political scientist, and a historian collaborated on this narrative overview of the experiences of female candidates in American politics. Written from the vantage point of 1992's "Year of the Woman," this work contains useful information on Feinstein's political career at the state and national level, including a telling assessment of her appeal among women voters.

Verbie Lovorn Prevost

628

GERALDINE FERRARO

Born: August 26, 1935; Newburgh, New York

Area of Achievement: Government and politics
Contribution: In 1984, Ferraro became the first woman to be nominated to the vice presidency by a major political party.

Early Life
Geraldine Anne Ferraro was born to an Italian American family in Newburgh, New York, on August 26, 1935. Her father, Dominick Ferraro, operated a nightclub in Newburgh, which had a reputation of being a wide-open town. In 1944, he was arrested and charged with operating a numbers racket. He died of a heart attack the day he was to appear for trial.

Antonetta Corrieri Ferraro, the major influence on Geraldine's early life, was left to rear her two children alone. She and the children left Newburgh in order to make ends meet; they relocated in a modest home in the somewhat less desirable South Bronx. Education was traditionally a way up and out for the children and grandchildren of immigrant families, and Antonetta Ferraro worked hard as a seamstress to provide an education for her children. Geraldine Ferraro attended Marymount Manhattan College and was graduated in 1956. She worked as a schoolteacher to support herself while attending law school at night and received her law degree from Fordham University in 1960, the same year she married John Zaccaro, a real estate developer. In honor of her mother, Ferraro kept her maiden name.

In the years that followed, three children were born to Ferraro and her husband. Although she passed the New York bar examination in 1961, she chose to practice law part-time while rearing her children. It was not until 1974 that she entered public service and accepted a post as an assistant district attorney in Queens County, New York, specializing in cases involving women, children, and the elderly.

Life's Work
Running as a Democrat, Geraldine Ferraro was elected to the United States Congress in 1978, and was reelected in 1980 and 1982. During those years she devoted her considerable energies to serving her working-class district in Queens, New York, by obtaining federal assistance for roads and subways, pure water and pollution control, control of illicit drugs, and other urban issues.

As one of the few women in Congress—there were only eleven Democrats and six Republicans in 1979 and a total of twenty-four women in 1983—she also became an obvious symbol for the feminist movement that had begun to transform American society. Ferraro denied that she wanted to be solely a women's representative, but she did speak out on the feminization of poverty, the discrimination affecting salaries and pensions awarded to men and women, and the problems of single-parent households headed by women.

Ferraro was not the first woman to have made her mark in Congress. In 1916, Jeannette Rankin was the first woman elected to Congress, and she voted against American involvement in both world wars. Pat Schroeder of Colorado and Barbara Milkulski of Maryland were two Democratic representatives rising to prominence at the same time as Ferraro. Outside of Congress, women were also achieving positions of political power. By the 1980's, Sandra Day O'Connor sat on the United States Supreme Court, Elizabeth Dole and Margaret Heckler were in the cabinet, Dianne Feinstein was the mayor of San Francisco, and many male politicians were asking their female colleagues to speak for them in election campaigns.

The year 1984 was a presidential election year and the conservative Republican Ronald Reagan was running for reelection. Most observers believed it would be a difficult challenge to defeat the former actor, who enjoyed notable popularity as president and was recognized for his skills of communication. After enduring a bruising series of primaries, Walter Mondale, former vice president under Jimmy Carter and one-time senator from Minnesota, emerged as the leading Democratic challenger and came to the San Francisco convention in July with the Democratic presidential nomination assured. The only remaining question was who would be his vice presidential running mate.

Traditionally, vice presidential candidates were selected to bring balance to the ticket. With Mondale's roots in the upper Midwest it could be expected that he might well choose someone from one of the big coastal states such as New York or California. Age, experience, and ideology could also play a part. In the past, however, balancing gender had never been seriously considered, and the Democratic and Republican parties had never chosen a female candidate for either the presidency or the vice presidency. When he appeared before the National Women's Political Caucus in 1983, Mondale himself had indicated that he would consider a woman as his vice presidential candidate if he received the Democratic nomination.

In November of 1983, several influential women met with Ferraro in hopes that she would consent to accept the vice presidential nomination if it were offered. Other Democratic women had been considered, but most were rejected as unsuitable because of geography, their stand against abortion, their brief tenure in elective office, or their lack of national and foreign policy experience. Ferraro nicely complemented Mondale: An Italian American Catholic from urban New York, she had completed three terms in Congress representing a conservative ethnic and blue collar constituency. Ferraro had struck a balance between her role as a wife and a mother of three children and her career as a politician. She had also made an impact within Democratic party circles. In her position as secretary of the Democratic Caucus in 1982, Ferraro had served as House liaison to the National Party Conference; in 1984, she was the chair of the Platform Committee at the Democratic National Convention and oversaw the selection of presidential and vice presidential nominees.

The prospect of a female as the Democratic vice presidential nominee was widely discussed. In June of 1984, *Time* magazine featured Ferraro and Feinstein on the cover as possible candidates. By the end of the month, there was considerable pressure on

Mondale to choose a woman as his running mate: The National Organization for Women (NOW) was seemingly threatening a convention fight if a woman was not selected. Mondale, however, did not have to be threatened. Always supportive of women's issues, Mondale knew that as a long-shot candidate against a popular incumbent he had little to lose and possibly much to gain by choosing a woman running mate. Many, including some Republicans, believed that a woman nominee would attract votes to the Democratic ticket.

On July 19, 1984, Ferraro made history when she was nominated as the Democratic vice presidential candidate. She and Mondale knew that the campaign would not be easy, but they believed that Reagan was vulnerable on both his foreign policy, which they deemed too belligerent toward the Soviet Union and thus endangering the world's peace, and on the domestic issues of unfairness and lack of opportunity for the less privileged members of American society. Unfortunately for Ferraro, much of the ensuing campaign revolved not around the issues of public policy but rather on herself and her personal history.

Sadly, it might have been predicted that a woman candidate would be treated differently, and not only by representatives from the opposite political party. Ferraro had difficulties with Mondale's own campaign staff, and other problems arose which, she argued, would not have occurred if she had been a male. More troubling were claims that she had acted unethically and perhaps illegally in the financing of her first congressional campaign, with her congressional disclosure statements, and with her family's past taxes and tax returns. These issues quickly dominated her campaign. She questioned whether such charges would have received such credence and publicity if she were a male candidate. Her husband was initially willing to release his financial statement, but not his personal tax returns, which he had been filing separately for several years. His reluctance to release this information led to charges that he had something sinister to hide. Over the next several weeks accusations were made that Zaccaro's father had rented office space to an underworld figure and that Zaccaro himself had borrowed money from an estate in which he was the legal conservator. In late August, after the various tax and financial statements were finally made available for public scrutiny, Ferraro held an open press conference in the attempt to put the issue to rest. This tactic was only partially successful.

Ferraro was also criticized by members of the Catholic hierarchy for her stand in favor of personal choice in the controversial matter of abortion. This, too, she believed reflected a double standard: Male Catholic politicians had not been personally criticized for similar stands on the abortion issue, and, in the past, Catholic bishops had generally abstained from political comment. Given the Mafia stereotype closely connected to the image of the Italian American community in the popular mind, Ferraro also was exposed to charges that she and her husband and their families had ties to organized crime. What was most galling for Ferraro was that other Italian American politicians did not come to her defense. The final blow to Ferraro's dignity was the report in October that her father had been arrested shortly before his death, charged with participation in a numbers racket.

Despite these personal attacks and the physical challenges of the 1984 campaign, Ferraro found her activities to be highly rewarding. In three months, Ferraro traveled more than 55,000 miles and spoke in 85 cities. Her campaign raised $6 million for the national Democratic ticket. Crowds were invariably large and enthusiastic wherever she appeared. In November, however, the country voted overwhelmingly for Ronald Reagan and George Bush. The polls and political commentators had early predicted the outcome, and Ferraro realized that she and Mondale were going to lose even before election day.

After the 1984 campaign, Ferraro chose to keep a low political profile and passed up the opportunity to challenge Alphonse D'Amato, the incumbent Republican senator from New York, in 1986. Still under public scrutiny, her husband pleaded guilty to overstating his net worth in getting a loan and was sentenced to community service. Later, Ferraro's son, John, a college student, was arrested on cocaine charges. In 1990, Ferraro chose to campaign aggressively on behalf of female Democratic candidates in New York. Next, Ferraro launched her own political comeback in 1992, when she entered the New York Democratic primary as a candidate for United States Senate. Competing against three other candidates in the primary, including New York state comptroller and former congressional representative Elizabeth Holtzman, Ferraro faced a tough battle. Typically upbeat and optimistic to the end, Ferraro finished second, less than one percentage point and fewer than 10,000 votes behind the winner, who was ultimately defeated in the general election.

Summary

For many women—and for some men—Geraldine Ferraro's 1984 campaign for the vice presidency was a watershed, a defining moment in their lives. Never before had a woman been chosen for such a high office by a major political party. During and after the campaign, Ferraro received thousands of letters from women, young and old, who saw her campaign as a symbol of equality, recognition, and opportunity for American women. Gloria Steinem, one of America's most respected feminists, noted during the campaign that "In the long run, the importance of the Ferraro factor may be the talent and dreams it unleashes in others." As an attorney in private practice after the campaign, Ferraro found time to encourage numerous women candidates by raising funds through public appearances on their behalf. Within a decade of the 1984 election, California, the largest state in the union, had chosen two women to represent the state in the U.S. Senate—a political first made possible, in part, by the example of Geraldine Ferraro.

Bibliography

Adams, James Ring. "The Lost Honor of Geraldine Ferraro." *Commentary* 81 (February, 1986): 34-38. This article explores the press and media coverage Ferraro received during the 1984 campaign and concludes that part of the press resorted to sensationalism but some of the media failed to adequately delve into Ferraro's controversial family history.

Blumenthal, Sidney. "Once upon a Time in America." *The New Republic* 194 (January 6, 1986): 28-36. In this important article, Blumenthal explores Ferraro's past and her family history and notes that, in spite of her claims, there are numerous criminal connections to both her and her husband's history.

Drew, Elizabeth. *Campaign Journal*. New York: Macmillan, 1985. Drew covered the 1984 election campaign for *The New Yorker* magazine. Her comments on Ferraro's campaign are insightful, including the observation that some exit polls indicated that Ferraro's controversial candidacy lost votes for the Democratic party.

Ferraro, Geraldine A. *Ferraro: My Story*. New York: Bantam Books, 1985. Ferraro, with the assistance of Linda Bird Francke, writes primarily of the 1984 vice presidential campaign and the various vicissitudes which she experienced. It also covers more superficially her earlier life, particularly her political career.

Ferraro, Susan. "What Makes Gerry Run?" *The New York Times Magazine*, March 22, 1992, 46. The author, no relation to the subject, discusses the early stages of the 1992 New York Democratic Senatorial campaign where Ferraro was attempting a political comeback. In addition, Ferraro's story since 1984 is summarized.

Witt, Linda, Karen M. Paget, and Glenna Matthews. *Running as a Woman: Gender and Power in American Politics*. New York: Free Press, 1993. A journalist, a political scientist, and a historian collaborated on this sweeping narrative of the experiences of female candidates in American politics. Throughout this work, Geraldine Ferraro's political career serves as one of the key case studies. The book contains numerous references to Ferraro's 1984 campaign, her career outside of public office, and her heroic efforts to encourage the political aspirations of other female Democratic candidates during the 1990 election year.

Eugene Larson

DOROTHY FIELDS

Born: July 15, 1904; Allenhurst, New Jersey
Died: March 28, 1974; New York, New York
Area of Achievement: Music
Contribution: One of the most gifted lyricists during the golden age of American popular music, Dorothy Fields collaborated with Jerome Kern, Jimmy McHugh, and Cy Coleman on enduring standard songs. She also wrote the libretto for such musicals as *Annie Get Your Gun* (1946) and *Sweet Charity* (1964).

Early Life

Dorothy Fields was born in Allenhurst, New Jersey, on July 15, 1904, the youngest of the four children of Lew Fields and his wife Rose. Dorothy's father was a famous vaudeville performer whose partnership with Joseph Weber made Weber and Fields one of the favorite show business acts of the 1890's. Lew Fields's real name was Lewis Maurice Schanfield, and he had worked his way to success from the Lower East Side of Manhattan and a background as the son of Polish immigrants.

After attending public school in New York City, Dorothy was graduated from Benjamin Franklin High School. Her parents did not want their children to make show business a career. When Dorothy auditioned for a part as an actress, her father saw to it that she failed. During her early twenties, Dorothy made ends meet by selling her poems to magazines while she worked as a drama teacher at Franklin High. Among her friends were the songwriting team of Richard Rodgers and Lorenz Hart. At the time they were collaborating with her brother Herbert in writing a Broadway show. She recalled that Rodgers and Hart had "bright, fresh, wonderful ideas," but her father, by that time a Broadway producer, was slow to see the potential of either Rodgers and Hart or his own daughter.

Life's Work

By the late 1920's, Dorothy Fields had been introduced to songwriter Jimmy McHugh. They began a partnership and wrote material for the nightclub performances of Duke Ellington and his jazz orchestra at the Cotton Club in Harlem. One song Fields and McHugh wrote was "I Can't Give You Anything but Love, Baby." The idea for the song came to them one afternoon when they were standing outside Tiffany's, the New York jewelry store that catered to wealthy clients. They heard a couple talking about diamonds, and the young man told his girlfriend that the only thing he could give her was love. With the title, the song soon followed. The tune, however, was not a success in the first show in which it was featured. The team of McHugh and Fields were then hired to write *Blackbirds of 1928*, an all-black musical revue on Broadway. Again, the critics panned their song, but the show eventually became a long-running hit. "I Can't Give You Anything but Love, Baby" caught on, and sold three million copies in sheet music. It was the first success for Fields as a lyric writer.

During the next seven years, Dorothy Fields wrote hit after hit with McHugh. Their popular favorites included "Exactly Like You," "On the Sunny Side of the Street," and their biggest success from 1935, "I'm in the Mood for Love." By the mid-1930's, Dorothy Fields had risen to the top of the songwriting profession.

For the next four decades, Dorothy Fields had an outstanding career in show business that made her an integral part of the national culture. Her words reflected what fellow songwriter Johnny Mercer called her intuitive sense of how a lyric should work. "She has a *feel* for the tune," Mercer told interviewer Max Wilk during the 1970's. Fields was very methodical in her approach to her craft. She recorded her ideas in a book to which she would often refer when working on a song or a show. "I'm not out to write popular song hits," she confided to Wilk, "though I've written songs that have *become* popular. I'm writing a song to fit a spot in the show. To fit a character, to express something about him or her . . . to move that story line forward."

She had married surgeon J. J. Werner in 1925, but they were divorced in 1932. Six years later, Dorothy Fields married Eli Lahm, a New York apparel manufacturer. They had a son, David, and a daughter, Eliza. Dorothy was a tall, thin woman with hazel eyes and chestnut hair. Interviewers described her as soft-spoken and prone to understatement about her formidable talent. She was hard-working and energetic throughout the day. As she put it, "You keep on writing; if the one you've written doesn't work, you write another."

The success of McHugh and Fields led to offers from Hollywood to work on motion picture musicals. While she was on the West Coast, Fields was asked to provide a lyric for a melody that Jerome Kern had written for the 1935 film version of his Broadway hit *Roberta*. Told that the melody was "curiously uneven," Fields came up with the words for the song "Lovely to Look At," and the producer promptly added it to the picture before telling Jerome Kern of the decision. When Kern heard her words, he was delighted. For the next picture Kern was writing, he decided that he wanted to work with Dorothy Fields.

The film that best embodied the Kern-Fields collaboration was the Fred Astaire-Ginger Rogers classic *Swing Time* from 1936. The score contained a number of enduring tunes such as "Pick Yourself Up," "A Fine Romance," and "Bojangles of Harlem." The melody and lyrics that Kern and Fields provided suited the Astaire-Rogers singing and dancing style perfectly, and the result was a delightful blend of comedy, music, and dance.

Swing Time also included a song that has attained a place as one of the most popular standards of the century. Alec Wilder, in his analysis of the American popular song, said of "The Way You Look Tonight" that it was "a lovely, warm song with a lovely, warm lyric." As Dorothy Fields remembered it, "the first time Jerry played that melody for me, I went out and started to cry. The release [last eight bars of melody] absolutely killed me. I couldn't stop, it was so beautiful." When the Academy Awards for 1936 were presented, "The Way You Look Tonight" was honored with the award for best song. Although the Kern-Field team wrote songs for another four years, none of their other efforts equaled the success they achieved in *Swing Time*.

At the end of the 1930's, Dorothy Fields decided to work with her brother Herbert

Fields in writing the libretto (or "book") for Broadway shows. She returned to New York to pursue this phase of her career. From her father, she had developed a shrewd sense of how a play should be constructed with the songs designed to advance the plot. These talents helped when she and her brother collaborated with the famous songwriter Cole Porter on shows during the early 1940's such as *Let's Face It, Mexican Hayride*, and *Something for the Boys*. Porter paid little attention to the plots of these musicals, and Dorothy and Herbert Fields accepted that approach as his working style that led him to compose hit songs.

The Fields siblings collaborated on the libretto for another show in 1945 with prominent composer Sigmund Romberg, who had earlier written "Lover, Come Back to Me" and *The Desert Song* (1926). The theme for the new musical was the development of New York City's most famous park during the political corruption of the 1870's. *Up in Central Park* was a success, but not a runaway hit. In addition to cowriting the book for the show, Dorothy crafted lyrics to Romberg's melodies.

Dorothy Fields had long planned to work with Jerome Kern again on a dramatization of the life of Annie Oakley, the famous western trick-shot artist who had toured with Wild West shows at the turn of the twentieth century. Kern died suddenly in late 1945, whereupon Dorothy and Herbert Fields asked Irving Berlin if he would like to write the songs for the show. Since Berlin usually wrote the words and the music for his songs, Dorothy and Herbert concentrated on the script. This collaboration between the Fields siblings and Berlin proved unusually fruitful. Berlin used some of the dialogue that Dorothy and Herbert had devised and transformed their ideas into a lilting and tuneful score. Ethel Merman starred in *Annie Get Your Gun*, which opened in 1946. Such hits as "There's No Business Like Show Business" enthralled audiences, and the show ran for almost twelve hundred performances.

Dorothy Fields returned to lyric writing when she added the words to the music of Arthur Schwartz in the show *A Tree Grows in Brooklyn*, which opened in April of 1951 with the actress Shirley Booth as one of the stars. Based on a novel about the lives of Irish immigrants in Brooklyn around 1900, it was a critical success and a commercial failure that closed after 270 performances. The score that Schwartz and Fields provided for the show, however, was one of the classics of the modern musical stage. In such numbers as "I'll Buy You a Star" and "Make the Man Love Me," Dorothy Fields attained a grace and simple poetry that had marked her work a decade earlier with Jerome Kern.

From the late 1950's until the end of her career, Dorothy Fields was associated with other hit shows designed to showcase the talents of the dancer-singer Gwen Verdon. The first was *Redhead* in 1959 for which Dorothy won a Tony Award. Next came *Sweet Charity* in 1964 with the composer Cy Coleman, which included the popular hit "Hey, Big Spender." Her last show in 1973 was a musical adaptation of the William Gibson play *Two for the Seesaw*, also written with Cy Coleman. A heart attack took her life in the spring of 1974.

Great Lives from History

Summary
Dorothy Fields wrote the lyrics for some of the most enduring popular songs in the nation's history. Her career spanned half a century, and her writing at the end of her life was as fresh and contemporary as it had been during the 1920's when she first achieved fame. Her songwriting colleagues recognized the sophistication and wit of her lyrics during her lifetime. She was also an important contributor to the literature of the musical theater in the shows she wrote with her brother. In the male-dominated songwriting profession of the years between 1920 and 1975, Dorothy Fields was a woman of taste and insight who left the world songs that were still being sung two decades after her death.

Bibliography
Boardman, Gerald. *American Musical Theatre: A Chronicle.* 2d ed. New York: Oxford University Press, 1992. A thorough treatment of almost every show that Fields either wrote or to which she contributed the lyrics.
Bowers, Dwight Blocker. *American Musical Theater: Shows, Songs and Stars.* Washington, D.C.: Smithsonian Collection of Recordings, 1989. This guide to accompany the Smithsonian Collection of recordings of the musical theater is a rich source of data about the most popular shows for which Dorothy Fields either wrote the book, contributed the lyrics, or did both for the same musical.
Croce, Arlene. *The Fred Astaire & Ginger Rogers Book.* New York: Galahad Books, 1972. The chapter on *Swing Time* is very useful for Fields's contribution to this classic musical with its excellent score of the songs she wrote with Jerome Kern.
Laufe, Abe. *Broadway's Greatest Musicals.* New York: Funk and Wagnalls, 1967. Discusses the long-running hits with which Dorothy Fields was associated during her Broadway career.
Wilder, Alec. *American Popular Song: The Great Innovators, 1900-1950.* Edited by James T. Maher. New York: Oxford University Press, 1990. The best guide to the development of popular songwriting, with insightful analyses of the composers with whom Dorothy Fields worked during her career.
Wilk, Max. *They're Playing Our Song.* Mount Kisco, N.Y.: Moyer Bell, 1991. This anthology of interviews with famous songwriters and lyricists contains a chapter on Dorothy Fields that provides a good summary of her life and career along with her own personal comments.

Lewis L. Gould

ELLA FITZGERALD

Born: April 25, 1918; Newport News, Virginia

Area of Achievement: Music
Contribution: Described as having perhaps the most extraordinary jazz voice in the world, Fitzgerald is a musical innovator as well as a pioneer in American jazz and popular music.

Early Life

Ella Fitzgerald has an extremely enigmatic past. Her reticence about family, friends, and personal history makes it almost impossible to give a definitive account of her early life, which has become the stuff of American myth. Although the place of Fitzgerald's birth is not disputed, the date of her birth has been the subject of some controversy. It has been argued that she was actually born in 1920 (a claim she has neither confirmed nor denied) and thus is two years younger than is usually reported, the reason for this being the child labor laws that were in force when she began her professional career. Her early relationship with her mother has also been disputed: In some accounts, she is described as having been orphaned as a young child and reared by her aunt. Fitzgerald's own account disputes this rendition of her early life, however, and she indicates that her mother was a powerful force in her childhood.

Nevertheless, it is known that her father died when Ella was an infant and that her mother took her to Yonkers, New York. Her mother worked as a cook and in a laundry. Fitzgerald describes her aunt, Virginia Williams, as a second mother. It was in New York that Fitzgerald developed an interest in music and in performing. The Boswell Sisters were Fitzgerald's favorite group, and she expressed an interest in emulating their success.

Fitzgerald's musical career began when she entered a talent contest at the Apollo Theater in Harlem in 1934. She entered, on a dare, as a dancer, but because she was too frightened to dance, she chose to sing instead. The song she sang in this contest has been the object of dispute, but in an interview Fitzgerald said it was "The Object of My Affection" (a song popularized by Connee Boswell). The early laughter of the audience turned into applause, and her march to stardom had begun. She continued to enter and win amateur contests throughout Harlem (the center of the city's music scene). It was at this time that her high school education came to an end, and with it, her stated ambition to become a physician. An abortive attempt to be a featured performer on CBS radio in 1934 ended with the death of her mother. Fitzgerald was too young to work legally.

Life's Work

In 1935, Ella Fitzgerald's early successes led to an audition with Chick Webb, a popular bandleader. After giving a warmly received performance at Yale University, Fitzgerald entered the ranks of professional singers. Webb was not only her band leader but also her legal guardian and chief adviser. She rose to national attention while the vocalist of the Chick Webb band. Live radio broadcasts and popular recordings on the Decca label made her known across America. Some of her earliest recordings (1935-1938) were "Love and Kisses" (her first song, recorded June 12, 1935), "Sing Me a Swing Song," "Rock It for Me," and "My Heart Belongs to Daddy." Singing was not her only talent; she also began to write lyrics. The singer Billie Holiday recorded one of Fitzgerald's first efforts as a lyricist, "You Showed Me the Way." Another early songwriting effort (cowritten with Webb), "A Tisket, a Tasket" (1938), became Fitzgerald's first major hit as a recording artist. Nat King Cole and Duke Ellington both had lyrics written for their music by the young writer.

In 1939, Webb died and Fitzgerald became the leader of his band. She continued to record popular songs for Decca, including "Cabin in the Sky" and "Baby Won't You Please Come Home." After the band disintegrated in 1941 (as a result of the military inductions of most of the band members), she struck out on her own and sang with a number of bands, including the Ink Spots, the Mills Brothers, and the Delta Rhythm Boys. She also appeared in the motion picture *Ride 'Em Cowboy* (1942). She continued to record and write music. While generally known only as a vocalist, Fitzgerald was inducted (the youngest person to ever have this honor) into the American Society of Composers, Authors, and Publishers (ASCAP) in 1943, thus demonstrating her significance as a lyricist.

It was while performing in the early 1940's that Fitzgerald perfected the style of singing that was to become her signature: scat singing. This technique, which involves using the voice as a musical instrument and emphasizing the quality of the sound rather than recognizable words (using improvised syllables instead of lyrics), gave her performances a unique and exciting power.

During the war era, Fitzgerald was one of the most popular performers in America. After World War II, her reputation traveled worldwide when she toured with the Jazz at the Philharmonic group. She consistently was voted "best vocalist" in polls featured in *Down Beat* (a popular jazz magazine) and sang with the most important popular and jazz bands of the 1940's and 1950's.

In 1949, Fitzgerald married bassist Ray Brown, the leader of a jazz band with which she played. Their marriage lasted only four years, during which time they adopted a child, Ray Brown, Jr., who remains Fitzgerald's only child. It is not entirely clear how many times Fitzgerald has been married. Some sources indicate once, some twice (including a marriage to Bernie Korngay, a shipyard worker, in 1941 followed by divorce in 1943), and some three times (with an early marriage ending in annulment). It is generally agreed, however, that Ray Brown was her last (if not her only) husband.

After her divorce from Brown, Fitzgerald began to work more closely with Norman Granz, who had been the head of the Jazz at the Philharmonic project. Granz became her manager, and Fitzgerald began to record on his label, Verve. This ended her recording relationship with Decca, which had produced more than 230 records. Her first Verve recording was "The Cole Porter Songbook" (1956), a two-album set that was to begin the period during which she produced her most influential and well-known work. With Granz, she released a series of recordings, each focused on the works of a particular composer or writing team, thus showcasing her vocal talents and the writers' musical and lyrical abilities. Her recordings of many songs were considered definitive, and they often renewed public interest in composers whose popularity had waned. Songbooks featuring the music and lyrics of Harold Arlen, Irving Berlin, Duke Ellington, George Gershwin and Ira Gershwin, Moss Hart, Jerome Kern, Frank Loesser, Johnny Mercer, and Richard Rodgers appeared during the twelve-year period from 1956 to 1968.

While working on the songbooks, Fitzgerald appeared in several motion pictures, *Pete Kelley's Blues* (1955), *St. Louis Blues* (1958), and *Let No Man Write My Name* (1960). She continued to tour nationally and internationally and to appear on television and radio. Hard and constant work have been a consistent part of Ella Fitzgerald's life for more than fifty years. Well into the 1980's, she worked more than forty weeks a year giving concerts, despite numerous health problems, and continued to release recordings on Granz's Pablo label.

Ella Fitzgerald has endured as a performer and has grown into an icon (a role she has accepted but with which she has never been comfortable). She continues to perform, though in a greatly diminished capacity, and continues to receive honors for her past and present contributions to American music and to the arts in general. Among the honors she has received are national awards from the governments of the United States (including the Kennedy Center Award) and France (the Ordre des Artes et des Langues) as well as innumerable awards from her peers (including "best vocalist" honors from all the major music magazines and a number of lifetime achievement awards). Although she completed only two years of high school, she is now the possessor of at least eight honorary doctorates. The most significant doctorate (according to an interview she gave in 1991) was the one she received in 1991 from Yale, the site where her professional career began.

Summary

Ella Fitzgerald has created the standard by which other popular singers are judged. She has been termed the "voice of the century" and the "first lady of song," and few critics disagree with these assessments. Bing Crosby's famous line about Fitzgerald sums it up well: "Man, woman, and child, Ella Fitzgerald is the greatest!"

Yet Fitzgerald's contributions go beyond her natural ability and her innovation. She has been a significant force within American entertainment for a number of reasons. Fitzgerald was one of the first women to lead a major band in the United States (the Chick Webb band after Webb's death). Her popularity knows no racial boundaries, though she has been criticized for turning her back on black music and black audiences. In addition, the lines between popular music and jazz have been blurred by her unique vocal style, which has not compromised either form.

Fitzgerald's improvisational singing style has influenced many jazz and popular vocalists. Scatting has become a regular part of the grammar of jazz, but no one scats as well as Fitzgerald does. Her sheer energy and desire to perform have inspired many people, and she has demonstrated that talent does not necessarily diminish with time. Her concerts and her albums have been consistently popular throughout her career, and she has proved that race, gender, and age (neither youth nor maturity) do not have to impede an individual's path to success. Fitzgerald occupies a place in the pantheon of popular stars and in American culture that is uniquely and permanently her own.

Bibliography
Colin, Sid. *Ella: The Life and Times of Ella Fitzgerald.* London: Elm Tree Books, 1986. This brief biography presents few new insights but does provide an overview of Fitzgerald's life up to 1985. It includes a number of photographs, a discography, and a bibliography. Colin, a music scholar from England, provides a useful, non-American view of the "Ella Phenomenon."
Crowther, Bruce, and Mike Pinfold. *The Jazz Singers: From Ragtime to the New Wave.* New York: Blandford Press, 1986. Crowther and Pinfold survey the role of vocal performances in jazz and provide a meaningful context within which Ella Fitzgerald can be analyzed. Although Fitzgerald's central role as an innovator and as a key definer of vocal jazz performance is made clear, only a small amount of text is devoted specifically to her.
Diamonstein, Barbaralee. *Open Secrets: Ninety-four Women in Touch with Our Time.* New York: Viking Press, 1972. This book provides fascinating insights into Fitzgerald's personal opinions and interests. One chapter is a series of responses by Fitzgerald to questions about race, gender, and power. Although the work is dated, it offers one of the frankest glimpses into this secretive star's mind.
McDonough, John. "Ella at Seventy-five: What Becomes a Legend Most: Ella Fitzgerald." *Down Beat* 60 (June, 1993): 22-25. This is an excellent, up-to-date discussion of Fitzgerald's place in the jazz world. A box in the article provides "Ella for Beginners," a discussion of the compact disc recordings released in celebration of her seventy-fifth birthday. It was *Down Beat* that gave Fitzgerald her first national recognition in its 1937 readers poll.
Pleasants, Henry. *The Great American Popular Singers.* New York: Simon & Schuster, 1974. Pleasants puts Fitzgerald's voice into the context of the other "great voices" of American popular music, including, among others, Judy Garland, Frank Sinatra, and Barbra Streisand. This work provides the most detailed and insightful discussion available of the specific qualities of Fitzgerald's voice and performance that have given her "a nearly universal popularity."

Timothy J. McMillan

WILLIAMINA PATON STEVENS FLEMING

Born: May 15, 1857; Dundee, Scotland
Died: May 21, 1911; Boston, Massachusetts
Area of Achievement: Astronomy
Contribution: Skilled in the analysis of stellar spectral photographs, Fleming discovered several new variable stars and novae and was the leader of a group of women doing similar work.

Early Life

Williamina Paton Stevens, daughter of Robert Stevens and Mary Walker Stevens, was born in Dundee, Scotland, on May 15, 1857. Her father had a successful picture framing business and was an early experimenter in photography. He died when Williamina was seven years old. Her mother's family were of Scottish stock and were noted for "energy, perseverance and loyalty"—a heritage that would manifest itself throughout Williamina's life. She received her early education in the Dundee public schools. At the age of fourteen, Williamina began to assume the dual role of teacher and student. She continued to teach for five years, until she married James Orr Fleming on May 26, 1877. The young couple moved to Boston in 1878. Their marriage failed and they separated in early 1879, by which time she was pregnant.

Needing to support herself, Fleming took employment as a housemaid in the residence of Edward C. Pickering, director of the Harvard College Observatory. She returned to Scotland in the fall of 1879 for the birth of her son, whom she named Edward Pickering Fleming, and later returned to the Pickering household, where her diligence and intelligence were greatly appreciated.

Life's Work

In 1881, Williamina Fleming became a member of the Harvard College Observatory staff. The story of her promotion from housemaid to staff member is a curious one: One day, Pickering, exasperated by the ineptitude of a male assistant in examining a photographic plate, said that his Scottish maid could do a better job—which she did, when called into his office. Thus, without any formal training in astronomy, she gradually assumed more and more of the responsibility for examining and cataloging the photographic records that were accumulating at the observatory. She was not the first woman to be employed at the Harvard College Observatory, but she became the first to achieve international renown for her work there—work that required diligence, care, and dedication. Fleming had all these qualities in abundance.

The timing of Fleming's joining of the observatory staff was fortuitous. Astronomers had only just learned that by connecting prisms and cameras to their telescopes they could gather vast amounts of a new kind of stellar information in permanently recorded form. The resulting photographic plates showed that each star exhibited its own characteristic spectrum when the light passed through a prism mounted within the telescope. These spectra could be analyzed and compared with those of other stars, allowing stars with similar spectra to be grouped into classes. Stellar spectra yielded information on stellar temperatures and chemical composition, allowing astronomers, traditional viewers of the heavens, to become astrophysicists, students of the physical conditions and processes taking place on individual stars.

The Harvard College Observatory, with observing stations in Peru as well as in Cambridge, had the necessary equipment to carry out a full-scale survey of both hemispheres of the heavens. Money became available to Harvard to finance such a program in 1887 through the Henry Draper Memorial—a fund established by Draper's widow, Mary Anna Draper, to enable the continuation of her late husband's work.

Henry Draper was a New York physician and amateur astronomer who had his own observatory. In 1872, he was the first person to photograph the spectrum of a single star. His hopes and plans to obtain photographs of the spectra of a large number of stars were cut short by his untimely death at age forty-five in 1882. His wife, who had been his assistant in this work, came from a wealthy family and was in a position to endow Harvard sufficiently to carry out his plans.

Williamina Fleming, with no previous training in astronomy but with native intelligence and under the tutelage of Edward Pickering, gradually came to assume more and more responsibility for the preparation of the stellar catalog that had been planned to memorialize Henry Draper. In 1890, *The Draper Catalogue of Stellar Spectra*, which had 10,351 entries, was published by the Harvard College Observatory. The spectra were cataloged according to the "Pickering-Fleming" system, which had been devised jointly by the two scientists and was used for more than two successive decades.

Fleming was required to examine, qualify, and catalog the spectra on all the photographic plates obtained by Harvard. In the course of her work over the thirty years that she worked at the observatory, she also discovered 222 new variable stars (stars whose brightness, or "magnitude," varied with a definite period of time) and ten novae (stars that suddenly increased in brilliance before dying away). In addition, she discovered fourteen of 107 rare stars known as "Wolf-Rayet" stars.

In recognition of Fleming's remarkable achievements, she was appointed "Curator of Astronomical Plates" in 1898 by the Harvard University Corporation—the first such appointment Harvard ever gave to a woman. At the time of Fleming's death in 1911, there were 200,000 plates in the collection.

Fleming was assisted in her work on the photographic plates by a corps of more than a dozen women employed by the observatory whom she hired and supervised. She exhibited considerable administrative skill and was highly respected as a friendly but strict disciplinarian. One of her younger assistants was Annie Jump Cannon, who was especially good at the work and carried on, after Fleming's death, as curator.

As the years passed, Pickering came to rely more and more on Fleming's assistance, particularly in preparing and editing for publication issues of the *Annals of the Harvard College Observatory*, some of which contained results of Fleming's spectral studies.

Pickering was scrupulous about giving Fleming credit in the various publications. As a result, she became well known throughout the worldwide community of astronomers. She was elected in 1906 to the Royal Astronomical Society of Great Britain—the first American woman to be so honored. She was also elected to the French and Mexican Astronomical Societies. The latter awarded her their Guadalupe Almendaro Gold Medal in 1911. In 1898, she was one of the founding members of the American Astronomical and Astrophysical Society. At the society's first meeting, held at Harvard, a paper by Fleming was read by Pickering. It was so well received by the audience that, after a burst of applause, Fleming came forward and responded to questions from the audience. She was also made an honorary fellow of Wellesley College.

Fleming was an indefatigable worker who was devoted to Pickering and the Harvard College Observatory. She rarely took vacations. She knew that her work was valued and appreciated but did wish that her salary of $1,500 per year were higher, since she was providing the care and education of her son, who studied at the Massachusetts Institute of Technology to become a mining engineer and was graduated in 1901.

Fleming's health declined in her later years. She died of pneumonia in Boston on May 21, 1911, at the age of fifty-four.

Summary

Williamina Paton Stevens Fleming was one of the large number of immigrants who came in the late nineteenth century to the United States, where they found the opportunity to develop their potential skills.

Fleming's case was unusual in that, as a divorced woman with a child to take care of, she rose from being a housemaid to become the most famous American woman astronomer during her lifetime. Some of her success must be ascribed to her good fortune in being associated with astronomer Edward C. Pickering. Nevertheless, it was her own abilities, coupled with devotion and hard work, that made possible her success.

The late nineteenth century was a time of increasing opportunity in America for women in both education and employment, but the numbers of women who benefited thereby were small. Fleming was very cognizant of the plight of most of her fellow women. Her own field of astronomy, at least at the Harvard College Observatory, was singularly hospitable to women, at least in having them do certain kinds of calculating and cataloging work.

In 1893, Fleming was invited to participate in the Congress of Astronomy and Astrophysics, which was held in conjunction with the World Columbian Exposition in Chicago. She delivered there an address entitled "A Field for Women's Work in Astronomy," which was later published in the journal *Astronomy and Astrophysics*. She detailed her own work in astronomy at the Harvard College Observatory and urged other observatories to open their doors to women workers. At that time, some women's colleges, such as Vassar and Wellesley, were offering courses in astronomy and had their own observatories. The major American observatories, however, were being built and run by men.

A number of magazine articles written for the general public took up Fleming's story, describing her work and her views on women's work. She was herself a distinguished career woman and a staunch woman suffragist.

She was clearly a public figure and an inspiration to younger women, especially those who came under her supervision at the Harvard College Observatory. Yet she retained, and even boasted of, her traditional feminine skills of cooking and sewing, frequently entertaining friends at her home, located near the observatory. Her son's success as a mining engineer was also a source of satisfaction to her. Williamina Fleming remains a model to be admired for her intelligence, industry, and strong character.

Bibliography
Jones, Bessie Z., and Lyle Gifford Boyd. *The Harvard College Observatory: The First Four Directorships, 1839-1919*. Cambridge, Mass.: Harvard University Press, 1971. Chapter 11 discusses the work and lives of women astronomers at Harvard, including Fleming. Other chapters provide extensive information on E. C. Pickering and the Henry Draper Memorial.
Mack, Pamela E. "Straying from Their Orbits: Women in Astronomy in America." In *Women of Science: Righting the Record*, edited by G. Kass-Simon and Patricia Farnes. Bloomington: Indiana University Press, 1990. Emphasizes the years up to 1920 and contains a section on the work of Fleming at the Harvard College Observatory.
Mozans, H. J. *Woman in Science: With an Introductory Chapter on Woman's Struggle for Things of the Mind*. New York: D. Appleton, 1913. Reprint. Notre Dame, Ind.: University of Notre Dame Press, 1991. A historical sourcebook for women's contributions to science dating back to ancient Greece. Chapter 4, "Women in Astronomy," details the work of talented women astronomers, up to and including Fleming, placing her in the context of previous and contemporary women astronomers. Includes a bibliography and an index. H. J. Mozans is the pseudonym of John A. Zahm.
Ogilvie, Marilyn Bailey. *Women in Science—Antiquity Through the Nineteenth Century: A Biographical Dictionary with Annotated Bibliography*. Cambridge, Mass.: MIT Press, 1986. The profile on Fleming summarizes the scientist's career and achievements, and provides a list of sources.
Rossiter, Margaret W. *Women Scientists in America: Struggles and Strategies to 1940*. Baltimore: The Johns Hopkins University Press, 1982. A scholarly survey of the opportunities and difficulties encountered by American women scientists and would-be scientists of the nineteenth and early twentieth centuries. Specific, referenced examples, including Fleming, are cited in detail. Includes publication data on popular articles related to Fleming.

Katherine R. Sopka

ELIZABETH GURLEY FLYNN

Born: August 7, 1890; Concord, New Hampshire
Died: September 5, 1964; Moscow, Soviet Union
Areas of Achievement: Trade unionism, social reform, and women's rights
Contribution: A great orator and champion of the socialist and communist movements in the United States, Flynn dedicated her life to fighting for the rights of the working class and women.

Early Life

Elizabeth Gurley Flynn was born in August, 1890, in Concord, New Hampshire. Her father, Thomas Flynn, was a first-generation Irish American who, as a young boy, worked in the granite quarries of New England. The self-educated Thomas passed the entrance examinations of Dartmouth College and enrolled to study engineering. After the death of his father two years later, he withdrew from college in order to support his mother and siblings. Flynn married Annie Gurley, an Irish immigrant who worked as a tailor to support her younger siblings. Annie Flynn was an advocate of equal rights for women who enjoyed attending public lectures and speeches on suffrage and civil rights issues.

The Flynn family was poor. During the first ten years of Elizabeth's life, her father's sporadic employment forced the family to move frequently. In 1900, Annie Flynn demanded more stability for the family, and the South Bronx, New York City, became their home. Although living in squalid conditions, the Flynns encouraged their children to read, learn, and be concerned with political and social issues. Elizabeth attended public school; a good student, she excelled in debate, English, and essay writing. Inspired particularly by what she learned about the United States Constitution and the Bill of Rights, she intended to become a constitutional lawyer.

Elizabeth's political education began at an early age. As a child, she heard stories of the Flynns' and Gurleys' roles in the Irish resistance to British rule. Thomas was often involved in socialist politics and causes. He openly opposed the Spanish-American War (1898), joined the Anti-Imperialist League, and voted for Eugene V. Debs, the Socialist Party candidate for president in 1900. Thomas and Annie Flynn, with their children, regularly attended the Sunday night meetings of the Bronx Socialist Forum. Annie encouraged Elizabeth to read widely, including socialist literature and philosophy. To the young Elizabeth, socialism called for the abolition of banks, landlords, and capitalists. She believed that the poverty, harsh working conditions, and despair of her family and neighbors could be eradicated through socialized, collective ownership.

The Flynn family joined the Harlem Socialist Club in 1906. Soon afterward, Elizabeth was invited to make a speech to the club's membership. With her mother's encouragement, fifteen-year-old Elizabeth made her first public speech: "What Socialism Will Do for Women." This title reflects a belief that Elizabeth maintained throughout her life: Economic and political freedom for women is possible only through socialism. Another milestone in Elizabeth's life occurred in 1906. On the basis of a special provision for "juniors and women," she joined the Industrial Workers of the World (IWW), a radical labor union for which she worked as a major organizer for twenty years.

Life's Work

Elizabeth Gurley Flynn's speech at the Harlem Socialist Club marked the beginning of her career as a public orator and militant organizer. After this speech, she received invitations to speak at socialist clubs in many East Coast cities. These clubs, however, seemed old-fashioned and staid to the young Flynn. By contrast, the IWW was exciting and militant, because it attempted to organize all wage-earners into "One Big Union" and understood that the rights and interests of women should not be separated from the interests of the working class.

In 1907, Flynn was a delegate at the IWW Convention in Chicago. Although the convention was uneventful, Flynn became a traveling labor union organizer. An acquaintance from the convention invited Flynn to the Mesabi Range, Minnesota, to organize iron ore miners. Flynn traveled to Minnesota and began her work as an organizer for the IWW.

A full-time IWW organizer, Flynn traversed the country and made numerous well-received speeches. Determined to organize the working class, especially those people (women, children, and minorities) often ignored by the more traditional labor unions, Flynn campaigned in every major urban area. She played a major role in most of the landmark labor actions of the early twentieth century, including the massive strikes in Lawrence, Massachusetts (1912); Paterson, New Jersey (1913); the Mesabi Range, Minnesota (1916); and Passaic, New Jersey (1926). Flynn's speeches inspired thousands to leave their jobs and protest for better wages and working conditions.

The role of women and women's issues in labor action were of special concern to Flynn. The IWW had only four women organizers, but that was more than any other union had. Flynn encouraged women wage-earners and the wives of wage-earners to organize and strike on issues such as food prices, day care, child labor, and housework. She also urged the IWW leadership to be more responsive to the role of women as workers and organizers.

Flynn also used her flair for political writing to promote IWW and socialist views; she published numerous pamphlets and newspaper columns. In 1914, Flynn became involved in organizing defense committees and fund drives to fight politically moti-vated legal action used against immigrants, workers, and those involved in militant activities. The Workers Defense Union (1918-1924), organized by Flynn, provided legal assistance and aroused public support for various groups and individuals, including African Americans threatened by the newly strengthened Ku Klux Klan and Italian immigrants targeted by the New York Palmer Raids (1920).

Almost twenty years of organizing, speaking, and writing exacted an emotional and physical toll on Flynn's health. After a ten-year (1926-1936) hiatus from public life, she returned to New York City in 1937 eager to resume her political activism. The

IWW had disbanded for the most part, as had many other socialist unions and clubs. With the support of several longtime friends, Flynn applied for membership in the Communist Party of the United States of America. Her membership was approved, and she was given a salaried Party position. The Party's Popular Front (1935-1939) campaign was appealing to Flynn. This campaign, which had received broad support as an early effort to fight fascism in Europe, was the Party's effort to create a more traditional, American-based appeal. Coalitions with labor unions and the adoption of traditional symbols and slogans of democracy were part of this effort. The Party was authoritarian in structure, however, and its members were expected to conform to the "party line." Although Flynn continued to see herself as a populist agitator, she remained faithful to the Communist Party, even though the Party often ignored many issues pertinent to women.

Flynn's Party activities included raising funds for the Spanish Republicans and promoting New Deal programs intended to fight hunger and fascism. She maintained a hectic speaking schedule and wrote columns for the *Daily Worker*, the Communist Party newspaper. Flynn's interest again focused on the role of women in the Party, unions, government, and the household.

With the beginning of the Cold War, the United States government sought to neutralize any influence or popularity won by the Communist Party during World War II. In 1948, President Harry S Truman ordered the arrest of the twelve leading Party officials for violating the Smith Act. Flynn organized and led the defense for the accused, portraying the charges as undermining their right to free speech and assembly. On June 20, 1951, Flynn was arrested, along with fifteen other lesser Party officials, for violating the Smith Act. During the ensuing trial, Flynn's self-defense impressed even those who opposed her. She served a thirty-day sentence, during the trial, for refusing to identify other Party members and supporters. Convicted in 1955, Flynn served twenty-eight months in the Federal Reformatory for Women in Alderson, West Virginia.

After her release from prison Flynn remained a Communist Party leader. In 1960 and 1961, she completed an eight-month tour of European socialist and communist countries, ending in the Soviet Union. Flynn was changed by this experience. She unhesitatingly praised the practice of communism in these countries. In the *Daily Worker* and in her private correspondence, she portrayed the Soviet Union as a progressive, increasingly democratic state. During this trip she was treated as a celebrity, a heroic fighter for workers.

On her return to the United States, Flynn was elected chairperson of the Communist Party. In this new position, she initiated a series of lectures aimed at more liberal, middle-class audiences. Flynn believed that the Party could establish a populist appeal by forming coalitions with the newly emerging civil rights and student groups. Yet one final legal battle remained. The U.S. government revoked Flynn's passport for failure to comply with the McCarran Act, an anticommunist piece of legislation that required that communist-led organizations make public the names of their officers and members, among other things. Flynn, with the assistance of fellow radical Herbert

Aptheker, argued her case to the Supreme Court, and her passport rights were reinstated. Needing a quiet vacation, Flynn traveled again to the Soviet Union. On September 4, 1961, less than one month after arriving in Moscow, Flynn died in the Kremlin Hospital. The Soviet Union gave her a full state funeral. Flynn's ashes are buried in the Kremlin Wall and in Waldheim Cemetery, in Chicago, Illinois.

Summary

Elizabeth Gurley Flynn lived an unconventional, militant life, committed to the values and principles of socialism. An extremely intelligent and gifted speaker, at a young age she became dedicated to fighting for the rights of the working class, the poor, women, and immigrants—those she believed were most exploited by capitalism. Flynn did not see herself as a philosopher or great leader. She liked to be described as a self-educated, revolutionary agitator—someone who could inspire the masses to radical action. Encouraged by a loving family to exercise her personal and political freedom, Flynn challenged conventional ideas about a woman's role in society. She joined primarily male-dominated organizations but often used her position to emphasize and articulate the problems and interests of women as workers, wives, citizens, and mothers. Although Flynn had a son and numerous relationships with men, her time, energies, and concern were directed primarily toward political activities. Flynn has been criticized by feminists for her participation in organizations that were often sexist in principle and action. Flynn, however, was convinced that true equal rights for women could be realized only through socialist organization and collective ownership. Fighting for women's rights separately from those of the working class, for Flynn, was counterproductive.

Bibliography

Buhle, Mari Jo. *Women and American Socialism: 1780-1920*. Urbana: University of Illinois Press, 1981. A critical history of socialist and women's movements in the early twentieth century United States. Flynn's role in the early labor movement, her positions on feminist issues, and her leadership in the Communist Party are discussed in terms of how socialist movements are often supported by feminist ideas and philosophies.

Dubofsky, Melvyn. *We Shall Be All: A History of the Industrial Workers of the World*. 2d ed. Urbana: University of Illinois Press, 1988. A thorough and detailed history of the IWW from a radical perspective. Flynn's roles in major labor strikes and free speech movements are well documented.

Flynn, Elizabeth Gurley. *The Rebel Girl: An Autobiography, My First Life (1906-1926)*. Rev. ed. New York: International, 1973. An exhaustive account of Flynn's early life as an IWW organizer and political activist. She provides an interesting and engaging view of her personal life as well. The "second life" autobiography was never published. Flynn provides some of the best descriptions available of the Lawrence (1912) and Paterson (1913) strikes.

——————. *Words on Fire: The Life and Writing of Elizabeth Gurley Flynn*.

Edited by Rosalyn Fraad Baxandall. New Brunswick, N.J.: Rutgers University Press, 1987. This, the first published collection of Flynn's writings, includes many early essays. A long, thorough biographical introduction and a conclusion that offers a feminist perspective on Flynn's life are also included.

Renshaw, Patrick. *The Wobblies: The Story of Syndicalism in the United States.* Garden City, N.Y.: Doubleday, 1967. A history of the IWW as a radical labor union that attempted to organize workers no other union would allow as members. Flynn is noted as a major organizer, but her work is mentioned only briefly. The book, however, provides a good short history of the development and decline of the IWW.

Tax, Meredith. *The Rising of the Women: Feminist Solidarity and Class Conflict, 1880-1917.* New York: Monthly Review Press, 1980. A review of the major political struggles involving women (1880-1917). The chapters "Rebel Girls and the IWW" and "Lawrence, 1912" provide insight into Flynn's union activity. The book also offers a critical feminist discussion regarding the relationship between gender and class.

Karen A. Callaghan

JANE FONDA

Born: December 21, 1937; New York, New York

Area of Achievement: Film

Contribution: Fonda is a high-profile film star who became a political activist and a leading figure in the anti-Vietnam War protest movement of the 1960's, a spokesperson for women's rights, and a hugely successful businesswoman.

Early Life

Jane Seymour Fonda was born on December 21, 1937, in New York City to Henry Fonda and Frances Seymour Brokaw Fonda. Her mother had inherited a considerable fortune, and her father, already a successful film star, was also to become wealthy in his own right. The marriage lasted until 1949, when Fonda fell in love with another woman, Susan Blanchard, and asked his wife for a divorce. After Frances committed suicide in April of 1950, Fonda married Susan Blanchard (in 1957, he was married to Afdera Franchetti). Jane Fonda then lived with her grandmother in Connecticut and attended the Greenwich Academy. In 1951, she enrolled at the Emma Willard School in Troy, New York, then later attended Vassar. In 1957, she left Vassar to study art at the Académie Julian in Paris. For a while, she took up modeling and was twice featured on the cover of *Vogue*, but she ultimately decided on an acting career and began to study with Lee and Paula Strasberg in New York at the Actors Studio.

Life's Work

Jane Fonda's stage debut came in 1955 when she appeared with her father in Omaha, Nebraska, in *The Country Girl*. Her Broadway debut came in 1960 in the Daniel Taradash play *There Was a Little Girl*, directed by Joshua Logan, a friend of her father's, who also directed her in her first screen role as a love-crazy cheerleader in *Tall Story* (1960) in which she starred with Anthony Perkins. Although it launched Fonda's screen career, *Tall Story* was not a hit, and *There Was a Little Girl*, a play about a girl who is raped, was too brutal and controversial for its time and closed after three weeks. Logan, impressed by Fonda's talents, considered her an "instant professional."

Other films soon followed. She was directed by Edward Dmytryk in *Walk on the Wild Side* (1962) and by George Cukor in *The Chapman Report* (1962). In 1965, she made her film debut in France with *La Ronde*, directed by Roger Vadim, whom she married that year; they were divorced in 1970. In 1965, she made the popular *Cat Ballou* in America, but by 1967 she was starring in the cartoonish *Barbarella*, made by Vadim, who transformed his wife into a sex goddess. Yet Fonda's image was also changing in other ways.

Her films of the late 1960's began to reflect a new seriousness, particularly Sydney Pollack's *They Shoot Horses, Don't They?* (1969), which earned for her an Academy Award nomination for Best Actress; she was also named Best Actress by the New York film critics for that role. She won the Academy Award as Best Actress for *Klute* in 1971, under the direction of Alan Pakula. As her career was peaking, however, the actress became political in a way that alienated her from many American viewers for the next twenty years.

Fonda's political instincts attracted her to the radical French director Jean-Luc Godard, who featured her in *Tout va bien* (1972). Godard at that point had vowed never to make a film that was not critical of the American presence in Vietnam, and Fonda shared his attitude. Protesting the Vietnam War in 1971, she formed an antiwar troupe (Entertainment Industry for Truth and Justice) that toured Southeast Asia and produced a filmed record entitled *F.T.A.*, completed in 1972 with a visit to North Vietnam, which led conservative Americans to question her patriotism. In 1974, Jane Fonda and activist Tom Hayden joined forces with Haskell Wexler to produce a documentary entitled *Introduction to the Enemy*, which was a chronicle of Fonda's second trip to Vietnam. Fonda had the courage of her convictions and was willing to put her career on the line. It took years for her to recapture her popular audience.

Her opposition to the Vietnam War characterized her as a radical in the minds of many Americans, as did her marriage in 1973 to Tom Hayden, an antiwar militant who was a highly visible spokesman for the radical Left and the antiwar movement. Her political agenda carried over into the films that she made, such as *Coming Home* (1977), which concerned the physical and psychological effects of war on a returned veteran who had been wounded in Vietnam; *Julia* (1977), with Fonda playing Lillian Hellman in a story of artistic integrity and moral responsibility; and *The China Syndrome* (1979), an antinuclear film dramatizing the danger of a meltdown at a nuclear power plant, released, as luck would have it, just before the near meltdown at the Three Mile Island plant in Pennsylvania. Conservative critics attempted to ridicule the film, but the picture was not so easily dismissed after the threatened meltdown at Three Mile Island. Even in the midst of her Vietnam period, however, Fonda also worked with director Joseph Losey, taking the lead in David Mercer's screen adaptation of Henrik Ibsen's *A Doll's House* in 1973.

During the course of her career through the 1980's, Fonda had starred in nearly forty films, leaving a record of some remarkable performances. She was nominated seven times for Academy Awards and won the Oscar twice, for *Klute* and *Coming Home*. Her television film *The Dollmaker* (1983, adapted from a novel by Harriette Arnow, published in 1954) earned for her an Emmy award. The pictures that earned for her nominations for the Academy Awards included *They Shoot Horses, Don't They?*, *Julia*, *On Golden Pond*, and *The Morning After*, directed by Sidney Lumet in 1986.

During the Reagan years of the 1980's, Fonda transformed herself into a conventional businessperson, capitalizing on the popular interest in physical fitness by launching an extremely successful line of videotapes featuring her own personal exercise programs and aerobics workouts as well as a line of exercise clothing. Concerned about the rigorous content of the workouts she promoted, Fonda consulted with fitness experts to ensure the safety of the exercises she performed. Profits from her fitness enterprises allowed Fonda to explore the possibilities of developing her own film production company.

Throughout the 1980's, Fonda worked hard to distance herself from the negative reaction to her political period. By the middle of the decade, she had advanced to the number 4 position (up from number 10) in the Gallup Poll roster of America's Most Admired Women, and the 1984 *World Almanac* listed her as America's third most influential woman. After *On Golden Pond* (1981), her reconciliation picture with her father, she played some memorable roles, first as the chain-smoking psychiatrist in Norman Jewison's 1985 film adaptation of John Pielmeier's play *Agnes of God*, in which she had splendid support from Anne Bancroft and Meg Tilly as the novitiate nun who murders her newborn baby, and then as an alcoholic in Sydney Lumet's *The Morning After* (1986). Her performance in Alan J. Pakula's *Rollover* (1981), however, was perfunctory, and she won no acclaim for her portrayal of Harriet Winslow in *The Old Gringo* (1989) or her performance with Robert De Niro in *Stanley and Iris* (1989). During the 1990's, it almost seemed that Fonda had gone into retirement.

Fonda was still very much aware of her celebrity image when, during the early 1990's, she went on national television with a sympathetic Barbara Walters to tell the American public that she was sorry for at least part of what damage she might have done to the American war effort in Vietnam. It took her a long time to shake the image of "Hanoi Jane."

The film that had helped rehabilitate her popularity was the feminist satire *Nine to Five* (1980), a comic spoof of the male-dominated world of business. Dabney Coleman played her sexist boss as a perfect caricature, and the picture became tremendously popular. Perhaps her most successful picture was *On Golden Pond*, a sentimental and nostalgic favorite directed by Mark Rydell, adapted by Ernest Thompson from his own play. In this drama, Jane Fonda took a secondary role to her father and Katharine Hepburn. This was to be Henry Fonda's last film, but his performance was touching. The film offered a thoughtful examination of the problems of old age and the need for reconciliation between parents and children. Hanoi Jane had disappeared and Hollywood Jane had reappeared. In 1991, Fonda married television mogul Ted Turner.

Summary

Jane Fonda's career might seem exploitative and contradictory, since she has changed her screen persona and image so frequently with the times. The popularity of her father, Henry Fonda, prepared the way for her entry into motion pictures as a Hollywood starlet with a recognizable name, but by the mid-1960's she turned from Hollywood to France, first coming under the influence of Roger Vadim, who exploited her sex appeal, then under the influence of director Jean-Luc Godard, who radicalized her and made her an international antiwar figure.

Fonda was also influenced by the actor-teacher Lee Strasberg at the Actors Studio in New York, who completed her professional training. She has been influenced by various men in her life: her father, Vadim, Godard, Lee Strasberg, Tom Hayden, and

Ted Turner. Critic Richard Dyer has divided Fonda's career into six phases—her father, sex, acting, politics, independence, and middle age—but these phases tend to overlap. Although Fonda's career has been constantly influenced by her father, her mentors, and her husbands, she has always strived for independence as an artist, producer, and entrepreneur. As an independent producer, she has achieved critical and popular success, though not necessarily at the same time, with such pictures as *Coming Home*, a first step toward reconciliation after the end of the Vietnam War; *On Golden Pond*, which seemed to work a reconciliation with her father; and other pictures, such as *Nine to Five*, which facilitated her return to the popular mainstream.

Bibliography
Andersen, Christopher. *Citizen Jane: The Turbulent Life of Jane Fonda*. New York: Henry Holt, 1990. The most complete treatment of Fonda's career, this book includes coverage of *The Old Gringo* (1989), her last film before her marriage to Ted Turner, which seemed to mark the end of her acting career.
Dyer, Richard. *Stars*. London: British Film Institute, 1979. Dyer, who considers stars "signifying entities," examines Fonda's "iconographical significance" as shaped by her ideology, which he traces through six phases of her career.
Fonda, Henry. *Fonda: My Life: As Told to Howard Teichmann*. New York: New American Library, 1981. Teichmann tells the life story of Henry Fonda, based on 200 hours of taped material and 117 interviews with Fonda's family and friends. The father's relationship with his daughter can be traced throughout the book, which ends with a consideration of *On Golden Pond* (1981).
Guiles, Fred Lawrence. *Jane Fonda: The Actress in Her Time*. Garden City, N.Y.: Doubleday, 1982. A very competent star biography, arguably the best early book on Fonda's life and career. Her career is followed through *On Golden Pond* (1981).
Herman, Gary, and David Downing. *Jane Fonda: All American Anti-Heroine*. New York: Quick Fox, 1980. This is the sort of book that has at least one, and often three or four, pictures on every page. It celebrates left-leaning Jane and her achievements as a radical activist up to *The Electric Horseman* (1979).
Vadim, Roger. *Memoirs of the Devil*. Translated by Peter Beglan. New York: Harcourt Brace Jovanovich, 1976. Vadim, whose work reminded the bluenoses of America that French films were supposed to be naughty, was the director who created *And God Created Women* and turned Brigitte Bardot into an international sex symbol. In this book, he celebrates his relationships with "the world's most beautiful women"—Catherine Deneuve, Bardot, and Fonda.

James M. Welsh

EILEEN FORD

Born: March 25, 1922; New York, New York

Area of Achievement: Business and industry
Contribution: Vice president and cofounder of the prestigious Ford Model Agency, located in New York and Paris, Eileen Ford wrote several books on modeling and is known for her ability to discover and develop talent. Ford has also been instrumental in the standardization of business practices in modeling.

Early Life
Eileen Otte was born on March 25, 1922, the only daughter of Nathaniel Otte and Loretta Laine Otte. Eileen grew up along with her three brothers in the affluent New York City suburb of Great Neck on Long Island. Eileen was a good student and lived a carefree life. She was fun-loving and was known as a prankster. At sixteen, she moved address and name signs from one property to another in her neighborhood to confuse visitors.

As a teenager, Eileen's goal was to enjoy life. She had a car, lots of boyfriends, and plenty of invitations to parties. Eileen was engaged eleven times and stated that her engagement depended on whose fraternity pin she was wearing. She later described her younger life as "perfectly marvelous" with little thought concerning future work or career.

Eventually, Eileen's mother, herself a former model, encouraged her daughter to go to college to study pre-law. After graduating from high school in 1939, Eileen enrolled in Barnard College and majored in political science. Studying, however, was not a priority. Eileen was more concerned about fashion and spent most of her free time knitting sweaters to wear. Her one academic interest was reading. She read at least one book a week and enjoyed historical novels and adventure stories. She favored ancient history and marveled at the feats accomplished by the ancient Babylonian, Greek, and Roman civilizations.

It was in college that Eileen first became acquainted with the modeling profession. She began modeling during the summer for the then-popular Conover Model Agency, which specialized in the wholesome coed look. Although her modeling experience was limited to only one month in each of two summer vacations, Eileen did become familiar with various business practices and met several photographers and other models.

In 1943, Eileen was graduated from college with a bachelor's degree in psychology. She met her future husband and business associate, Jerry Ford, in 1944. Ford was a college student and talented football player at Notre Dame who met Eileen when he went to the East to finish his education. Eileen and Jerry had a whirlwind courtship and eloped on November 20, 1944, only four months after their first meeting.

Eileen's work experience had varied after her graduation from college. She worked for an American export company, and later for photographer Elliot Clark as secretary and stylist. Next, she worked as a copywriter for a department store and as a fashion reporter for the Tobé Reports. Eileen's exposure to photography and fashion gave her further insight into the modeling industry.

In 1946, Eileen Ford became pregnant and quit formal employment. To help support the family, Eileen decided to earn extra income on the side by handling bookings for two of her model friends for a fee. Within a year, this new business boomed, and Ford Model Agency made its debut. Eileen's husband, Jerry, joined her shortly thereafter to help manage the agency. Within one year, Eileen and Jerry Ford were managing twenty-two models.

Life's Work

Eileen Ford and her husband grossed an incredible $250,000, in revenues during their first year of business in 1946. Life was busy for the Fords, manning seven telephones and answering about 275 calls a day. The Ford Agency's enormous popularity and growth were partly attributable to its unique business practices. Eileen Ford was determined to treat all of her models with respect and expected everyone else she dealt with to do the same. Specializing in "high fashion" modeling, she refused to let her models pose for cheap or suggestive photographs. This practice encouraged top models to leave other agencies and to join the Ford Agency.

The agency can attribute most of its recognition and success, however, to Eileen Ford's uncanny ability to find and develop talent. Candice Bergen, Lauren Hutton, Ali McGraw, and Jane Fonda all worked as famous Ford models before pursuing their acting careers. Supermodel Christie Brinkley launched her career as a Ford Agency model. Finding a "star" model, however, does not happen by chance. The Ford Agency devotes substantial resources and time to the discovery and development of talent.

The Ford Agency staff has developed a process of reviewing numerous portfolios every day looking for potential models. In addition, Eileen Ford and her staff travel throughout the United States and Europe in search of new talent. Among the first things they look for are certain desirable physical traits in candidates—height, weight, wide-set eyes, straight noses, and long necks. These individuals must also photograph well. The agency also looks for "star" quality—models who can project their person-alities and who have unique looks. By the early 1990's, the agency was receiving solicitation letters and personal visits from thousands of would-be models every year, but less than fifty were selected annually to go through a try-out.

During the interview process in the early years of the agency, Ford established a rule of being candid with the interviewees. When she rejected a model, she thoroughly explained the reasons why so that the candidate was not given false hopes later by a dishonest agency. By stating "it (modeling) is just a job and not that important," Ford encouraged prospective employees to keep modeling in perspective.

After she located promising candidates, Ford's model-making process began. Upon arriving in New York, Ford candidates were expected to move into the Ford's personal residence (especially if they were young) or be placed in a Ford-provided apartment.

All new candidates were closely supervised and were required to take a series of classes using *Eileen Ford's Book of Model Beauty* as a textbook at the Ford Agency. The classes lasted three months and taught the models how to use makeup, to pose in front of the camera, to demonstrate professional behavior in the studio, and to observe proper diet and exercise. Frequently, Eileen Ford attended the sessions personally in order to give her advice. Upon completion of the course, the Ford staff selected the few models who were invited to become part of the "Ford" family.

After the training process was completed, the Ford staff assigned each new model to a "booker," who was responsible for setting up appointments and introducing the model to various magazine editors and photographers through interviews. In the "booking" room (where all appointments were scheduled), the model's chart was posted containing her vital information and appointments. The bookers were expected to know their models thoroughly, and match and schedule them for jobs.

As part of the family, the models were expected to abide by strict standards of discipline. Eileen Ford wanted her models to be healthy and to look good. During flu season, she was often known to pass out vitamins as a form of preventive medicine. If a model was discovered to be breaking the agency's rules of behavior, Ford often acted as a surrogate mother, issuing a warning to make amends. If undisciplined behavior persisted, Ford took the initiative to send the offender home.

Over the years, Ford has earned a reputation as being somewhat inflexible and narrow-minded. She favors young models between the ages of fifteen and twenty who possess a Scandinavian look. Nevertheless, she has allowed the Ford Agency to create other divisions in order to satisfy market demand. In the 1970's, she added a children's division with the introduction of eight-year-old model Brooke Shields. Upon the request of her older models, Ford began the "Classic Woman" Division for women over forty. Most recently, famous designers such as Liz Claiborne have been marketing larger-sized clothing. Thus, Eileen formed a division for heavier models. The agency also has a men's division that is managed by Ford's husband.

For nearly five decades, Eileen Ford has dedicated her life to the modeling industry. She continues as president of the Ford Agency, which in the early 1990's reported $40 million in gross revenues. Ford's modeling genius and vigor, complemented by the business talent of her husband, have made the Ford model agency into a multimillion dollar business.

Summary

Eileen Ford's most significant contribution to the modeling industry related to the standardization of several business practices. In the 1940's, standards concerning payment of models and agencies were minimal. At that time, models were responsible for setting and collecting their own fees. As a result, many models were not paid for their work. Thus, the Ford Agency instituted several payment policies that eventually became the norm in the industry.

Ford pays every model in advance on a voucher system, and the agency collects the fee from clients later. Weekend jobs are voluntary and pay time-and-a-half or double time. One special category of bookings is called "weather permitting" where models are paid half their fees if the booking is canceled because of bad weather. The model could have been doing an indoor job. On the other hand, if the model cancels the job, no fee is required.

Ford Agency and other agencies have also pushed up market prices for modeling services. The four most prestigious agencies—Ford, Wilhelmina, Elite, and Zoli—control 60 percent of the industry's billings. Since these firms control modeling in New York City, the lack of competition causes high hourly rates for models. Ford Agency remains first in billings despite strong competition from the other agencies.

Eileen Ford's writings have also contributed to the training and preparation of models. Her modeling books have been best-sellers both here and abroad. Her most popular books include *Eileen Ford's Book of Model Beauty* and *Secrets of the Model's World*.

Eileen Ford established her reputation as the industry's foremost modeling expert through determination and her unerring eye for talent. Her involvement with and control of her models have contributed to Ford Agency's success. The Ford rules, techniques, and billing practices have also been geared to take into account the model's welfare. Models appreciate Eileen's personal touch, and as a result, Ford Agency has been the most prestigious and popular modeling agency for almost five decades.

Bibliography
Brannum, Mary. *When I Was 16*. New York: Platt & Munk, 1967. Excellent biographical sketch of Eileen Ford during her younger, more formative years. The author describes Eileen Ford's life as carefree and uncomplicated. The author extensively writes about Ford's view of the modeling industry during the late 1960's and the way she managed her agency.
Cohen, Scott. *Meet the Makers: The People Behind the Product*. New York: St. Martin's Press, 1979. The collection of interviews with the "Makers"—in Eileen's case, the Model Maker.
Ford, Eileen. *Eileen Ford's Book of Model Beauty*. New York: Trident Press, 1968. This classic is given to every new Ford model. It is a complete instructional guide to nutrition, beauty, posture, makeup, skin and hair care, and more.
—————. *Secrets of the Model's World*. New York: Trident Press, 1970. An advice book for would-be models. Ford thoroughly describes the industry, detailing what is expected from models and explaining the various career opportunities. She writes about the pros and cons of a modeling career and the importance of working with a reputable agent or agency. The foreword, written by a Ford assistant, lends insight into the behind-the-scenes action at the Ford Agency.
"The Godmother." *Life* 69 (November 13, 1970): 63. A lengthy profile of Eileen Ford. Although dated in its details, this article emphasizes her management philosophy, her values, and her standards for evaluating modeling work that she finds acceptable.

Rosenbaum, Ron. *Manhattan Passions: True Tales of Power, Wealth, and Excess.* New York: Beech Tree Books, 1987. Contains an essay about the arrival of a new foreign-born model in the United States to work for the Ford Agency. Much of the piece serves as an exposé of Ford's management style as the new model's training program progresses.

Schonauer, David. "Ford's Famous 'X-factor.'" *American Photo* 4 (May-June, 1993): 72-77. As a veteran in the search for new modeling talent, Ford assesses the gamine and grunge looks of the 1990's, reviews the changes that have revolutionized the modeling world since the 1950's, and dismisses rumors that her agency is up for sale. Illustrated with photographs of some of the Ford Agency's top models.

Marsha M. Huber

CHARLOTTE FORTEN

Born: August 17, 1837; Philadelphia, Pennsylvania
Died: July 22, 1914; Washington, D.C.
Areas of Achievement: Education, literature, and civil rights
Contribution: Charlotte Forten, an African American educator, author, and abolitionist, spent her life furthering the cause of fellow African Americans.

Early Life

Charlotte Lottie Forten was born on August 17, 1837, in Philadelphia, Pennsylvania. Representing the fourth generation of Fortens born free in the United States, she was the only child of Robert Bridges Forten, and his first wife, Mary Virginia Woods Forten. Acknowledged as the most prominent and wealthy free black family in America, the Fortens avidly pursued reform, equality, and the abolition of slavery. Mary Virginia Woods Forten died when Charlotte was three. After her mother's death, Charlotte grew up under the tutelage of her aunts and other relatives.

The ideals and influences of Charlotte's family shaped the rest of her life. Her grandfather, James Forten, Sr., petitioned the United States Congress in 1800 to end the African American slave trade, establish guidelines to abolish slavery, and provide legislation that would weaken the Fugitive Slave Act of 1793. Congress denied the petition with a vote of eighty-five to one. Forten and his friends were not easily discouraged as they continued their pursuit for equality. Forten actively criticized legislation that would ban free blacks from Pennsylvania and the Colonizationists' efforts to move free blacks to Africa. James Forten, Sr., believed that blacks in the United States were entitled to the country's resources and equal protection under the law. Similarly, Charlotte Forten's father, her aunts, and her uncles played vital roles in the abolitionist movement. The family also supported women's rights.

Surrounded by the most prominent intellectuals of the era, Charlotte knew the importance of scholarly achievement. Robert Forten arranged for his daughter to have private tutors until she could have an excellent public education in Salem, Massachusetts. At the age of sixteen in 1854, she moved to Salem, where she prepared herself for a teaching career. Determined to please her father, Charlotte applied herself to her studies. Residing with prominent black abolitionist Charles Lenox Remond and his wife in Salem, Charlotte acquainted herself with William Lloyd Garrison, Wendell Phillips, John Whittier, Abigail and Stephen Foster, and many other notable figures of the time. She thrived in her intellectual duties at the Higginson Grammar School. In 1855, she entered Salem Normal School and was graduated in 1856. Gaining a reputation as a local poet, she often submitted poems for publication. One of her poems, written in praise of William Lloyd Garrison, was published in the *Liberator* magazine in March, 1855.

Life's Work

After graduation, Charlotte Forten began teaching and continued studying in her free time. She practiced French, German, and Latin and studied European and Classical history. She also enjoyed literature, including the works of her contemporaries.

The pursuit of knowledge became Forten's primary interest. As a deeply religious person, she believed that God intended her to uplift and educate the people of her race. Her self-sacrificing nature made it difficult for Forten to appreciate herself and the contributions she made. She was aware of the racial hostility around her and sometimes allowed it to influence her self-image, in spite of compliments on her appearance, her manners, and her intelligence. Furthermore, her father's move to Canada in 1853 left her somewhat estranged from her immediate family.

During her stay in Salem, Forten began the first of her series of five journals in which she discussed all aspects of her life including family, politics, education, and important leaders of the time. In 1856, she accepted a teaching position at Epes Grammar School in Salem. Soon, however, she had to return to Philadelphia after suffering from a respiratory illness and severe headaches. By July of 1857, she was back at Epes, only to resign in March, 1858, because of her recurrent health problems.

Again Charlotte returned home where she rested and taught privately. The extra time allowed her to write poetry and essays for publication. In May of 1858, her poem entitled "Flowers" was published in *Christian Recorder* magazine. In June of that year, her essay "Glimpses of New England" appeared in the *National Anti-Slavery Standard*. "The Two Voices" and "The Wind Among the Poplars" were printed in 1859. In January of 1860, "The Slave Girl's Prayer" was published in the *National Anti-Slavery Standard*.

Forten regained her health sufficiently to return to Salem in September of 1859, to accept a teaching post at the Higginson Grammar School. During the next spring, however, she again fell ill. While battling to regain her health, she taught briefly in a school for black children. She visited John Whittier upon her return to Salem in the summer of 1862. During this visit Whittier proposed that Forten could further the cause of her people if she went to teach the contraband slaves in the South.

On October 22, 1862, Charlotte Forten sailed to Port Royal, South Carolina. Stationed on St. Helena Island, she secured a position as a teacher among the slaves. With a fond regard for her students, she sought to prepare them for life as freed men and women. Her primary task included teaching the fundamentals of a formal education to contraband children of all ages. Forten taught reading, writing, spelling, history, and math. She emphasized the importance of proper moral and social behavior to the older blacks. She leaned toward assimilation, believing that blacks would find it difficult to interact with society if they remained culturally different.

Charlotte also met with prominent whites during her stay on St. Helena. As the first black teacher among the slaves, she had to face the reactions of white teachers and Union soldiers. Usually she was politely received, and people associated with her even more when abolitionist friends and acquaintances arrived. Among some of her close friends were Colonel Thomas Wentworth Higginson, who commanded the First South Carolina Volunteers, and Colonel Robert Gould Shaw, commander of the all-black Fifty-fourth Massachusetts regiment. Forten also had a very close friendship with Dr. Seth Rogers, a white surgeon in Higginson's First South Carolina Volunteers. Charlotte's friendships and the teaching she accomplished made her stay on St. Helena a rewarding one; eventually, however, her health failed her once again. Her declining health and news of her father's death from typhoid fever on April 25, 1864, convinced Forten to move back to the North permanently. Although she still suffered from poor health, she accepted a position as secretary of the Teachers Committee of the New England Branch of the Freedmen's Union Commission in October of 1865. She continued to further her own education by studying and translating French literature. Her translation of *Madame Thérèse: Or, The Volunteers of '92*, a novel by Emile Erckmann and Alexandre Chatrain, was published by Scribner in 1869. Charlotte's role as secretary of the Teachers Committee required her to act as a liaison between teachers in the South who taught former slaves, and the people in the North who sent financial and material support. In October of 1871, she resigned from that position to teach at the Shaw Memorial School in Charleston, South Carolina. Forten then moved to Washington, D.C., where she taught in a black preparatory high school from 1872 to 1873. She left that position and accepted a job in the Fourth Auditor's Office of the United States Treasury Department as a first-class clerk. Although poor health continued to frustrate her, she continued to work in Washington, D.C.

Charlotte Forten married Francis Grimké on December 19, 1878. The Princeton-trained minister was twelve years her junior; he was described as intelligent, noble, and morally upright. The couple had one daughter who died in infancy. Charlotte and Francis Grimké worked hard to dispel discrimination in society. They attacked racial oppression in numerous essays and sermons. In 1885, they moved to Florida, where Francis Grimké accepted the pastorate at Laura Street Presbyterian Church. After four years they returned to Washington, D.C., and continued missionary work.

Although Charlotte Forten Grimké combined her efforts with those of her husband, she did not abandon her interest in writing poetry and essays. Several poems from that period include "A June Song" (1885), "Charlotte Corday" (1885), "At Newport" (1888); some essays that survive are "On Mr. Savage's Sermon: 'The Problem of the Hour'" (1885), and "One Phase of the Race Question" (1885). Evidently essays and poetry remained an important facet of her life. Throughout her life she continued writing her journals, of which there are five, titled by number, date, and the locations of her residence.

She spent her last years surrounded by family and friends. Her home was enlivened socially and intellectually with well-known political activists. She also enjoyed a close relationship with her niece Angelina Grimké, who lived in Washington, D.C., with the Grimkés. In spite of her illnesses, Charlotte lived a full, happy life. She died on July 22, 1914, in her home at the age of seventy-six.

Summary

Charlotte Forten did not complete one monumental task for which she is well known. Instead, she worked diligently to help others. In spite of frequent illnesses and insecurities, she willingly dedicated her time and energies to further the cause of her oppressed race. As a woman, Charlotte Forten far exceeded the intellectual expectations of the time. She tirelessly pursued knowledge and shared it with others. As a poet and writer, she voiced her opinions and interests to the American public. It was her philanthropic deeds, however, that she performed in the name of her race. As a free black woman, she tirelessly sought liberation, equality, and education for her people.

In an era when the white society oppressed the black, Charlotte stood out as a person who tried to correct injustices. Her quiet demeanor belied the active mind and spirit that were revealed by her pen. Her unassuming personality and eagerness to please led her in a life of service to others. The quiet dignity of Charlotte Forten and her lifelong efforts made her one of America's notable women and an inspiration to all Americans.

Bibliography

Barker-Benfield, G. J., and Catherine Clinton. *Portraits of American Women: From Settlement to the Present.* New York: St. Martin's Press, 1991. This publication is a combined volume presenting biographies of American women, arranged according to historical eras. Each biography discusses the impact each woman made on her contemporaries. The book is amply illustrated.

Braxton, Joanne M. "Charlotte Forten Grimké and the Search for a Public Voice." In *The Private Self: Theory and Practice of Women's Autobiographical Writings*, edited by Shari Benstock. Chapel Hill: University of North Carolina Press, 1988. An analysis of Forten's complete journals, based on archival research and a personal appreciation of the journals. The author maintains that, as a young woman, Forten used her journal as a means to try out different poetic voices.

Forten, Charlotte L. *The Journals of Charlotte Forten Grimké.* Edited by Brenda Stevenson. New York: Oxford University Press, 1988. This volume comprises the five journals written by Charlotte Forten. They provide insight into the politics and people of the abolitionist era. The editor provides an introduction and notes for each journal, as well as a chronology and brief biographies of people mentioned.

McPherson, James M. *The Struggle for Equality: Abolitionists and the Negro in the Civil War and Reconstruction.* Princeton, N.J.: Princeton University Press, 1964. A complete and thorough analysis of the abolitionists, including Forten, and the roles they played during and after the Civil War. Includes a bibliographic essay describing the manuscripts, correspondence, publications, and archives used.

Quarles, Benjamin. *Black Abolitionists.* New York: Oxford University Press, 1969. Reprint. New York: Da Capo Press, 1991. Providing the reader with a thorough background of the African American abolitionists, the author covers the early efforts of black preachers and writers to the antislavery underground; the book also describes the organizational efforts of later abolitionists. This volume includes detailed bibliographic notes separated by chapter.

Dover C. Watkins
Elisabeth A. Cawthon

DIAN FOSSEY

Born: January 16, 1932; San Francisco, California
Died: December 26, 1985; Karisoke Research Institute, Rwanda
Area of Achievement: Anthropology
Contribution: Through her firsthand study of Central Africa's mountain gorillas, Fossey established their classification as a subspecies and courageously struggled to forestall their extinction.

Early Life

Eventually to earn renown as one of the world's leading primatologists, Dian Fossey recalled having a passionate rapport with animals from her earliest childhood. A lonely child, she recorded that her parents had denied her pets, except for a goldfish whose death she recalled with sorrow even as an adult.

The Fosseys divorced when Dian was six, after which time she was reared in what later seemed to her a comfortably wealthy San Francisco household by her mother, Kitty, and stepfather, Richard Price. Both parents believed that what suited her was a career in business, and after her graduation from high school, it seemed that Dian might become a businessperson. Supporting herself with income from clerical, laboratory, and industrial jobs, Dian enrolled in a business course at Marin Junior College.

Having learned horseback riding, she landed "the best job" she ever had when she was twenty-one, working on a dude ranch in Montana, where she was surrounded by animals. Unfortunately, the job ended when she was stricken by chicken pox. In 1950, she flatly rejected her parents' advice and enrolled in the preveterinary course at the University of California, Davis, but she withdrew during her second year in the face of difficulties with chemistry and physics. Accordingly, she transferred to San Jose State College, from which institution she was graduated in 1954 with a degree in occupational therapy, a calling close to her heart, since she had always adored children. Interning in California hospitals during the next nine months, she worked with ill and impaired children; then, anxious to leave California forever, she found a post at Korsair Children's Hospital in Louisville, Kentucky.

A growing interest in Africa and its animals increasingly preoccupied Dian during her years at Korsair. She was already showing signs of the loner's intrepidity. By renting a farm cottage in the country near Louisville to avoid the urban living she disliked intensely, she made it possible to surround herself with the animals that she had never been allowed to possess.

Fossey read extensively about Africa and was particularly excited by George B. Schaller's *The Year of the Gorilla* (1964). Although she had been introduced to Louisville's prominent bachelors by Mary White Henry, secretary to Korsair's chief administrator and the daughter of a noted heart specialist, Fossey generally limited her interests in men to those who satisfied her curiosities about Africa. Invited but unable to afford to join Mary Henry's safari trip to Africa in 1960, Dian nevertheless determined to save for a journey of her own by 1963, a goal she met by September of that year. Her trip, which she financed by mortgaging her hospital income for the next three years, marked a pivotal point in her life and soon launched a remarkable career.

Life's Work

Dian Fossey's safari, conducted despite her serious allergies, a proneness to pneumonia, and the added complications of dysentery, vertigo, a broken ankle, and exhaustion, took her into the wild animal preserves of Kenya, Tanganyika, the Congo, Uganda, and Southern Rhodesia. Before her safari concluded, she met the distinguished British paleoanthropologists Louis S. B. Leakey and Mary Leakey, at the site of their famed discoveries in Tanzania's Olduvai Gorge. Leakey, a man of immense knowledge and enthusiasm, encouraged Fossey to pursue the still-neglected study of the great apes.

Inspired by Leakey's advice, Fossey moved on to mountain gorilla territory on the slopes of the Virungas volcanic chain adjacent to the borders of the Congo, Rwanda, and Uganda. There she met hotelier Walter Baumgartel, himself an amateur expert on gorillas. Baumgartel introduced Fossey to noted wildlife photographers Joan and Alan Root. At the Roots' invitation, Fossey climbed Mount Mikendo with them and, awestruck, encountered her first mountain gorillas—a group of six of them—about whom she vowed immediately to learn more.

Returning to her post at Children's Hospital in Louisville, Fossey spent her spare time during the next three years writing about her African experiences and developing a novel with an African setting. Despite her enthusiasm, however, she had little success with publication, although the Louisville *Courier Journal* weekend color edition, which ran some of her stories and photographs, brought her considerable local notability and persuaded her to improve her writing by enrolling in the Famous Writers' School. In the interim, her long-standing engagement to a well-born Austrian who was studying in the United States foundered as her fiancé repeatedly postponed the marriage date.

In March, 1966, Louis Leakey, with whom Fossey had had no contact since their meeting in the Serengeti National Park at the Olduvai Gorge, came to lecture in Louisville. Fossey attended the lecture, waiting until its closing to reintroduce herself to Leakey and to press her articles upon him. Leakey vividly remembered Fossey, with her good looks and her intensity. Fossey reminded Leakey that she intended to commit her life to working with animals, particularly with gorillas. While others waited backstage to meet Leakey after the lecture, he and Fossey planned Dian's future.

It was an ecstatic meeting for both. Leakey reiterated his strong desire to see women, because of their care and patience, become animal researchers and urged her to pursue her curiosities about gorillas just as Jane Goodall, whom he had also sponsored, had with chimpanzees. Within weeks, Fossey received a letter from Leakey in which he agreed to pay her travel expenses to Africa and to provide money to establish a research camp complete with assistants, food supplies, and photographic equipment. With his backing, too, she was prompted to seek sustained support from the Wilkie Foundation, which had funded Goodall, as well as from the National Geographic Society.

Ill with pneumonia, heavily dosed with antibiotics, and leaving behind her hospital job and her profoundly distressed parents, Fossey flew to Africa on December 16, 1966. After having a reunion with the Leakeys and receiving assistance from Alan Root, she established her first research campsite at an elevation of 10,200 feet at Kabara meadow, below the chilly rain forests of the Congo's (Zaire's) Mount Mikeno. Two pioneer students of the mountain gorilla had preceded her at Kabara. The American naturalist Carl Akeley, who had persuaded the Belgian government to create the Albert National Park in the 1920's, was buried there, and George Schaller, whose works had been an inspiration to Fossey, had done research there in the early 1960's. Like Akeley and Schaller, Fossey, assisted by the superb tracker and park guard Sanwekwe, made contact with the mountain gorillas. She also encountered other local wildlife, including elephants, buffalo, and giant forest hogs. At last she was with animals and had become, in Leakey's phrase, "the gorilla girl."

The harrowing political situation that erupted as the Congo passed from Belgian control to independence and subsequent internecine warfare drove Fossey from Kabara in 1967. Again, with aid from Leakey, her funding agencies, and other friends, she built a campsite on the Rwanda side of the Virungas chain that became the famed Karisoke research center, named for the saddle between Mt. Karisimbe and Mt. Visoke. She directed this center for the next dozen years, breaking her residence only long enough to complete work toward a doctorate at Cambridge University—an essential scholarly attainment if her work was to be viewed seriously by the scientific community. Meanwhile, Fossey attracted a succession of young research assistants to Karisoke; they came both to aid Fossey and to pursue their own research. Funding for Fossey and her research assistants came from the National Geographic Society and the Wilkie Foundation, thanks often to Leakey's support, in exchange for articles and photographs chronicling Fossey's experiences with mountain gorillas. At times, those funds were supplemented by Fossey's own money.

Rather quickly, Fossey established close personal contact with a number of gorillas and gorilla families. In time, she would intensively study fifty-one individuals in several groups, thanks to her amazing patience and ingenuity in imitating gorilla behavior with sufficient skill to warrant their acceptance of her. Among those animals that became familiar to Fossey's readers were Uncle Bert, Flossie, Macho, Old Goat, Rafiki, Beethoven, Effie, Marchessa, Icarus, Pantsie, Puck, and her beloved Digit, whose slaughter by poachers led Fossey to launch an international effort—led by the Digit Fund—to preserve the world's remaining mountain gorillas.

More effectively than anyone before her, Fossey was able to identify mountain gorillas as a subspecies. Disproving the image of gorillas as the ferocious primates depicted in innumerable stories and films, she demonstrated that, on the contrary, mountain gorillas were immensely shy vegetarians and thus were all the more vulnerable to depredations caused by Rwanda's farmers, by poachers, by illegal collectors (including zoos), and by exposure to government-sponsored tourism. Her battles against these menaces were a tribute to her personal bravery and tenacity.

An intense and independent personality, obsessed with both her research and protection of the gorillas, Fossey made as many enemies as friends among government officials, poachers, illegal collectors, and her own research assistants. Exhausted and seriously ill from thirteen years of lonely, physically and intellectually demanding work, she accepted a visiting assistant professorship at Cornell University in 1981, largely to recuperate. While she was at Cornell, she worked to promote her book and the Digit Fund, to lecture, and to negotiate with her sponsors. She returned to Karisoke in 1983 and was murdered in her quarters on December 26, 1985.

Summary

At the close of her career, Dian Fossey had joined company with Jane Goodall and Birute Galdikas as the world's leading primatologists in their respective specialties: Fossey for her studies of the mountain gorillas, Goodall for her research on chimpanzees, and Galdikas for investigations of orangutans. The studies produced by these remarkable women reached international audiences, and popularly the three were dubbed "the trimates."

Fossey preferred the African bush country and its rigors to civilization. She independently pursued her unslakable curiosities about the animals to which she devoted her life with loving fervor. She made protection of the mountain gorillas an international cause, eventually enlisting the volunteer efforts of college and university students, governments, wildlife organizations, scientists, scientific organizations, and diplomats. She helped to train and inspire a generation of fledgling primatologists. Fossey did so against formidable opposition, not only from Rwandan farmers, poachers, and some officials but also from elements within academia and the scientific community. To some of these people, she was "a wild woman"; to others, obsessed, domineering, and uncooperative; to still others, an unscientific researcher who anthropomorphized observations of her subjects.

Whatever her faults, Fossey's calling was a high one, and the strength of character she brought to it will serve as a model for future researchers.

Bibliography

Fossey, Dian. *Gorillas in the Mist*. Boston: Houghton Mifflin, 1983. The fascinating saga of Fossey's African experiences, complete with rich descriptions of her "gentle giants," their behavior, and their environment. Superb illustrations and color photos are included, as is an invaluable bibliography. Indexed.

Goodall, Jane. "Explorations: Mountain Warrior." *Omni* 8 (May, 1986): 132-134. A detailed appreciation of Fossey's work and hardships by a distinguished fellow primatologist with whom Fossey visited and lectured.

Hayes, Harold. *The Dark Romance of Dian Fossey*. New York: Simon & Schuster, 1990. An able, if somewhat melodramatic, biographical portrait of Fossey, her friends, and her enemies. Includes a sound discussion of her specific contributions to the study of gorilla behavior. A valuable bibliography and an index are provided.

Morrell, Virginia. "Called 'Trimates:' Three Bold Women Shaped Their Field." *Science* 260 (April 16, 1993): 420-425. The author places Fossey in context with Jane Goodall and Birute Galdikas as founders of modern primatology and discusses the unique contributions of each.

Mowat, Farley. *Woman in the Mists: The Story of Dian Fossey and the Mountain Gorillas of Africa.* New York: Warner Books, 1987. An excellent biography, written with Mowat's skilled interweavings of engaging excerpts from Fossey's diary and notes. Concentrates on Fossey's personal development more than on the specifics of her scientific work. Includes an index.

Clifton K. Yearley

JODIE FOSTER

Born: November 19, 1962; Los Angeles, California

Area of Achievement: Film
Contribution: One of Hollywood's major actresses, Foster won two Academy Awards for Best Actress and a nomination for Best Supporting Actress before she reached the age of thirty.

Early Life
Alicia Christian "Jodie" Foster, born in Los Angeles, California, on November 19, 1962, was the youngest of four children resulting from the marriage of Evelyn "Brandy" Foster and Lucius Foster III. Jodie's parents divorced before her birth. Living with her mother, two sisters, and a brother, Jodie rarely saw her father during her formative years.

Jodie's mother Brandy, a producer's publicist, became the dominant force in her life. At the age of three, Jodie accompanied her brother Buddy to a tanning commercial audition. Instead of hiring Buddy, advertising agency executives noticed Jodie, who became the bare-bottomed "Coppertone child": It was an auspicious beginning for a sensational career.

When Jodie was very young, her mother introduced her to a wide variety of cultural experiences, including exotic foods, foreign films, and the fascinating people who moved in Hollywood's "fast lane." Television commercials became a regular staple of her professional life as she supplanted Brandy and Buddy as the principal provider for the family of five. She later recalled that the family adopted the slogan "All for one and one for all."

Not suspecting that Jodie's career would last beyond childhood, Brandy Foster carefully guided and protected her youngest daughter. First came the television commercials: Jodie made forty-five in five years before Brandy declared her ready for more serious challenges. May 19, 1969, marked the beginning of the second stage of Jodie's acting career—a role on the television show *Mayberry, R.F.D.* Between 1969 and 1973, Jodie appeared in numerous television dramas, ranging from *Gunsmoke* and *Bonanza* to a starring role in the Emmy Award-winning *Rookie of the Year.*

Jodie's mother also carefully nurtured her daughter's education, enrolling her first in California's gifted child program and then in Lycée Français, a bilingual preparatory academy. Jodie never took an acting class, but she loved school and developed rapidly in its disciplined intellectual environment. She particularly exhibited a flair for literature and writing, talents that resulted in the *Esquire* magazine article she wrote before reaching the age of eighteen.

Jodie's Hollywood film debut occurred in 1972, when she made the first of two pictures for Walt Disney, *Napoleon and Samantha*, which featured an aging lion. On screen, Jodie's androgynous appeal produced critical acclaim. Offscreen, the lion turned rough as they played together, lifting Jodie by his teeth, leaving scars on her stomach and putting her in the hospital. The next Disney production, *One Little Indian* (1973), offered a much safer role.

Life's Work

Jodie Foster's appearance as Raquel Welch's neglected daughter in *Kansas City Bomber* (1972) marked the beginning of her successful transition to films that appealed to adult audiences. Although critics labeled as children's entertainment some of her early films, such as the Mark Twain classic *Tom Sawyer* (1973), in which she played Becky Thatcher, they also praised Foster's maturity. Film critic Richard Schickel, identifying her emerging contribution to the film industry, noted that Foster was the only member of the *Tom Sawyer* cast who remembered "what it is like to be a real person in a real world." She was on her way.

It was this ability to project realistically—especially Foster's unusual mixture of innocent youthfulness and precocious sexuality—that caught Martin Scorsese's eye when she auditioned for a bit part in *Alice Doesn't Live Here Anymore* (1975). Scorsese, who had just produced the critically acclaimed *Mean Streets* (1973), needed someone uniquely qualified to play the role of Iris, the teenage prostitute, in *Taxi Driver* (1976). He picked Foster to play the part.

Taxi Driver became a turning point in Foster's career in several respects. It placed her in the $100,000 salary class and earned for her an Academy Award nomination for Best Supporting Actress. It also demonstrated her wide range of appeal, because, while Foster's sexual magnetism attracted men, the role of Iris also brought her into sync with society's growing empathy for abused or neglected women.

The fact that Foster could play such a complicated part also said much about her personal maturity at the age of thirteen. Although the film represented a distinct challenge for all its cast, including veteran actors Robert De Niro and Harvey Keitel, the censors worried about its severe emotional impact upon such a young girl. The Los Angeles Welfare Board subsequently subjected her to an intense psychiatric interrogation. When she easily passed the battery of examinations and answered all the psychiatrist's questions, he pronounced her fit to appear in "the most cathartic treatment of violence in America since *Bonnie and Clyde.*"

After making *Taxi Driver*, Foster continued to play unfortunate, abandoned, or neglected girls in somewhat less controversial roles such as that of Tallulah, who ran a speakeasy in *Bugsy Malone* (1976), and Deirdre, the terminally ill daughter in *Echoes of a Summer* (1976). Neither of these efforts nor her first starring role as Rynn, an orphan who survived a corrupt adult world, in *The Little Girl Who Lives down the Lane* (1977), produced the praise elicited by her acclaimed performance as Iris, so Foster, beginning in *Carny* (1980), returned to the steamy roles in which she seemed to thrive.

In 1981, after her graduation as Lycée Français' class valedictorian, Jodie Foster entered Yale University. There, she encountered John Hinckley, Jr. Hinckley, who had become obsessed with her performance as Iris, tried unsuccessfully on numerous occasions to make Foster's acquaintance. On March 30, 1981, the frustrated Hinckley shot President Ronald Reagan in an insane attempt to impress her.

A lesser actress might have wilted under the pressure that the media focused on her, but Foster kept both her career and her college education on track. She did not even withdraw from her college play, despite the presence of a copycat would-be assassin, another obsessed fan with a gun in the audience. She continued her recovery from the trauma by writing a December, 1982, *Esquire* article entitled "Why Me?" As her college career neared its end, she busied herself with films, making *The Hotel New Hampshire* and *The Blood of Others* in 1984.

Despite the Hinckley incident, Foster played more victim roles. In the space of two years, from 1987 to 1989, Foster made five films, including *Five Corners* (1987), in which she played the target of a violent psychopathic rapist (John Turturro), and *The Accused* (1988), in which she gave an Academy Award-winning Best Actress performance as the gang-raped Sarah Tobias. In the latter role, Foster called national attention to the myriad problems created by rape and the degrading process of victimization. Both on screen and in real life she exhibited courage in the face of fear.

Then came *The Silence of the Lambs* (1991), in which Foster, as the novice FBI agent Clarice Starling, transformed herself from the hunted to the hunter, tracking down a psychopathic murderer. The performance, which won for her a second Academy Award as Best Actress, brought her to the top of her profession.

By the time Jodie Foster turned thirty in November, 1993, she had grown from child to adult, victim to victor, and actor to producer-director. Although acting remained her primary activity, she also established her own company, Egg Pictures, which allowed her to produce and directe *Little Man Tate* (1991).

Although she did not avoid controversial roles, Foster played a more traditional part with Mel Gibson and James Garner in a 1994 motion picture remake of the old television series *Maverick*. The film was a commercial success at the box office, and critics praised Foster's comedic skills.

Summary

Jodie Foster's career has transcended the level of achievement experienced by the vast majority of Hollywood actresses. By the time Foster reached the age of thirty, she had done more films than many much older and more highly paid actresses had. The actress who never took an acting lesson won two Best Actress Oscars and a third Best Supporting Actress nomination. Furthermore, she has become a feminist hero because of her gritty determination to overcome adversity posed by dangerous males both on and off the screen.

On March 30, 1992, when Foster accepted her second Oscar for her role as Clarice Starling in *Silence of the Lambs*, she expressed her gratitude to an Academy willing to embrace "such a strong feminist hero that I'm proud to have portrayed." Jodie Foster had become a phenomenon very rarely seen in Hollywood: a child star who stood on the verge of becoming one of America's most controversial, productive, and powerful actresses. It is perhaps even more significant that Foster has used her power to change the way America views women.

Bibliography
Aylesworth, Thomas G. *Hollywood Kids: Child Stars of the Silver Screen from 1903 to the Present.* New York: E. P. Dutton, 1987. This work, which examines the "child star syndrome," includes several brief analyses of Foster's early career.
Cameron, Julia. "Burden of the Gift." *American Film* 16 (November/December, 1991): 44-48. A brief but penetrating analysis of Foster's transition from actress to producer-director. This work offers insights into Foster's portrayal of victims/heroines and the way she views men.
Corliss, Richard. "A Screen Gem Turns Director." *Time* 138 (October 14, 1991): 68-72. The author traces Foster's career, predicts great success for the actress as a director, and pronounces *Little Man Tate* "an audacious winner."
Crivello, Kirk. *Fallen Angels: The Lives and Untimely Deaths of Fourteen Hollywood Beauties.* Secaucus, N.J.: Citadel Press, 1988. This collection of brief biographical chapters offers penetrating insight into the "woman as victim" role in which Foster increasingly specialized throughout her career.
Foster, Jodie. "Has Jodie Foster Lost Her Mind?" *Esquire* 94 (October, 1980): 40. This perceptive piece is a good example of the pre-Hinckley youthful exuberance and optimism that Foster took with her to Yale.
_____. "Why Me?" *Esquire* 98 (December, 1982): 101-108. This work provides a very illuminating analysis of Foster's early transition from victim to heroine.
Hirshey, Gerri. "Jodie Foster." *Rolling Stone.* no. 600 (March 21, 1991): 34-36. This cover story includes an incisive look at Foster's identification with ignored, neglected, and abused women in general and those depicted in *Silence of the Lambs.*
Johnson, Brian D. "The Reality of Rape." *Maclean's* 101 (October 24, 1988): 60-62. This work analyzes Foster's career since the Hinckley incident and the problems surrounding abused women.
Miller, Linda R. "Victor of Circumstances." *American Film* 14 (October, 1988): 26-31. A good piece by a freelance writer who successfully analyzes the way Foster overcame complex problems connecting her life and the films she made.
Segell, Michael. "What's Driving Miss Jodie?" *Redbook* 178 (November, 1991): 76-79. A lucid discussion of Foster's views regarding female sexuality, parenting, and how *Little Man Tate* showed a side of her personality never previously revealed to the public.
Sischy, Ingrid. "Jodie Foster." *Interview* 21 (October, 1991): 78-85. Examines Foster's career following the completion of *Little Man Tate.*

J. Christopher Schnell

LYDIA FOLGER FOWLER

Born: May 5, 1822; Nantucket, Massachusetts
Died: January 26, 1879; London, England
Areas of Achievement: Medicine and women's rights
Contribution: The first woman to become a professor at an American medical school, Fowler became a well-known lecturer on physiology, temperance, and women's rights during the years in which the medical field gradually opened to the entry of women.

Early Life

Lydia Folger, the daughter of Gideon and Eunice Macy Folger, was born on May 5, 1822, on the small island of Nantucket off the coast of Massachusetts. Her father, who had spent various periods in his life as a mechanic, a farmer, a candle maker, a ship owner, and even a sometime politician, was a direct descendant of Peter Folger, who had arrived on Nantucket in 1663 as one of the earliest settlers of the island. The Folger clan, which also includes Benjamin Franklin, can be traced back to English nobility in the person of the Earl of Shrewsbury.

Another well-known relative of Lydia Folger Fowler was her distant cousin Maria Mitchell, who grew up in Nantucket as a contemporary of Fowler's and who would one day become a professor of astronomy at Vassar College. In fact, it was through Maria Mitchell's father, a popular teacher in the community, that Fowler gained a consuming interest in her studies, particularly in math and science. Additionally supported by an uncle who fancied himself an amateur astronomer, Lydia Folger Fowler felt a special devotion to the field in which her cousin Maria would find such distinction. All in all, Fowler's early education, with its inclusion of subjects generally thought of as unsuitable for women students, appears to have been quite extensive when compared to that of other women of the era.

One possible explanation for this circumstance is the distinctive character of the community in Nantucket. For the most part, the men of Nantucket worked in seafaring trades—trades that demanded that they leave the island for weeks and months at a time. Such necessities helped to form an atmosphere of independence and self-reliance among the women of the island, who were often forced to run the affairs of the community while the men were away. Lucretia Mott, one of the early leaders of the women's rights movement and a native of Nantucket, is a good example of the kind of attitudes fostered there. Add to this the fact that the island at this time was inhabited primarily by Quakers, who were defined by an openness to social reform and a devotion to the ideal of equality, and one can begin to imagine more clearly the environment from which Lydia Folger Fowler emerged.

Life's Work

Lydia Folger left Nantucket in 1838 to study for a year in Norton, Massachusetts, at the Wheaton Seminary, where she would later spend two years (1842-1844) as a teacher. This stint ended with her marriage, on September 19, 1844, to Lorenzo Niles Fowler. They would have but one child together, a daughter named Jessie Allen, born in 1856.

Lorenzo Fowler was at this time one of the most well-known and vocal proponents of the budding science of phrenology. He and his brother Orson had been exposed to phrenological theories during the 1830's while they were both studying at Amherst College in preparation for a life in the ministry. Convinced of the tenants of this new science, the brothers became two of its most famous adherents by embarking on numerous lecture tours and even establishing the publishing house of Fowlers and Wells in 1842 in order to become the publishers of the *American Phrenological Journal*. Beginning in 1845, Lydia Folger Fowler accompanied her husband during the journeys to his speaking engagements, and later, in 1847, she began to give lectures of her own at the opening of each congregation. These lectures covered such topics as anatomy, physiology, and hygiene, and formed the basis for the two books Fowler would publish in 1847 through the auspices of her husband's publishing operation. *Familiar Lessons on Physiology* and *Familiar Lessons on Phrenology* (to be followed in 1848 by a third volume, *Familiar Lessons in Astronomy*) appeared as books intended for young readers and enjoyed some sales success.

Heartened by her successes as a lecturer and author, Lydia Folger Fowler decided to pursue a medical degree and enrolled at Central Medical College in November, 1849. Located first in Syracuse, New York, and later moving to Rochester in 1850, Central was the first medical school to make a regular policy of admitting women. The school even included a so-called "Female Department," of which Fowler served as principal during her second term of study. Although there was this emphasis on Central's campus and though there were several other women who joined her entering class, Lydia Folger Fowler was the lone female graduate in June of 1850, making her only the second woman ever, after Elizabeth Blackwell, to receive a medical degree in the United States.

Fowler was soon to gain a first of her own. After she had worked briefly as a "demonstrator of anatomy" to students at Central, Fowler was promoted in 1851 to the position of professor of midwifery and diseases of women and children, thereby becoming the first woman professor at an American medical college. The professor-ship was not long-lived, however, because Central Medical College merged with a rival institution in 1852 and Fowler left to practice privately in New York City. While in New York, Fowler resumed teaching, and in 1854, she began a series of private medical lectures for women at Metropolitan Medical College, a physiopathic school that existed between 1852 and 1862. Fowler also succeeded in publishing three articles in the pages of Metropolitan College's alternative medical journal. These articles were entitled "Medical Progression," "Female Medical Education," and "Suggestions to Female Medical Students." These articles argued the necessity of women physicians, noting that women needing medical care were often precluded by their modesty from seeking help from the heretofore exclusively male profession.

The early 1850's also witnessed Fowler's increased politicization, as she became involved in several causes for reform. Twice she served as secretary to national women's rights conventions (1852 and 1853), and once she was a delegate to a meeting of the state Daughters of Temperance (1852). In February of 1853, Fowler presided over a women's temperance meeting in New York City, during which she utilized her well-honed skills at public speaking. In addition to supporting these reform movements, Fowler continued to give public lectures on the topics of physiology and hygiene. She remained in New York City until 1860, when she left with her husband as he embarked on a speaking tour of Europe. After spending the year studying and working in Paris and London, Fowler returned to New York in 1861. In 1862, she became an instructor in midwifery at the New York Hygeio-Therapeutic College. The next year, Lorenzo Fowler left the publishing house, and he and Lydia Fowler moved to London, where they would spend the rest of their days.

While in London, Lydia Folger Fowler chose not to practice medicine but continued to remain extremely active within the temperance movement, becoming an honorary secretary of the Woman's British Temperance Society. This period also allowed Folger the leisure to focus on her writing. *Nora: The Lost and the Redeemed*, a temperance novel that earlier had been serialized in America, appeared in book form in 1863. A series of Folger's lectures on child care was published in 1865 as *The Pet of the Household and How to Save It*. Finally, in 1870, a book of poems entitled *Heart Melodies* became Folger's last published work. Lydia Folger Fowler died in London of pleuropneumonia on January 26, 1879.

Summary

Lydia Folger Fowler's list of accomplishments easily leads one to see her as an inspiring symbol of women's determination to break down the social and institutional barriers that excluded them from the study and practice of medicine. That she made such great strides and enjoyed so much success at Central Medical College, becoming the second American woman to receive a medical degree and the first to become a professor in an American medical school, secures forever Fowler's place among the early pioneers of women's rights within the medical field. To stress her symbolic importance, however, is to misrepresent the true nature of her influence upon the other women of her era. Lydia Folger Fowler's efforts were of a much more practical kind. During her many extended tours of public lectures, Fowler addressed wide and varied audiences, meeting and speaking with countless admirers and skeptics. It was during these moments, when she brought her message and personal example so immediately to those in attendance, that Lydia Folger Fowler had her greatest impact. No other woman physician of the moment could claim to have influenced so many people in so direct and intimate a manner. While it is true that much of Fowler's lecturing was done in connection with the thoroughly debunked science of phrenology and that she continually found herself working in alternative or marginal situations, this does not seem so surprising if one considers the hostility she must have felt emanating from a medical institution that sensed that its days as a closed fraternity were numbered.

Bibliography

Hume, Ruth Fox. *Great Women of Medicine*. New York: Random House, 1964. Fowler is mentioned as an able practitioner though a graduate of an eclectic college. The portrayals of the six women in the book—Elizabeth Blackwell, Florence Nightingale, Elizabeth Garrett Anderson, Sophia Jex-Blake, Mary Putnam Jacobi, and Marie Curie—provide the reader with a good introduction to the medical profession in the 1800's.

Lopate, Carol. *Women in Medicine*. Baltimore: The Johns Hopkins University Press, 1968. In the first chapter, Lopate gives good background concerning the entrance of American women into the medical profession. She explains the importance of eclectic schools such as the one Lydia Folger Fowler attended in offering women entrance.

Morantz-Sanchez, Regina Markell. *Sympathy and Science: Women Physicians in American Medicine*. New York: Oxford University Press, 1985. The best discussion of Lydia Folger Fowler appears in this comprehensive history of women in American medicine. Morantz-Sanchez explores the role of feminism in this history as well as the unique contributions women made to the field of medicine.

Walsh, Mary Roth. *"Doctors Wanted: No Women Need Apply": Sexual Barriers in the Medical Profession, 1835-1975*. New Haven, Conn.: Yale University Press, 1977. In this work, Lydia Folger Fowler is mentioned on the first page as the first American woman to be graduated from an American medical college. This book is an excellent study of the barriers women faced in entering the medical profession in the United States as well as a good overview of the progress of medicine in the nineteenth century, helping to put Fowler in perspective.

Wilson, Dorothy Clarke. *Lone Woman: The Story of Elizabeth Blackwell, the First Woman Doctor*. Boston: Little, Brown, 1970. Wilson shows how Elizabeth Blackwell's achievement led to the adoption of a coeducational policy by the Rochester Eclectic College of Medicine. Fowler was the first woman graduate of Rochester and thereby benefited from Blackwell's endeavor.

Bonnie Ford

HELEN FRANKENTHALER

Born: December 12, 1928; New York, New York

Area of Achievement: Art
Contribution: An innovator in painting, printmaking, and sculpture, Frankenthaler is the inventor of stain painting and is recognized as the forerunner of color-field painting.

Early Life
The youngest of three sisters, Helen Frankenthaler was born on December 12, 1928, in New York City. Her father, New York Supreme Court justice Alfred Frankenthaler, and her mother Martha (née Lowenstein), a talented amateur painter, recognized Helen's talent early and nurtured her abilities by sending her to the experimental and progressive schools Horace Mann, Brearley, and Dalton. At Dalton, she quickly became a favored student of the well-known Mexican painter Rufino Tamayo, with whom she studied until she entered Bennington College in the spring of 1946. Studying with the painter Paul Feeley at Bennington, Frankenthaler was introduced to the cubist aesthetic, which continued to influence her throughout her college years. While still a student, Frankenthaler worked for *Art Outlook*, a review magazine, studied at the Art Students League with Vaclav Vytlacil, taught art at Hale House, Boston, and worked as a writer for *The Cambridge Courier* during nonresidential terms. After graduation, Frankenthaler took several courses at the Graduate School of Fine Arts at Columbia University.

In 1950, Frankenthaler was asked to organize a benefit exhibit of Bennington College alumnae paintings at Jacques Seligmann and Company. Among the invited guests attending was the influential Clement Greenberg, a critic who wrote for *The Nation* and *Partisan Review*. Greenberg introduced Frankenthaler to David Smith, Lee Krasner, Jackson Pollock, Willem and Elaine de Kooning, Franz Kline, Adolph Gottlieb, and Barnett Newman, all of whom were abstract expressionists of the first generation of the New York School. The year 1950 was also significant in that Frankenthaler's work was selected for inclusion in *Fifteen Unknowns*, an exhibition at the Kootz Gallery, New York, the first of her professional exhibitions. Soon afterward, she became involved with New York's Tibor de Nagy Gallery, which held her first solo exhibition in New York in 1951 and helped establish her as a major new painter.

Most important to Frankenthaler's development as an artist, however, was Jackson Pollock's 1950 show at the Betty Parsons Gallery in New York. Unlike Willem de Kooning's paintings, which at that point used thick, thrusting brush strokes of paint sweeping across the canvas in what has come to be known as gestural abstraction or action painting, Pollock's mural-sized paintings contained no brush strokes at all. Thick paint was dripped directly onto the canvas, an innovative technique that was both abstract and expressionist. Forcing the viewer's eyes through implied movement along convoluted paths, the paintings suggested constant and somewhat frenetic movement across a canvas that dissolved the distinction between the background and the foreground.

Life's Work

Impressed by Pollock's new technique but not wanting to become simply an imitator, Helen Frankenthaler, in October of 1952, developed the soaked paint technique for which she is famous. *Mountains and Sea*, often described as a landmark painting, was the first work to be created with this technique. Thinning oil paint to a watery consistency, Frankenthaler poured the paint directly onto a raw canvas stapled to the floor. The resulting delicate colors—pale greens, blues, grays, oranges, and pinks—created the effect of light but intense watercolor softly flowing across the immense seven-by-ten-foot canvas that showed through in spots. The expressionist landscape did not fill the canvas as other expressionist works of the time did; instead, it floated in the center of the canvas, the white edges neither framing nor limiting the painting.

Although *Mountains and Sea* was the most celebrated of her paintings shown at her second solo exhibition, which was also held at the Tibor de Nagy Gallery, Frankenthaler did not become an immediate success. Throughout the 1950's, her audience consisted primarily of fellow artists such as Kenneth Noland, Morris Louis, Al Leslie, and Grace Hartigan—all, like Frankenthaler, second-generation members of the New York School. Nevertheless, she continued to work and to travel extensively throughout Europe. In 1958, she married the painter Robert Motherwell, and later that year she began teaching art in an adult education program at Great Neck, New York, along with other members of the Tibor de Nagy Gallery. Her solo exhibition at the André Emmerich Gallery in New York, in 1959, was the first in what has become a long-standing association. The next year saw her first retrospective.

During the 1960's, Frankenthaler's work became much better known and appreciated. She had solo exhibitions in Los Angeles, Paris, Milan, and London, and she represented the United States in the Venice Biennale. In 1968, she was named the first woman fellow of Calhoun College at Yale University, and in the following year, the Whitney Museum in New York held her second retrospective. Additionally, she was awarded her first honorary doctorate from Skidmore College in 1969, one of more than fourteen doctorates that she has received.

It was during the 1960's that Frankenthaler began to experiment with acrylic paints, although her overall technique remained essentially the same. Instead of using thinned oil paints, she diluted her acrylic pigments and poured them directly onto unprimed canvas, using sponges, mops, and squeegees to position the color. Consisting of bright splashes of two or three colors on the white canvas, the works are much starker and consciously geometric than her earlier oil paintings.

Since the 1960's, Frankenthaler has received even more acclaim and a further expansion into other artistic media: paper, bronze, clay, ceramic, and set making. Her awards during this period include the Spirit of Achievement Award from Yeshiva

University (1970), the Garrett Award of the Art Institute of Chicago (1972), the Art and Humanities Award from the Women's Forum of Yale University (1976), an Extraordinary Woman of Achievement Award from the National Conference of Christians and Jews (1978), and the New York City Mayor's Award of Honor for Arts and Culture (1986), to name only a few. She was a member of the National Council on the Arts (1985-1991) and was the subject of several national films and videos, including Barbara Rose's *American Art in the '60s* (1973) and Perry Miller Adato's *Frankenthaler: Toward a New Climate*, one of seven in a series of programs focusing on women in art and produced by WNET/Thirteen, New York (1978). In 1985, she was commissioned to design sets and costumes for the Royal Ballet, Royal Opera House, Covent Garden production of *Number Three*, set to Sergei Prokofiev's Third Piano Concerto, a major project done while helping to organize a retrospective of her works on paper at the Guggenheim Museum in New York.

Moving to printmaking, Frankenthaler has avoided simply making spinoffs or studies of her better-known paintings. Instead, these expressionistic works, among which are etchings, lithographs, *pochoirs*, and woodcuts, continue to explore the use of open space and color. Often these works employ mixed media. In one eight-foot-wide work, three panels are mounted in a cast bronze screen. The screen, front and back, functions as one unified work of art, relating the graphics in the triptych format to the back, which is flat bronze with a chemical overpainting; sculptural drawing is welded or painted onto the frame, which corresponds to the interior graphics. Additionally, Frankenthaler has made use of techniques well before they have become generally popular—for example, making unique impressions for each color used in a lithograph rather than one impression for all colors. She has completed five print editions and a sculpture relief using the Mixografia process, a process involving the use of wax, copper, and paper to create a three-dimensional effect.

Summary

Helen Frankenthaler is recognized as the key transitional figure between abstract expressionism and color-field painting. The technique of stain painting influenced many artists. Indeed, fellow artists Kenneth Noland and Morris Louis were so impressed with Frankenthaler's ability to spread color on the surface of the picture without creating an illusion that the three began a series of studio visits to experiment with the technique. Pouring the pigment into schematic patterns, Noland and Louis began to create paintings of almost pure color and thus pioneered the color-field school of painting. Critics agree that Frankenthaler's stained paintings were and are innovative and provide a major contribution to modern art. Unlike the work of the male painters of her generation, Frankenthaler's 1950's work has a subtle delicacy of color and light. The stained color fills the canvas, leading the viewer to focus on the materials and processes of the painting while responding to the intense color. Moving to other media, Frankenthaler continues to be a vital proponent of expressionistic color, and her novel explorations with mixed media and Mixografia are extensions of her innovation. Two retrospectives, the 1989 retrospective at the Museum of Modern

Art in New York and the 1993 retrospective of her printmaking at the National Gallery of Art in Washington, D.C., have brought her works to the widest possible audience and confirmed her place as one of America's major artists.

Bibliography
Arnason, H. H. *History of Modern Art: Painting, Sculpture, Architecture, Photography.* 3d ed. New York: Harry N. Abrams, 1986. An extensive history of the modern period that includes a useful index, a large, categorized bibliography, and color plates of major modern works. It provides a good overview of abstract expressionism, color-field painting, and Frankenthaler's role in them.
Carmean, E. A., Jr. *Helen Frankenthaler: A Paintings Retrospective.* New York: Harry N. Abrams, 1989. A catalog edition of the 1989 tour sponsored by the Modern Art Museum of Fort Worth. Besides including color plates of selected works of the exhibit, it contains an insightful interpretation of each of the works, along with a selected biographic chronology, a selected exhibition history, and a selected bibliography.
Elderfield, John. *Frankenthaler.* New York: Harry N. Abrams, 1989. A monumental volume that explores Frankenthaler's paintings. Providing the most extensive number of color illustrations of Frankenthaler's work, it also features numerous black-and-white photographs of the artist at work in the very thorough chronology. Elderfield provides a comprehensive commentary on Frankenthaler's work and her methods. Particularly useful is the bibliography, which lists films, videos, periodicals, and catalogs.
Fine, Ruth E. *Helen Frankenthaler: Prints.* New York: Harry N. Abrams, 1993. An exhibit catalog with a text that focuses on providing a history and commentary of Frankenthaler's printmaking. It includes a good overview of her etchings, woodcuts, monotypes, and Mixografia, as well as a brief reference section, a chronology, an exhibition history, and useful workshop and technical references.
Munro, Eleanor. *Originals: American Women Artists.* New York: Simon & Schuster, 1979. An outgrowth of the 1978 Public Broadcasting System (PBS) series on American Women Artists, this critical study of more than forty women artists includes detailed interviews of each, a brief general bibliography, and a selected artists' bibliography. The chapter on Frankenthaler focuses particularly on her day-to-day technique.
Rose, Barbara. *American Art Since 1900: A Critical History.* New York: Frederick A. Praeger, 1967. A major critical overview of the period that concisely explains Frankenthaler's historical importance in relation to abstract impressionism, color-field painting, and the New York School. A good overall reference work with 244 black-and-white illustrations and 37 color illustrations, it provides a brief selected bibliography and an index. Rose is also the author of the first monograph done of the artist, in 1972, which has been eclipsed by more recent works.
Sandler, Irving. *The New York School: The Painters and Sculptors of the Fifties.* New York: Harper & Row, 1978. Focusing on the artists of the second generation of the

New York School, this work provides a historical overview of the evolution of these artists beyond the first generation as well as their influence on those that followed. The work includes a comprehensive bibliography and two useful appendices.

Wilkin, Karen. *Frankenthaler: Works on Paper, 1949-1984.* New York: George Braziller, 1984. An exhibition catalog with critical commentary focusing on Frankenthaler's oil and acrylic works on paper. Provides a good overview of this material in its historical context as well as many color plates, a selected bibliography, and a selected exhibition history.

Marlene San Miguel Groner

ARETHA FRANKLIN

Born: March 25, 1942; Memphis, Tennessee

Area of Achievement: Music

Contribution: Franklin transcended her gospel music roots to create a unique and powerful vocal style that made her one of the most popular and respected female vocalists to emerge during the late 1960's and led to her recognition as the "Queen of Soul."

Early Life

Aretha Louise Franklin was born on March 25, 1942, in Memphis, Tennessee, to the Reverend Clarence LaVaughan Franklin and Barbara Siggers Franklin. Aretha was the fourth child born to the couple, who had two older sons, Vaughn and Cecil, and an older daughter, Erma. Aretha's father, known as C. L. Franklin, was a widely respected Baptist minister and singer. When Aretha was two years old, the family moved to Buffalo, New York, before eventually settling in Detroit, Michigan, where her father became the founding minister of the New Bethel Baptist Church. Aretha's childhood security was shattered when her mother, a fine gospel singer, deserted the family when Aretha was six years old; Barbara Franklin died four years later.

In addition to his ministry, C. L. Franklin began to make gospel recordings for Joe Von Battles, a local Detroit record producer. Battles in turn leased the majority of these recordings from his own JVB label to Chess Records, a Chicago-based recording company that catered to black listeners. By the mid-1950's, Aretha's father had become known as the "Man with the Million-Dollar Voice" and was in such demand that he was able to command $4,000 per appearance when his revival singing troupe went on tour. During her father's lifetime, he recorded more than seventy albums of his inspirational sermons.

As a result of his own musical activities, Aretha's father created an atmosphere in which his daughter could blossom artistically. Aretha began playing the piano when she was eight years old and continued to practice even though she found it difficult to endure the rigid discipline of formal music lessons. Through her father, Aretha met some of gospel music's most prominent singers. After the loss of their mother, Aretha and the other Franklin children often found themselves cared for by a number of women who were active with the gospel activities of C. L. Franklin's church. Mahalia Jackson, Clara Ward, and Marion Williams all served—at one time or another—as substitute mother and friend to the young and impressionable Aretha. It was her father, though, who continued to be the dominant figure in her life. An imposing and charismatic individual, he was a spiritually minded man who took pride in showing the world that a religious man could achieve success without sacrificing his principles.

Another influential figure in Aretha Franklin's life was the Reverend James Cleveland. A prominent force in gospel music during the 1960's and 1970's, Cleveland entered Aretha's life when she was about nine years old as a result of moving in with the Franklin family. Cleveland became one of Aretha's first mentors, teaching her rudimental piano chords and helping her to expand her vocal range. By the time she was thirteen, Aretha was touring with her father's gospel revival shows. The grueling schedule and the tough environment of the touring circuit encouraged Aretha to pursue a career as a performer and completed her precocious transition from childhood into early maturity.

Life's Work

When Aretha Franklin was twelve years old, she sang her first solo in her father's New Bethel Baptist Church. She impressed the audience with mature and expressive singing talents that belied her young age. Franklin made her first solo recording for the Chess Records label when she was fourteen. As a gospel singer, she recorded various hymns at her father's church. It soon became evident that Franklin was an extremely gifted singer with a vocal range that spanned five octaves. Whether playing the piano or singing, Franklin was a sensation and generated additional publicity for her father's church.

At the age of fifteen, Aretha became pregnant and had to drop out of high school. Although Aretha's family continued to support her during this difficult time, some members of her father's church believed that Aretha's involvement in her father's touring shows had led to her predicament. In 1958, she gave birth to a son and named him Clarence Franklin in honor of her father. During this period, Franklin explored a variety of musical styles and became an avid listener of blues singer Dinah Washington. Convinced that she could establish herself as a mainstream secular singer, Franklin decided to move to New York City.

With encouragement from family friends such as Sam Cooke, former lead singer with the Soul Stirrers gospel group who had already made the transition to popular music, and jazz bassist Major Holley, Franklin moved to New York in 1960. Holley helped Franklin secure an audition with the legendary producer John Hammond. An executive with Columbia Records, Hammond had been responsible for directing the recording careers of many famous jazz musicians, including Billie Holiday and Count Basie. Impressed with Franklin and convinced that she could be a major recording star, Hammond was instrumental in putting her under contract with Columbia Records from 1960 to 1966. During her tenure at Columbia, Franklin recorded ten albums including *The Electrifying Aretha Franklin* (1962), *Unforgettable—A Tribute to Dinah Washington* (1964), and *Soul Sister* (1965). Although Hammond encouraged Franklin to retain her gospel approach to songs, he persuaded her to record material that was directed squarely toward the jazz market. Unfortunately, the phenomenal success that was envisioned by Columbia Records never materialized, and Franklin was obliged to work with various producers who pushed her further away from her gospel roots.

During her years at Columbia Records, Franklin's personal life was filled with turmoil. In 1961, she married Ted White, a thirty-one-year-old record promoter. Although Jo King had been Franklin's manager for several years, White took over the management of his wife's career soon after their marriage. White was particularly opposed to the direction in which various Columbia producers were pushing Franklin. In 1962, however, *Down Beat* magazine published its annual critics' poll naming Franklin as the best new star in the jazz vocal category. That same year, Franklin was also one of the headline vocalists to appear at the 1962 Newport Jazz Festival. Although jazz critics were praising Franklin for her vocal talent, she was not convinced that jazz was her best style. In 1964, Franklin gave birth to her third child (her second with Ted White). Confused about the direction of her career, saddened by the death of close friend Dinah Washington in 1963 from an overdose of sleeping pills, and increasingly unhappy in her marriage, Franklin sought a new direction in her life.

In 1966, Franklin left Columbia Records and signed a recording contract with Atlantic Records, one of the leading labels, particularly in the area of rhythm-and-blues music. Franklin collaborated with noted producer Jerry Wexler and began to mold a more comfortable and popular style of singing built upon her gospel and blues background. The heavy orchestration that had been used to back her recordings on the Columbia label were scrapped; in its place, Wexler and Franklin adopted a hard-edged soul sound. In 1967, Franklin released her debut album with Atlantic: *I Never Loved a Man (the Way I Loved You)*. Recorded at Atlantic's studio in Muscle Shoals, Alabama, which was famous as the site of the soul sound, the album featured sessions with accomplished blues musicians including saxophonist King Curtis. The title single was released in February of 1967, sold an amazing quarter of a million copies in two weeks, and reached number one on the charts. Her next single, "Respect," matched that performance on Billboard magazine's rhythm-and-blues chart and also reached number one on its pop music chart. Franklin won her first two Grammy Awards for "Respect"—in the categories of best R&B recording and best R&B performance by a female.

Because of her large crossover appeal, Franklin was able to attract a broad audience of white listeners in addition to her loyal following among black listeners. By the late 1960's, the white music-buying public, primarily composed of teenagers, showed signs that it was eager to spend money on black recording stars. Like Ray Charles before her, Franklin struck a chord among music lovers that transcended racial barriers. The albums that followed her first Atlantic release were also big sellers, including *Lady Soul* (1968), *Aretha Now* (1968), *Aretha Live at Fillmore West* (1971), *Young, Gifted, and Black* (1972), and *Amazing Grace* (1972). On each of these recordings, Franklin reached the height of her musical powers and was showcased as a confident and compelling performer. She was able to meld the spiritual and popular impulses in her music in order to create an authentic sound without artifice. Whether she was singing about love or the loss of love, about joy or pain, Franklin captured the essence of such emotions in songs such as "Chain of Fools," "Baby, I Love You," "(You Make Me Feel) Like a Natural Woman," "I Say a Little Prayer," and "Amazing Grace." Although Franklin was forthright and uninhibited as a singer, she was an extremely private individual in her private life. It had been rumored that Ted White had mistreated her, and their marriage ended in 1969. Although they were never married, Franklin had a six-year relationship with Ken Cunningham following her divorce and gave birth to her fourth son, Ketcalf, in 1970. Franklin continued her recording career throughout the 1970's, but her albums of the late 1970's failed to generate the same emotional power or financial success as her earlier efforts. In 1978, she was married to actor Glynn Turman, but the marriage ended in 1982. Tragedy struck in 1979, when Franklin's father was shot by a burglar. She moved back to Detroit to care for him, but he died in 1984 after having been in a coma for five years. The financial burden of his medical care had been enormous, so Franklin chose to give two benefit performances in 1979 and 1981 in order to raise sufficient funds to cover his expenses, continuing a tradition of donating time and money throughout her career in support of charitable causes.

In 1980, Franklin left Atlantic Records to sign with producer Clive Davis' Arista Records label. That same year, she had a cameo role in the film comedy *The Blues Brothers*, which paid tribute to many notable blues singers. Franklin's musical career seemed to find new energy with such albums as *Who's Zoomin' Who?* (1985) and *Aretha* (1986), and she found a new legion of fans among viewers of the MTV cable music video station. Franklin was eventually inducted into the Rock and Roll Hall of Fame and was honored with the Lifetime Achievement Award at the Grammy Awards ceremony held in 1994. She continued to remain active professionally into the 1990's and received an honorary doctorate from Detroit's Wayne State University in 1991. In December of 1994, Franklin was recognized for her musical contributions to the performing arts as one of five recipients of that year's Kennedy Center Honors.

Summary

Aretha Franklin earned her title as the "Queen of Soul" as a measure of the public's admiration for her compellingly honest and gripping songs released during the late 1960's and early 1970's. As an entertainer working during these years of great social upheaval in the United States—years that witnessed the height of the Civil Rights movement and the emergence of the Black Nationalist and Black Power movements as well as the turmoil surrounding the Vietnam War—Franklin made her own efforts to support the cause of social justice for African Americans. Drawing upon the honesty and vitality of her roots in gospel music, Franklin produced a singing style that touched the hearts and souls of her vast listening public. Although Franklin was blessed with a remarkable voice, it was much more than just musical talent that catapulted her to stardom. When she performed, it was her integrity and her conviction that won over even the most skeptical critics and listeners. Although her career declined somewhat during the late 1970's, Franklin did not abandon her pursuit of musical perfection, and she returned to top form by the mid-1980's. Known for her gritty improvisational style and her celebration of the rich African American musical tradition of her gospel and rhythm-and-blues heritage, Franklin served as an inspiration to many female singers who followed, including Natalie Cole, Bette Midler, and Whitney Houston. Franklin established a high musical standard by which all other female soul and popular singers will be compared.

Bibliography

Bego, Mark. *Aretha Franklin: The Queen of Soul*. New York: St. Martin's Press, 1989. The most thorough full-length biography of Franklin that exists in print. It details how Franklin has managed to overcome many personal crises and career obstacles. Includes photographs and a useful discography.

Busnar, Gene. "Aretha Franklin." In *The Superstars of Rock: Their Lives and Their Music*. New York: Julian Messner, 1980. Although directed at a juvenile audience, this book contains a chapter on Franklin that provides a useful introduction to her career. Includes excerpts from various interviews as well as a brief discography that stops at 1978.

Gaar, Gillian. *She's a Rebel: The History of Women in Rock and Roll*. Seattle: Seal Press, 1992. An insightful study of how difficult it has been for women to succeed in the male-dominated world of rock music. This book details Franklin's rise to international fame and the price she paid in pursuit of that fame.

Gersten, Russell. "Aretha Franklin." In *The Rolling Stone Illustrated History of Rock and Roll*, edited by Jim Miller. Rev. ed. New York: Random House/Rolling Stone Press, 1980. Gersten, a well-respected rock journalist, has written a perceptive profile of Franklin that explains her place in popular culture. He points out that no matter how erratic Franklin's career has been, her best work stands as some of the finest popular music ever produced.

Guralnick, Peter. "Aretha Arrives." In *Sweet Soul Music: Rhythm and Blues and the Southern Dream of Freedom*. New York: Harper & Row, 1986. A well-researched work that presents a detailed profile of Franklin; points out how she transformed her private torment and personal experiences into remarkably heartfelt music.

Hirshey, Gerri. "Aretha Franklin: A Woman's Only Human." In *Nowhere to Run: The Story of Soul Music*. New York: Times Books, 1984. A richly detailed conversational chapter on Franklin's rise to fame that discusses the many people around her who helped her as well as those who all too often abused her.

Jones, Hettie. "Aretha Franklin." In *Big Star Fallin' Mama: Five Women in Black Music*. New York: Viking Press, 1974. In addition to its profile of Franklin, this juvenile-level book includes chapters on Gertrude "Ma" Rainey, Bessie Smith, Mahalia Jackson, and Billie Holiday. Jones presents these five African American women in the context of the times in which they lived and points out the ways in which each one served as an instrument for social change.

Wallace, Virginia Wilson. "Aretha Franklin." In *Epic Lives: One Hundred Black Women Who Made a Difference*, edited by Jessie Carney Smith. Detroit: Visible Ink Press, 1993. A solid five-page biographical entry on Franklin that chronicles her career through the early 1990's.

White, Timothy. "Aretha Franklin." In *Rock Lives: Profiles and Interviews*. New York: Henry Holt, 1990. In addition to the basic facts of Franklin's career, this biographical profile interjects many fascinating asides that offer perspective on Franklin's struggle to remain professionally active.

Jeffry Jensen

JESSIE BENTON FRÉMONT

Born: May 31, 1824; near Lexington, Virginia
Died: December 27, 1902; Los Angeles, California
Area of Achievement: Government and politics
Contribution: As the daughter of a powerful senator and wife of an explorer and general, Frémont participated in Jacksonian politics, the opening of the West, abolitionism, and the Civil War. In her behind-the-scenes work, she challenged the constraints of nineteenth century roles for women.

Early Life

Jessie Ann Benton was born on May 31, 1824, at Cherry Grove, her mother's family plantation near Lexington, Virginia. She was the second daughter of the five children born to Thomas Hart Benton and Elizabeth McDowell Benton. Her father had moved as a young man from his native North Carolina to Tennessee, where he became a friend and protégé of Andrew Jackson. In 1815, Benton migrated to St. Louis, Missouri, where he practiced law and was elected the new state's first senator, in 1820. In 1821, Benton married Elizabeth McDowell, whom he had courted for six years. Elizabeth's Scotch-Irish Presbyterian family had settled in a Blue Ridge mountain valley near Lexington, Virginia, in 1737, and had become prominent in local and state politics.

As Jessie grew up, the family moved between households in St. Louis, Cherry Grove, and Washington, exposing the curious child to an array of personalities, from Washington insiders to southern aristocrats to rough frontiersmen. Jessie was privately tutored in languages, piano, history, and classics. Her father's favorite child, she was taken along to the Capitol and White House, where she absorbed the elder Benton's democratic convictions. A champion of the common people, her father advocated western expansion and opposed the extension of slavery.

Jessie displayed a willful and independent spirit, which her father encouraged as long as she was a child. As she approached womanhood with no sign of diminishing assertiveness, he realized that allowing her to exercise her mind and personality freely had ill prepared her for the submissive role expected of nineteenth century women. At age fourteen, Jessie was sent to Miss English's Female Seminary in Georgetown, a fashionable finishing school which she despised.

In 1840, Jessie met John Charles Frémont, a handsome young officer with the Army's Topographical Corps. Frémont had all the qualities of courage, impulsiveness, and willfulness that would make him a great explorer and attractive to the ladies, including sixteen-year-old Jessie. Her father was alarmed, since Frémont lacked the status and wealth that Benton thought important in a suitor for his daughter. Frémont was the illegitimate son of a French immigrant and had been reared in poverty by his mother in South Carolina. Despite efforts by her father to prevent a romance, Jessie eloped with the dashing Frémont on October 19, 1841. Eventually reconciled to the marriage, Thomas Hart Benton welcomed his new son-in-law as a willing partner in his campaign to open the West to American expansion, and in his daughter Benton recognized a talented and driven helpmate who would advance Frémont's career.

Life's Work

Unable to participate in politics in her own right, Jessie Benton Frémont devoted her considerable energies to promoting her husband's career. Like her father, she believed fervently that the destiny of the United States was to expand across the continent. John Charles Frémont shared this goal and embodied the resolve necessary to achieve it. Through Benton's influence and his own credentials as an explorer, Frémont was appointed to head a series of expeditions to chart the West. The first of these assignments sent Frémont into western Wyoming in 1842, where he surveyed South Pass and climbed one of the highest peaks of the Wind River range. Upon his return, Jessie helped him write the report of the expedition which was published in 1843. While the scientific observations were John Frémont's, the dramatic flair and poetic touch added by Jessie made the report a romantic adventure story. Their collaboration produced results reflecting the strengths of each, although the credit reverted to John. Jessie, like other women of the day, measured her own success by her husband's triumphs.

At the start of John's second expedition in 1843, an incident occurred which revealed Jessie's capacity for audacious actions on her husband's behalf. While John was preparing to leave Missouri, Jessie intercepted a message from the War Department instructing Frémont to return to Washington. Withholding the order, Jessie sent word to John to set out immediately on his journey. The expedition, which traveled to Oregon and California, was a huge success. The report, written by Jessie from John's dictation, sold in the tens of thousands and served as a guidebook for settlers moving West on the Oregon Trail.

In the meantime, Jessie began to raise a family. A daughter, Elizabeth Benton, was born in 1842. Jessie saw two children die before their first birthdays: Benton (1848) and Anne Beverley (1853). Two healthy sons were born: John Charles in 1851, and Frank Preston in 1854.

John Charles Frémont's third expedition altered the fate of the family. Ending up in California in 1846, John was on hand to participate in the Bear Flag Revolt, an uprising in which American settlers seized power from Mexican officials prior to the actual outbreak of war between the two countries. Caught in a dispute between superior officers, Frémont disobeyed a direct order and was sent East for court-martial. Jessie went in person to President James K. Polk to argue vigorously in her husband's defense. The court found John guilty and recommended his expulsion from the Army, though Polk rescinded the dismissal. The Frémonts refused to accept clemency, however, and John resigned in indignation from the Army. Embittered, the Frémonts moved to California, where John had purchased an estate called Las Mariposas near Yosemite Valley.

Life was rough in California during the Gold Rush, with occasional food shortages and few reliable servants available. The rewards, however, greatly outweighed the inconveniences when several rich veins of gold were discovered on Las Mariposas. Despite legal disputes over the title of the estate, the Frémonts found themselves millionaires, able to travel to Europe as celebrities in 1852. After returning to America in 1853, John headed yet another western expedition, while Jessie settled the family in New York.

In 1856, the new Republican Party chose John Charles Frémont to run for president. The Frémonts favored the Republicans' free-soil position of prohibiting slavery in the new territories of the West. For the first time in American history, the candidate's wife figured prominently in the presidential campaign. Republican banners proclaimed "Frémont and Jessie" and "Jessie's Choice," with illustrations of the attractive Jessie and her handsome husband. While in public she played the decorous role expected of her, behind the scenes Jessie masterfully managed John's campaign. She helped to write his campaign biography, read and answered all of his mail, and received his visitors. Her prominent role was criticized by Frémont's opposition, yet it also galvanized women into political activity as never before. Women attended political rallies, and a few went on the lecture circuit for Frémont and free-soil. Although Frémont lost the election, the strong Republican showing in the party's first national election revealed the rising strength of the free-soil movement and the growing rift between North and South.

Jessie, exhausted from the campaign and upset over her father's refusal to endorse Frémont for president, reluctantly followed her husband to California once more. Her depression was compounded by her father's death in April, 1858.

When the Civil War broke out in 1861, Abraham Lincoln appointed John C. Frémont as Union commander of Missouri. Jessie joined her husband in St. Louis, acting as his unofficial adviser and assistant. Beset with shortages of men and supplies and surrounded by Confederate sympathizers, John had difficulty controlling the state. Largely as a military strategy, Frémont proclaimed the emancipation of all slaves belonging to disloyal Missourians. When a storm of protest erupted, Jessie traveled to Washington to plead John's case personally with President Lincoln. Speaking forcefully and emotionally, she antagonized Lincoln and failed to help her husband. John lost his Army command and retired to New York to wait out the war. In an effort to save her husband's reputation, Jessie wrote *The Story of the Guard: A Chronicle of the War* (1863), a book about John's exploits.

After the war, a series of financial disasters eroded the Frémont fortune, and by 1873, the family was destitute. Jessie wrote to support her family, contributing reminiscences and fiction to magazines such as *Harper's*, *Century*, and *Atlantic Monthly*. She produced a number of books based upon her travels, adventures, and acquaintances, including *A Year of American Travel* (1878), *Souvenirs of My Time* (1887), *Far-West Sketches* (1890), and *The Will and the Way Stories* (1891).

In 1887, the Frémonts moved to Los Angeles. After John died in 1890, Jessie continued to work on her memoirs and other writing and lived with her daughter Elizabeth, who acted as her nurse and companion until Jessie's death in 1902.

Summary

The life of Jessie Benton Frémont reveals the limited roles allowed women of the nineteenth century and the efforts they made to find fulfillment within those narrow boundaries. Reared by an indulgent father who encouraged her natural curiosity and independence, Jessie never comfortably fit into the passive role than commonly expected of women. While she did marry and raise a family, she acted out her own ambitions through her dynamic husband. She promoted his career by capitalizing on her own attributes, winning influence for him by calling upon her own political connections. She transformed his dry scientific reports into romantic adventure stories with her skilled pen. When he stumbled, she stepped beyond accepted propriety of the time to defend him brashly in front of presidents. When his ineptitude in business bankrupted the family, she quietly but competently went to work to bring in an income.

Jessie Benton Frémont often felt frustrated with the limited roles available to women. When she could, she gave generously to support the suffrage movement. She lamented that as a woman, she was not taken seriously in politics. Nevertheless, she did help to expand the opportunities for women through her example of feminine brilliance and assertiveness. Her role as the active wife of the presidential candidate in the 1856 campaign inspired women to demand the right to participate in politics. Like others of her generation, she responded to the Civil War with patriotism, public action, and compassion.

Bibliography

Chambers, William Nisbet. *Old Bullion Benton, Senator from the New West: Thomas Hart Benton*. Boston: Little, Brown, 1956. Though somewhat dated, this work is still the most thorough biography of Jessie's father, Thomas Hart Benton. Useful for Benton and McDowell family background, political context, and relationship between Benton and John Charles Frémont.

Frémont, Jessie Benton. *The Letters of Jessie Benton Frémont*. Edited by Pamela Herr and Mary Lee Spence. Urbana: University of Illinois Press, 1992. A delightful collection of letters written by Frémont which gives first-hand insight into her personality. The editors have written an excellent biographical sketch of Frémont and have provided detailed chapters introducing each section of her life.

Herr, Pamela. *Jessie Benton Frémont: A Biography*. New York: Franklin Watts, 1987. An up-to-date biography of Jessie Benton Frémont that makes valuable use of letters and papers of the Frémont and Blair-Lee families. Highly readable account of Frémont placed within the political and social context of her time, reflecting new scholarship on women.

Nevins, Allan. *Fremont; Pathmarker of the West*. Reprint. Lincoln: University of Nebraska Press, 1992. This reprint of a classic biography of John Charles Frémont portrays him in heroic proportions. This work also gives Jessie Benton Frémont deserved credit for contributing to John's career. Useful for meticulous detail on both John and Jessie's lives, though poorly documented.

Stone, Irving. *Immortal Wife: The Biographical Novel of Jessie Benton Fremont.* Garden City, N.Y.: Doubleday, Doran, 1944. A fictionalized account of Jessie Benton Frémont's life. Despite its fictional format, Stone's novel is based upon the papers and published works of Frémont, thus ensuring a relatively high degree of factual accuracy.

Lynne M. Getz

BETTY FRIEDAN

Born: February 4, 1921; Peoria, Illinois

Area of Achievement: Women's rights
Contribution: Betty Friedan's first book energized thousands of women and helped to initiate the feminist movement in the late 1960's. Since that time, she has been a leader in the continuing struggle for women's rights.

Early Life
Betty Naomi Goldstein was born on February 4, 1921, to jeweler Harry Goldstein and former journalist Miriam Horowitz Goldstein in Peoria, Illinois. She remembers the fact that her mother gave up a career in journalism to be a housewife. This, she believes, explains her mother's enthusiastic encouragement of young Betty's journalistic endeavors in high school, college, and beyond.

Betty graduated from Smith College in 1942, summa cum laude, and later did graduate work at the University of California at Berkeley. After college, she worked in New York City as a reporter for a labor press. It was wartime, and women were encouraged to fill jobs while the men were overseas as soldiers.

Once the war ended, however, women were expected to give up their jobs so that the returning veterans could find work. She lost her reporting position and had to find work as a researcher. This was a "woman's job," which involved doing the research and often much of the writing for articles that were then published under the male authors' bylines.

In the postwar era, women were expected to return to their traditional domestic roles—to get married, settle down, and have children. Thus began a time when women were presented with idyllic visions of being happy housewives at home in the suburbs raising families and caring for their homes and husbands. Betty accepted this vision, married Carl Friedan in 1947, and had three children: David, Jonathan, and Emily. She had, however, kept her job, taking a year's maternity leave after her first child's birth. When she requested her second leave, however, she was fired.

Friedan now tried to live up to the ideals of the day, working very hard to find the feminine fulfillment her mother had never found in domestic life. Eventually moving to a house on Long Island, Friedan reared her family, but she also continued to write, contributing articles to several women's magazines.

Life's Work
A popular topic in the media began to be the notion that women's education was not preparing them adequately for their roles as women. That is, women went to colleges where they received educations they would never be able to apply in careers, since their proper role as women was to be housewives. Too much education was making them discontent with this role in life. The focus was on the inappropriateness of women's education, but Betty Friedan began to see that what was wrong was not

the education but the role that limited the choices of educated women.

Based on a 1957 survey she had been asked to conduct among her fellow classmates from Smith College, Friedan wrote an article for *McCall's* on this issue, but her work was rejected by the male editor as too unbelievable. She was then asked to write the same information for *Ladies' Home Journal*. When the article went to print, however, it had been changed to say the very opposite of what Friedan had originally written. *Redbook* also considered and refused to do the story. Betty Friedan realized that she would have to write a book to get her ideas into print, because they threatened the very identity of women's magazines.

In her first book, *The Feminine Mystique* (1963), Friedan coined this now-famous term to describe the prescribed female role of the post-World War II years. The book caused shock waves throughout the country, because thousands of American women identified immediately with her words. These women were to become part of the energy that would instigate the feminist movement beginning in the late 1960's.

By 1966, Friedan, sensing that words were not enough, began putting her energies into organizing for women's rights. In that year, she attended a conference in Washington, D.C., of all the state Commissions on the Status of Women. Because of the frustrations of these women delegates at their inability to have any impact on the government, they began at that meeting organizing what was to become NOW, the National Organization for Women. Friedan wrote NOW's statement of purpose. The organizing conference of the new group was held in October of 1966, with about three hundred members, and Friedan was elected the first president, a post she held until 1970, a year after her divorce in May, 1969.

Continuing her activism, she became a major organizer of the Women's Strike for Equality, which took place on August 26, 1970, the fiftieth anniversary of the date women were granted the right to vote. During this time, Friedan was arguing against what had been termed "sexual politics," which included anger at males as oppressors of women, notions of female separatism, and vocal support of lesbianism as a political issue. Her argument against sexual politics was that it was divisive and that it diverted attention away from the real political and economic issues of most women.

In 1971, Friedan helped organize and was the coconvenor of the National Women's Political Caucus, formed to encourage and support women and pro-women candidates for public office. By 1972, however, she was beginning to back out of political activism, focusing her energies on writing, speaking, and teaching. In that year, she was invited to teach as a visiting professor at Temple University. This was followed by invitations to Yale in 1974 and Queens College of the University of the City of New York in 1975.

At this point, Friedan was exploring ideas about what she called the "second stage," which she defined as the sex-role revolution that must include men. This new focus was reflected in the course titles at Temple, Yale, and Queens: "The Sex-Role Revolution, Stage II."

In 1975, Betty Friedan was named Humanist of the Year by the American Humanist Association, and she received an Honorary Doctorate of Humane Letters from Smith

College. The following year saw the publication of her second book, *It Changed My Life: Writings on the Women's Movement* (1976). In this book, Friedan described her work over the previous years and included a journal of her experiences.

Her third book, *The Second Stage* (1981), further explored Friedan's growing concern with the need to overcome the polarization between the sexes and to achieve the human wholeness that she saw as the ultimate promise of feminism. In addition, she was concerned about a damaging myth she saw growing in American culture— that of the superwoman who could have it all: career, marriage, and family. Her book argued that the time for reacting against male dominance and focusing on work outside the home was passing as women's goals were being won, and that now women needed to begin to unite with men in building a new society of male-female equality.

Although it was a logical extension of her previous work and concerns, this book unleashed a great controversy. Many feminists turned on Friedan, saying that she had betrayed the women's movement by buying into popular ideas about the importance of the traditional family and the need to gain the approval of men.

Betty Friedan's next book was *The Fountain of Age* (1993). This book was undertaken as a way to understand her own denial and dread of aging, but in the process of her research she found a major contradiction between the typical view that aging is a time of loss and debility and the realities of the lives of the aging people she interviewed.

She notes that for women the process of aging is changing because of the changes in the ways women are defining themselves (changes, of course, that she herself helped bring about with her leadership in the feminist movement). She calls the new generativity that both women and men are experiencing as they grow older the fountain of age, in a play on the idea of the fountain of youth.

Summary

Betty Friedan's effect on the American women's movement has been immeasurable. Since she first gave voice to the dissatisfaction of housewives caught in the postwar ideology of the "feminine mystique," throughout her work in founding and leading movements such as the National Organization for Women, and into her later years as her ideas have focused first on the second stage and then on aging, she has always been willing to be controversial, has always followed her own star, and has always spoken for many who identify with her insights.

Betty Friedan has taught at New York University and the University of Southern California and continues to lecture worldwide. Her personal papers have been collected at the Schlesinger Library of Radcliffe College.

Bibliography

Behm, Barbara. *Betty Friedan: Speaking Out for Women's Rights*. Milwaukee: Gareth Stevens, 1992. This book discusses Betty Friedan's impact on the women's movement and her views of women's rights.

Friedan, Betty. *The Feminine Mystique*. New York: W. W. Norton, 1963. This book,

Friedan's first, chronicles her own experiences and those of many other women in trying to live up to the feminine ideal of the American postwar era.

—————————. *The Fountain of Age*. New York: Simon & Schuster, 1993. In this book, Friedan explores concepts of aging—discovering that the process of growing older carries positive connotations for many people and giving many insights into her own life experiences.

—————————. *It Changed My Life: Writings on the Women's Movement*. New York: Random House, 1976. Perhaps the most autobiographical of Friedan's books, this work documents her activism in the women's movement and presents various entries from her journal.

—————————. *The Second Stage*. New York: Summit Books, 1981. Like all of Friedan's books, this one gives the reader further insight into her life and personal journey as well as into her thoughts on the progress of the women's movement, which she believed, at the time she wrote this work, was entering a second stage.

Krichmar, Albert. *The Women's Rights Movement in the United States, 1848-1970: A Bibliography and Sourcebook*. Metuchen, N.J.: Scarecrow Press, 1972. This useful book provides a wealth of material regarding the women's movement in which Friedan played so important a part.

Eleanor B. Amico

LOIE FULLER

Born: January 15, 1862; Fullersburg, Illinois
Died: January 1, 1928; Paris, France
Area of Achievement: Dance
Contribution: A pioneer in the art of modern dance, Loie Fuller created choreography that featured the manipulation of fabric and novel lighting effects. Her spectacular dances helped to create an enthusiastic audience for solo American dance performers.

Early Life
Loie Fuller, née Marie Louise Fuller, was born in rural Fullersburg, Illinois. She apparently took a few dance lessons as a child, but it is doubtful that either the quality of instruction or her own interest in dance was high. She took singing lessons and appeared as a child performer at temperance lectures, holding colored charts depicting the liver. From this unlikely background emerged one of the pioneers in American modern dance.

In the mid-nineteenth century, the United States was a nation in the midst of reform fervor: dress reform, health reform, temperance, utopian communities, "physical culture"—all movements destined to intertwine with the women's suffrage movement and influence the course of both theater and dance in the twentieth century. Loie Fuller, a shrewd, ambitious, and innovative young woman, was able to capitalize on these unique currents in health, politics, and the arts and create a novel form of theatrical presentation that was widely imitated.

Loie Fuller did not set out to become a dancer. Dance as a performing art in the mind of the American public was either ballet (which was imported from Europe) or a combination of folk and social dances, acrobatic tricks, and burlesque performed as variety acts in vaudeville theaters or as part of touring pageants. Dance contests were popular entertainment, and men were the featured performers through the 1870's and 1880's. Audiences came to see familiar dance forms done by those who could do them better than they could themselves. Women seldom appeared without a male partner until the 1890's, when a new form of entertainment called "skirt dancing" captivated audiences and legitimized solo women performers.

Large theatrical spectacles, part circus and part pageant, dominated the touring circuits. With names such as *Nero and the Destruction of Rome* (1886) and *Egypt Through the Centuries* (1892), these extravaganzas were often loosely based on historical events, with scant regard for authenticity. They included ballet, pantomime, acting, special technical effects, sets, costumes, and fantastical stories and legends, and they often featured casts of hundreds.

An actor who worked her way into the profession more by determination than by talent, Fuller entered the theater at a time when women with distinctive personalities were successful: All the major stars had, according to Elizabeth Kendall in *Where She Danced* (1979), "an unmistakable personal style. All the women headliners were idiosyncratic performers." Fuller appeared in a variety of theatrical presentations, including comedies such as *Little Jack Sheppard* (1886), Buffalo Bill's Wild West Show, and even her own play *Larks*. It was while rehearsing *Quack, M.D.* at the Harlem Opera House in New York City in 1889, however, that she made the discovery that was to catapult her to world fame: The manipulation of silk fabric created fleeting impressions of flowers, animals, wind, water, and fire. (Fuller gave several accounts of the exact time and place of her fateful discovery over the course of her career, but 1889 is the most likely date.)

Life's Work

Loie Fuller was quick to recognize the marketability of her invention. She had an innate ability to understand what it was that an audience wanted to see and how to capture the spirit of the time and reflect popular taste. Sensing that her discovery was "artistic," Fuller decided that the best place to showcase her art was Europe, the center of western arts and culture. In 1892, she made her debut at the famous Folies Bergère in Paris. With special sticks hidden under yards of silk, she twirled, undulated, and waved her arms to music. Her body, hidden by the voluminous fabric, lit by electric lights under frosted panels of glass, performed the simplest of dance motions, accompanied by arm gestures. According to Kendall, "What she had found . . . was actually more an idea than a new method. It was ordinary dancing concealed and surrounded by veils."

The dances Fuller choreographed all involved the creation of spectacular visual effects through the manipulation of fabric, color, light, and motion. Her "Serpentine Dance" of 1892 consisted of twirling around under yards of draped silk: Lights that shone onto the silk created the impression of clouds, butterflies, birds, flames, and flowers. Equally successful was her "Fire Dance" when she stood on a glass panel that was lit from below, the changing red, yellow, and orange lights illuminating the silk made her appear to be consumed by fire, to the delight and astonishment of her audiences.

Fuller's dances, with their curvilinear forms and organic shapes, combined with her use of technology, made her the darling of the Art Nouveau and the artistic circles of Paris. Toulouse-Lautrec made a lithograph of her, Raoul Larche modeled her in an ormolu lamp, Art Nouveau glassworkers consulted her about colors and dyes, and poets and artists William Butler Yeats, Stéphane Mallarmé, and Auguste Rodin publicly praised and admired her.

A pioneer in technical lighting design, Fuller was fascinated by science and technology. She had her own laboratory in the basement of her house, where she worked on new discoveries, corresponded with scientists Pierre and Marie Curie about the use of newly discovered radium as a costume enhancement, and designed slide projectors with slides painted with liquid gelatin to create unusual lighting effects. Her first film, made in 1905 for Pathé, used slow motion, shadows, and negative printing.

From her success at the Folies Bergère, Fuller went on to perform at the Paris

Exposition in 1900, return in triumph to the American stage, and tour Europe with a group of young dancers, billed as "Loie Fuller and her Muses." In Paris, Fuller's work was seen by future dance pioneers Isadora Duncan and Ruth St. Denis. According to Joseph Mazo (1977), Fuller predated Duncan in discarding the corset, using classical music, and training a company of dancers in her own style. Duncan joined Fuller's troupe briefly, traveling with Fuller to Berlin and Vienna following the Paris Exposition.

Fifteen Years of a Dancer's Life, Fuller's autobiography, was published first in France in 1908 and then reprinted in English in London in 1915. In it, she describes her philosophy of art and dance, reflecting the aesthetics and enthusiasms of the early twentieth century. For Fuller, dance was motion, expressive of sensation and emotion. She wrote, "In the dance . . . the human body should . . . express all the sensations or emotions it experiences." She believed that her art was naturally expressive, and disparaged formal dance training. Her dance, like Art Nouveau, attempted a return to natural and organic forms, using the discoveries of science and technology.

Although she was American, "La Loie" spent most of her performing career in Europe, where she was revered. Only after she acquired the cachet of a star "foreign" dancer was Fuller acclaimed in the United States. In this way, she was much like the slightly younger dance pioneers Isadora Duncan and Ruth St. Denis. Of the three, only St. Denis returned home from European success to create and sustain an American audience for modern dance. For the European audiences, jaded by centuries of academy-based ballet and art, these three American women were astonishingly vibrant. In Europe, according to Kendell (1979), "They were thought to be not just new kinds of artists but new kinds of personalities . . . they found in Europe the approval of an old, refined, and self-aware culture; Europe found in them a pre-civilized freshness."

In 1909, Loie Fuller toured New York and Boston, accompanied by fifty electricians and her group of women dancers. She performed her "Fire Dance" and danced as Salomé to the music of the Peer Gynt Suite. Although reviews in the New York *Dramatic Mirror* complained about the flimsiness of the women's costumes, the shadowy effects of the lighting kept serious scandals at bay. True to her dress-reform upbringing, Fuller denounced the corset and proclaimed the dignity of her dances.

In the 1920's, Fuller returned to her laboratory, finding further technological innovations to inspire her dances. Her "Shadow Ballets," performed in London in 1923, featured dancers who were sometimes only partially visible, and included an ominous, large shadow of a hand reaching for terrified dancers. Other dances from this period include choreography in which only certain parts of the dancer's body are visible through streaks of light across the stage. In these and other dances, Fuller clearly demonstrates a multimedia approach to dance that was to be expanded in the 1960's by choreographer Alwin Nikolais.

Fuller died in Paris of pneumonia in 1928. She had kept working until her death, always searching for new ideas and new methods of expression. She had many imitators, but none who created the same degree of magic and illusion.

Summary
    Loie Fuller's pioneering spirit as an artist provided the inspiration for a second generation of American women dancers. She demonstrated that a woman alone on stage could command the attention of an audience and that other forms of dance besides classical ballet could be expressive and artistic. Her innovations in lighting design and stage technology influenced theatrical production for decades after her death. Fuller paved the way for later dance artists and their audiences to perceive dance as a serious art form capable of evoking deep emotions. Although her technique was not sophisticated, her emphasis on dance as a medium of expression that integrated music, motion, lighting, and costume paralleled the revolutionary ideas of the Russian ballet choreographer Michel Fokine and the innovations of the Ballets Russes.
    American dancers Isadora Duncan and Ruth St. Denis both admired her work and drew inspiration from it. They also profited from the fact that Fuller's popularity opened up venues for performance that had not existed previously and prepared audiences for an appreciation of the new dance forms.
    Loie Fuller's rise to fame coincided with the rise of the woman suffrage movement, and she shared much of the missionary zeal of its founders and supporters. In championing women's right to wear clothing that was healthy and liberating, in her unconventional life as a lesbian, artist, and celebrity, and in her emphasis on the dignity and importance of women, Loie Fuller was a pioneer in all aspects of her life, not simply as a dancer.

Bibliography
Anderson, Jack. *Ballet and Modern Dance: A Concise History.* Princeton, N.J.: Princeton Book, 1986. An overview of the development of theatrical dance forms which is easy to read and entertaining. Although Anderson's material on Loie Fuller is not substantial, he does help place her work within the context of the emergence of modern dance.
Brown, Jean Morrison, ed. *The Vision of Modern Dance.* Princeton, N.J.: Princeton Book, 1979. A compilation of essays by important modern dance choreographers and dancers, edited and introduced by Brown. The chapter on Loie Fuller features an excerpt from Fuller's autobiography and gives a clear sense of what Fuller thought about her art.
Kendall, Elizabeth. *Where She Danced.* New York: Alfred A. Knopf, 1979. A thorough history of the emergency of modern dance at the turn of the century, with an emphasis on the social, political, economic, and aesthetic forces that shaped the women who were the pioneers of this art. Although Kendall focuses more on Isadora Duncan and Ruth St. Denis than she does on Fuller, the social and historical information that she includes provides an essential background for understanding Fuller's importance and contributions.
Kraus, Richard G., et al. *History of the Dance in Art and Education.* 3d ed. Englewood Cliffs, N.J.: Prentice Hall, 1991. A general text that helps to contextualize the

pioneers of Fuller's generation and the early development of dance education in America.

Mazo, Joseph H. *Prime Movers: The Makers of Modern Dance in America*. Princeton, N.J.: Princeton Book, 1977. Mazo features eleven choreographers, from Loie Fuller to Twyla Tharp, whom he considers trailblazers of modern dance. The chapter on Loie Fuller is detailed and anecdotal, and it contains photographs of her dancing.

Cynthia J. Williams

MARGARET FULLER

Born: May 23, 1810; Cambridgeport, Massachusetts
Died: July 19, 1850; at sea near Fire Island, New York
Areas of Achievement: Journalism and social reform
Contribution: A pioneering feminist far ahead of her time, Margaret Fuller was a perceptive literary and social critic, and America's first woman foreign journalist.

Early Life

Sarah Margaret Fuller was born on May 23, 1810, in Cambridgeport, Massachusetts, the first of the nine children of Timothy Fuller and Margaret Crane Fuller. Her father, a prominent figure in Massachusetts politics, was a graduate of Harvard College and the absolute authority in his household. Keenly disappointed that his first child was a girl, Timothy Fuller nevertheless determined to educate her according to the classical curriculum of the day—an experience usually afforded only to boys.

Even as a small child, Margaret was directed by her father in a rigorous schedule of study. She learned both English and Latin grammar and, before she was ten years old, read Vergil, Ovid, and Horace as well as Shakespeare. At age fourteen, Margaret went briefly to Miss Prescott's School in Groton but soon returned home to immerse herself again in study. Although Margaret was intellectually developed far beyond her years, the girl's intensity caused trouble in friendships, a pattern that continued throughout her life. Margaret was also uncomfortable with her physical appearance. Therefore, she decided to cultivate her intellect, spending fifteen-hour days reading literature and philosophy in four languages, breaking only for a few hours of music and walking each day.

By the late 1820's, Margaret was forming strong friendships with Harvard students such as James Freeman Clarke and Frederic Henry Hedge, many of whom would later become involved, as she did, with the Transcendentalist movement. She was becoming known in intellectual society in Cambridge and at Harvard as a formidable conversationalist. The same determination that brought her such success, however, also brought criticism. Margaret tended toward sarcasm, offending even close friends in intellectual discussions, and the great demands that she placed upon herself she also placed upon others.

In 1833, Timothy Fuller moved his family to a farm in Groton. Margaret taught her younger siblings and, when her mother's health declined, took over the household. She continued to read, particularly German literature and philosophy, but her life at that time was a strain. Early in 1835, Margaret fell seriously ill, then recovered; in October of that year, her father died.

At this turning point, Margaret's future seemed uncertain and difficult. She had planned a European trip to expand her horizons but had to cancel it in order to support the family. After a three-week visit at the home of Ralph Waldo Emerson (a Transcendentalist and a literary figure) in Concord, she decided to take a teaching position at Bronson Alcott's experimental Temple School in Boston. In 1837, Margaret accepted a teaching position in Hiram Fuller's (no relation) Greene Street School in Providence, Rhode Island.

During her two years in Providence, Fuller also continued her scholarly work—often at the expense of her health—translating Johann P. Eckermann's *Conversation with Goethe*, for example, and publishing poems and international literature reviews in a liberal, Unitarian journal edited by James Freeman Clarke. In addition, she wrote her first piece of important criticism, which was published a year later in the first issue of the Transcendentalist publication the *Dial*. Although Margaret was a successful teacher, she missed the intellectual stimulation of Boston, so in 1839 she moved back to Jamaica Plain, a Boston suburb, where she was joined by her mother and younger siblings.

Life's Work

When Margaret Fuller moved back to Boston, her involvement with Transcendentalism (which began when she met Emerson in 1836) increased. As a movement, Transcendentalism focused around a common perspective on religion and philosophy rather than any particular doctrine, and intellectuals met regularly for discussion about the nature of freedom and spirit. In 1840, Fuller became the first editor of the Transcendentalist literary quarterly the *Dial*. She also wrote much of the copy and kept the periodical alive—almost single-handedly—until she resigned her editorship two years later.

Fuller supported herself during this time by conducting "Conversations," highly successful weekly discussions attended by the society women of Boston. Fuller believed that women were not taught how to think, and she determined to remedy this with discussions of topics from Greek mythology to ethics to women's rights. Through these "Conversations," which continued until she moved to New York in 1844, Fuller became known as a powerful speaker and intellectual critic. During this time, she was also involved with Brook Farm, a Transcendentalist experiment in the nature of ideal community that began in 1841 (she did not actually live there).

Fuller was frequently Emerson's houseguest in Concord. She said of Emerson, "From him I first learned what is meant by the inward life." They had a strong friendship, and through their discussions, both were able to develop their knowledge and appreciation of literature. The friendship was complex, however, and Fuller and Emerson were not always comfortable in each other's presence, much less with each other's ideas.

During this period, Fuller traveled outside the boundaries of New England. Her journey to the Midwest is recorded in Fuller's first book, *Summer on the Lake* (1843), in which she investigated the relationship between nature and society, focusing on people and social manners. While conducting research for this book, Fuller became the first woman to receive permission to enter the library at Harvard University. The book also brought Fuller to the attention of Horace Greeley, editor of the *New York Tribune*. He invited her to become the newspaper's literary critic, and—against the advice of friends such as Emerson—Fuller accepted. In December, 1844, she moved to New York, leaving the constraints of family and friends behind, to become the first female member of the working press in the United States.

Horace Greeley said that Fuller was, in some respects, the greatest woman America had yet known, and he gave her almost a free hand with her writing. Fuller's style became more solid, and her thinking deepened even further as she wrote regularly on major authors and ideas of her time. While at the *Tribune*, Fuller also became concerned about public education and social conditions. She visited prisons, poorhouses, and asylums, and her front-page articles about them moved people's feelings and laid the foundation for reforms.

In 1845, Greeley published Fuller's *Women in the Nineteenth Century*, the first American book-length discussion of equal rights for men and women. The book became a public sensation and made Fuller's name known throughout the English-speaking world. A classic in American feminist literature, it combined the spiritual focus of a transcendental vision with the need for practical action and was influential in the Seneca Falls conference on women's rights in 1848. In 1846, Fuller published *Papers on Literature and Art*, a compilation of her critical reviews which set a high standard for American literary criticism.

The strain of writing on deadline made Fuller's chronic headaches worse, however, and she was also trying to recover from a broken romance. In August, 1846, Greeley commissioned her as America's first foreign correspondent, and she visited first England, then France, and finally Rome, in April, 1847. Everywhere she went, Fuller met with major figures of the time and sent dispatches back to the *Tribune*. Fuller was disturbed by the misery that she saw around her, particularly that of working-class women. More and more, life—not art—became her preoccupation, and Fuller's articles on the common worker appeared prominently in the *Tribune*.

In the summer of 1847, Fuller made an extended tour of Italy. She was drawn into the Italian struggle for independence, and in the course of her travels she met Giovanni Angelo Ossoli, a young Italian count who was committed to the liberal cause. Ossoli and Fuller became lovers and, it seems, planned for a life together. Because Ossoli would have been disowned by his aristocratic family for marrying a non-Italian and a non-Catholic, however, the marriage was delayed for more than a year.

Ossoli and Fuller spent the winter of 1848 involved in the Republican struggle in Rome. Fuller continued to send detailed articles about the revolution to the *Tribune*, but she kept her relationship with Ossoli a secret for a long time, even from family and friends in America. Fuller was expecting a child, so she moved to Rieti, outside Rome, where she gave birth to a son, Angelo, on September 5, 1848. Fuller stayed with the child until April, then left him with a nurse and returned to Ossoli and the fighting in Rome, where she directed an emergency hospital and ran supplies to her husband's fighting unit. When the Italian liberals were finally defeated in July, 1849, Ossoli and Fuller were forced to leave Rome. They took Angelo and fled to Florence, where Fuller wrote what she thought was the most important work she had done to date: a history of the Italian Revolution.

Fuller wanted to publish the manuscript in the United States, so the family set sail for New York City on May 17, 1850, despite Fuller's deep foreboding about the journey. Difficulties started soon after they set sail: The ship's captain died of smallpox; then Angelo became sick with the disease, and he almost died. On July 17, just after land was sighted, a storm came up and the inexperienced captain ran the ship aground near Fire Island, New York. Whenever the storm abated, people tried to swim to shore, only a few hundred feet away, but Fuller resigned herself to death and refused to leave the ship. She eventually allowed a sailor to try to save the baby, but Fuller and her husband stayed on board as the ship was pulled apart by the sea. Angelo's body finally washed ashore, but Fuller, Ossoli, and Fuller's manuscript were never found.

Summary

Those who remember Margaret Fuller most often do so within the context of her association with New England Transcendentalism, but her most significant contributions were in the areas of literary criticism and social reform. Despite the fact that her own writing style was inconsistent, Fuller is nevertheless considered to be one of the two real literary critics of the nineteenth century, along with Edgar Allan Poe. She developed a theory of criticism that combined perspectives of realism and romanticism, and she held to high standards that did not fluctuate with the prevailing winds of the times.

Fuller was also a pioneering journalist and perceptive social critic on both the national and the international level. In *Tribune* columns, her commentary on public education and social conditions looked deeply into American values. She visited and wrote about Sing Sing and Blackwell's Island prisons, for example, which led to the establishment of the first halfway house for newly released female convicts. Her dispatches from Europe—especially her account of the Italian revolution—helped Americans grow in their understanding of the world around them.

Although Fuller did find fulfillment as a wife and mother, her powerful character was not circumscribed by these traditional female roles. In her behavior, Fuller questioned economic, social, and political assumptions about women; in her writing, she propagated her belief in equality through. Her major work, *Women in the Nineteenth Century* (1845), is generally considered to be the first important feminist work by an American woman. Fuller fascinated the readers of her day and challenged their ideas about what a woman could and should be. More than a century later, her argument that people should be able to express themselves as individuals, not simply as representatives of their gender, continues to offer insights into the unlimited potential of human nature.

Bibliography

Allen, Margaret Vanderhaar. *The Achievement of Margaret Fuller*. University Park: Pennsylvania State University Press, 1979. This biography presents probably the most strikingly feminist perspective on Fuller's life and work. Allen concludes that Fuller was easily the equal of Emerson and Thoreau.

Blanchard, Paula. *Margaret Fuller: From Transcendentalism to Revolution.* New York: Delacorte Press, 1978. This biography is written from a clearly feminist perspective, though with a more subtle voice than Margaret Allen's. It has helped to make Fuller more accessible to the general reading public.

Chevigny, Bell Gale, comp. *The Woman and the Myth: Margaret Fuller's Life and Writings.* Old Westbury, N.Y.: Feminist Press, 1976. The major study changed Fuller scholarship in the mid-1970's and is essential reading for anyone who is seriously interested in Fuller.

Edwards, Julia. *Women of the World: The Great Foreign Correspondents.* Boston: Houghton Mifflin, 1988. This work presents a lively and vivid account of Fuller's activities in Europe and quotes liberally from her communiques to the *Tribune.* It gives a real sense of Fuller within the context of the times.

James, Laurie. *Why Margaret Fuller Ossoli Is Forgotten.* New York: Golden Heritage Press, 1988. James, an actress, has done extensive research in preparing her original one-person drama about Fuller, which has toured internationally. In this sixty-five-page book, James presents her thesis that Fuller has been buried in history because the authors of her "definitive" biography *Memoirs of Margaret Fuller Ossoli* (1852) intentionally misrepresented her life and works. James builds quite a case against Ralph Waldo Emerson, William Henry Channing, and James Freeman Clarke. She elaborates further in her *Men, Women, and Margaret Fuller* (1990).

──────────, ed. *The Wit and Wisdom of Margaret Fuller Ossoli.* New York: Golden Heritage Press, 1988. This selection of quotations is organized around topics such as "love," "equality," "revolution," "toys," and "faith and soul." Fuller's astute, often wry observations have not gone out of date, and the reader can get a real taste of Fuller from this small book. It also includes a list of Fuller's major achievements and a bibliography.

Myerson, Joel, comp. *Critical Essays on Margaret Fuller.* Boston: G. K. Hall, 1980. These articles represent Fuller criticism from 1840 to the date of this publication. As Myerson observes, it is obvious that from the start, critics were more interested in Fuller's personality than in her work. The fifty-three mostly short selections make interesting reading.

Watson, David. *Margaret Fuller: An American Romantic.* New York: Berg, 1988. This is a useful account of Fuller's life, work, and reputation. Watson examines Fuller's roles as romantic, feminist, and socialist, suggesting that she deserves to be taken seriously as a contributor to historically important bodies of thought. Of particular interest is Watson's examination of modern feminist Fuller scholarship. He concludes that modern attempts to "rescue" Fuller do not always escape the myopic traps to which they are opposed. Includes a chronology, an index, and a bibliography.

Jean C. Fulton

META VAUX WARRICK FULLER

Born: June 6, 1877; Philadelphia, Pennsylvania
Died: March 13, 1968; Framingham, Massachusetts
Area of Achievement: Art
Contribution: As an African American sculptor, Meta Fuller drew upon her heritage for many of the themes in her work. She is recognized as a forerunner of the Harlem Renaissance of the 1920's.

Early Life

Meta Vaux Warrick, the youngest of three children, was born in to a well-to-do Philadelphia family. Her mother, Emma Jones Warrick, managed a hairdressing parlor in her home to which fashionable women from the upper class came. Meta was named for one of them, the daughter of Senator Richard Vaux, who had encouraged Emma to name her expected child after her. Meta's father, William H. Warrick, owned a chain of barbershops both in Philadelphia and in Atlantic City, New Jersey, where the family spent their summers. Her parents gave their children a good education and took an interest in their upbringing. Meta remembered that when she was a child, her father took her for long walks in the park and to the Philadelphia Academy of Fine Arts, where he explained paintings and sculptures to her. This she regarded as her introduction to the fine arts.

Meta's older siblings, William and Blanche, also contributed to her artistic development. Her brother told her fascinating horror stories that fed her imagination and later in life inspired some of her more realistic sculptures, earning for Meta the nickname "sculptor of horror." Her sister, who was interested in watercolor and woodcarving, would encourage Meta's creativity by giving in to her younger sister's begging for art materials to play with, especially pieces of clay.

Meta went to an all-black public school until she won a three-year scholarship to the Pennsylvania Museum and School of Industrial Art (later the Philadelphia College of Art). When she graduated in 1898, her metalwork *Crucifixion of Christ in Agony* won a prize. She was granted an additional year of postgraduate study during which she modeled a fine, powerful, horrible head of Medusa in clay. Meta was already becoming a "sculptor of horror." After her fourth year of study, she received the George K. Crozier first prize in modeling for *Procession of Arts and Crafts*, a bas-relief frieze showing thirty-seven figures dressed in medieval costume.

Meta had clearly demonstrated her talent. Encouraged by her teachers to study abroad, she approached her mother—her father had died in 1897—with a bold statement: "I think I'll go to Paris." One of her teachers had apparently paved the way, because her mother consented.

Life's Work

In September of 1899, aboard the *Belgianland*, Meta Vaux Warrick sailed to France to study for two years. In Paris, she went to the American Girls' Club, where she had reserved a room. She arrived there and was introduced to the director, Miss Acley, who asked her why she had not written that she was colored and not a white girl. Meta replied that she had been informed that the club was open to any American girl who came to Paris to study, which was her intention. She would not partake in the club's social life. Although Miss Acley said that she herself was not opposed, there were some Southern girls who might object.

The outcome of this humiliating experience, which Meta vividly recalled all her life, was that she had to find other lodgings. She eventually was able to sublet a studio from two English women and soon became friends with a young Parisian woman, realizing that she could not expect friendship from her American compatriots.

Her study in Paris was fruitful but slow. Miss Acley had been helpful in putting her in contact with American sculptor Augustus Saint-Gaudens, who gave her advice in her study. In her third year—she had received her mother's permission to stay on another year—she had advanced sufficiently to summon up the courage to contact Auguste Rodin, the foremost sculptor in Europe at the time. She brought with her a piece called *Secret Sorrow* (c. 1902, also known as *Man Eating His Heart*), which was inspired by Stephen Crane's poem "The Heart," which deals with despair and desolation.

When Rodin turned the little sculpture in his hand and had examined a photograph of another piece, *The Impenitent Thief*, he uttered the words that she would remember for the rest of her life: "Mademoiselle, you are a sculptor. You have the sense of form in your fingers." With this encouragement, Meta Warrick's career took off. She soon was able to both exhibit and sell her work. One important mentor was Samuel Bing, an art dealer who exhibited Meta's work in his new gallery, L'Art Nouveau. He also bought some of her sculptures. The Salon of 1903 showed several of Meta's pieces, including *Man Carrying a Dead Comrade* and *The Wretched* (c. 1903). The latter, which is regarded as one of her most powerful works, depicts seven figures, each representing a form of human suffering.

Meta was praised for her ability to make clay come alive under her hands. Thriving from this success and with three years of study concluded, she returned to Philadelphia with great expectations as well as with money earned from her sales. Her native country, however, did not greet her with the same enthusiasm that she had encountered in France. American art dealers showed no interest in buying her work. Meta realized that it was the racial issue that hindered her progress.

Nevertheless, in 1907, Meta received a prestigious commission. She was asked to execute a memorial for the Tercentennial Exposition in Jamestown, Virginia, to commemorate the arrival of black men and women in America. The group consisted of fifteen tableaux with a total of 150 figures. Her work in documenting the development of the black peoples of humankind makes Meta Warrick a forerunner of the Harlem Renaissance of the 1920's.

About the time she was creating the *Jamestown Tableaux*, she met her future husband, Solomon Carter Fuller. Born in Liberia, he became the first black psychiatrist in the United States (a mental health center in Boston bears his name). They were married in 1909, and they settled in Framingham, Massachusetts, where Meta Warrick Fuller lived until her death in 1968. The couple had three boys, and with the responsibility of rearing them as well as running a household, Meta had little time for sculpture.

In 1910, she also suffered a severe blow when sixteen years' worth of her work was destroyed by a fire in a Philadelphia warehouse. At least twenty-five pieces of finished sculpture, models and studies, her tools, and memorabilia from her Parisian years were among the items lost in the fire.

The loss discouraged her until, in 1913, the prominent black leader W. E. B. Du Bois, whom she knew from Paris, asked her to execute in full scale the *Spirit of Emancipation*, representing a young man and woman standing in the shelter of a gnarled tree. Du Bois wanted it for the celebration in New York of the fiftieth anniversary of the Emancipation Proclamation.

In 1914, Fuller exhibited some thirty pieces, including genre scenes portraying her young boys as well as a portrait of her husband. She had moved from the earlier "horrible" themes to social subjects, such as *Immigrant in America*. *Ethiopia Awakening* (1914), another pivotal work, showed the new direction her art had taken.

She also made religious works, such as *The Good Shepherd*, *The Crucifixion*, several depicting the Madonna, and *Mother and Child*. A work that falls between social and religious themes is the moving *The Talking Skull* (1937), which depicts an African American boy kneeling in communication before a skull. In May of 1917, the powerful work *Peace Halting the Ruthlessness of War* took a second prize in a competition under the auspices of the Massachusetts Branch of the Woman's Peace Party.

Although her husband enjoyed the attention her sculpture received, he did not encourage her as an artist. He regarded caring for home and family as her first duty. Eventually Fuller felt such a strong need to devote more time to sculpture that she decided to build her own studio. With money she inherited from her mother, she bought land on the Learned Pond near Warren Road, where they lived. In secret she built the studio. It took her two years. In 1929, she was ready to sculpt, and she also began to teach. Her refuge soon became a gathering place for friends.

Meta Fuller also enjoyed translating poetry into sculpture. Her two interpretations of *Waterboy*, based on the song of the same name, exemplify this kind of work. She also wrote poetry when she was not working, such as the work "Departure" (1964), in which she reflects on and accepts death.

Fuller was active to the end of her life, planning works and executing pieces for the community. The Framingham Public Library has her *Storytime*; St. Andrew's Episcopal Church, of which she was a member, has several of her sculptures; and the local hospital has a medallion of her husband, Solomon Carter Fuller. Meta Vaux Warrick Fuller died in Framigham, Massachusetts, on March 13, 1968, at the age of ninety.

Summary

An unusually talented sculptor, Meta Vaux Warrick Fuller, a tribute to both her gender and her race, was able to overcome many obstacles that were placed in her way. The citation given to her when she was made an honorary life member of the Framingham Business and Professional Women's (BPW) club noted her as a generous teacher of youth and as a sculptor recognized in Europe, her nation, her state, and her town. The BPW headquarters in Washington, D.C., received a work by Fuller, *Madonna*, which was commissioned by the local club. Other honors came to Fuller in her later years. In 1962, a week before her eighty-fifth birthday, Livingstone College, in Salisbury, North Carolina, of which her husband was a graduate, awarded her the honorary degree of Doctor of Letters.

Meta Warrick Fuller's memory lives on. In 1973, a public park in Framingham was dedicated to honor her and her husband. In 1985, an exhibition of sixty pieces of her work was shown both in the local Danforth Museum of Art and in the Museum of the National Center of Afro-American Artists, in Boston. In 1987, her work was included in an exhibition on the Harlem Renaissance, a recognition she deserves as an early promoter of the achievements of the African American race.

Bibliography
Brawley, Benjamin. "Meta Warrick Fuller." *The Southern Workman* 47 (January, 1918): 25-32. This article is useful for interpreting and listing Fuller's sculpture up to 1918, including those pieces that were lost in the fire of 1910. The author has written many short pieces on Meta Fuller.
Dannett, Sylvia G. L. "Meta Warrick Fuller." In *Profiles of Negro Womanhood*. 2 vols. New York: N. W. Lads, 1964-1966. This is the most complete biographical summary of Meta Fuller's life available. The author includes several anecdotes from Fuller's early life and cites the honors she received.
Hoover, Velma J. *Meta Vaux Warrick Fuller: Her Life and Art*. Washington, D.C.: Association for the Study of Afro-American Life and History, 1983. The author, the director of Multidisciplinary Program for Minorities, Dr. Solomon Carter Fuller Mental Health Center, knew the artist in the last fifteen years of her life. He provides a thoughtful portrait of Fuller as a friend and neighbor. Includes illustrations of five of Meta Fuller's sculptures and a picture of the artist in her home.
Igoe, Lynn Moody. *Two Hundred Fifty Years of Afro-American Art: An Annotated Bibliography*. New York: R. R. Bowker, 1981. This reference work, the most thorough available, lists Meta Warrick Fuller's works and tells where illustrations of them can be found.
Kennedy, Harriet Forte. *An Independent Woman: The Life and Art of Meta Warrick Fuller*. Framingham, Mass.: Danforth Museum of Art, 1984. A catalog published in connection with an exhibition of sixty of Meta Fuller's works, mainly bronzes and painted plaster works, shown from December 16, 1984 to February 24, 1985, at the Danforth Museum of Art in Framingham, Massachusetts, and from May 5 to July 7, 1985, at the Museum of the National Center of Afro-American Artists in Boston.
Logan, Rayford W. "Meta Vaux Warrick Fuller." In *Notable American Women: The*

Modern Period, edited by Barbara Sicherman et al. Cambridge, Mass.: The Belknap Press of Harvard University Press, 1980. This article is important, since the author has corrected mistakes with regard to Meta Fuller's birth and death; he obtained a birth certificate from Philadelphia and consulted an obituary.

Ovington, Mary White. *Portraits in Color.* New York: Viking Press, 1927. This book contains twenty profiles of prominent black personalities, including Meta Fuller. The author states that she has written of no one whom she has not met and seen at work. Provides information not included in other writings and appears to be the source for several later citations.

Porter, James A. *Modern Negro Art.* New York: Dryden Press, 1943. Reprint. New York: Arno Press, 1969. Includes brief evaluations of many of Meta Fuller's works.

Elvy Setterqvist O'Brien

MARY HATWOOD FUTRELL

Born: May 24, 1940; Alta Vista, Virginia

Area of Achievement: Education
Contribution: Futrell, a dedicated educator, worked her way up through the ranks to become the first African American to lead the National Education Association (NEA), a national teachers union representing 1.9 million members.

Early Life
Mary Alice Hatwood was born on May 24, 1940, in Alta Vista, Virginia, and grew up in Lynchburg, Virginia. She is the second daughter of Josephine Austin Hatwood. Her father, John Ed Calloway, died when she was four. Brought up by her mother, Futrell recalls a childhood filled with caring and discipline. From her mother's example, Futrell learned that hard work and sacrifice are often required in direct correspondence to the talents and responsibilities one gets in life. Josephine Hatwood gave up a lifelong ambition to become a nurse and worked as a cleaning lady for three families and several churches in order to support her children.

Josephine Hatwood was a tough taskmaster, especially for Mary, the most academically gifted of her children. According to Futrell, "Mama's toughness with me always left me feeling as if I pleased her less than her other children and that I could never entirely gain her good wishes." Later, Futrell would understand that her mother pushed her to work harder than her three sisters because she sensed that Mary's future success would depend upon her ability to channel her strong will.

The second most influential person in Mary's early life was Miss Jordan, her tenth grade teacher at Dunbar Public High School in Lynchburg, Virginia. Jordan's contribution to Mary's development is best illustrated by a single event, which began as a punishment. As a consequence of talking too much in class, Mary was told to write an essay based on the impact of education on the economy. After Mary had completed the assignment, Jordan read it through and informed the young girl that her first effort was not good enough. Consequently, she forced Mary to revise the essay five times, each time focusing upon a different element of good writing. At the end of this process, Jordan entered Mary's polished essay in a contest. It won third prize.

This dramatic and singular incident typified Jordan's expectations for Mary. Futrell recalls, "Except for Mama, she was the person I most wanted to please in this world."

After being graduated from high school, Mary Hatwood entered Virginia State University on a $1,500 scholarship. Four years later, she received a bachelor's degree in business education. Hatwood then entered George Washington University, where she earned a master's degree in her chosen field. Subsequently, she took additional graduate courses at various institutions of higher learning: the University of Maryland, the University of Virginia, and Virginia Polytechnic Institute and State University. In 1977, she married Donald Futrell, also a teacher. In August of 1989, Mary Hatwood Futrell began a doctoral program in educational policy studies at George

Washington University and simultaneously became associate director of the Center for the Study of Education and National Development at the university.

Life's Work

In 1963, Mary Hatwood Futrell joined the professional staff of an Alexandria, Virginia, high school as a teacher of business education. Early in her career, she secured a place for herself in the Education Association of Alexandria (EAA) and so distinguished herself through service that in 1973 she was elected president of the organization. Her interest in educational policy issues led her to join forces with teachers' unions in larger arenas, both state and national. In 1976, Futrell became the first African American president of the Virginia Education Association (VEA), and in 1978 she was elected to a seat on the board of the National Education Association. Continuing her commitment to serve at higher levels in teacher unions, in 1980 Futrell became secretary-treasurer of the NEA. Finally, on July 2, 1983, Futrell was the uncontested candidate for NEA president. In succeeding years, Futrell was voted back into the national leadership position twice, serving an unprecedented three terms, or six years. On August 31, 1989, Futrell resigned from office as head of the largest teacher's union in the country.

Much of Futrell's educational philosophy is revealed in the monthly presidential statements she wrote for *NEA Today*, the union's main publication. In these open letters to her membership, she was forthright in her appraisal of a public that she believed sometimes condoned social barriers to quality education for all children, and she was fervently critical of the federal government's failure to provide the kind of fiscal support she believed was needed to correct such problems as the huge national drop-out rate, the dearth of special education programs, insufficient Head Start programs, and inadequate child care for young families. Nevertheless, she remained enthusiastic about the positive effects that she believed rank-and-file educators could have in setting the stage for excellence in education through their advocacy for change.

Futrell believed that many members of society were in a state of denial when it came to recognizing, as part of the national drop-out statistics, the thousands of students who are pushed out of school by in-school discrimination. In her opinion, many ethnic and linguistic minority students often find themselves not well assimilated in their school environments. In the March, 1988, issue of the *NEA Today*, she argued:

> [W]hen these students can no longer endure messages that erode their self-esteem and demean their native heritage, they seek escape. We add these students to the dropout statistics. They don't belong there. They're pushouts. Only when we're honest enough to call them pushouts will we begin to solve their problem, which is our problem.

Futrell's concerns for quality special educational programs were exacerbated by national government policies that she thought were especially insensitive during most of the period of her tenure as a national leader. For example, she was sorely disappointed by the actions of President Ronald Reagan's Administration when, in 1987, it cut the federal education budget, thereby ending federal support for vocational education, shrinking funds for handicapped students by $336 million, and cutting by half aid for needy college students. In the March, 1987, issue of *NEA Today*, she wrote: "For the seventh time in seven years, this President seeks to gut public education. Slashing federal education funds by 30 percent, says Senator Lawton Chiles (D-Fla), is 'like cashing in your life insurance policy to take skydiving lessons.'" She concluded, "The day we really long for is the day we are offered not skydiving lessons, but lessons that lift us toward the lofty ideals our six previous Presidents embraced."

Futrell was further dismayed by the Reagan Administration's passing the Stewart B. McKinney Homeless Assistance Act, which provided only five million dollars for the education of homeless children. In her opinion, this nominal support virtually guaranteed the elimination of federal help to states for the education of approximately 700,000 clients. In April of 1988, she outlined what she saw as the deficiencies in the act for homeless children. She accurately pointed out that the current initiative could provide only about $7.14 to each homeless child, barely enough for a six-month supply of pencils and paper for each student.

Futrell was more encouraged by the promises of George Bush when, upon becoming president, he dubbed himself the education president. She developed a cordial working relationship with the Bush Administration, but, over the course of time, she was not impressed by the president's reluctance to push for educational reform by providing the necessary dollars. By way of contrast, near the end of her third term, her hopes for progress down the road of quality education for the nation's children soared when, during the 1988 presidential campaign, she enthusiastically supported the Democrats' educational platform, which included plans for the continuation and expansion of college loans. She eagerly endorsed the COSTEP program conceived by Democratic Senator Lloyd Bentsen, and she was heartened by the program's plan to bring banks and businesses together in a cooperative effort to provide college loans for deserving students.

As Futrell neared the end of her third presidential term, she began to look for trends and changes in areas of education that had been clearly developed across the past several years of her national leadership, and what she saw was a ray of sunshine in the area of drug abuse. Reviewing a recent national survey, she charted a decline in drug use among all students. Although elated by the obvious good news, she could not overlook the fact that the battle had left many wounded and in need of rescue. Voicing her concern for students who had been early victims of the waning drug culture, Futrell pointed out that too few rehabilitation centers existed to serve them. She stressed that support for these unfortunate students should be more of a national priority.

Futrell took great pride in the Mastery Learning Project, a cooperative venture established during her terms in office as NEA president. The project involved the NEA and International Business Machines (IBM) Corporation. In this pilot program, twenty-six schools nationwide participated. Educators created and packaged the curriculum, and IBM provided the electronic hardware to implement it. Futrell saw this joint effort involving educators and members of the business world as the necessary first step toward expanding the use of technology in academic learning. In commenting on the success of the project, Futrell remarked, "Our challenge now is to nurture and expand the relationship we've begun. Our challenge is to merge the traditional 3R's with a new technological three R's. . . . [C]omputers offer our schools the promise of profound change."

As Futrell stepped down from her NEA leadership position in 1989, she envisioned the future for education. Noting that the 1990 budget included allocations for good new programs, she then compared the shares that education and the military would receive and concluded that, "In real dollar terms, education . . . [would end] up with less federal support." Optimistically, Futrell hoped that a steady focus on the needs of education in the future would continue to inspire and invigorate educators who would be at the forefront of the struggle.

In one of her final messages to her membership, Futrell wrote about how she "thinks often of our tomorrows—of challenges that remain, of dreams still unrealized and hopes still unfulfilled. It is an exhilaration that comes of knowing that our journey must continue, because we have promises to keep."

Summary

Under Mary Hatwood Futrell's leadership, the national membership of the NEA increased dramatically. She is credited with building the NEA into America's largest union, adding 250,000 members during the six years she held office. It is generally conceded in educational and political circles that her reform positions changed the orientation and goals of the NEA and gave momentum to legitimate calls for educational reform and change from rank-and-file educators.

Futrell was widely recognized and honored for her achievements as a national leader in education. The accolades bestowed upon her include the Human Relations Awards, National Conference of Christians and Jews, 1976, 1986; Outstanding Black Business and Professional Person, *Ebony*, 1984; One of the Country's 100 Top Women, *Ladies' Home Journal*; One of the Most Influential Blacks in America, *Ebony*, 1985, 1986; Anne and Leon Shull Award, Americans for Democratic Action, 1986; and a number of honorary doctorates from such institutions of higher learning as George Washington University, Virginia State University, Spelman College, Adrian College, Central Connecticut State University, Eastern Michigan University, Lynchburg College, North Carolina Central University, University of Lowell, and Xavier University.

Bibliography

Bender, Steve. "They Teach Our Children Well." *Southern Living* 25 (June, 1990): 85-90. An article that profiles two Southern leaders in education. Focuses on the messages of discipline and respect for learning that Futrell tries to give students.
Futrell, Mary Hatwood. "Mama and Miss Jordan." *Reader's Digest* 135 (July, 1989):

75-80. Futrell relates how two strong, caring, uncompromising women taught her discipline and inspired her to excel.

Howard, Michael E. "A Conversation with Mary Hatwood Futrell." *Black Enterprise* 20 (October, 1989): 30. In an exclusive interview conducted after she announced her decision to step down as president of the NEA, Futrell discusses a wide range of subjects, from union organization to politics in education. Futrell speculates on the future of the NEA after her departure.

Lee, George L. *Interesting People: Black American History Makers*. New York: Ballantine, 1992. A collection of original illustrated short biographies from the national black press. Includes a brief profile of Mary Hatwood Futrell.

Olson, Lynn. "Losing 'The Most Effective Spokesman Ever.'" *Education Week* 8 (June 14, 1989): 1, 24. Provides a personal profile of Futrell in the wake of her announcement that she would step down from the presidency of the NEA after a six-year tenure. This article assesses Futrell's achievements as an educator and as a skilled spokesperson for one of the nation's largest unions representing schoolteachers.

Smith, Jessie Carney, ed. *Notable Black American Women*. Detroit: Gale Research, 1992. This biographical source contains a sketch of the NEA president that includes a summary of her early life, a critical look at her educational philosophy, and an assessment of her influence as a national leader.

Sarah Smith Ducksworth

MATILDA JOSLYN GAGE

Born: March 25, 1826; Cicero, New York
Died: March 18, 1898; Chicago, Illinois
Area of Achievement: Women's rights
Contribution: Matilda Joslyn Gage's scholarly work provided much of the woman suffrage movement's literature. Her countless speeches and writings on behalf of the movement made her one of its most important leaders.

Early Life

Matilda Joslyn was born in Cicero, New York, on March 24, 1826. She was the only child of two well-educated, liberal parents, who were both actively interested in social reform. Her father, Hezekiah Joslyn, was a physician who educated Matilda at home, teaching her Greek, mathematics, and physiology, while her mother, Helen Leslie Joslyn, an educated Scotswoman, similarly encouraged her daughter. Matilda was also influenced by the wide variety of scientists, theologians, and philosophers who were entertained in the Joslyn home.

Realizing that home education was insufficient, Matilda's parents sent her to the Clinton New York Liberal Institute for further schooling. She ended her formal education when she married Henry H. Gage, a merchant, at the age of eighteen, but she continued to read and write in order to educate herself further. She was particularly interested in theology, continuing to refine her Greek and teaching herself Hebrew in order to examine the Bible in the original. The Gages lived initially in Syracuse, New York, but later moved to Fayetteville, New York, where they reared one son and three daughters.

Matilda's life was marked by the interest in social action that she inherited from both of her parents. When she moved to Fayetteville, her house became a stop on the Underground Railway, a route used to smuggle runaway slaves north to Canada and freedom. She was also active in the temperance movement, which worked to abolish alcohol. She gave speeches, wrote articles, and helped to organize meetings and conventions.

Life's Work

Matilda Joslyn Gage entered the women's movement in 1852, when she was the youngest speaker at the Third National Woman's Rights Convention in Syracuse, New York. Her speech, which was later distributed as part of the movement literature, outlined and lauded the accomplishments that women had already made, despite their legal and economic encumberments. She stressed the need for women to achieve economic independence, seeing this as the key to women's elevation. She drew parallels between the state of slaves and that of women, declaring that they faced the same enemy. The audience, which included her five-year-old daughter, listened with interest.

Over the next ten years, Gage became an important actor within the woman suffrage movement, which she saw as the most important social reform movement of the century. She gave speeches, held office within the organization, and wrote articles, short stories, and letters. In 1862, when asked to present a flag to the 122nd Regiment of New York Volunteers, she seized the opportunity to deliver a speech on the importance of ending slavery. When the National Woman Suffrage Association (NWSA) was created in 1869, she was a member of its first advisory council. In 1870, she published *Woman as Inventor*, which celebrated the creativity and past achievements of women while denouncing the men who had usurped the fruits of women's labors.

When Susan B. Anthony was arrested for trying to vote illegally in 1873, Gage helped Anthony speak to prospective jurors in New York. The women split the townships between them, and Gage repeatedly delivered a cogent and impassioned speech, "The United States on Trial, Not Susan B. Anthony."

In May, 1875, Gage was elected head of the National and the New York suffrage associations. She testified on behalf of a suffrage bill that came before Congress that year, and when Congress failed to act, she wrote a protest that was distributed at the following year's January NWSA convention in Washington. The protest, which stated the women's intent not to celebrate the country's centennial because the country remained "an oligarchy of sex" rather than a true democracy, was widely circulated. Police threatened to close down the woman suffrage convention, declaring it an illegal assembly, but Gage refused to stop the proceedings, declaring to the cheering crowd that if she were arrested, she would simply hold a woman's rights convention in jail. That May, Elizabeth Cady Stanton replaced her as head of the NWSA, since both Gage and Stanton believed it to be important that the most publicly known suffragist be head of the organization during the centennial.

In 1880, Gage's pamphlet "Who Planned the Tennessee Campaign of 1862?" demonstrated that a woman, Anna Ella Carroll, had planned the military strategy that had altered the course of the Civil War but had received no credit for it.

From 1878 to 1881, Gage edited and published the *National Citizen and Ballot Box*, the four-page official monthly newspaper of the NWSA. Her articles spanned a wide spectrum of topics, including prostitution, women's collectives, and women's experiences in the prison system. She often wrote about the oppression of American Indians, and she was made an honorary member of the Council of Matrons of the Iroquois. Her writing influenced the formation of NWSA policy, and some of it became the basis for testing rights in court.

Many of her articles dealt with theology and her analysis of the Church. Early in 1878, Gage spoke at a Free Thought convention and was well received. She had always seen Christianity as a primary force in women's oppression, and the Free Thought movement offered the opportunity to confront Christianity directly. She did not abandon the suffrage movement; in 1879, she and other members of an NWSA delegation met with President Rutherford B. Hayes to discuss the importance of suffrage. Although he refused to take any action, Hayes was nevertheless impressed by the clarity and strength of Gage's arguments. When Belva Lockwood ran as the

Equal Rights Party's presidential candidate in 1881, advocating votes for women, immigrants, and American Indians, Gage threw her full support behind Lockwood and was one of two electors-at-large on the ticket.

Gate not only worked on the national level but also devoted time and effort to campaigns on the state level. She helped to form the Virginia State and New York State suffrage associations. She worked on gaining women the right to vote and run for office in elections in New York in 1880 and saw one of her daughters elected school clerk as part of an all-woman platform that year.

In 1878, Gage gave up the *National Citizen and Ballot Box* in order to continue collaborating with Anthony and Stanton on the *History of Woman Suffrage*, the first volume of which was published in 1881. The huge work, mostly written by Gage and Stanton while Anthony worked to secure its publication, initially consisted of three volumes, averaging a thousand pages each. Gage also worked with Stanton on *The Woman's Bible* and, as a member of the Revising Committee, helped to research and analyze the Old Testament.

Gage's *Woman, Church, and State* was published in 1893. The book, the result of a lifetime of research, explores the role of the Church in women's oppression, addressing itself to "all Persons, who breaking away from custom and the usage of the ages, dare seek Truth for sake of Truth." Gage believed that the Church provided a framework that justified and perpetuated the position of women, citing such events and doctrines as witch-burnings, the enslavement of women, the elimination of women deacons from the early Church, the concept of original sin, and the sexual double standard. In her book, Gage was one of the first feminist thinkers to propose that in the ancient past there had existed matriarchal societies in which women had held considerably greater power than that held by the women of her day.

By 1888, the NWSA faced internal difficulties caused by the struggle between conservative and radical members of the association. At the convention sponsored by the NWSA for the International Council of Women that year, Gage spoke at several sessions. She began the session she chaired with a prayer addressing a female deity, shocking some members of her audience. Gage insisted that women should not exclude themselves from any vision of a supreme deity, but conservative members of the council saw Gage's action as indicative of an unacceptably radical position.

Distressed by the upheavals and compromises caused by the reunion of the NWSA with its counterpart, the more conservative American Woman Suffrage Society, to form the National-American Woman Suffrage Association in 1889, Gage formed the Women's National Liberal Union (WNLU), which she called her "grandest and most courageous work." The organization called for numerous reforms, including the separation of church and state, the abolition of prayer in public schools, prison reform, and unionization. Stanton and Anthony believed that the WNLU's existence challenged the authority of the NAWSA and denounced Gage for her actions, going so far as to edit mention of her achievements out of the fourth volume of the *History of Woman Suffrage*.

Gage continued to work with the WNLU and other reform movements, but ill health gradually confined her activities to her daughter's home in Chicago, where she died of a brain embolism in 1898.

Summary

Matilda Joslyn Gage was one of the most influential women among the leaders of the woman suffrage movement, but she received little attention from later historians. It is only today that scholars are beginning to recognize her impressive achievements in writing and speaking, which make her a major feminist theorist and historian. Her writings redefined women's struggle, and her perceptive and accurate analysis helped to shape the policy of the NWSA. She emphasized the importance of women's knowledge about themselves and their past in achieving equality, and she devoted her life to researching that past.

Bibliography

Buhle, Mari Jo, and Paul Buhle, eds. *The Concise History of Woman Suffrage: Selections from the Classic Work of Stanton, Anthony, Gage, and Harper*. Urbana: University of Illinois Press, 1978. This varied selection of speeches and writings includes some material that provides the context for each piece. Gage is not well represented, but the text does include enough of her writing to give an accurate indication of her style and emphases.

Campbell, Karlyn Kohrs, ed. *Women Public Speakers in the United States, 1800-1925: A Bio-Critical Sourcebook*. Westport, Conn.: Greenwood Press, 1993. This text includes an article on Gage by Sally Roesch Wagner that focuses on Gage's rhetoric and provides a chronology of her speeches.

Flexner, Eleanor. *Century of Struggle: The Woman's Rights Movement in the United States*. Cambridge, Mass.: The Belknap Press of Harvard University Press, 1975. Although Flexner only briefly mentions Gage, the book provides a useful overview of the woman suffrage movement, allowing Gage to be placed in context.

Gage, Matilda Joslyn. *Woman, Church, and State*. Watertown, Mass.: Persephone Press, 1980. This reprint of Gage's book showcases a number of her foci and displays the rigor and clarity of her writing. In includes a detailed introduction by Sally Roesch Wagner that discusses Gage's impact on the woman suffrage movement and why she came to be overlooked by many of its historians.

Spender, Dale. *Women of Ideas and What Men Have Done to Them*. Boston: Pandora Press, 1988. Spender eloquently analyzes how and why Gage was written out of the history of the woman suffrage movement and discusses the philosophy expressed in *Woman, Church and State*.

Spender, Lynne. "Matilda Joslyn Gage: Active Intellectual." In *Feminist Theorists*, edited by Dale Spender. New York: Pantheon Books, 1983. This essay provides an overview of Gage's work, emphasizing the relevance of her writings to contemporary feminists and the manner in which many of her ideas echo contemporary concerns.

Wagner, Sally Roesch. *A Time of Protest: Suffragists Challenge the Republic, 1870-*

1887. Sacramento, Calif.: Spectrum, 1987. Wagner's book contains a thorough account of the suffrage struggle during this period, which emphasizes Gage's importance to the movement.

Catherine Francis

MAVIS GALLANT

Born: August 11, 1922; Montreal, Quebec, Canada

Area of Achievement: Literature
Contribution: One of Canada's best-known writers, Gallant has produced intelligent and subtle stories that have been widely influential.

Early Life
Mavis de Trafford Young was born in Montreal, Quebec, in 1922. Not much is known of her childhood, which was marked by family instability. The family's frequent moves to various parts of Canada and the United States enabled Mavis to be fluent in both French and English. By the time she was eighteen, Mavis had attended seventeen schools, her father was dead, and she was no longer on speaking terms with her mother. Critics have speculated that these early experiences may have colored the themes of cosmopolitanism, exile, and displacement found in her mature work.

Mavis' juvenile odyssey ended at age eighteen, when she moved to Montreal. For a few years, she held a variety of transitory jobs. In 1944, she had her first experience as a writer, working for the newspaper the Montreal *Evening Standard*. Mavis wrote many feature articles for the *Standard*, covering the lifestyle and culture of postwar Montreal as she wrote about subjects ranging from literature to the challenges faced by new immigrants to Canada. She began to develop her distinctive writing style, scrupulously realistic yet laden with a creative opacity. In 1948, Mavis married Johnny Gallant, a pianist who played in nightclubs in Montreal and New York. By 1950, this marriage had failed. Dissatisfied with the secondary status accorded women journalists at the *Standard*, Mavis decided to live in Europe. At the same time, she decided to shift her focus from journalism to fiction.

Life's Work
Mavis Gallant's career as a fiction writer was launched in 1950, when she had a story accepted for publication by *The New Yorker*. Gallant continued to publish stories in *The New Yorker*; most of the stories later collected in her books were first published there. Her life in Europe was different from what it had been during the *Standard* years and provided ample material for her stories. Gallant lived in Rome and London during the 1950's before settling down for good in Paris in 1960. This city inspired the stories in her first book, *The Other Paris* (1956). Gallant's early stories are not "set" in Paris in the conventional sense; rather, they hang suspended in a kind of borderline zone between Canada and Europe, security and exile. Gallant's acerbic and detached style in these stories underscores the alienated lives of the expatriates she depicts.

Gallant published a short novel, *Green Water, Green Sky*, in 1959. In her next book, *My Heart Is Broken: Eight Stories and a Short Novel* (1964), Gallant moved beyond the comparatively simple narratives of *The Other Paris*. In stories such as "Its Image in the Mirror" and "Sunday Afternoon," Gallant probes beneath the narrative surface to explore what is tacit, repressed, or latent in the lives of her characters. In contrast to the first book, the stories do not possess an obvious, quasi-anecdotal "point"; rather, the reader must pause at the end of the tale, assess the impact of what has happened, and make his or her own effort to decipher the meaning of the story. This second story collection also established that Gallant's principal medium would be the short story, a form ideally suited for her linguistic craft.

Paradoxically, Gallant's next work was a novel, *A Fairly Good Time* (1970). As Gallant's longest single work to date, the novel broke new ground in its representation of the subordinate role of women in patriarchal French society. Nevertheless, Gallant's story collection *The Pegnitz Junction* (1973) proved to be her real breakthrough work. Moving away from the domestic and psychological territory that had characterized her earlier stories, Gallant plunged into the maelstrom of twentieth century European history. At the center of this volume is World War II and the Holocaust. Gallant uses both her distance (as a young, Gentile Canadian woman, she was not directly involved in either of these events at the time) and her proximity (lent by her residence in Europe and her psychological familiarity with human malice) to outstanding effect, generating a striking amalgam of irony and passionate commitment.

Gallant's next major work, *From the Fifteenth District: A Novella and Eight Short Stories* (1979), is set in the same historical period; it leaves the moral and ethical foreground and goes into the more quotidian background of people's ordinary lives. In stories such as "The Four Seasons" and "The Latehomecomer," Gallant explores the displacements of memory and the unreliability of perception and judgment among a notably international set of characters.

Gallant's next book, though, was vigorously applauded as a return home. In *Home Truths* (1981) Gallant for the first time sets a significant part of her work in her native Canada. This setting was, in a way, both a cause and an effect of the quantum growth of Gallant's critical reputation. Previously marginalized with faint praise in the 1950's and 1960's as a lapidary dry wit, Gallant was now hailed as one of Canada's leading writers and was widely anthologized and taught in college courses. Part of this acclaim was a tribute to the quality of her work. In addition, Gallant, as a woman and a Canadian, had profited from the rise of feminism and Canadian nationalism as topics of interest within literary criticism during the 1970's. Yet Gallant had rarely written about Canada itself. Despite this situation, some commentators had concluded that her interest in history and the conflicts of personal and national identity were oblique references to issues of bilingualism and sovereignty in Quebec. Nevertheless, Gallant's lack of material Canadian settings was felt. This lack was ameliorated with the publication of *Home Truths*, and Gallant consequently became a staple of the Canadian literary circuit.

At the center of *Home Truths* are the memorable "Linnet Muir" stories. Linnet Muir is a young girl growing up in the Montreal of Gallant's youth. Although they are not directly autobiographical, the stories obviously have autobiographical meaning for Gallant. The saga of Linnet Muir constitutes a *Bildungsroman*, or "story of growing up," although the segmented nature of the narrative, broken up as it is into individual stories which themselves move back and forth unpredictably in time, militate against the overarching unity often deemed typical of this genre and suggest that there is more to Linnet's mind and experience than readers might immediately conclude. Linnet's life is also bound up with issues of Canadian identity. From the mistaking of a statue of a Canadian railroad magnate for the British King Edward VII in "In Youth Is Pleasure" to Linnet's ambivalent fascination in "Varieties of Exile" with the figure of a British "remittance man"—a feckless young scion of a wealthy family who has been dispatched to the colonies to redeem himself—the Linnet stories are filled with telling incidents that vividly depict the convoluted relationship between Canada and the mother country. Here, Gallant approaches the issues later to be widely analyzed under the banner of post-colonial fiction.

During the 1980's, Gallant's renewed currency in Canada helped boost her growing international reputation, as she came to be regarded as one of the senior and most accomplished short-story writers in English. Despite her celebrity in her home country, Gallant continued to reside in Paris. Even during her fifties and sixties, Gallant continued to be an adept observer of the minute social and political changes in the contemporary Parisian scene. In *Overhead in a Balloon* (1985), Gallant once again devotes much of the book to a sequence of connected stories. Instead of the innocent Linnet, Gallant employs a more worldly protagonist. Édouard, a Parisian who is aware of tragedy and loss at an early age, can never quite bring all the elements in his life together at one time. A powerful story outside the Édouard sequence is "Speck's Idea," a farcical look at cultural nostalgia and literary hucksterism.

Still working primarily with Parisian settings, Gallant's books *In Transit: Twenty Stories* (1988) and *Across the Bridge: Nine Short Stories* (1993) are at once humorous, plangent, and challenging. "Dédé" in the latter book has been particularly acclaimed; a portrait of communication problems within a middle-class French family, it reveals Gallant's talent at its most offhandedly imaginative. In the early 1990's, Gallant was rumored to be working on a novel as well as a nonfiction account of the nineteenth century Dreyfus affair, a historical incident in France involving the court-martial of a Jewish soldier, Alfred Dreyfus. This latter project once again reveals Gallant's interest in history as well as fiction.

Summary

Beginning her writing career as a journalist and essayist, Mavis Gallant found her literary voice to be well suited to the polished brevity of the short story form. As a Canadian writer best known for her observations of life in her native Montreal as well as in France, Gallant has excelled in creating portraits of various individuals— particularly girls and women—who are seeking to define themselves within a circum-scribed social landscape. Gallant's stories, with their historical reach and philosophi-cal depth, depict the fragile personal lives of believable individuals. She succeeds in creating fictional worlds that are recognizable and yet somehow remote and foreign in their stylistic detail. Many of her stories contain some of the most daring and impressive narrative gestures to be found in contemporary fiction. In Gallant's works, the narrative is not resolved with a single, magical "epiphany," as in many modern short stories; instead, the reader is left with an enigma in the story which he or she has to reflect upon, intellectually or emotionally, and then solve. As Gallant has said in one of her own essays, no life is more interesting than any other; what really matters is what is revealed and how.

Bibliography
Besner, Neil K. *The Light of Imagination: Mavis Gallant's Fiction.* Vancouver: University of British Columbia Press, 1988. In a comprehensive and insightful discussion, Besner surveys the entire Gallant canon in both formal and thematic terms. Perhaps the best introduction to Gallant criticism.
Hancock, Geoff. "Interview with Mavis Gallant." *Canadian Fiction*, no. 28 (1978): 18-67. This is the fullest of Gallant's many interviews, one that contains much that is relevant to research into her works. The entire issue is a good resource to explore early criticism of Gallant.
Keefer, Janice Kulyk. *Reading Mavis Gallant.* Toronto: Oxford University Press, 1989. Keefer is a contemporary Canadian novelist and critic, residing in the Maritime Provinces, who is herself a significant writer; thus her book is valuable for what it says about Keefer as well as its discussion of Gallant. Keefer superbly situates Gallant's explorations of emotion, psychology, and history.
Merler, Grazia. *Mavis Gallant: Narrative Patterns and Devices.* Ottawa: Tecumseh Press, 1978. This early study devotes most of its attention to the structural logic of Gallant's writing, stressing the patterns of formal organization that Gallant uses to communicate her narratives to the reader.
Smythe, Karen E. *Figuring Grief: Gallant, Munro, and the Poetics of Elegy.* Montreal: McGill & Queen's University Press, 1992. This book, written under the full influence of postmodern critical theory, especially the ideas of the influential Canadian critic Linda Hutcheon, examines the way short-story writers such as Gallant and her fellow Canadian Alice Munro are influenced by the high-poetic tradition of the elegy. Especially interesting is Smythe's treatment of the more deliberately complex late stories.

Nicholas Birns

GRETA GARBO

Born: September 18, 1905; Stockholm, Sweden
Died: April 15, 1990; New York, New York
Area of Achievement: Film
Contribution: A major star in early Hollywood, Garbo was able to exert economic, social, and symbolic influence in a way that no other film actress has. Garbo was one of the few performers to survive the transition from silent to sound films.

Early Life
Greta Lovisa Gustafsson (she changed her name to Garbo in 1923) was born on September 18, 1905, in Stockholm, Sweden. The poor south side of Stockholm was her home, and her youth was spent in poverty. Her father, Karl Alfred, was a laborer (according to some reports, a butcher), and her mother, Anna Lovisa, a house cleaner. Garbo's lifelong frugality may be related to the impoverished circumstances of her youth.

Greta was the youngest of three children; she had a sister Alva and a brother Sven. Although she was a good student, Greta's studies ended at the age of fourteen when her father became terminally ill. Working in a barber's shop as a lather girl provided her with money to supplement the family's income after her father's death in 1920. By July of 1920, she had found a better job as a shop clerk at Paul U. Bergstrom (known as PUB), a major Stockholm department store. Even at this early date, Garbo had ambitions toward a career in acting. PUB proved to be instrumental in furthering her goals.

Garbo's first job before the cameras was as a hat model for a PUB catalog. This led to work in filmed commercials for the store and then in 1922 to a theatrical film entitled *Luffar-Peter* (*Peter the Tramp*). Garbo quit her job as a shop clerk and concentrated on acting. Her theatrical career progressed rapidly with her acceptance into the Royal Dramatic Theatre Academy, the most highly respected drama school in Sweden. Before she could complete the two-year course, she had left the school to appear in *Gösta Berling's Saga* (1924), directed by Moritz Stiller (one of Europe's greatest directors). When Stiller became Greta's mentor, he convinced her to change her name to Garbo, a more theatrical name. *The Joyless Street* (1925), which was Garbo's last European film, was a critical and box-office disaster.

Stiller and Garbo caught the attention of Louis B. Mayer, the vice president of Metro-Goldwyn-Mayer (MGM) studios, and were offered contracts to work at MGM in the United States. Mayer was interested in obtaining Stiller as a director but showed little interest in Garbo; he said that she was too fat for an American audience. Stiller refused to come to the United States without Garbo, and thus MGM grudgingly acquired what was to be one of its brightest stars.

Life's Work
The United States did not greet Greta Garbo with open arms. Only one photogra-

pher met her and Stiller upon their arrival in New York. After two months, they were called to Hollywood and Garbo was put to work on her first American motion picture, *The Torrent* (1926), in which she shared the star billing with Ricardo Cortez, a popular actor of the time. The film was an immediate success, in part because of her aloof eroticism, and Garbo became a household name in the United States. Her second MGM film, *The Temptress* (1926), was a rehash of the first; she had already been typecast as a vamp (sexual vampire). Garbo quickly wearied of the role of "bad woman" and of Hollywood. It was at this time that her image as reclusive, distant, and uncommunicative began. Whether this was a brilliant marketing device, her true personality, or a combination of the two is impossible to determine, but her air of mystery, her role as the "Swedish Sphinx," and her unwillingness to give interviews became the centerpiece of her persona and added greatly to her mystique (and her box-office value).

After her third American film, *Flesh and the Devil* (1927), became a major financial and critical hit, Garbo went on strike for a higher salary and for more control over the roles she was to play. Her strike lasted for seven months and resulted in a pay raise from six hundred dollars a week to five thousand dollars a week. Within two years, Garbo had become a major power in Hollywood, one of the few who successfully bucked the studio system then in place.

Whereas Greta Garbo had become a star, her friend and former director, Moritz Stiller was unable to work in the American film industry. He returned to Sweden in 1928 and died shortly thereafter. Garbo made seven more silent films—*Love* (1927), *The Divine Woman* (1928), *Mysterious Lady* (1928), *A Woman of Affairs* (1929), *Wild Orchids* (1929), *The Single Standard* (1929), and *The Kiss* (1929)—and became one of the most popular female stars in Hollywood. She brought in large revenues from both American and European markets.

The transition to sound film was greatly feared by many silent-film actors, and Garbo's voice was eagerly anticipated. She maintained her on-screen silence for two years after sound came to Hollywood. Her first vocal vehicle was carefully chosen to use her Swedish accent to best effect. The film that introduced Garbo's voice to American audiences was Eugene O'Neill's *Anna Christie* (1930), a story about a young Swedish immigrant and her reunion with her father, who is unaware of her sordid past. The script was written to create the maximum suspense; Garbo does not appear until well into the picture, and then she stands without speaking for another minute. The advertising campaign for the film emphasized the novelty that "Garbo Talks!" and the English-speaking world listened. Her first spoken words on screen were "Gif me a Viskey. Ginger Ale on the side. . . . And don't be stingy, baby." A German-language version of *Anna Christie* was made to introduce the "voice heard 'round the world" to a non-English-speaking audience as well.

Garbo's conquest of sound films placed her firmly at the center of MGM's pantheon of stars but did nothing to change her public reclusiveness. To capitalize on her success, MGM gave her six films in the next two years: *Romance* (1930), *Inspiration* (1931), *Susan Lennox: Her Fall and Rise* (1931), *Mata Hari* (1931),

Grand Hotel (1932), and *As You Desire Me* (1932). It was in *Grand Hotel* that she uttered what was to become her defining phrase: "I vant to be alone."

As a result of her popularity, she was able to negotiate a contract that made her the highest-paid actress in Hollywood ($250,000 per film in 1933). She also demanded creative control over her films. The role of *Queen Christina* (1933) reflected many aspects of Garbo's persona: sexual ambiguity, solitude, and reclusiveness. The final shot of *Queen Christina* is one of the most powerful images of Garbo: She is gazing out to sea, her face completely blank, the audience writing its own story on her canvas.

Her next film, *The Painted Veil* (1934), was a financial and critical failure. Against the wishes of the studio, Garbo chose to star in yet another costume drama, *Anna Karenina* (1935). The film was a success. She received the New York Film Critics award for "best feminine performance" for *Anna Karenina* and another in 1937 for *Camille* (1936). The latter is considered to be her finest performance. After *Camille*, Garbo made only three more films. Europe was preparing for war, and the market for screen goddesses was changing. The failure in 1937 of *Conquest* was followed by a transformation of Garbo's screen persona with the release of *Ninotchka* (1939), her first comedy since *Luffar-Peter*. The picture was marketed with the slogan "Garbo Laughs" and was a commercial and critical success. In an attempt to recast Garbo as an "all-American" girl, *Two-Faced Woman* was released in 1941 to disastrous reviews and to almost universal condemnation and censorship for its apparent condoning of adultery.

With European markets closed by war and with the failure of *Two-Faced Woman*, Garbo parted from MGM and from filmmaking. In all, Garbo made twenty-five films (including the German version of *Anna Christie*) for MGM. According to critics, only a few of these were worthy vehicles for an actress of her caliber.

From 1941 to 1990, Greta Garbo stayed in retirement, living on the money she had invested. Although she never married, Garbo was romantically linked to a number of men and women throughout her life; her strong desire for privacy makes confirmation of any details of her personal life almost impossible. In 1951 she became an American citizen, and in 1954 she was awarded a special Academy Award "for a series of luminous performances." Although she was photographed from time to time as she walked the streets of her chosen home, New York City, her career before the public eye had ended.

On Easter Sunday in 1990, Greta Gardo died as secretively as she had lived. Her remains were cremated at an undisclosed location. The official cause of death was not released.

Summary

Greta Garbo's influence on American and European culture was enormous. One of the largest box-office draws of all time, her face and name were instantly recognizable throughout the Western world. Yet Garbo's celebrity was achieved without constant media hype, without press conferences and interviews; her fame derived, in great part, from her secrecy. She granted her only major interview in 1928.

In the 1930's, her on-screen hairstyles and clothing (the latter were designed by the Hollywood costumer Adrian) were copied by women around the world. Caricatures of her appeared in the cartoons; she was the central topic of a James Thurber story, "The Breaking Up of the Winships"; her salary was mentioned in the Cole Porter tune "You're the Top"; and her image was cast in plaster and sold to decorate mantels and pianos. More than fifty years after her retirement from motion pictures, her film revivals continued to command large audiences, and numerous books have been published exploring her film career and her image.

Garbo is considered to be one of the great actresses of the modern era, even though her films themselves are not always viewed as being exemplary. *Camille*, however, often appears on film critics' lists of the best films of all times.

Perhaps Garbo's greatest significance was as a major power player in Hollywood. Even in a male-dominated industry she was able to enforce her standards of filmmaking. She chose the roles she wanted to play, and she was able to demand a salary comparable to any actor, because her name alone was enough to ensure a film's profitability. Garbo commanded a level of respect and economic clout that no other actress could approach.

Bibliography
Affron, Charles. *Star Acting: Gish, Garbo, Davis.* New York: E. P. Dutton, 1977. An excellent overview of three important actresses from the early period of Hollywood. This work puts Garbo's acting ability and star power into perspective by comparing her with her contemporaries. This book focuses more on Garbo's craft as an actress and less on her role as a star.
Bainbridge, John. *Garbo.* Garden City, N.Y.: Doubleday, 1955. This is the best and most widely available biography of Garbo. There is some discussion of the early, pre-Hollywood period, but this work mainly documents her rise as a star, though focusing on her essential humanity. It has only a few illustrations.
Conway, Michael, Dion McGregor, and Mark Ricci. *The Films of Greta Garbo.* New York: Bonanza Books, 1963. A complete, fully illustrated discussion of all of Garbo's films. Stills from each film are accompanied by a synopsis of the script and representative reviews by contemporary critics. The opening essay by Parker Tyler is an excellent exploration of Garbo as icon.
Daum, Raymond W. *Walking with Garbo: Conversations and Recollections.* New York: HarperCollins, 1991. This most recent biography of Garbo includes some of her last recorded thoughts. This book is well illustrated and filled with personal asides by the author, a friend and confidant of Garbo's.
Gronowicz, Antoni. *Garbo.* New York: Simon & Schuster, 1990. This intimate account of Garbo by poet Gronowicz was withheld from publication until after her death. This provocative book attempts to address the questions of her early childhood, her sexual proclivities, and her reasons for leaving Hollywood. What liberties have been taken with reality cannot be determined, since both Gronowicz and Garbo are dead; however, the book is fascinating.

Walker, Alexander. *Garbo*. New York: Macmillan, 1980. A lavishly illustrated book filled with early (pre-Hollywood) photographs, stills from Garbo's films, advertisements, and post-Hollywood photos. This is the MGM-authorized version of Garbo's career; thus, it includes memos, contracts, and other documentation not available to earlier authors. The text is interesting, but the photographs are the major reason to choose this book.

Timothy J. McMillan

ISABELLA STEWART GARDNER

Born: April 14, 1840; New York, New York
Died: July 17, 1924; Boston, Massachusetts
Area of Achievement: Patronage of the arts
Contribution: Isabella Stewart Gardner, one of the greatest collectors of European art
of her day, built a fascinating museum to house her collections.

Early Life

Isabella Stewart was born in New York City on April 14, 1840, the oldest of the four
children of David and Adelia Smith Stewart. Her mother's ancestors were Puritan
colonists; her father, a wealthy coal mine owner, was descended from Mary, Queen of
Scots. Isabella, a high-spirited and rebellious girl, was educated privately and traditionally in her Manhattan home. She spent summers at the family farm on Long Island,
where she developed a taste for outdoor sports.

At sixteen, she entered a finishing school in Paris. There she met a Boston girl
whose brother, John Lowell Gardner, fell in love with her when she returned to
America. Gardner's family was not only wealthy but also socially prominent. Isabella
Stewart and John Gardner married at Grace Church (Episcopal) in New York on
April 10, 1860, and settled on Boston's Beacon Street in a house built for them by
David Stewart.

They were young, well connected, and rich. Nevertheless, things did not go well
for them. Isabella's health was not good, and she did not immediately fit into Boston
society. A child was born in 1863, but he died within two years; Isabella was told she
could have no more children. She became despondent and lapsed into depression.
European travel was prescribed for her. When in 1867 Isabella was carried up a ship's
gangway on a mattress, she did not know that she was embarking on her life's work.

Life's Work

In Europe, Isabella Gardner (known as "Mrs. Jack") emerged from her low spirits.
The Gardners sailed up the coast of Norway and then visited St. Petersburg, Vienna,
and Paris. Along the way, she began to develop a passion for art of all kinds. Some
scholars believe that this passion was born in Copenhagen when she viewed the
sculptures of Albert Bertel Thorwaldsen. The trip invigorated Isabella Gardner in
many different ways. When she returned in 1868, Boston society saw not a social
failure nor even a budding art patron, but a forceful and adventurous member of the
best society. She was not conventionally beautiful. Her face could be called plain. Yet
her figure was perfect and full; her manners were vivacious and alluring. Her dress
was daring, her jewels (especially her strings of pearls) were dazzling, her dancing
was graceful, her parties were famous, and her behavior was flamboyant, eccentric,
and even reckless. Her flirtations and possible love affairs inspired gossip, envy, and
outrage, but she was too wealthy and powerful to be ignored. (Whether any of her
protégés or admirers became her lovers is still unknown.)

Gardner did not let society cut her off from other interests. She helped raise three orphaned nephews. She did church work (she was a high-church Episcopalian). She liked football, baseball (she was a Red Sox fan), and prize fights; she conversed with the boxer John L. Sullivan. Later in life, she frequented the Boston Zoo and liked to play with the lions. Her husband, far from disapproving of his wife's activities, enjoyed them and encouraged her.

Her flamoyant and charming social exterior was captured beautifully by Anders Zorn's painting *Mrs. Gardner in Venice* (1896). She is depicted bursting from a balcony into a room of her palazzo, telling everyone to come and watch the fireworks. More of her sensual appeal, as well as her friendly charm, can be gathered from John Singer Sargent's full-length portrait (1888), which outlines her figure, mutes her facial features, and shows some of her famous pearls around her waist. The reception of this portrait was so sensational that John Gardner had it removed from the show, and it was never exhibited in his lifetime.

Both Zorn and Sargent became Isabella Gardner's friends. In her Boston home (and in her Venetian palazzo), she entertained writers and intellectuals such as historian Henry Adams, poet James Russell Lowell, author and philanthropist Julia Ward Howe, physician and author Oliver Wendell Holmes, Irish author Lady Augusta Gregory, and the James brothers, William the psychologist and Henry the author. Henry James, who could discern Gardner's essential innocence, became a particularly close friend, and she had a serious flirtation with novelist F. Marion Crawford. Musicians such as pianist Ignace Jan Paderewski and singer Madame Nellie Melba visited and performed in her salon. Even the Boston Symphony presented concerts there. Charles Eliot Norton of Harvard preached there the wonders of Italian culture. Isabella Gardner also joined the Dante Society and began collecting rare books. The highlight of the Gardners' trip around the world in 1883 was a visit to the ruins of Angkor Wat, then newly discovered in Cambodia. As a result of this trip, they began to collect oriental art.

It was studying and collecting works of European art, however, that more and more captured Gardner's attention. She knew great galleries from her schoolgirl days, and in the 1880's she studied paintings in Munich, Vienna, Venice, and Florence, and bought works from the American artist James McNeill Whistler.

In 1891, her father died. Her substantial inheritance enabled her to translate her educated tastes into action. Under the guidance of the young Harvard graduate Bernard Berenson, she began to collect in earnest, principally paintings by Old Masters. Her life during the 1890's was one of searching and bargaining for works for her collection. She bought old chairs, tapestries, Persian rugs, terra-cotta reliefs, carved chests, and altar pieces. She bought, usually with Berenson's help, Jan Vermeer's *Le Concert*, Whistler's *Harmony in Blue and Silver*, Sandro Botticelli's *The Death of Lucretia*, Guardi's *View of Venice*, Rembrandt's self-portrait as a young man, a bust by Benevenuto Cellini, Titian's *Rape of Europa*, Diego Velázquez's portrait of Philip IV, and portraits by Raphael and Peter Paul Rubens.

She entered into the second stage of her life's work when these works threatened to overwhelm the Beacon Street house. As early as 1896, the Gardners began to plan to locate a museum in the outskirts of Boston on a recently drained swamp. In Europe in 1897, they bought architectural items to incorporate into that building: columns, balconies, capitols, frescoes, mirrors, and a mosaic pavement. When John Gardner died in 1898, his widow, though temporarily in seclusion, hardly broke stride. She bought more works: Paolo Veronese's ceiling painting *Psyche Received into Olympus*, Hans Holbein and Albrecht Dürer portraits, Fra Angelico's *Death and the Assumption of the Virgin*, Botticelli's *The Madonna and Child of the Eucharist*, a panel by Giotto, and a Raphael pietà.

She bought the swampland in the Fenway region of Boston and then, as secretly as possible, began to build Fenway Court (the museum's official name). She supervised the construction in every intricate detail; though she may have driven her architects and workmen to despair, the result was spectacular: a Venetian palace, modeled in particular on the Palazzo Bardini and on the Palazzo Barbero, where Zorn had painted her. On the museum's official seal was Isabella Gardner's personal motto: *C'est mon plaisir* (it is my pleasure).

The Isabella Stewart Gardner Museum in the Fenway was opened by invitation on January 1, 1903. Guests were welcomed at the top of the main staircase by Gardner, dressed in black and wearing two large diamonds mounted on springs so that they waved about her head like antennae. Only after a concert in the music room were the guests permitted to enter the rest of the building, a four-sided courtyard lit by candles and torches and topped by a glass roof. The floor of the courtyard was the Roman mosaic; on it rested fragments of sculpture from the ancient world; banks of flowers were everywhere. What amazed her guests even more were the rooms that surrounded the courtyard, rooms filled with the Gardner collections in arrangements designed by Gardner herself: the Raphael Room, the Dutch Room, the Titian Room, the Gothic Room.

From that time on, Gardner lived comparatively modestly in private quarters on the fourth floor of the museum, though in the museum itself she hosted many suppers, luncheons, dances, and concerts. The public was allowed in four weeks a year. She continued to buy works of art, though at a reduced pace: Piero della Francesca's *Hercules*, a madonna and child by Giovanni Bellini, and portraits by Velázquez, Édouard Manet, and Edgar Degas. She added a Spanish Cloister in 1916 to house Sargent's large painting *El Jaleo*. She even learned to drive an automobile.

Gardner was slowed but not stopped by a paralytic stroke in 1919. Sergent's affectionate watercolor of 1922, which shows her swathed in white with only her gaunt face showing, does not give adequate testimony to the energy she continued to feel. She died in July, 1924, and willed that Fenway Court be open to the public, with the proviso that its contents must remain intact and be displayed substantially as she arranged them.

Summary

As an energetic, attractive, and even reckless woman with money and high social status, Isabella Stewart Gardner shocked and fascinated the Boston aristocracy. She represented on a grand scale the new kinds of social freedom that some American women were achieving after the Civil War. She also embodied new American attitudes toward Europe; she was able to collect European works of art and craftsmanship and bring them to a new home in America. She was like a Henry James heroine in her enthusiastic embrace of Europe; she was unlike James's heroines in that, rather than being corrupted by the old world, she triumphed. Perhaps a fitting symbol of her greatness is Mount Gardner in Washington state, which was named for her.

Her lasting influence on Boston and on American culture is the result of her collections and the building she built to house them. Both display a personal taste that, though extravagant and eclectic, was educated and imaginative. Gardner was able to discern (and often acquire) art objects of the highest quality. The critic Aline Saarinen believes that she and Bernard Berenson estabilshed the contemporary taste for American collections of Italian art. Meanwhile, Fenway Court, the exquisite embodiment of her dreams, is a repository of priceless European art, one of the greatest collections in the United States.

Bibliography

Berenson, Bernard. *The Letters of Bernard Berenson and Isabella Stewart Gardner, 1887-1924, with Correspondence by Mary Berenson,* edited by Rollin Van N. Hadley. Boston: Northeastern University Press, 1987. Bernard Berenson, eminent art authority, and Isabella Gardner exchanged hundreds of letters between 1887 and her death. The letters reflect their friendship and give a blow-by-blow account of their struggles in putting together the Gardner collection. Illustrated.

Brooks, Van Wyck. *New England: Indian Summer, 1865-1915.* New York: E. P. Dutton, 1940. This famous work of literary history gives a superficial and largely unfavorable view of Mrs. Gardner's activities.

Carter, Morris. *Isabella Stewart Gardner and Fenway Court.* Boston: Houghton Mifflin, 1925. An authoritative, sympathetic, and detailed first biography, full of Gardner's correspondence, written by a man who worked for Gardner in her last years. Many illustrations, mainly early photographs.

Edel, Leon. *Henry James.* 3 vols. New York: J. B. Lippincott, 1953-1972. Many scattered references show James's affection for Mrs. Gardner, his paradoxical judgments of her, and how her life echoed his major themes. Edel thinks Henry James draws upon Gardner and upon Palazzo Barbaro for details in *The Wings of the Dove.*

Hardy, Philip. *European and American Paintings in the Isabella Stewart Gardner Museum.* Boston: Trustees of the Isabella Stewart Gardner Museum, 1974. This illustrated catalog is useful in demonstrating Gardner's taste and achievements as a collector. Contains reproductions of the Sargent and Zorn portraits.

Saarinen, Aline B. *The Proud Possessors: The Lives, Times, and Tastes of Some Adventurous American Art Collectors.* New York: Random House, 1958. The informative chapter on Gardner is the best short introduction of her life and achievements. The book places her in the context of other great American collectors.

Tharp, Louise Hall. *Mrs. Jack: A Biography of Isabella Stewart Gardner*. Boston: Little, Brown, 1965. Well researched and readable. Tharp gives much more background information than Carter does on the Gardner family and on many intimate aspects of Isabella Gardner's life: the Boston gossip about her, her jewelry, and her friendships.

George Soule

JUDY GARLAND

Born: June 10, 1922; Grand Rapids, Minnesota
Died: June 22, 1969; London, England
Areas of Achievement: Film and music
Contribution: An entertainer with a magnificent voice that attracted a worldwide audience, Judy Garland appeared in films, on television, and in concert. She is remembered for her powerful singing and dramatic flair.

Early Life

Judy Garland's father and mother, Frank and Ethel Gumm, had worked in vaudeville but, after having two daughters, settled down and leased the motion picture theater in Grand Rapids, Minnesota. In the era of silent films, organists provided music to accompany the action. For this reason, when sound became available for films, theaters continued to provide entertainment for audiences in the intermission between films. The Gumms entertained their audiences with Ethel's piano playing and their daughters' singing.

Judy, born two weeks overdue on June 10, 1922, was named Frances Gumm. Though her parents would have preferred a son, Judy's childhood was reasonably happy, and she was pampered. When she was two and a half, Judy made her stage debut at her father's theater, and soon the parents had created an act for the three Gumm sisters. In 1926, they moved to California, leasing a theater in Lancaster, north of Los Angeles on the edge of the Mojave Desert.

Ethel had great ambition for her children and devoted much attention to her daughters' careers. She gave them dance and music lessons. In 1927, she enrolled them in a dance school in Los Angeles that had been a springboard for many stars. Judy liked the school, but her older sisters soon dropped out.

The Gumm sisters, now named the Garland sisters, still performed as an act together, and word began to spread (even in the press) about the child with the incredible voice. Ethel took Judy for auditions, and Judy sang for Joseph Mankiewicz, for Ida Koverman, who worked for Louis B. Mayer (the head of Metro-Goldwyn-Mayer, or MGM), and eventually for Mayer himself, who signed her without a screen test in September, 1935, when she was thirteen.

Life's Work

MGM needed to produce fifty-two films each year to fill the theaters it controlled (the Loew's theater chain). Some three thousand people worked to produce these films, and the company operated much like an efficient factory. Developing stars was an important task, for stars would attract audiences to the films. MGM became, therefore, one of the most extraordinary finishing schools in the world. As it did for all of its young stars, the company provided for Judy Garland's education, even building a small classroom near the set when she was working on a film. She had a voice coach, was given dance lessons, diction lessons, drama lessons, makeup lessons, and deportment lessons, and had a physical therapist and specialists to help her lose weight.

Garland was short and plump, with scoliosis (a slight curvature of the spine, which ran in her mother's family). Her teeth were crooked and her nose was a problem. (She had to wear removable caps on her teeth and rubber discs in her nose on screen.) She also had constantly to fight excessive weight. Garland was humiliated by all these judgments and by comparison with her peers. She soon came to believe that she was not physically attractive nor sexually desirable to men and that she was inferior to the other teenagers there (who included Lana Turner, Elizabeth Taylor, and Hedy Lamarr). Ethel Gumm would remind Garland that she was signed for her voice. Garland's voice coach, Roger Edens, developed her skills as a singer, and her mother, now devoting herself entirely to Garland's career, came to the studio every day to rehearse and accompany her.

Garland's first two small roles were in *Every Sunday* (1936) and *Pigskin Parade* (1936). Her first major film role was in *Broadway Melody of 1938* (1937), and for this motion picture the studio began giving Garland benzedrine and phenobarbital to help her lose weight and to sleep at nights. These were new wonder drugs for the film colony in California, and no one was aware of their addictive potential. For Garland, using them for *Broadway Melody* began her lifelong dependence on drugs.

Broadway Melody was released in the fall of 1937, and the reviews of Garland's performance were enthusiastic. After making several more films, usually with Garland cast as the girl who never gets the man she loves, MGM decided to build a film vehicle especially for Garland, *The Wizard of Oz* (1939). Work on *The Wizard of Oz* began in mid-1939, the film was released in August, and in the spring of 1940 Judy Garland received a special Oscar for best juvenile performance. Later that year, Louis Mayer gave her an eighteenth birthday party at his house and raised her salary from $750 to $3,000 a week.

In this early period, Garland appeared in several films with the young Mickey Rooney, and the pairing was so popular that a part for Garland was written into the Andy Hardy films, in which the title character was played by Mickey Rooney. *Babes in Arms* (1939), starring the two of them, cost $600,000 to make and grossed more than $2 million in the United States alone.

Judy Garland married David Rose, the leader of an orchestra, in July, 1941, but they separated in 1943 and divorced in 1944. She married the film director Vincente Minnelli in 1945, and a daughter, Liza Minnelli, was born to the couple in 1946. Minnelli directed several successful films starring Garland, including *Meet Me in St. Louis* (1944), *The Clock* (1945), *Ziegfeld Follies of 1946* (1946), and *The Pirate* (1948). This marriage ended in 1950, and the divorce became final in 1952.

Garland married Sidney Luft in June, 1952, already pregnant with Lorna, who was born in November, 1952. (A son, Joey, was born in 1955.) Sid devoted himself to Garland, abandoning his career in order to manage hers. They separated in 1958 and began a seven-year period of fights, reconciliations, and separations. There were two brief marriages with younger men, Mark Herron and Mickey Deans; the latter marriage ended with Judy Garland's death in 1969.

In 1942, Garland appeared in her first film with dancer Gene Kelly, *For Me and My Girl* (1942), which introduced Kelly to the screen. In this film, and in later films with Fred Astaire, Garland's talent as a dancer was showcased. In perhaps the best of these, *Easter Parade* (1948), with music by Irving Berlin, Judy Garland ably complemented Astaire.

By the time she was twenty-two, Garland had been in nineteen films. From 1943 through 1945, she was voted one of the five most popular screen actresses in the United States. Garland's drug and emotional problems, however, began to interfere with her work. She was usually late to work, if she arrived at all, and was temperamental. MGM paid a psychiatrist to be with her on the set in 1947. MGM suspended her frequently and fired her from three films (including *Annie Get Your Gun*). In September of 1950, MGM canceled her contract, almost fifteen years to the day after they signed her.

It was four years before she appeared in another film. The first was *A Star Is Born* (1954), made by an independent company and released by Warner Bros., which critics hailed as a triumphant comeback for Garland at the age of thirty-two. The film has an eighteen-minute sequence, "Born in a Trunk," which traces the success story of a vaudeville star, and features "The Man That Got Away," which became one of Judy's trademark songs. In *Judgment at Nuremberg* (1961), Garland played a small but key dramatic role and earned an Oscar nomination for Best Supporting Actress. *A Child Is Waiting* (1963), which featured another fine dramatic performance, was followed by Garland's last film, *I Could Go on Singing* (1963), a film about a concert singer tormented by personal problems.

Judy Garland had little ability to handle her financial affairs. Despite advice from her mother and financial experts, she was continually in debt. After her divorce from Vincente Minnelli and her firing from MGM, she and Minnelli owed $60,000 in back taxes and thousands more to friends. In 1966, her assets were listed as $12,000 and her liabilities to 120 creditors as $122,000.

The result was that she had to work in order to pay her bills. With the film studios reluctant to hire her, Garland moved to the nightclub and cabaret circuit and appeared in concerts and on television shows. Her first concert was in 1943 in Philadelphia, and she toured for the USO. In 1951, she had successful runs at the London Palladium, the leading theater in London, England, and at the Palace in New York City. Her finest performance was at Carnegie Hall in 1961, a concert that was recorded and released as an album. Her drug addiction and increasing psychological disturbance, however, led her to cancel performances and walk out on contracts, so that often she could not even cover the expenses of her current tour. Though some of her concerts were outstanding, during others she collapsed on stage or was booed.

Judy Garland first appeared on television in 1955 in *The Ford Star Jubilee*, a spectacular sponsored by the Ford Motor Company. CBS began a one-hour musical-variety series, *The Judy Garland Show*, in 1963. The show had to compete against NBC's very popular *Bonanza*, but it ran for twenty-six shows before it was canceled.

Garland was addicted to amphetamines and barbiturates and also abused alcohol. She had frequent stays in hospital and sanatoriums, often to dry out after a physical or psychological collapse, and eventually she developed kidney and liver problems. She suffered from depression, and she made frequent attempts at suicide. On June 22, 1969, her husband found her in the bathroom, dead from an overdose at the age of forty-seven. Some people believe that the overdose was accidental; others, that her death was suicide.

Summary
Despite her psychological problems, Judy Garland is remembered for her film performances (as a child in *The Wizard of Oz* and as an adult in *A Star Is Born*) and for her concert performances. Her singing was magnificent, and her later film work showed that she was also capable of fine dramatic performances. She was successful in films, in concerts, and on television. She blended her personal problems into her performances, so that a few of her films seemed autobiographical, and her admiring audiences longed for her next comeback. If Garland could recover, maybe they could too. Her recording of "Somewhere over the Rainbow," made late in her life, in the midst of which she breaks down crying, became a classic as soon as it was released, perhaps because it expressed what everyone feels at times.

Her daughter, Liza Minnelli, has pursued a career similar to her mother's, appearing in films and on the stage.

Bibliography
DiOrio, Al. *Little Girl Lost*. New Rochelle, N.Y.: Arlington House, 1974. This biography of Judy Garland is similar to several others but also has a complete listing of every record, television show, and film she made, noting the songs she sang on each occasion.

Frank, Gerold. *Judy*. New York: Harper & Row, 1975. This biography provides a thorough examination of Judy Garland's life, giving details of her many illnesses and psychological problems. It does not attempt to evaluate her career in film and entertainment.

Meyer, John. *Heartbreaker*. Garden City, N.Y.: Doubleday, 1983. John Meyer, a songwriter, was in a relationship with Judy Garland from October 18, 1968, to January 31, 1969, at which point he lost her to her soon-to-be fourth husband, Mickey Deans. Meyer gives a detailed account of his life with Judy, complete with re-created conversations.

Morella, Joe, and Edward Z. Epstein. *Judy: The Films and Career of Judy Garland*. New York: Citadel Press, 1969. This is a scrapbook detailing Judy Garland's career, with a listing of the films in which she appeared, photographs of her in different roles, extracts from reviews of her work, and comments by friends and colleagues.

Spada, James. *Judy and Liza*. Garden City, N.Y.: Doubleday, 1983. This biography focuses on the relationship between Judy Garland and her daughter, Liza Minnelli. The quality of the relationship between mother and daughter is documented from

Judy's pregnancy through to Liza's adolescence and the growing emergence of Liza as a star in her own right. The book ends with the development of Liza Minnelli's career after the death of her mother.

Torme, Mel. *The Other Side of the Rainbow: With Judy Garland on the Dawn Patrol.* New York: William Morrow, 1970. This is a personal account of Mel Torme's experiences with Judy Garland. He first met her in 1943, and he worked with her in 1963 and 1964 as a writer of special musical material and adviser for the CBS television program *The Judy Garland Show.*

David Lester

ERNA GIBBS

Born: March 5, 1904; Bad Homburg, Germany
Died: July 23, 1987; Chicago, Illinois
Area of Achievement: Medicine
Contribution: Erna Gibbs, with her husband, Frederic A. Gibbs, played key roles in the use of the electroencephalograph (EEG) as a diagnostic tool. Their application of the EEG was instrumental in understanding the cause of epilepsy.

Early Life
Erna Leonhardt was born March 5, 1904, in Germany, the seventh of eight children. Erna's parents, Jean Emil Leonhardt and Ida Schneider Leonhardt, had invested wisely in a number of industries, enabling their children to receive excellent private school educations. As part of their studies, Erna and her siblings became fluent in several languages, including English.

After Germany's defeat in World War I and the subsequent hyperinflation that followed, the Leonhardt family entered a period of financial difficulties. Hoping to ease the financial burden on her family, and looking forward to the adventure of traveling to another country, Erna emigrated to the United States in 1927. After Erna's arrival in the United States, a friend pointed out a "want ad" placed in a newspaper by Dr. William Lennox, a member of the Harvard Medical School faculty and founder of the American Epilepsy League. Erna applied for the position and was hired as a research assistant by Lennox.

Though Erna Leonhardt had no formal science training, she had a quick, astute mind and soon mastered the tasks assigned to her by Lennox. At one point she considered applying to the medical school, even enrolling in some courses. As the only woman in the class, however, she was generally ignored or at best given rudimentary help and attention. Discouraged by such treatment, Erna gave up on the idea of a medical career.

Working with Lennox, Erna quickly developed into an excellent technician. She became particularly adept at blood work, including analysis of blood sugar and gases. She also developed a friendship with a neuropathologist at the medical school named Frederic A. Gibbs. She and Gibbs would marry on December 16, 1930, forming an inseparable team until her death.

Erna Leonhardt and Frederic Gibbs remained at Harvard until 1930, he as an assistant neuropathologist, and she as a research assistant with a joint appointment at Boston City Hospital. Working with both Lennox and Gibbs at Harvard, Leonhardt continued her blood analysis; she and Gibbs soon established themselves in the field as the first researchers to demonstrate that nourishment for the brain is entirely dependent on the glucose carried within the bloodstream.

Following their marriage in 1930, the Gibbses moved to the University of Pennsylvania. It was here, through the Johnson Foundation for Medical Physics, that they began their groundbreaking work in the study of epilepsy.

Life's Work

Erna and Frederic Gibbs were to spend two years at the University of Pennsylvania, and it was during this period that they firmly established themselves as experts in the study of epilepsy. To do so, it was necessary to establish a correct pathological basis for the illness. Prior to the 1920's, the cause of epilepsy was believed associated with interruptions of blood flow to the brain. Indeed, it was well known that seizures could be stimulated in animals through shutting off of the blood supply; similar "spasms" were thus suggested to result in epileptic seizures in humans. Nevertheless, several experiments carried out by Erna and Frederic Gibbs failed to support the prevailing theory. For one thing, they were unable to observe any difference in oxygenation levels within the blood either before or after seizures. What finally put the blood flow theory to rest were the measurements of actual blood flow carried out by the Gibbses. Taking advantage of her clinical experience, Erna inserted a flow meter into the carotid artery of epileptic patients and measured the rate of blood flow during epileptic seizures. Although this eventually became a commonplace procedure, it was rarely attempted during the 1930's. Erna Gibbs observed that the rate of blood flow showed no relationship with formation of seizures, effectively demonstrating the outmoded nature of the former theory. In 1938, she and her husband received the Mead Johnson Award for their studies on blood flow.

The question still remained as to what actually was occurring during epileptic seizures. It was here that the Gibbses effectively applied the methodology of the electroencephalograph (EEG), much of their work being carried out following their return to the Harvard Medical School in 1931.

The first evidence for electrical activity occurring in the brain was discovered in 1874, when R. Caton in England first measured electrical changes in the brains of rabbits. Similar studies were applied in the ensuing years to other animals, but no correlation with pathological activity was suspected, other than the observation that sensory stimuli would result in changes in the electrical patterns.

Psychiatrist Hans Berger in Germany carried out the first successful recordings of electrical activity in the human brain in 1924 and published his work in 1929. Berger was able to demonstrate that the human brain has an electrical "beat" associated with the neurons, or nerve cells. This "beat" was characterized by a specific rhythm, characterized by fluctuations in the frequencies of waves, and the voltages associated with those waves. The slower waves he called alpha waves and the faster waves he designated beta waves. Berger called these patterns, in German, the elektrenkephalogramm; this term was translated into English as electroencephalogram.

As a psychiatrist, Berger published much of his work in psychiatric journals. As a result, the significance of his discovery was overlooked by many in the neurological field. Erna and Frederic Gibbs, however, recognized the potential application of Berger's observations to their own work. Following a visit with Berger, they began applying EEG technology to their studies of epilepsy.

The first steps required an improvement in the sensitivity of the instruments used to measure brain waves. Berger had produced his EEG by attaching electrodes to the skulls of his subjects, connecting the leads to a modified radio receiver powered by vacuum tubes. In this manner, he had improved the sensitivity of the procedure by a factor of a million. Even so, measurement of minute changes in brain activity was at times still beyond the abilities of the instrumentation available to the Gibbses. Fortuitously, Albert Grass at the Massachusetts Institute of Technology (MIT) had been developing amplifiers and feedback circuits for his own studies of earthquakes—work that led to the creation of the Grass Instrument Company. Grass and the Gibbses developed a collaborative relationship that led to the design of a homemade device effective at recording brain wave patterns with sufficient sensitivity. With some modifications, the resulting instrumentation continued to be used as the standard device for measuring brain waves well into the 1970's.

The Gibbses remained at Harvard from 1931 to 1944, founding, in 1934, the first American laboratory in clinical electroencephalography. In 1944, they joined the faculty at the University of Illinois School of Medicine, Erna as a research assistant, and Frederic as associate professor. During their years at Harvard, and later in Illinois, they perfected their analysis of brain wave patterns, correlating patterns of change with specific pathological conditions. Much of their work involved the study of epilepsy, but their studies also extended into other areas of brain neuropathies: injuries, blood sugar levels, strokes, and even sleep patterns.

It was Erna who carried out most of the EEG analysis. During the course of her career, she read more than 100,000 brain wave recordings, exhibiting an unusual ability to recognize patterns quickly and to correlate such patterns with the patient's history. It was said she could observe the folded paper that contained the recording and easily establish a diagnosis. (Recordings from the pen could be seen in the folds; the size of the marks were indicative of the type of electrical activity.) During these years, it was she who classified patterns, gathered statistics, and even began the use of punch cards for early computers. Their work resulted in the 1941 publication of the *Atlas of Electroencephalography*, which eventually comprised four volumes. Among the methodologies that Erna and Frederic developed was a procedure to predict an epileptic seizure in certain patients twenty-four hours in advance.

Though much of the intuitive analysis of the work was Erna's, she was one member of a team during these years. She and Frederic together authored hundreds of books and articles. They had a large number of dedicated technicians to help them. Their numerous awards, even when presented to an individual, were clearly recognizing the work carried out by many individuals.

In 1944, Erna and Frederic Gibbs established the Epilepsy Clinic at the University of Illinois School of Medicine, in addition to the independent Gibbs Laboratories. Their independent laboratory was responsible for establishing nearly all the recognized standards in the monitoring of drug levels of epileptics.

After a long career, Erna Gibbs died at her home in suburban Chicago in 1987.

Summary

The work of Erna Gibbs and her husband contributed much of the scientific knowledge associated with use of the electroencephalogram and its application to the understanding of brain waves. There is no question that development and use of the EEG as an effective physiological tool was directly a result of her analysis. Through her recordings and studies of brain wave patterns, Erna Gibbs was able to classify a variety of pathologies, including several forms of epileptic seizures. Indeed, it was she who first recorded such a seizure in 1933. In an attempt to extend this work to the medical community at large, Gibbs devoted much of her time to training the scientific community in analysis and application of these electrical recordings.

The *Atlas of Electroencephalography*, the first edition of which was published in 1941, served as a pioneer work in the field of electroencephalography. In addition to its usefulness as a single reference for analysis of brain wave activity associated with epilepsy, the *Atlas* also cataloged the electrical activity associated with other states, from low blood sugar to strokes. The correlation of these activities with gross cerebral lesions continues to serve as an important diagnostic tool. The atlas served as the standard in the field for decades and continued through multiple editions to be a vital reference.

The foundations and societies with which Erna and Frederic Gibbs were associated continued their work. Within this list may be found the American EEG Society and the Brain Research Foundation at the University of Chicago, which supports the Brain Research Institute. The Epilepsy Clinic at the University of Illinois School of Medicine is also a monument to the Gibbses' work. Their involvement with these societies could be personal, as well as professional, as evidenced by their willingness one year to allow their home to serve as the packaging site for 70,000 boxes of Halloween candy to be used in raising funds for research into brain disorders.

Bibliography

Brazier, Mary. *The Electrical Activity of the Nervous System.* 2d ed. New York: Macmillan, 1960. A detailed text on nerve impulses and the nervous system. However, several chapters provide a history of development and use of the EEG. Particularly useful are highlights of the work of Hans Berger.

Gibbs, Frederic A., and Erna L. Gibbs. *Atlas of Electroencephalography.* Cambridge, Mass.: L. A. Cummings, 1941. The first edition of what would become a classic work in the field. While much of the work is clinical (though of interest to those who wish to observe sample EEGs), the initial chapters provide a good history of the subject.

——————— . *Medical Electroencephalography.* Reading, Mass.: Addison-Wesley, 1967. A book designed for physicians, the text contains numerous examples of EEGs and their correlation with brain disorders. However, the introduction contains a good description of how the EEG is used in clinical practice.

Glaser, Gilbert. *EEG and Behavior.* New York: Basic Books, 1963. An exploration of the relationship between EEG patterns and normal or abnormal behaviors. Though the clinical aspects of the book are somewhat dated, its descriptions of the basis for EEG activity provide a good general review of the subject. The book also provides

historical material on the subject in the introductory sections for each chapter.
Heise, Kenan. "Erna Gibbs; Developed Brain Scan." *Chicago Tribune*, July 31, 1987,
p. C11. In the absence of a full-scale biography on Gibbs, this obituary provides
one of the few sources of information regarding her life. Gives a concise assessment
of her career and achievements.

Richard Adler

ALTHEA GIBSON

Born: August 25, 1927; Silver, South Carolina

Area of Achievement: Sports
Contribution: The first African American to win a Wimbledon singles title, Althea
Gibson was an important figure in establishing blacks as equal competitors at the
highest levels of the tennis world. She overcame the prejudice of the tennis world
at a time when racial barriers in the sport still operated. She should be remembered
as one of the stellar performers in the history of women's tennis.

Early Life
Althea Gibson was born on August 25, 1927, in Silver, South Carolina, the eldest
of the five children of Daniel Gibson and Anna Washington Gibson. Her parents
worked in the South Carolina cotton fields; their families were sharecroppers and poor
farmers. When Althea was three, her parents moved to New York City, and she grew
up in Harlem during the 1930's. She was a rebellious child who was often absent from
school. Her relationship with her father was stormy, and his treatment of her verged
on physical abuse at times. She learned to defend herself in the dangerous world of
the streets and honed the skills of courage and self-reliance that would carry her to the
top of women's tennis.

Her athletic career began on the paddle tennis courts of a Police Athletic League
"play street" near her home. As she learned tennis on regular courts, she competed in
local tournaments in the New York area. After she won the American Tennis Association girl singles crown in 1944 and 1945, and was runner-up for the women's title in
1946, she moved to North Carolina with the family of R. W. Johnson. There she
attended high school and practiced her game. In 1948, she won the national American
Tennis Association's women's title. She won the championship of this African American tennis association for the following nine years.

Life's Work
Althea Gibson entered Florida A & M University in 1949 on a tennis scholarship.
Meanwhile, she pursued her tournament career. She played well in the National
Indoor Tennis Championships in 1949, and she won the Eastern Indoor championship
of the U.S. Lawn Tennis Association (USLTA) in March of 1950. Nevertheless, she
faced an informal racial barrier because of the unwillingness of the USLTA to invite
a black player to participate in the U.S. Open at Forest Hills. The USLTA used the
excuse that Althea had not played in enough tournaments to prove herself.

A former women's champion, Alice Marble, provided a decisive boost to Gibson's
career at this key moment. In a hard-hitting editorial for *American Lawn Tennis*
magazine, Marble urged that Gibson be given a chance to prove herself in genuine
competition. "If Althea Gibson represents a challenge to the present crop of women's
players, it is only fair that they should meet that challenge on the courts, where tennis

is played." The USLTA relented, and Gibson was invited to the U.S. Open in August of 1950, the first African American to participate in the tournament. Her debut was a memorable one. In her second-round match, she was ahead of the noted player Louise Brough in the third set when rain stopped play. She was on the verge of upsetting a Wimbledon and U.S. Open champion. The night's interval and a tense press conference after the match was suspended worked against Gibson's concentration. The next day Brough came back to beat Gibson, 6-1, 3-6, 9-7. Despite the setback, Althea Gibson had proved that she could play at the highest level of tennis.

For the next six years, however, Gibson did not live up to the expectations that her first appearance at the U.S. Open created. She played at Wimbledon in June of 1951, the first African American to do so, but lost in the quarter-finals. She rose to a ranking of ninth in the United States in 1952 and moved up to seventh a year later. She then fell back to thirteenth in 1954. In the meantime, to support herself in an era when tennis was still ostensibly an amateur sport, she taught in the physical education department at Lincoln University in Missouri during 1954 and 1955. By now, she had given serious thought to retiring from tennis and pursuing a military career.

Althea Gibson then received an offer to be one of the American tennis players on a goodwill tour of Asia for the State Department in late 1955. Playing tennis on such a sustained basis revitalized Gibson's game, and she found that her talents were still sharp. She went on a run of victories that impressed the tennis world. In 1956, she won sixteen of the eighteen tournaments she entered before Wimbledon, including the Asiatic women's singles crown, the Indian national title, and the French indoor doubles championship with Angela Buxton. Gibson won her first Grand Slam tournament, the French Open, on the red clay of Roland Garros Stadium over Angela Morton, 6-0, 12-10. Her streak of singles victories came to an end when Shirley Fry beat her in the quarter-finals at Wimbledon. The British crowds rooted against her, and their journalists denounced the evident display of racial intolerance that so unnerved Gibson. Nevertheless, she won the doubles title, again teaming with Angela Buxton.

Althea Gibson continued her strong play throughout the remainder of 1956. She won several grass court singles titles, and reached the finals of the U.S. Open in September. She lost to Shirley Fry, 6-3, 6-4, in a match in which she did not play her best. The tennis circuit then led her to Australia, where she teamed with Shirley Fry to win the doubles crown at the Australian Open. Unfortunately, she lost to Fry in the singles of the tournament several days later.

The rest of 1957 saw Althea Gibson reach the top of the world of women's tennis. Shirley Fry had retired, and Gibson sensed that she could defeat the other players that she faced. She won several warm-up tournaments for Wimbledon and came into the fortnight's competition as the odds-on favorite. She reached the finals and played against Darlene Hard. The match was played in 96-degree heat. Gibson's serve worked well, and she was in command from the early points. When her 6-3, 6-2 victory was secured, she exclaimed, "At last, at last." Queen Elizabeth II presented Althea Gibson with the trophy. Gibson also won the doubles championship with Darlene Hard.

When Althea Gibson returned to the United States, she received a ticker-tape parade in New York City. It was, she said, the greatest honor she had ever received. She capped her championship year with a victory at the U.S. Open over Louise Brough, 6-3, 6-2. Vice President Richard Nixon presented her with the trophy, and the crowd gave her a sustained round of applause.

The following year brought more victories for Gibson. She took the Wimbledon crown for the second time. She won over Angela Mortimer of Great Britain, 8-6, 6-2. Gibson went on to win the U.S. Open again with a three-set victory over Darlene Hard, 3-6, 6-1, 6-2. She then announced that she was retiring from amateur tennis. The trophies were nice, she said, but she had to make a living.

In her prime, Althea Gibson was an overpowering tennis player. She stood five feet, ten inches tall, and her powerful serve reminded many people of the speed and force of the serves of male players. Her volleys and overhead smash were also devastating. She exuded confidence on the court, a quality that sometimes irritated those who competed against her. Billie Jean King has said that Althea Gibson is one of the most underrated champions in women's tennis. Given the obstacles she had to over-come at a time when racial bias permeated the sport, her record becomes even more impressive.

After her departure from amateur tennis, Gibson played professionally as an attraction with the Harlem Globetrotters during 1959. She competed on the Ladies Professional Golf Association tour for a time and coached tennis in New Jersey. She also served as the State Athletic Commissioner of New Jersey during the 1970's. Althea had a supporting role in a John Wayne film, *The Horse Soldiers* (1958). She married William Darben in 1965, and her second marriage was to Sidney Llewellyn in 1983. Althea Gibson was named to the Lawn Tennis Hall of Fame and Museum in 1971, to the Black Athletes Hall of Fame in 1974, and to the International Women's Sports Hall of Fame in 1980. Gibson continues to teach and to play tennis, although she no longer competes in the professional arena.

Summary

Althea Gibson has earned a reputation as the greatest African American woman tennis player of all time. Despite the prejudice and discrimination that confronted her during a period before the Civil Rights movement of the 1960's, she surmounted the obstacles that were placed in her path to become a dominant player of her era. From 1956 through 1958, she mastered the world of women's tennis, and she could have added more titles to her record if she had so desired.

Unfortunately, Gibson's example did not lead to a surge of black women tennis players. The tennis establishment failed to encourage the development of young African Americans with potential to be top-flight players. The next great African American star would be the male player Arthur Ashe, who emerged in the following decade. Althea Gibson was an outstanding champion. Her courage, will to win, and perseverance deserve more attention than they have received from historians of tennis and from students of women athletes.

Bibliography

Biracree, Tom. *Althea Gibson*. New York: Chelsea House, 1989. As one of the entries in the publisher's American Women of Achievement series for juvenile readers, this biography provides a fine introduction to Gibson's life and career and includes useful information regarding her activities after her retirement from professional competition.

Brown, Gene, ed. *The Complete Book of Tennis*. New York: Arno Press, 1980. This compilation of *The New York Times* coverage of tennis during the twentieth century contains excellent accounts of Althea Gibson's major tournament victories during the 1950's.

Collins, Bud. *My Life with the Pros*. New York: E. P. Dutton, 1989. A longtime reporter of tennis, Collins covered Gibson's emergence as a tennis star, and his book gives a good sense of the obstacles Gibson faced from the white media and tennis establishment.

Gibson, Althea. *I Always Wanted to Be Somebody*. Edited by Ed Fitzgerald. New York: Harper & Brothers, 1958. A vivid account of Gibson's rise to the top of the tennis world. Its depiction of her formative years makes it an important contribution to African American autobiographies.

King, Billie Jean, and Cynthia Starr. *We Have Come a Long Way: The Story of Women's Tennis*. New York: McGraw-Hill, 1988. The section on Althea Gibson is a perceptive assessment of her career and her effect on women's tennis during the 1950's. It makes the persuasive argument that Althea Gibson has not received the recognition she deserves.

Lumpkin, Angela. *Women's Tennis: A Historical Documentary of the Players and Their Game*. Troy, N.Y.: Whitston, 1981. This survey of writing about women's tennis and the history of the sport provides references to the major published articles regarding Althea Gibson during her years at the top of women's tennis. A valuable source of information about her career.

Wade, Virginia, with Jean Rafferty. *Ladies of the Court: A Century of Women at Wimbledon*. New York: Atheneum, 1984. Has a very informative chapter on Gibson's successes at Wimbledon.

Karen Gould

CHARLOTTE PERKINS GILMAN

Born: July 3, 1860; Hartford, Connecticut
Died: August 17, 1935; Pasadena, California
Areas of Achievement: Literature and journalism
Contribution: In highly original literary and social scientific works, Charlotte Perkins
Stetson Gilman addressed both women's contemporary status and the social and
economic changes necessary to improve it.

Early Life
Charlotte Anna Perkins was born on July 3, 1860, in Hartford, Connecticut. Her
intellectual father, Frederick Beecher Perkins, tried a variety of careers, including
teaching, writing, and library work. Her mother, Mary Westcott Perkins, like most
young women of her time and class, had not prepared for any career besides domesticity. Unfortunately, Frederick found family responsibilities confining and had difficulty sticking to a career. From her earliest years, Charlotte saw her family coping
with unpaid debts, frequent moves, dependence on friends and relatives, and a tense
emotional environment. In 1869, her parents agreed to separate, and in 1873, when
divorce was rare and considered shameful, Mary divorced Frederick so that he could
remarry. In spite of her family's problems, however, Charlotte enjoyed a rich intellectual environment. Through her father, she had family ties to the famous Beecher clan,
including clergyman Henry Ward Beecher, writers Harriet Beecher Stowe and Catherine Beecher, and suffragist Isabella Beecher Hooker. Although these Beecher
women extolled images of domesticity, their lives of achievement in the world
undermined their rhetoric. Charlotte learned to read before she was five and in her
teens took pleasure in writing fanciful stories and poetry. Her mother, who saw herself
as having been critically wounded by emotion, strongly discouraged this activity. At
seventeen, Charlotte wrote to her father requesting a reading list; he responded with
suggestions of works on history, anthropology, and evolutionary science, to which she
applied herself diligently.

She studied art at the Rhode Island School of Design and at twenty-one was
supporting herself as a commercial artist. In 1882, she met Charles Walter Stetson, an
aspiring artist who proposed marriage within three weeks of their meeting. She
approached marriage warily, mindful of her parents' unhappy experience. Despite her
doubts, they married in 1884. She gave birth to a daughter, Katharine, a year later and
soon fell into a nearly incapacitating depression. She improved during a long vacation
away from her husband and child but declined after her return; indeed, she almost
went mad during a "rest cure" with nerve specialist S. Weir Mitchell. In 1887, she and
Walter agreed to separate; that fall, she and her daughter moved to Pasadena, California, where she began to work seriously on her writing.

Life's Work
The combination of her excellent though informal education, her Beecher heritage

of independent thinking, and her family experiences fitted Charlotte Stetson well for the work she would soon do. Her wide reading had converted her to Charles Darwin's theory of evolution, though definitely not to laissez-faire Social Darwinism. Instead, she subscribed wholeheartedly to the ideas in Lester Frank Ward's *Dynamic Sociology* (1883), which stressed human responsibility to mold the social environment rationally for optimal human evolution. She especially liked Ward's discussion of women's crucial role in evolution and of how women's potential had been stunted by artificial social constraints. Her Beecher heritage encouraged her to trust her own ideas and express them publicly. Finally, as a daughter, she had seen that the prescribed family roles did not always work, while her experiences as a wife and mother almost cost her her sanity. She used her life as material for her writings, drawing on the powerful emotions her experiences had bequeathed. Although she considered herself a rationalist, her best work often derived its energy from her unacknowledged anger toward those she loved, including her parents and child.

In Pasadena, Stetson moved near her close friend Grace Channing and determined to be self-supporting. Her finances were always shaky, so she supplemented her writing with tutoring, lecturing, and commercial art projects; for a time, she supported herself and Katharine by managing a boarding house. She initially allowed some poems to be published without pay, for the exposure led to speaking engagements and other opportunities. She became increasingly active in Nationalism, an all-American socialist movement, inspired by Edward Bellamy's best-seller *Looking Backward* (1888), which flourished through Nationalist clubs around the country. This work brought her speaking engagements and contacts in San Francisco, where she moved in 1891. There she met and impressed many well-known feminists and reformers. Her newfound prominence allowed her to become a full-time writer and speaker, and in 1893, she published her first volume of poetry, *In This Our World*.

The following year, 1894, brought several changes. Charlotte's mother, whom she had nursed through her struggle with cancer, died, and Charlotte's obsessive relationship with a woman friend collapsed around the same time. Her divorce from Walter, following negative press coverage and legal complications, became final in April, and Walter promptly married her friend Grace. Far from being distressed by their marriage, Charlotte seemed almost relieved, and relations among the three remained cordial. By mutual agreement, she sent Katharine, at age nine, to live with Walter and Grace, on the grounds that they could care for her better. Charlotte was now free to travel and concentrate on her own career.

In her writing and public speaking, she focused on ideas rather than on aesthetics or entertainment value. She preferred all writing, whether poetry, fiction, or analysis, to have a didactic purpose. This is apparent in her most important early works. In 1892, she published the terrifying short story "The Yellow Wall-Paper." Superficially, it describes a woman's descent into madness during a medical treatment resembling Mitchell's rest cure. More profoundly, the story depicts the disastrous effects on women of stifled sexual and verbal expression, enforced passivity, and externally imposed roles.

She explored these same themes in another context in *Women and Economics* (1898), the book that firmly established her reputation. By then, she had attended the first national women's rights convention in 1896, traveled throughout the United States and England, and established friendships with leading reformers of the day. In 1897, she had experienced another bout of severe depression but this time had sought relief by writing; within seventeen days, she had drafted her first prose book. Based on Ward's ideas and her own observations, *Women and Economics* criticized how women were defined by their sexual function and described the negative consequences of women's dependence on men. Women who did not develop to their potential could not contribute fully to the evolutionary progress of society, as mothers or anything else. Winning the vote, while important, could not undo centuries of economic dependence. Women would discover their true social role only when they could support themselves outside the home, which would simultaneously liberate men and allow society to evolve without distortion. Naturally, such a change would require major social modifications, especially in the home. Though considered radical, the book was an immediate success in the United States and abroad. Charlotte became increasingly popular as a writer and speaker, and her own economic independence was assured.

Her new financial security may have persuaded her to try marriage again. She and her cousin Houghton Gilman, a New York banker, married in June, 1900. They quickly implemented some ideas from *Women and Economics*, including a "home without a kitchen." Their happy marriage modified Charlotte's nomadic lifestyle, allowed her to spend more time with her daughter, and lasted until Houghton's death.

Charlotte Gilman continued writing about women's status, family roles, and work. In 1900, she published *Concerning Children*, which discussed the influence of environment on children but unfortunately reflected the nativism of the period. *The Home: Its Work and Influence* (1903) elaborated on themes from *Women and Economics*, while *Human Work* (1904) focused on the interdependency of the human community and the need for the contributions of all. Gilman also participated in an International Congress of Women in 1904, gave a lecture tour throughout Europe in 1905, and wrote articles and poems for periodicals.

In 1909, she launched her own monthly magazine, *The Forerunner*, and wrote virtually everything that appeared in it—editorials, poetry, fiction, reviews, and more. This allowed her to express herself freely without editorial constraint and to serialize works in progress. One of her most interesting works was the utopian novel *Herland* (1915). In this dramatization of her theoretical ideas, Gilman envisioned three American men discovering a completely female society in which the institution of the family does not exist—only individuals and the community. She discontinued the magazine in 1916.

Whether because of the general disillusionment following World War I or the sense that the "woman question" was resolved once the vote had been won, Gilman's later works, on topics such as birth control, urban planning, and religion, were not well received. Still, she kept writing. In 1926, she wrote her autobiography, but she found a publisher for it only in the last year of her life. She seemed to have been largely forgotten by the postwar generation. In 1932, she was diagnosed with breast cancer, and, in 1934, after Houghton died, she moved to Pasadena to be near Katharine. When the cancer spread and a painful death was approaching, Gilman chose to commit suicide on August 17, 1935.

Summary

Charlotte Perkins Gilman made major contributions to the development of feminist thought in her own time and for later generations. For her contemporaries, she developed a scathing critique of the Victorian family, whose damaging effects on women she had observed. More important, she went beyond describing what was wrong with women's social roles to envision how to improve relations between the sexes for the good of society as a whole. In her fiction, poetry, and analysis, she drew on her own experiences and pain to come up with solutions that many of her contemporaries saw as far more radical than the successful goal of woman suffrage.

After years of being ignored, her work was rediscovered during the women's movement of the 1960's and 1970's, speaking even more clearly to that generation than to her own. Not only her words but also her life itself had resonance for modern feminists. They too grappled with practical questions of reproductive freedom, child care, sexual expression, and the role of supportive same-sex relationships. They too sought to strike a balance between family and work responsibilities, between the personal and the political, between nurturing others and maintaining a sense of self. They also understood, probably better than her contemporaries, the critical importance of economic independence. Gilman's energetic and passionate struggle made her truly a forerunner of the modern feminist movement.

Bibliography
Cooper, James L., and Sheila McIsaac Cooper, eds. *The Roots of American Feminist Thought*. Boston: Allyn & Bacon, 1973. Presents well-selected passages from *Women and Economics*, along with a useful analysis of the development of Gilman's thinking. Places Gilman in the context of feminist thinkers such as Mary Wollstonecraft, John Stuart Mill, and others.
Degler, Carl N. "Charlotte Perkins Gilman on the Theory and Practice of Feminism." *American Quarterly* 8, no. 1 (Spring, 1956): 21-39. This crucial work in the rediscovery of Gilman, written in the context of the new wave of feminism inspired by Simone de Beauvoir concentrates on Gilman's writing, not on her life.
Gilman, Charlotte Perkins. *The Living of Charlotte Perkins Gilman*. New York: Harper & Row, 1975. The author's autobiography is especially good on her unconventional childhood and adolescence, her breakdown, her work life, and her theories of child rearing, but it contains little but platitudes about her second marriage.
Hill, Mary A. *Charlotte Perkins Gilman: The Making of a Radical Feminist, 1860-1896*. Philadelphia: Temple University Press, 1980. This is the first major biogra-

phy to make use of Gilman's personal papers and to reveal the passionate relationships that Gilman purposely left out of her autobiography. Occasionally, the book
slights Gilman's published works in order to restore the missing personal aspect of
her life.

Karpinski, Joanne B., ed. *Critical Essays on Charlotte Perkins Gilman*. New York:
G. K. Hall, 1992. A useful collection of essays by both Gilman's contemporaries
and recent scholars. Carol Ruth Berkin's essay "Private Woman, Public Woman:
The Contradictions of Charlotte Perkins Gilman" is a particularly fine assessment
of Gilman's character and work.

Lane, Ann J. *To Herland and Beyond*. New York: Pantheon Books, 1990. A sensitive,
intuitive, scholarly biography that examines Gilman in the context of her most
intimate relationships and the ways in which these shaped her work; the personal
approach and organization are somewhat jarring but offer fascinating insights.

Scharnhorst, Gary. *Charlotte Perkins Gilman*. Boston: Twayne, 1985. Concentrates
primarily on analyzing Gilman's fiction and poetry, rather than her life or her works
of social criticism. Includes a useful annotated bibliography and a chronology.

Susan Wladaver-Morgan

LAURA GILPIN

Born: April 22, 1891; Austin Bluffs, Colorado
Died: November 30, 1979; Santa Fe, New Mexico
Area of Achievement: Photography
Contribution: Gilpin was best known for her photographs of the American Southwest, particularly for her portraits of Pueblo and Navajo Indians, and received considerable acclaim as the most important woman photographer of the southwestern landscape and Native American culture.

Early Life

Laura Gilpin was a native westerner, born in Colorado. Her grandfather's cousin, William Gilpin, served as the area's first territorial governor. Laura's mother, Emma, seems to have been something of an intellectual, with progressive views about the role of women in society. Frank Gilpin, Laura's father, was an outdoorsman and rancher. Laura had one brother, Francis Gilpin, Jr., born in 1899. Another brother, John, died five months after his birth in May of 1892.

Unfortunately, Laura's father was never very successful as a rancher, and he changed jobs frequently. In 1896, the family moved to Colorado Springs, and Frank commuted to Cripple Creek, where he managed a mine. In spite of her father's lack of financial success, Laura's family found acceptance among Colorado Springs social circles because of their connection to the former governor. Laura attended the private Ferris School and in later years recalled her childhood as a happy one.

Laura's father was a distant relative of the famous survey photographer, William Henry Jackson; so perhaps Laura's proclivity for photography should not seem surprising. Laura was given her first camera, a Kodak Brownie, for her twelfth birthday, in 1903. Soon after, her parents gave her a developing tank.

The following year, 1904, Laura attended the Louisiana Purchase Exposition in St. Louis, Missouri. This trip evidently piqued her interest in native peoples, and she was fascinated by the "displays" of Filipino natives living in a reconstructed village on the fairgrounds. With her Brownie, she recorded these intriguing people, thereby anticipating her later career.

Another early influence occurred in 1905, when Emma Gilpin took Laura and her brother to New York City. While there, Laura's mother arranged to have the children photographed by the celebrated portraitist, Gertrude Käsebier. This sitting helped to shape Laura's future.

Laura was educated in the East, first at the Baldwin School in Bryn Mawr, Pennsylvania, and then at Rosemary Hall in Greenwich, Connecticut. Unfortunately, she never received a high school diploma because her studies were interrupted by illness. She did return to the East briefly, however, to study violin at the New England Conservatory of Music in Boston from the fall of 1910 to the early winter of 1911. At that time, she was called home by her parents, and the family moved to an 1,800-acre ranch in Austin, Colorado. From 1911 to 1915, Laura ran a successful poultry business on the ranch. Indeed, it was money from the sale of her turkey enterprise which eventually allowed Laura to study photography.

Life's Work

Laura Gilpin began experimenting with the newly introduced Autochrome process of photographic development in the summer of 1908 while home from school in Colorado Springs. She and two friends devised a crude home darkroom and, following the instructions on the box of commercial plates, achieved remarkable success with this early color process. Her earliest work, not surprisingly, is in the pictorialist mode favored by Gertrude Käsebier and her colleagues in the Photo-Secession. This painterly, romantic approach appealed to Gilpin, who saw parallels between photography and music in terms of pattern, harmony, and tone values.

In 1915, Gilpin visited California and attended the Panama-Pacific Exposition in San Francisco and the Panama-California Exposition in San Diego. In May of 1916, a photograph taken at the latter venue earned for Gilpin her first award in a competition sponsored by *American Photographer* magazine.

In 1916, with money from her poultry business, Gilpin set out for New York to study photography at the Clarence H. White School. White, formerly a member of Alfred Stieglitz's famous Photo-Secession, was recommended to Gilpin by Gertrude Käsebier. The White School was quite progressive, offering complete training in photographic technique, photo chemistry, design, and even art history. Gilpin remained in New York until the winter of 1917-1918, when she fell victim to an influenza epidemic. She returned home to Colorado Springs, and her mother hired Betsy Forster, a young nurse, to care for her. This was to become the central relationship in Gilpin's life, a friendship which lasted more than half a century.

After recovering from her illness, Gilpin embarked upon a career as a professional photographer. Portrait commissions from Colorado Springs "society" were her bread and butter. Gilpin also began exhibiting widely during the 1920's. Most of her success came from western landscapes, a subject for which she felt a great affinity. In the mid-1920's, Gilpin turned away from the soft focus of pictorialism and her work became clearer. This shift in style seems to have been precipitated when Gilpin accidentally dropped her soft-focus Pinkham and Smith lens overboard when she and an artist friend, Brenda Putnam, were setting off on a European tour in April of 1922. Although Gilpin was able to replace the lens a few weeks later, the experience made her realize she actually preferred the sharper image.

In the summer of 1924, Gilpin took a camping trip by car through the Southwest with Betsy Forster and Brenda Putnam, visiting Mesa Verde, Gallup, Zuni, Laguna Pueblo, Taos, and other sites. Gilpin's earliest photographs of Pueblo Indians date from this period. These early images of Native Americans are more romanticized than her later work, and Gilpin sought to depict the timeless quality of her subject.

In 1927, Gilpin issued a gravure folio of her southwestern photos. At about the same time, she began work on two photographically illustrated booklets: *The Pikes Peak Region* (1926) and *Mesa Verde National Park* (1927). She supplemented her income with commissions to photograph architecture for a Denver firm.

Three years later, in 1930, Gilpin and Betsy Forster made another photographic journey across the Southwest, this time making lantern slides. On this trip, they became acquainted with the Navajo, and the following year Forster accepted a position as field nurse to the Navajo community at Red Rock, Arizona. Gilpin visited often and began to photograph the tribe. Through Forster's close relationship with the Navajo, Gilpin came to understand them and was able to successfully collaborate with her subjects. Using an 8 x 10" view camera, she tried not to exploit or romanticize them. Although Forster lost her job at Red Rock in 1933, she and Gilpin returned there for a visit in 1934. The Navajo photographs made between 1931 and 1934 are among Gilpin's finest.

The Depression years were difficult, and Gilpin had a hard time earning a living. In the spring of 1932, she made a trip to the Yucatán to photograph archaeological sites, an interest stimulated by her contact with Native Americans. She made a remarkable series of views of Chichén Itzá using a 5 x 7" camera. Thirty-six of the Yucatán prints were subsequently purchased by the Library of Congress.

In 1935, Gilpin and Forster went into partnership, opening the Friendfield Turkey Farm eighteen miles from Colorado Springs. Poultry farming had been profitable before, and the two hoped it would see them through the Depression. Gilpin also continued to photograph, receiving a commission from Santa Fe architect John Gaw Meem in 1936. For several years, the turkey farm was a thriving enterprise; in 1939, however, it suddenly failed. Forster found employment by opening a guesthouse in Colorado Springs in 1940, and Gilpin began issuing her photos as postcard sets, marketing them through the Harvey hotel chain. It was at this time that Gilpin received a contract from Hastings House in New York for a book of her southwestern photos. *The Pueblos: A Camera Chronicle* was published late in 1941. During World War II, Gilpin searched for a way to use her photographic talents to aid the war effort. Finally, in November of 1942, she got a job as a public relations photographer with Boeing in Wichita, Kansas, a position she held until November of 1944. During this period, Forster, who had remained in Colorado Springs, contracted polio and encephalitis and had to be moved to her sister's home in Nebraska.

By the spring of 1945, Gilpin had little to tie her to Colorado Springs. Her parents and her brother Francis were all dead and her good friend had moved away. At this point, Gilpin received a contract to produce a book on the Rio Grande. She was assigned to work with an editor in Santa Fe; so, in the fall of 1945, at the age of fifty-four, Gilpin pulled up stakes and moved to New Mexico. By the following spring, Betsy Forster was beginning to improve and Gilpin brought her to Santa Fe to live with her.

Gilpin continued with the Rio Grande project, a portrait of the river with each page planned as a unit of picture and text. In 1948, her book *Temples of Yucatan* was published, and the 243-page *The Rio Grande: River of Destiny, an Interpretation of the River, the Land, and the People* went to press in 1949.

During the 1950's, Gilpin returned to photographing the Navajo. She had in mind a book based on her pictures and Forster's letters from the Red Rock years. By this time, Forster was strong enough to travel back to the reservation, and the book became a shared project. Unfortunately, its progress was constantly interrupted by the need to take on other assignments to earn money.

Eventually, in 1963, University of Texas Press and the Amon Carter Museum in Fort Worth picked up the Navajo book project. *The Enduring Navaho* was finally published in 1968, eighteen and a half years after Gilpin began the project. The book, dedicated to Forster, is 279 pages long and includes pictures made between 1931 and 1964. The work was widely praised.

Betsy Forster died on January 1, 1972, but Gilpin pressed on. That spring she began work on a new book about Canyon de Chelly. Increasingly, she was viewed as a celebrity. The Witkin Gallery in New York gave her a major exhibit in 1973. In 1974, her fifth attempt to win the Guggenheim grant was successful, and she was awarded $12,000 to make hand-coated platinum prints. The New Mexico Museum of Fine Arts gave her a major retrospective exhibition later that year.

Gilpin never finished the Guggenheim project or the Canyon de Chelly book. Old age and increasing requests for public appearances slowed her down. Yet, only two months before her death on November 30, 1979, Gilpin was taking aerial photographs of the Rio Grande Valley from a small airplane. She loved her work and pursued it with vigor until the end of her life. She left her photographic estate to the Amon Carter Museum, the institution that had helped her bring her most cherished project to fruition.

Summary

Laura Gilpin was a pioneer, both in landscape photography and in the depiction of Native Americans. A contemporary of Willa Cather and Georgia O'Keeffe, she responded as they did to the open spaces of the American West. Gilpin's talent for landscape photography, generally a male purview because of its links to male notions of exploration and conquest, set her apart from other women photographers of her day, many of whom had family responsibilities that restricted their movements.

As a photographer, Gilpin was particularly successful at capturing a sense of the land's impact on human conditions. Her images of the Pueblo and Navajo show a proud, enduring people, not the "vanishing race" depicted by her better-known colleague Edward S. Curtis.

Despite her accomplishments, Gilpin seems never to have been conscious of being a pioneer or a feminist. When interviewed by Gloria Steinem for *Ms.* magazine in 1974, Gilpin was reluctant to speak of her accomplishments or misfortunes and revealed that she did not think about women's liberation at all.

Bibliography

Coke, Van Deren. *Photography in New Mexico*. Albuquerque: University of New Mexico Press, 1979. Coke's book briefly mentions Gilpin and reproduces four of her photos.

Gilpin, Laura. *The Enduring Navaho*. Austin: University of Texas Press, 1968. This book, eighteen and a half years in the making, is dedicated to Betsy and was inspired by the letters she wrote during the years she served as a visiting nurse in Red Rock, Arizona.

_____. *The Pueblos: A Camera Chronicle*. New York: Hastings House, 1941. This is Gilpin's first major book, containing some seventy-six illustrations.

_____. *The Rio Grande: River of Destiny*. New York: Duell, Sloan and Pearce, 1949. This is one of Gilpin's major photoessays comprised of 229 photographs and 244 pages.

_____. *Temples in Yucatan: A Camera Chronicle of Chichén Itzá*. New York: Hastings House, 1948. This 124-page book includes numerous illustrations of the Mayan ruins taken on Gilpin's 1932 trip to Mexico.

Sandweiss, Martha. *Laura Gilpin: An Enduring Grace*. Forth Worth, Tex.: Amon Carter Museum, 1986. This monograph, produced in conjunction with the exhibit "An Enduring Grace: The Photographs of Laura Gilpin," is the most comprehensive study of Gilpin's career. It contains an extensive biography, detailed notes, a chronological list of exhibitions and publications, and numerous full-page plates.

Steinem, Gloria. "Laura Gilpin: The Compassionate Eye." *Ms.* 3 (September, 1974): 59-61. In this interview, Gilpin reflects upon her career. From her responses to Steinem's questions, it is evident that Gilpin was not entirely at ease in the pioneer feminist role that had been thrust upon her.

Vestal, David. "Laura Gilpin: Photographer of the Southwest." *Popular Photography* 80 (February, 1977): 100-105, 130-134. This brief profile of Gilpin's career includes six illustrations that highlight her photographic technique and artistic endeavors.

Gillian Greenhill Hannum

LILLIAN GISH

Born: October 14, 1893; Springfield, Ohio
Died: February 27, 1993; New York, New York
Areas of Achievement: Film and theater and drama
Contribution: A legendary and versatile performer for nine decades, Lillian Gish was
   hailed as the First Lady of the Silent Screen, starred in some of Broadway's most
   memorable productions, and performed regularly on television.

Early Life

Lillian Diana Gish was born on October 14, 1893, in Springfield, Ohio. She was
always vague about her birth date, never once mentioning it in her various autobiographical reminiscences. The years 1896 and 1899 frequently appear on biographical
material, though the earliest date is considered correct. Her father, James Leigh Gish,
married Mary Robinson McConnell, then living in nearby Urbana. He was twenty and
his wife was eighteen. At the time of his marriage, James Gish was a wholesale
grocery clerk. He quit to form his own confectionery business. He eventually moved
the business to Dayton, Ohio, where Lillian's sister Dorothy was born on March 11,
1898. The two sisters' lives remained inextricably linked, privately and professionally,
until Dorothy's death in 1968.

James Gish, a drifter at heart, was not temperamentally suited for fatherhood or
marriage. He also failed in his various business ventures in different cities until,
finally, he abandoned his wife and two young daughters in New York City. Mary Gish
was a strong-willed woman who always managed to find employment and to keep the
family together. Lillian often recalled that as a young child she learned the lessons of
security (mother), peace and love, and insecurity (father), which strengthened her
character and taught her to be self-reliant.

One day, the actress Dolores Lorne advised Mary Gish to become an actress and
seek employment on the stage. She did, taking the alias "Mae Bernard" so as not to
disgrace her family name. Lillian's earliest memories were of playing backstage in a
theater and watching her mother act. In time, the young Lillian was asked to perform.
She made her stage debut, billed as "Baby Lillian," in the melodrama *In Convict's
Stripes.* The year was 1902 and the place was Rising Sun, Ohio. Sister Dorothy
followed soon after in *East Lynne.* During the next ten years, Lillian, her mother, and
her sister performed together as well as apart. Lillian appeared in many plays, and she
did one stint as a dancer in a production starring Sarah Bernhardt.

Life's Work

The major turning point in Lillian Gish's professional career occurred in 1912. She
was introduced to D. W. Griffith, the visionary cinema pioneer, and their chance
meeting changed her whole life. Gish and her family had come to the American
Mutoscope and Biograph Company (Biograph) to pay respects to their old friend
Gladys Smith, who had become known as Mary Pickford. Pickford introduced Lillian

and Dorothy to Griffith. He was immediately taken by their purity and innocence, and he cast them in *An Unseen Enemy*. Despite Griffith's enthusiasm for her work, Gish continued with her stage career while she made films on the side.

The first important screen milestone for Gish came in 1913, when she starred in *The Mothering Heart*. Griffith refused to cast her at first because the woman was supposed to be about thirty, but the resolute actress persuaded the director. She convincingly portrayed a tragic wife whose baby died. It was the first of many heart-wrenching performances. Other important roles that year followed in a succession of pictures directed by Griffith, most notably the biblical story *Judith of Bethulia* and the Western *The Battle at Elderbush Gulch*. Gish's quick rise to prominence was no small feat, since Griffith had many outstanding actresses to choose from, including Pickford, Blanche Sweet, Mae Marsh, and Miriam Cooper.

The year 1914 proved to be important for Gish, Griffith, and the American cinema. Griffith, angry at Biograph because of its highly limited vision of film's future, quit suddenly and relocated to the Los Angeles area. More important to the studio, he took most of the talented players with him. Griffith wanted to make an American epic, and he did so in the fall of 1914. *The Clansmen* opened in California in January, 1915, with Gish cast as the Yankee heroine, Elsie Stoneman. Within two months, the title was changed to *The Birth of a Nation* for its New York premiere on March 3. Cinema, the "little toy," had come of age with this epoch-making motion picture. Thereafter, film had to be considered as a new art form.

The following year, Gish appeared in another Griffith masterpiece, *Intolerance* (1916). Her role, much smaller here, was the unifying symbol of the woman who rocks the cradle, lending cohesion to the four separate stories. She next starred in a series of pictures for Griffith, including *Hearts of the World* with Dorothy Gish, *The Great Love* (both 1918), *A Romance of Happy Valley*, *The Greatest Thing in Life*, and *True Heart Susie* (all three 1919). Gish's maturity and authority continued to increase, and her next film, the highly poetic *Broken Blossoms* (1919), witnessed her emergence as the quintessential waif-angel of the screen. With this work, she also came into her own as an acknowledged artistic collaborator with Griffith. *The Mothering Heart* had required Gish to age; now, the twenty-five-year-old actress had to play a young adolescent. She did so brilliantly. Gish brought fresh insights to the character during rehearsals and filming, continually delighting and inspiring Griffith. Her realistic portrayal of an innocent girl brutally battered by a sadistic father continues to shock audiences.

Gish's best screen work was still ahead of her. Griffith cast her as the plucky, jilted heroine in *Way down East* (1920). Her next major film, *Orphans of the Storm* (1922), directed by Griffith, also starred Dorothy Gish. They played unrelated "sisters" brought up in the same household during the French Revolution. Gish had persuaded Griffith to arrange it so that she and Dorothy could work together. It was their last joint screen appearance. Dorothy was a gifted comedian who preferred light material, whereas Lillian opted for dramatic fare.

Gish's artistic relationship with Griffith was a complex one. In different films, she assumed various responsibilities, including scriptwriting, bookkeeping, and even directing. She parted company with Griffith following *Orphans* and starred in two films without him, *The White Sister* (1923) and *Romola* (1924). In 1925, she signed with Metro-Goldwyn-Mayer (MGM) as a reigning star with complete creative control. Gish gave memorable performances as the heroine in *La Bohème* (1926), *The Scarlet Letter* (1926), and *The Wind* (1928).

After the arrival of Swedish love goddess Greta Garbo, MGM decided that Gish was too demure and sexless for their future film projects. They dropped her contract in 1928. She made several other motion pictures for other studios and then, in 1930, returned to the Broadway stage she had abandoned almost twenty years earlier. Over the next six decades, Gish returned to Hollywood occasionally to make films such as *Duel in the Sun* (1946), *The Night of the Hunter* (1966), *The Comedians* (1967), *Sweet Liberty* (1986), and *The Whales of August* (1987). Her first priority, however, was the theater, where she performed in countless productions.

Gish's first stage comeback occurred in Anton Chekhov's *Uncle Vanya* (1930). She then appeared in the title role of *Camille* (1932), as Ophelia in John Gielgud's acclaimed production of *Hamlet* (1936), and had a starring role in one of Broadway's most beloved and longest-running comedies, *Life With Father* (1939). Many other notable plays and costarring roles with famous stars followed over the years. The actress also starred in a number of television shows and specials; served as hostess of the series *The Silent Years* (1975); and found time to write two autobiographical books, *The Movies, Mr. Griffith, and Me* (1969), *Dorothy and Lillian Gish* (1973), and a book for young people, *An Actor's Life for Me* (1987).

The last years of Gish's life were laden with honors. She was awarded a special Lifetime Achievement Oscar in 1970 by the Academy of Motion Picture Arts and Sciences and was given a lavish film tribute by the Museum of Modern Art in 1980. In 1982, she received the Kennedy Center Honor. The American Film Institute gave her a special honorary salute in 1984. She was appointed a trustee of the American Academy of Dramatic Arts in 1966, and she received a Doctorate of Fine Arts from Rollins College and a Doctorate of Performing Arts from Bowling Green State University. The actress kept performing almost to the very end of her life. Gish died in New York City on February 27, 1993, just eight months short of her one hundredth birthday.

Summary

Lillian Gish achieved preeminence and recognition as a woman during her remarkable career. She became a legend in her own time. The actress began performing while still a child and continued working for nine decades. Her professional life contains the history of the film industry in this century. Gish has rightly been hailed as the First Lady of the Silent Screen. Pioneering director D. W. Griffith, who always referred to her as Miss Lillian, often said that she was the finest and most talented actress with whom he had worked.

Gish, more than any other actress, epitomized the ideal silent screen heroine. She had a fragile, ethereal beauty that was underscored by enormous sensitivity and talent. Equally impressive was the amount of research she undertook for each role. The physical demands she placed on herself, refusing to use stand-ins, always won for her the admiration of her coworkers, who also praised Gish for her cooperative spirit.

Gish's dedication to her career was total. Her one abiding passion was to perform and entertain audiences, whether on stage, screen, or television. The actress never married, despite scores of marital proposals. To all suitors her answer was the same: She was married to her profession.

Gish was a champion of women's rights in Hollywood. She became one of America's first female film directors as early as 1920 with *Remodeling Her Husband*, starring her sister Dorothy. The actress was one of the first to receive complete creative control over her films when she signed with MGM. She lived long enough to see women achieve major victories in all areas of the entertainment world. Lillian Gish will be remembered for her luminous presence and grace.

Bibliography
Gish, Lillian. *An Actor's Life for Me*. New York: Viking Kestrel, 1987. This reworking of the first part of Gish's autobiography for young people focuses on the early years of her career. The short book contains photographs and illustrations.

_____ . *Dorothy and Lillian Gish*. Edited by James E. Frasher. New York: Charles Scribner's Sons, 1973. A nostalgic look at Lillian and Dorothy Gish through hundreds of photographs, playbills, posters, clippings, and letters. The book is well organized by decades, devoting equal space to each sister. The last section is the most interesting; it examines Lillian's long career in pictures and closes with complete and separate filmographies and scenographies for the sisters.

_____ . *The Movies, Mr. Griffith, and Me*. San Francisco: Mercury House, 1969. Gish's valuable and intimate look at her noteworthy career. The actress provides biographical information on her parents, her early upbringing, and the economic conditions that brought her to the stage, as well as her subsequent career. She concentrates attention on Griffith, providing valuable insight into his films and working methods.

Paine, Albert B. *Life and Lillian Gish*. New York: Macmillan, 1932. An early, valuable biography of Gish that concentrates on her early stage work, her historic meeting with Griffith, and the flowering of her silent screen career. It closes with her triumphant return to the Broadway theater.

Silver, Charles, ed. *Lillian Gish*. New York: Museum of Modern Art, 1980. A loving tribute to Gish by the editor and various artists and colleagues, including Katharine Hepburn, Douglas Fairbanks, Jr., Francois Truffaut, Moira Shearer, Colleen Moore, and Mary Astor. It also includes Edward Wagenknecht's classic 1927 essay "Lillian Gish: An Interpretation." The work accompanied a retrospective showing of Gish's films at the museum.

Terry Theodore

WHOOPI GOLDBERG

Born: November 13, 1949; New York, New York

Areas of Achievement: Theater and drama, television, and film

Contribution: Whoopi Goldberg has overcome what many may consider insurmountable obstacles to emerge as a multitalented entertainer, the first African American female to win an Oscar, a Grammy, and a Golden Globe award.

Early Life

Whoopi Goldberg was born Caryn Johnson in the teeming metropolis of New York. The first of two children born to Emma Johnson, Goldberg spent her childhood in housing projects in the Chelsea section of New York. She and her younger brother, Clyde, were reared by their mother, a single parent. Little is known about Goldberg's father, who is said to have deserted his family when she was very young. His disappearance resulted in a lack of paternal influence on her life. Her mother took a variety of jobs in an effort to support her children. Emma Johnson ventured in the medical field as a nurse and at one point was involved in early childhood education after becoming a Head Start teacher.

As a child, Goldberg attended a parochial school in lower Manhattan. By the time she entered third grade, Whoopi's interest in the entertainment field was evident. She attended the Helena Rubinstein Children's Theatre. She was an admirer and fan of the old film classics, and her acting idols included Claudette Colbert and Carole Lombard. Goldberg remembers a childhood where her exposure to museums and ballet was frequent. She attended concerts conducted by Leonard Bernstein and Shakespearean plays produced by Joseph Papp in Central Park.

Goldberg has cheerfully described herself as being a child of the 1960's. She completed eight years of Catholic school before dropping out of school after two weeks in the ninth grade. Unaware that her learning difficulties were the result of dyslexia, Goldberg nevertheless believed that the outside world had much more to offer her than conventional education. Abandoning the rigid dress codes and strict morality of her parochial school upbringing, she opted to join the world of hippies. She was introduced to the drug scene at age seventeen, eventually becoming a heavy user. By 1969, Goldberg had checked herself into Horizon House in an effort to obtain help for her substance abuse. She decided to stop taking drugs because she believed her world was lacking focus and because she had been alarmed by the drug deaths of such rock luminaries as Jimi Hendrix and Janis Joplin. Some of her own friends and acquaintances were also becoming statistics of their fast lifestyles.

After undergoing drug rehabilitation, Goldberg became a political activist. She participated in civil rights marches at Columbia University and joined student protests throughout New York City. She worked at a summer camp in Peekskill, New York, as a counselor. In the early 1970's, Goldberg married her drug counselor and quickly had a baby. Her daughter was named Alexandrea Martin. Her marriage was brief; in 1974, she and Alexandrea moved to the West Coast. Before her West Coast relocation, Goldberg appeared in the Broadway choruses of *Hair, Pippin,* and *Jesus Christ Superstar.* Her one ambition after the demise of her marriage was to act.

Goldberg soon began to work at a variety of jobs in order to support herself and Alexandrea. She worked at a mortuary as a cosmetologist and was a bricklayer for awhile. She became a beautician and a bank teller. She also spent some time on welfare. Soon she would get off welfare permanently.

Life's Work

Whoopi Goldberg began to perform one-woman shows in the decade of the 1970's. One of her first and perhaps most memorable characterizations was based on Jackie "Moms" Mabley, a noted African American comedian whose work Goldberg admired. Goldberg wrote her first one-woman show with an author named Ellen Sebastian. For her performance as Moms Mabley, Goldberg won the Bay Area Theatre Award. She continued to perform across the country in similar shows.

Goldberg exhibited a unique knack for mimicry and possessed a biting wit. She brought to life a full range of characters based on situations she knew well, including a homeless woman on the street whose residence changed on a daily basis. Her characterizations were heralded by the critics. She endeared herself to the public and her audience. Her no-nonsense attitude not only was genuine but also won her many fans.

Goldberg's popularity grew as her visibility in the theater continued. Her 1985 Grammy award for best comedy album paved the way for her to collaborate with other comedic luminaries, including Billy Crystal and Robin Williams. With the aid of Crystal and Williams, Goldberg launched one of the most massive fund-raisers ever undertaken on behalf of the homeless.

Goldberg soon graduated to working in film. She was cast in her first film role as Celie in Steven Spielberg's 1985 adaptation of Alice Walker's novel, *The Color Purple.* In addition to garnering an Oscar nomination, Goldberg's depiction of Celie won her two awards: a Golden Globe and an Image Award from the National Association for the Advancement of Colored People (NAACP). Her film performance opened doors for Goldberg and marked a significant turning point in her life.

Goldberg immediately became a box office attraction and was cast in a variety of films. Her dramatic debut was followed by a comedic role in *Jumpin' Jack Flash* (1986), directed by Penny Marshall. She remained in the media limelight with films such as *Clara's Heart* (1988), *Burglar* (1987), *Fatal Beauty* (1987), *Homer and Eddie* (1990) opposite Jim Belushi, *The Telephone* (1988), and *Beverly Hills Brats* (1989). In 1991, Goldberg won an Oscar as best supporting actress for her role as Oda Mae Brown in the box office smash hit, *Ghost* (1990). It was fifty-one years earlier that another African American, Hattie McDaniel, had won an Oscar for best supporting actress in the film, *Gone With the Wind.* In October of 1990, Goldberg was given the Excellence Award by members and participants of the Women in Film Festival. In December of that same year, she was honored by the NAACP as their choice for Black Entertainer of the Year.

Goldberg extended her media exposure by venturing into television during the late 1980's. She co-starred with Emmy winner Jean Stapleton in the short-lived situation comedy called *Bagdad Café*, based on the 1988 film of the same name. She was also cast in a recurring role as Guinan, a wise alien bartender, on the syndicated hit series *Star Trek: The Next Generation*.

The decade of the 1990's began with additional challenges for Goldberg when she joined the talk show circuit. As host of her own late night show, Goldberg chose to adopt a different format with no live audience and no elaborate set. The half-hour conversation show drew many of Goldberg's well-known pals. Although it was well received by critics, the show lasted less than a year.

In the same year that she appeared in *Ghost*, Goldberg appeared in the film *The Long Walk Home* (1990) opposite Oscar-winning actress Sissy Spacek. The film, loosely based on events of the early Civil Rights movement, dealt with the relationship between a white woman and her black maid in Montgomery, Alabama, during the 1950's. Although not a blockbuster hit with the public, the film was critically acclaimed. Next, Goldberg returned to her comedic roots with a cameo role as a soap opera scriptwriter in the parody *Soapdish* (1991), a film that featured an ensemble cast including Sally Field and Kevin Kline. Goldberg expressed her pleasure in doing the part, enjoying the opportunity to work as part of a team regardless of the size of her role. Her next film appearance combined her interests in music and civil rights. As the star of the musical *Sarafina!* (1992), Goldberg portrayed a South African teacher who inspires her students to demonstrate their opposition to apartheid in South Africa.

She continued her role on *Star Trek* while starring in films. *Sister Act*, produced by Touchstone Pictures and distributed by Walt Disney, became a surprise box office hit. Although originally developed for Bette Midler, the lead role propelled Goldberg into the type of stardom which enabled her to name her price on future projects. She followed this role with a cameo appearance as a homicide detective in Robert Altman's film *The Player* (1992). The year 1993 marked the release of two films in which Goldberg had a leading role. *Made in America*, a comedy costarring Ted Danson, drew more attention for the romance between its two leads, but *Sister Act II: A Change of Habit* reaffirmed Goldberg's position as a box office draw and received critical praise for being a superior sequel. Regardless of their critical reception, Goldberg's roles have continued to exhibit her ability to create diverse characters rather than settling for stereotypes.

Goldberg has been in the media limelight since her discovery. She became a grandmother at thirty-five when her fifteen-year-old daughter, Alexandrea, gave birth. Her second marriage to Dutch cameraman, David Claessen, ended in divorce after two years. Her subsequent relationships with white males, particularly her much publicized romance with Ted Danson, drew criticism and tabloid attention. When Danson appeared in blackface at a Friars Club roast honoring Goldberg in New York City in 1993, the incident was nationally publicized. Danson's performance and Goldberg's refusal to condemn it created quite a backlash against the couple. African American luminaries such as talk show host Montel Williams and former New York mayor David Dinkins criticized Goldberg's judgment and behavior. A few months after the incident, the couple broke off their relationship.

Despite the negative publicity she received, Goldberg has continued to work. She followed the footsteps of her Comic Relief costar and close pal, Billy Crystal, by hosting the Academy Awards from the Dorothy Chandler Pavilion in Los Angeles on March 25, 1994. As she graced the stage and made the audience laugh with her, more than one billion individuals throughout the world viewed the program. Later in 1994, she awaited release of her film *Corrina, Corrina* and began production on her next film, *Boys on the Side*. Her trademark cornrow hairstyle and puckish smile continue to make her a likable and bankable performer.

Summary

Whoopi Goldberg has beaten the odds. The former welfare recipient and single mother has worked to achieve her stellar status. She has managed to overcome the limitations that dyslexia has imposed. She has become a spokesperson and advocate of antidrug legislation and education. Her own experience with drugs and drug rehabilitation have given her greater sensitivity to the challenges facing young people, and she has taken advantage of her own visibility in order to warn them about the dangers of substance abuse. Her success as a humanitarian is fast becoming legendary. Her Comic Relief program is considered one of the most successful charitable campaigns ever launched. As of 1994, Goldberg had organized and participated in six Comic Relief fund-raisers, collecting millions of dollars for the homeless.

Goldberg's determination to make people laugh resulted in a profitable career. Her ability to perform on stage, television, and film has enabled her to transcend the stereotype of simply being a "black" actor. She prefers to be known as a working actor and attributes her rise from the ranks to her hard work and tenacity.

Bibliography

Adams, Mary Agnes. *Whoopi Goldberg: From Street to Stardom.* New York: Macmillan, 1993. A readable biography aimed at juvenile readers, this work takes an honest, unblinking look at the gritty reality of Goldberg's early life while also focusing on the strength of character that helped Goldberg overcome numerous challenges. Discusses how Goldberg's comedic work particularly has reflected her individuality at the same time as it has expressed her attitudes and values.

Dunne, Sara. "Women as Children in American Comedy: Baby Snooks' Daughters." *Journal of American Culture* 16 (Summer, 1993): 31-35. Part of a special issue on humor, this article compares juvenile characters created by Fanny Brice, Whoopi Goldberg, Gilda Radner, and Lily Tomlin, and discusses how these personae have constituted striking departures from the conventional portrayals of young girls seen in film and on television over the course of the twentieth century.

Randolph, Laura B. "The Whoopi Goldberg Nobody Knows." *Ebony* 46 (March, 1991): 110-115. Interview with Goldberg that touches on her early life and her determination to overcome many obstacles in her pursuit of success. Provides insights into the way in which Goldberg learned to transform her observations of everyday life into a one-woman theatrical show that ultimately launched her career as a headlining comedian and film star.

Smith, Jessie Carney, ed. *Notable Black American Women*. Detroit: Gale Research, 1992. This book provides information on a range of famous African American women. Goldberg is featured as one of the contributors in the field of entertainment.

Unterbrink, Mary. *Funny Women: American Comediennes, 1860-1985*. Jefferson, N.C.: McFarland, 1987. A collection of profiles on women in the field of comedy from the heyday of the Gold Rush through the 1980's. Provides a useful overview of Goldberg's life up through her performance in *The Color Purple*. Somewhat dated source, particularly since Goldberg is discussed as one of the rising stars among female comedians.

Wenner, Jann S. "This Sister's Act." *US* (April, 1994): 58-64, 88. The author, founder of *Rolling Stone* magazine, discusses Goldberg's early childhood, her drug experience, and her struggle in Hollywood to achieve a level of respect and influence granted to few African American performers. Examines how Goldberg's performance in the box-office hit *Sister Act* enhanced her reputation as a film star capable of commanding a salary of $8 million per picture.

Annette Marks-Ellis

EMMA GOLDMAN

Born: June 27, 1869; Kovno, Lithuania
Died: May 14, 1940; Toronto, Canada
Area of Achievement: Social reform
Contribution: A leading member of the anarchic Left in the early twentieth century, Goldman was a critic of both capitalism and socialism and an advocate of women's rights.

Early Life

Emma Goldman was born on June 27, 1869, in Kovno (now Kaunas) in Lithuania, which was then part of the Russian Empire. Her parents, Abraham Goldman and Taube Binowitz Zodikow, were already rearing two daughters, Helena and Lena, from Taube Goldman's first marriage (she was a widow when she entered into an arranged marriage with Goldman). Beaten frequently by her father and denied comfort by her mother, Emma was unable to find either emotional or financial security in the Goldman household. For a time, she lived with relatives in Königsberg, a city in the northeastern corner of Germany. Her experience in her uncle's household was, if anything, worse, and Emma returned to her parents, who themselves moved first to Königsberg and then, in 1881, to St. Petersburg in Russia.

Emma did find some satisfaction in life. She was able to attend school in Königsberg, where a young teacher befriended Emma and introduced her to music and literature, both of which became lifelong sources of pleasure for her. In St. Petersburg, however, the family's economic privation meant that Emma had to abandon her hopes of continuing her education and becoming a doctor (her father could not understand why a woman needed an education) in order to work in factories that made gloves and corsets.

Rebelling against her father's authority and the Jewish religious and cultural traditions in which she was raised, Emma became fascinated with radicalism. An avid reader, she found inspiration in Vera Pavlovna, the heroine of Nikolai Cherny-shevsky's radical novel *What Is to Be Done?* (1863), who defied authority and convention. Especially meaningful to Emma, whose father suggested arranging a marriage for her, was Pavlovna's rejection of that practice as the auctioning of a sex object. Emma also admired the martyred young women who had been active partici-pants in the 1870's Russian radical movement, the People's Will.

Emma sought immediate relief from her despair by emigrating to the United States, the land of hope, departing Russia with Helena late in 1885. They intended to live with their sister Lena, who was married and living in Rochester, New York. To Emma's dismay, she soon seemed trapped in Rochester by the very things she wished to escape: monotonous, low-paying work in a clothing factory, further talk of an ar-ranged marriage, and the presence of her parents, who followed their daughters to the New World.

Again, Emma found inspiration in the story of martyred radicals: four men executed (a fifth committed suicide) in November, 1887, for the bomb murder of several Chicago policemen during a mass workers' meeting at the Haymarket Square in Chicago the previous year. What especially angered Emma was that the authorities never ascertained who threw the bomb, making it seem clear that the men who had been arrested were really being tried for their beliefs. If injustices similar to those that occurred in Russia could also take place in the United States, reasoned Emma, it was time for her to align herself with the opponents of capitalism and of its tools, the state and the church.

Emma had one more personal crisis to endure before making a commitment to activism. In her early teens, Emma had had her first sexual experience, a humiliating and painful one, with a young man she had considered her friend. She was still able to develop emotional attachments with men, however, and in Rochester she fell in love with a fellow worker, the handsome and seemingly intellectual Jacob Kersner, whom she married in February, 1887.

The marriage seemed to offer escape from familial pressures but did not succeed. Kersner proved to be impotent and took comfort in gambling with his cronies. For a time, Emma tried to avoid the stigma of divorce, but at age twenty, she divorced Kersner and moved to New Haven, Connecticut. She briefly returned to Rochester, remarried Kersner, divorced him a second time, and moved to New York City.

Life's Work

Among the new friends Emma Goldman made in the immigrant neighborhoods of New York's Lower East Side, two stood out: Alexander Berkman, who became her lover, and Johann Most, an older man who had made a name for himself in Germany and became a leading figure among anarchists in the United States. Although she was familiar with socialist thought, she regarded it as menacing to individual freedom because it accepted large state-owned industry as positive. Anarchism, in contrast, promised a society based on justice and reason and opposed both the centralization of the corporation and the centralization of the state.

Schooled by Most in both anarchist theory and public speaking, Goldman made her first speaking tour in 1890 and was delighted to realize that she had the power to sway people with the spoken word. She also came to realize, however, that the words she was speaking were not hers but Most's, and she repudiated his mentorship. Converts to anarchism and to the communal living that Goldman and Berkman advocated were disappointingly few, and the two thought of returning to Russia.

In 1892, a pressing new cause kept them in the United States: planning the assassination of tycoon Henry Clay Frick, who had violently suppressed a strike at the Homestead steelworks of Pittsburgh. They decided that Berkman would shoot Frick, while Goldman, who helped him plan the assassination attempt, would explain his actions. The affair went awry. Berkman merely wounded Frick, and other radicals, including Most, distanced themselves from Berkman and from assassination as a political weapon.

Goldman had now come to another turning point in her life. She thought of herself not as an exile from Russia but as a woman who could have a meaningful future fighting for change in the United States. Although she escaped prosecution for her role in Berkman's attack on Frick, she was arrested in 1893 and sentenced to a year in Blackwell's Island prison for her activities at a protest demonstration in New York's Union Square.

On her release, Goldman met a new lover, the Austrian-born anarchist Ed Brady, who wished to marry her. She rejected marriage, but did heed his suggestion to find another outlet for her compassion and sympathy for the downtrodden. To support herself, she was already working as a practical nurse (a skill she had learned in the prison hospital), and she went to Vienna to earn certificates in nursing and midwifery. During her year in Vienna (1895-1896) and another year in Paris (1899-1900) she also immersed herself in avant-garde literature and drama.

For some time, Goldman hoped to have two careers: the first as a nurse and midwife among the downtrodden in New York, the second as a radical lecturer. The two careers were not necessarily compatible, however, for as a lecturer she was attracting increasing fame as an opponent of war in 1898, of organized Christianity, and of conventional sexual morality. She became widely known as an advocate of free love, a term that added to her notoriety as "Red Emma." In using the expression "free love," Goldman meant not indiscriminate sexual activity but love without a legally recognized marriage, which she regarded as one of many devices society used to exploit women.

Goldman again faced prison in 1901 when she was arrested following the assassination of President William McKinley. She was not involved in the crime and was not held for trial, but with her characteristic defiance she could not resist asking Americans to show compassion for the condemned assassin, Leon Czolgosz. Public outrage made it impossible for her to book a lecture hall, and she was further embittered when radicals repudiated Czolgosz. For a while she retreated from public view. Using the pseudonym E. G. Smith, she tended to the poor in New York's slums.

By 1903, however, she was ready to resume lecturing. In 1906, she undertook a second commitment, that of publisher of a new periodical that she founded and named *Mother Earth*. She chose the name to suggest that the earth should provide the opportunity for all humankind to lead free and productive lives. *Mother Earth* would serve as a forum not only for anarchism but also for the issues of the Lyrical Left—personal liberation, freedom of artistic expression, and equality in sexual relations.

The journal, however, did not sell well enough to support Goldman—after one year it had two thousand subscribers—so she had to lecture more than ever. Often traveling with her new lover, Ben Reitman the hobo doctor, who acted as her booking agent, Goldman gave hundreds of speeches a year, reaching out to the "psychologically stifled middle class" as well as to the impoverished. Small of stature, she impressed listeners with her intensity and with her command of humor and sarcasm. In the question-and-answer sessions that usually followed her talks, she also showed a mastery of many subjects that came from countless hours of reading. English had long since become Goldman's primary language, but although her most publicized lectures were to American audiences, she insisted on making separate lectures in Yiddish.

From 1906 to 1916, Goldman continued to write and lecture on the sins of capitalism and also on art, drama, literature, and women's issues. She addressed the topic of birth control, criticized the institution of marriage, denounced the corset, and dared women to have more sexual experiences. Much of what she said infuriated social conservatives, but for good measure she also condemned suffragists as single-issue reformers. Ethical and social conventions, she maintained, were bigger obstacles to women's emancipation than were suffrage restrictions and other external barriers.

From 1914 on, World War I became an issue she had to address. As long as the United States remained neutral, Goldman could freely oppose the war, but even when the United States entered the war in 1917 she remained uncompromising in her opposition to it. No pacifist, she regarded war as more capitalist exploitation. The conscription law that the Wilson administration endorsed in 1917 was both repressive and illogical, she asserted, since it meant Prussianizing America in the name of democratizing Germany. Although she did not explicitly advocate resistance to the draft, she and Berkman (who had been released from prison in 1906 and was the editor of *Mother Earth*) were arrested on June 15, speedily tried, and sentenced to prison terms of two years. In a separate action, the government stopped the publication of *Mother Earth*.

In 1919 Goldman, Berkman, and more than two hundred other radicals of foreign birth were deported from the United States to Soviet Russia, but life there proved intolerable for her. Goldman did have an interview with communist leader Vladimir Lenin, but she soon concluded that a new era of statist repression was dawning.

She left Russia in 1921 and proceeded to relate her observations in lectures and in two books that were condemned by other leftists. At various times she lived in Sweden, England, France, and Canada, writing her memoirs and carrying on a large correspondence with many friends and members of her family with whom she had long before reconciled. In 1934, she was allowed to return to the United States, where she desperately wished to live, just long enough to make a speaking tour. In her last years, she expressed contempt for both Nazism and Stalinism, but when World War II began in September, 1939, she refused to make a choice between the evil of war and the evil of a dictatorship. An individualist to the last, she died in Toronto in 1940.

Summary

During Emma Goldman's lifetime, anarchism never became a mass creed. If anything, it declined in the United States because of government actions against radicalism, the growing appeal of trade unions, and because communism, especially after the Leninists had gained power in Russia, was able to win more converts. Nevertheless, Goldman was of major importance in the history of American radicalism, for her success lay not in contributing to the demise of capitalism or the state but in alerting people to issues involving personal liberation and self-fulfillment.

Unlike most members of the political left, who argued that the advent of the socialist state would emancipate women, Goldman demanded that women's issues be addressed immediately. Jeered, arrested, and threatened on many occasions, she won admirers among many middle-class Americans who might not have become converts to her causes but who believed in her right to advance them. She herself became a major spokesperson for free speech. It is therefore in the cultural history of twentieth century America that Goldman has most significance, for the issues she had raised prior to 1918 were issues that again seemed relevant in the 1960's, when a new generation of American dissenters and feminists rediscovered Goldman and celebrated her as a symbol of defiance and liberation.

Bibliography

Chalberg, John. *Emma Goldman, American Individualist.* Edited by Oscar Handlin. New York: HarperCollins, 1991. Written as part of an ongoing series of brief biographies of eminent Americans, this book provides the best introduction to Goldman's life.

Drinnon, Richard. *Rebel in Paradise.* Chicago: University of Chicago Press, 1961. Especially helpful for its explanation of the historical and social context in which Goldman lived. Shows the maturation of Goldman from youthful enthusiast to spokesperson for a cultural revolution.

Falk, Candace Serena. *Love, Anarchy, and Emma Goldman.* Rev. ed. New Brunswick, N.J.: Rutgers University Press, 1990. Falk concentrates on explaining the relationship between Goldman's various loves and her thinking on social and moral issues. Previously undiscovered correspondence between Goldman and Reitman helped give Falk new insights.

Goldman, Emma. *Living My Life.* 2 vols. New York: Alfred A. Knopf, 1931. Written while Goldman was residing in St. Tropez, France, this memoir is inaccurate and misleading in many areas but is still the best source for information about Goldman's childhood.

_____. *Nowhere at Home: Letters from Exile of Emma Goldman and Alexander Berkman.* Edited by Richard Drinnon and Anna Maria Drinnon. New York: Schocken Books, 1975. This topically organized compilation reveals much about Goldman's thoughts on communism and on the approach of World War II. Thoughtful editorial notes are included.

Shulman, Alix Kates. *To the Barricades: The Anarchist Life of Emma Goldman.* New York: Thomas Y. Crowell, 1971. This book for juvenile readers provides a lucid introduction to Goldman's life and thought.

Solomon, Martha. *Emma Goldman.* Boston: Twayne, 1987. Solomon analyzes Goldman's rhetorical style in both her written and spoken words. Provides insight into Goldman's thought, especially her evaluations of early twentieth century literature and drama.

Waldstreicher, David. *Emma Goldman.* New York: Chelsea House, 1990. This thoughtful book for young readers does an excellent job of presenting the main themes and events in Goldman's crowded life.

Wexler, Alice. *Emma Goldman: An Intimate Life.* New York: Pantheon Books, 1984.

In this three-hundred-page work, Wexler challenges many views of Goldman and seeks to explain the contradictions between the public Goldman and the private Goldman.

——————. *Emma Goldman in Exile*. Boston: Beacon Press, 1989. Wexler concludes her study of Goldman with this assessment of her last twenty years.

Lloyd J. Graybar

GREAT LIVES
FROM
HISTORY

AREAS OF ACHIEVEMENT